Film-Induced Tourism

ASPECTS OF TOURISM

Series Editors: **Chris Cooper**, *Oxford Brookes University, UK*, C. **Michael Hall**, *University of Canterbury, New Zealand* and **Dallen J. Timothy**, *Arizona State University, USA*

Aspects of Tourism is an innovative, multifaceted series, which comprises authoritative reference handbooks on global tourism regions, research volumes, texts and monographs. It is designed to provide readers with the latest thinking on tourism worldwide and push back the frontiers of tourism knowledge. The volumes are authoritative, readable and user-friendly, providing accessible sources for further research. Books in the series are commissioned to probe the relationship between tourism and cognate subject areas such as strategy, development, retailing, sport and environmental studies.

Full details of all the books in this series and of all our other publications can be found on http://www.channelviewpublications.com, or by writing to Channel View Publications, St Nicholas House, 31–34 High Street, Bristol BS1 2AW, UK.

ASPECTS OF TOURISM: 76

Film-Induced Tourism

2nd Edition

Sue Beeton

CHANNEL VIEW PUBLICATIONS
Bristol • Buffalo • Toronto

Nothing of him that doth fade,
But doth suffer a sea-change
Into something rich and strange.
(Shakespeare, The Tempest)

For Enid and Joe my guides through this rich and strange world

Library of Congress Cataloging in Publication Data
Names: Beeton, Sue.
Title: Film-Induced Tourism/Sue Beeton.
Description: 2nd Edition. |Bristol: CHANNEL VIEW PUBLICATIONS, [2016] |
 Series: Aspects of Tourism: 76 | Includes bibliographical references and index.
Identifiers: LCCN 2016022064| ISBN 9781845415846 (Hbk : alk. paper) | ISBN
 9781845415839 (Pbk : alk. paper) | ISBN 9781845415853 (Pdf) | ISBN 9781845415860
 (Epub) | ISBN 9781845415877 (Kindle)
Subjects: LCSH: Tourism and motion pictures. | Tourism—Decision making.
Classification: LCC G155.A1 B3835 2016 | DDC 338.4/791—dc23 LC record available
at https://lccn.loc.gov/2016022064

British Library Cataloguing in Publication Data
A catalogue entry for this book is available from the British Library.

ISBN-13: 978-1-84541-584-6 (hbk)
ISBN-13: 978-1-84541-583-9 (pbk)

Channel View Publications
UK: St Nicholas House, 31–34 High Street, Bristol BS1 2AW, UK.
USA: UTP, 2250 Military Road, Tonawanda, NY 14150, USA.
Canada: UTP, 5201 Dufferin Street, North York, Ontario M3H 5T8, Canada.

Website: www.channelviewpublications.com
Twitter: Channel_View
Facebook: https://www.facebook.com/channelviewpublications
Blog: www.channelviewpublications.wordpress.com

The policy of Multilingual Matters/Channel View Publications is to use papers that are
natural, renewable and recyclable products, made from wood grown in sustainable
forests. In the manufacturing process of our books, and to further support our policy,
preference is given to printers that have FSC and PEFC Chain of Custody certification.
The FSC and/or PEFC logos will appear on those books where full certification has been
granted to the printer concerned.

Typeset by Nova Techset Private Limited, Bengaluru & Chennai, India.
Printed and bound in the UK by the CPI Books Group.
Printed and bound in the US by Edward Brothers Malloy, Inc.

Contents

Figures and Tables

Figures

Tables

Introduction to the Second Edition

When planning the second edition of a book which represented research from the late 1990s to the early 21st century and was published over 10 years ago, it was tempting to undertake a complete re-write as there have been so many developments in the field of film tourism research. Most of the cases I studied are no longer on our screens, such as the Australian television series *Sea Change* (1998–2000) and the United Kingdom (UK) series *Heartbeat* (1992–2009), while others, such as *The Lord of the Rings* (2001, 2002, 2003), have been examined extensively in the ensuing years by numerous researchers; yet there remain aspects such as the role of film studio-based theme parks that continue to be understudied. However, due to the fact that this was the first research monograph on the topic, all of the studies in that first edition were important, even possibly seminal. While subsequent research has developed our knowledge of the field, many of these early findings remain relevant and have been observed elsewhere, as well as still presenting useful data and analytical approaches. So, I have retained these studies while presenting additional cases and literature to bring us into more contemporary times.

Furthermore, much of the work I presented in the first edition was Australasian based, a focus that I have retained, while acknowledging the extensive work being done in Europe and Asia. There are a number of reasons for this, the primary one being that this publication is based on my own primary research, which has had its focus in certain parts of the world; as I am based in Australia, I lean towards this region. In addition, as I discuss in Chapter 1, many of Australia's tourism icons were 'developed' in the age of film (that is, the early 20th century), including Ayers Rock (Uluru), which was not visited by tourists until a tour in 1936 led by Hardy Adventures, the Sydney Harbour Bridge and Opera House, completed in 1932 and 1963 respectively and even the Great Barrier Reef. As there are very few studies on Australian film-induced tourism, particularly in the theme park field, my studies remain important.

That said, I do include other cases that I have undertaken outside of Australia, in particular my aforementioned longitudinal research into *Heartbeat* (1992–2009) in the UK, along with film tours in the US, studies in Japan and theme parks around the world.

In the first edition of this publication, I concluded with a series of questions and areas that I felt required further research. When planning this second edition, I returned to the concluding chapter to see whether what I thought over 10 years ago has been studied, along with other aspects of film-induced tourism. I was pleased to find that, not only have I continued down the path directed by this research, but that others have also begun to address some of the points I raised.

> This work leaves many questions unasked and unanswered. The need to ascertain how, when and why a film (movie or TV series) inspires people to visit a particular locality is an important aspect that requires further study. Is film merely a variant of destination marketing (but without the formal strategy or advertising budget) at the time of release?...We need to consider what aspects people relate to and if it is their empathetic attachment to a story or place that facilitates tourism...The general public's desire for contact with 'celebrities' has also been suggested as a powerful tourism motivator. Is it the opportunity to live the fantasy of the celebrity status of film?...How can studies of the history of film and tourism assist in our understanding of tourism development as well as that of film-induced tourism? (Beeton, 2005: 237, 244)

Consequently, these developments are incorporated into this second edition, generally integrated into the appropriate areas, yet they are still questions we need to consider, and are reiterated in the concluding chapter. Certainly, I have looked at the historical dimension of the role of film in creating place images over time as well as cases of the longevity of the tourism that has been induced by film and television, which are also addressed in a recent publication, *Travel, Tourism and the Moving Image* (Beeton, 2015). A further area of study that I had not clearly articulated, yet inferred when identifying the different types of film tourists as primary, incidental and accidental (see Chapter 1), is that of the place of the fan and fandom. I have incorporated some of the interesting work now being undertaken in relation to fans and tourism in Chapter 2, as well as at other relevant points in the book.

At the time of writing the first edition, I also noted that there had been few, if any, studies of film-induced tourism in non-Western cultures. This is beginning to change, with the work of Kim (2011, 2012) and others looking at Korea, along with a large research project funded by the Japanese government looking at *contents tourism*, an emerging area of study in such a heavily mediatised (and fantasised) culture which is introduced in Chapter 2 and presented as an additional theme throughout the book.

So, Where's the Theory?

This is a question I regularly ask of the many papers and theses that I am invited to review and examine on this topic, so it is reasonable for it to be asked of me, as there may not appear to be a great deal of theory articulated in this publication. However, the entire work is underpinned by rigorous theoretical approaches, which I outline below.

The late Neil Leiper (2004) spoke of the simple fact that theory is everywhere – in order to learn how to hammer a nail, some theory is presented, such as the best angle to hold the nail, where to grip the hammer to get maximum velocity and how to actually strike that nail. Only after understanding this theory do we attempt the task. Leiper separates theory development into two areas, one where theory contributes to practice, while the other picks at practice, contributing to theory. What I have found is that, while I may start by looking at practice and developing theory to help understand it (grounded theory), which is where I began with film-induced tourism research in the 1990s, the process soon gets complicated. I have also located existing theories within other disciplines that could be applied to film-induced tourism, helping further to understand the phenomenon. Since that time, the theory-practice cycle has continued to feed back into itself, to a point where simple segregations such as Leiper's are no longer relevant. Neil and I often discussed this, agreeing that life is more complicated than many of the theoretical models we develop to describe it. This is evident in Stear's development of Leiper's (1979) tourism systems framework into a most complex system (Leiper *et al.*, 2008). But, I digress. A very simple, iterative model can illustrate this, where we can start anywhere, but in the end each iteration informs the next, ultimately contributing to our knowledge (Figure 0.1).

Much of the theory that underpins this book is inferred rather than specifically noted, assuming that the reader has some basic knowledge of tourism theory; however, where I have applied existing theories in a 'new' way, or developed an explanatory model, they are articulated. For example, the use of social representation theory (SRT) is demonstrated in the study of locals' attitudes towards *Sea Change* (1998–2000) (Chapter 6) along with the concept of 'demarketing' as a reimaging tool where a place becomes too popular (Chapter 7), while a postmodern perspective is taken when looking at film studio theme parks (Chapter 8), leading to the development of a theme park model based on MacCannell's (1973, 1976) and Pearce's (1982b) theoretical frontstage-backstage work (Chapters 8 and 9).

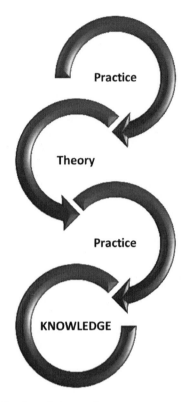

Figure 0.1 Theory-practice-knowledge cycle

Closely aligned with theory is the method of inquiry adopted for the material that is reported and analysed in this publication. I briefly outline this below.

Methodological Approaches: Autoethnographic, Participant-Observational Case Studies

This discussion leads me to speak about certain research approaches and methodologies that have relevance to the work presented here. I have already noted that much of the initial work presented in the first edition came out of a grounded theory approach, where I studied a range of cases, developing theoretical models to understand them; however, I also applied existing theories. When undertaking the research presented in this book, I have taken an emic case study approach, combined with participant-observation and autoethnography.

The case study

When I began to look at film-induced tourism, due to its situatedness I realised I needed to take a case study approach. So, I looked to the tourism literature in our top journals to gain some initial understanding of this method. Interestingly, while there were many 'case studies' there was no discussion about what a case study is, why it has been used or what it means. In fact, if it ever was mentioned as a research methodology, it was disparagingly. I then asked this question on Trinet, the major tourism academic Listserv with a breadth and depth of knowledge in its membership. At the time (the late 1990s), no one was able to help, with many asking if I could forward anything I discovered on to them...So, I delved into the sociological world, where I 'discovered' the influential work of Robert Yin, the 'father of the case study', whose work continues to guide me. First published in 1994, his seminal work, *Case Study Research: Design and Methods* is now in its fifth edition (2013), and became my methodological bible.

I have written about this in detail elsewhere (see Beeton, 2005), but briefly, Yin (2013) points out that there are two very distinct forms of case study, one being used as an instructional tool, the other for research, while I argue that there is a third form of case study used in journalism where a primary aim of the story is told to engage the reader (Beeton, 2005). The teaching case study is often manipulated to make a certain point or achieve an intended learning outcome along with the journalism case study, whereas the research case study is focused on finding out what is really going on. Yin notes that a case study is 'an empirical inquiry about a contemporary phenomenon (e.g. a 'case'), set within its real-world context – especially when the boundaries between phenomenon and context are not clearly evident' (Yin, 2009: 18). Consequently, in a case study the context is integral to understanding the case. Certainly, if we think about the relationship between film, tourism and place (the phenomenon and its context), the boundaries are not clear. Further supporting this approach, Yin describes three situations where it may be appropriate to adopt a case study methodology, namely

> ...when your research addresses a descriptive question – 'What is happening or has happened?' – or an explanatory question – 'How or why did something happen?'...Second, by emphasizing the study of a phenomenon within its real-world context...Third, the case study method is now commonly used in conducting evaluations. (Yin, 2012: 37–38)

While I am not using the case study for evaluations, except to test my proposed theme park model, I am certainly applying it to the first two aspects. Yin is at pains to explain that the case study is more than a method used merely in an exploratory phase of a research study, arguing that case study research goes

Table 0.1 Features of the case study

	Feature
1	Can explain why an innovation worked or failed to work
2	Has the advantage of hindsight, yet can be relevant in the present and to the future
3	Can illustrate the complexities of a situation by recognising more than one contributing factor
4	Shows the influence of personalities and politics on an issue
5	Can show the influence of the passage of time through longitudinal studies
6	The reader may be able to apply it to his/her situation
7	Can evaluate alternatives not chosen
8	Can utilise information from a wide variety of sources
9	Can present information in a wide variety of ways
10	Can illuminate a general problem through examination of a specific instance

beyond exploratory functions – a point with which I strongly concur. Table 0.1 (adapted from Hoaglin *et al.*, 1982) summarises the main features of the case study, many of which are relevant to my work outlined in this book.

Nevertheless, there remains the criticism of bias in case study research, and that it lacks rigor and applicability. I have argued elsewhere (ably supported by Yin and other luminaries) that a good case study is just as rigorous as any other well-conducted research – quantitative questionnaires and surveys can also be designed with a bias (Beeton, 2005). Unfortunately we have seen many poor case studies in our field, often due to the fact that the researcher simply does not understand the method. The steps in designing a case study are to define the 'case' (could be a person, event, organisation), select the design (single or multiple cases), and finally decide whether or not to use theory in the design of the study (Yin, 2013).

After my exploration into the case of the case study, I could only conclude that tourism research had treated this method in a cavalier and simplistic manner, subsequently dismissing it as less than useless in the discovery of knowledge by claiming that a 'case' could not be extrapolated into the broader population. I disagree – a well-designed study can illuminate other situations, develop theory and provide a significant test of theory. What concerns me more is when a group of students (for example) are surveyed and the results of that study are said to represent the entire community – an all too common feature of quantitative studies.

Autoethnography

As my knowledge further developed, I became increasingly frustrated with the accepted norm in much of the tourism literature of not using the personal pronoun in one's research. Again I turned to the social sciences, this time to anthropology where I discovered the use of, not only ethnography, but *autoethnography*, where the researcher examines him or herself as the 'data' – an approach that I had taken throughout my life, and certainly felt was a valid form of scholarly research and should be applied more to our work. In fact, I tend to spend a great deal of my allotted lifespan standing a little to the side of myself and reflecting on my emotions and experiences. To further this I began a blog, *The Feisty Flâneuse*, where I take the liberty of that space to recount and examine many of my thoughts and observations.

When I began to explore the concept of autoethnography some years back, not surprisingly, I encountered resistance from the academy, but also located some very interesting and valid research papers by outstanding scholars, including an illuminating case study from Holt (2003). This is certainly not a new phenomenon, with Denzin almost 20 years ago noting that, by taking an inward-looking (auto-)ethnographic approach (while maintaining a critical perspective), we can begin to understand '...the larger context where self experiences occur' (Denzin, 1997: 227). This certainly resonates with my own tourism scholarship and experiences, particularly in relation to film and popular culture. In fact, I see little point in trying to be an omnipotent observer in many research situations, as 'self-observation and reflexive accounts of experience cannot easily be disentangled, since, like sense and representation, they are mutually dependent' (Hackley, 2007: 102).

While autoethnography is not widely used in tourism research, it has been applied successfully by some in a range of research environments, including Noy (2003, 2004, 2007), Westwood (2005), Miller (2008), Scarles (2010), Buckley (2015), Frost and Laing (2015) and, in a more self-conscious early attempt, myself (Beeton, 2008a, 2010b) as well as more recently (Beeton, 2015). Noy in particular articulates the link I have seen between this approach and the tourist experience by explaining that '[e]xploring tourists' experiences autoethnographically...illuminates the fuzzy and liminal space that lies between tourism experiences and everyday experiences' (Noy, 2007: 352). Scarles (2010) goes so far as to discuss the concept of visual autoethnography, an area of inquiry that I feel will only grow in this era of self-photography and social media.

Tourism researcher Ralf Buckley published a most interesting paper in the journal, *Frontiers in psychology* (Buckley, 2015), where he argues that, when researching very personal, extreme emotional experiences where many people find articulating their emotions difficult, autoethnography can provide such insights, pointing out that

> Researchers can examine their own emotions in finer detail than those of research subjects. Using a retrospective approach, they can replay past experiences repeatedly from memory. Using a prospective or experimental approach, they can deliberately replicate particular experiences to analyse the associated emotions. (Buckley, 2015: 1–2)

While, for some, watching a movie or television series may not elicit extreme emotions, for others it certainly can, which I have experienced in many of the cases outlined in this book. As I note in Beeton (2015: 35), '...[b]y understanding how individuals respond to film, we are in a position to provide a stronger, more flexible and personal tourism experience for others'. That said, there are instances where so-called autoethnographic studies lack any true critical aspect, which is the key to valid research, and at times some of the cases I recount in this book fall into a less-than-critical narrative style. However, my reason for doing so is purposeful – I hope that, by not always being overtly self-critical, the reader will engage in that process (of themselves or of me). Ultimately, if I can get you, the reader, to be stimulated and challenged, I will be happy.

Participant-observation

Closely related to this autoethnographic case study approach is my continued insistence on participant-observation and the necessity to openly discuss the level of investigator immersion, which is part of ethnographic studies. So often I see research that claims to undertake participant-observation without any notable 'observation' or clear participation. While I have also discussed this elsewhere (see Beeton, 2005, 2007), in the interests of methodological comprehensiveness, I will briefly outline this concept.

Primarily, there a four 'states' of participant observation that we can place on a continuum, from a place of being a completely removed observer through to total immersion in the community and experience (Junker, 1960). We can certainly look at this in terms of the touristic aspects of visiting sites or sets of filming as well as when actually viewing the movie/television programme in the first instance (Beeton, 2015). In Figure 0.2, I illustrate my own level of immersion in many of the cases that I refer to in this book – I consciously worked to develop a strong relationship with the respective communities, but ultimately did not immerse myself totally in their communities.

Certainly, as a participating observer of film-induced tourism, my level of investigator immersion begins when viewing the media, be that at home

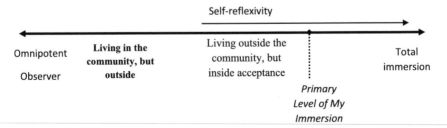

Figure 0.2 Level of investigator immersion

on television, in the cinema, or elsewhere, where I would argue I am completely immersed. Far from passively absorbing all that we see, today's (postmodern) viewer continually interprets their viewing experience, which can ultimately see them visiting the places where the story was filmed or set, which, of course, forms the basis of this book.

Situating tourism research

In Australia and much of the US and UK, tourism studies is situated in the business or management disciplines, which has encouraged a more detached, quantitative line of inquiry; but with more access to European sociological approaches and understanding of other disciplines, the use of the 'personal' has become more accepted in tourism research. Nevertheless, there are many, particularly those with a business management background, who struggle with this, but again I would argue that such criticism comes from reading work where the use of qualitative elements such as reporting in the first person has been approached and applied in a sloppy, non-reflexive manner.

I am not suggesting that all studies should be autoethnographic or participant-observation case studies, but there is a place for them alongside all other methodological approaches. Ultimately, the methodological approach is the one that most appropriately responds to the research questions or fields of inquiry.

Consequently, I have retained all of the case studies from the first edition, with updates where appropriate, while adding numerous participant-observation cases that enable us to take the discussion on film-induced tourism further. This includes studies on the long-running Australian TV series, *Neighbours* (1985–) and movies including *Oddball* (2015), as well as *The Hobbit's* (2012, 2013, 2014) influence in New Zealand along with the presentation of more business cases such as that of MovieTours in Hawaii, and introducing the work being done in Japan on contents tourism as well as other smaller cases. I also apply six cases to a study of the power relations between film companies and the destination marketing organisations in the places they film, which makes an important contribution towards understanding the success (or not) of the business of film-induced tourism

Regarding the Literature

Since undertaking the research that underpinned the first edition, there has certainly been an avalanche of students, scholars, researchers, journalists and the tourism (and film) industry looking at various aspects of film-induced tourism (or film tourism, cinematic tourism, television tourism, movie tourism, screen tourism, and so on). I refer to these studies where most relevant, but do not propose to provide a definitive review of what has become a large and broad-ranging literature – there are those who do that so much more effectively than I, including Heitmann (2010) and Connell (2012). That said, I have undertaken some thematic reviews of the literature in Beeton (2006a, 2011) as well as in the introduction to a special edition on film tourism in the journal *Tourism and Hospitality Planning and Development* (Beeton, 2010c), where many also presented some excellent perspectives on the literature. In that publication, rather than simply list the current literature, I undertook a discussion around the manner in which knowledge is developed in a 'new' field, using film-induced tourism as the case-in-point, which I will summarise here (Figure 0.3).

This model is seen from the perspective of a researcher based in a management and marketing paradigm, which is where most of the early literature emanated from, yet, over time, we searched out and engaged with other disciplinary studies. In particular I have found a great deal of relevant knowledge in the areas of communications, film and media studies.

As we moved from justifying the field as an appropriate area of research at the end of the last century, other questions became apparent, including those I posed at the end of the first edition. We also witnessed a group of

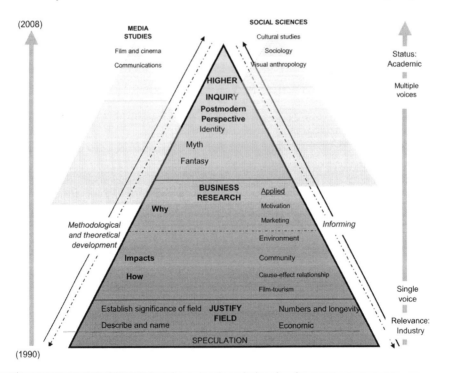

Figure 0.3 Model of film-induced tourism knowledge development
Source: Beeton (2010a: 4).

researchers moving away from the more quantitative approaches towards responding to qualitative questions of 'why?' and 'how?' That is not to say that the business and marketing research does not remain important, but the breadth and depth of inquiry expands over a period of time, in this instance around 20 years. While each 'level' tends to build on the knowledge developed by the levels below it, they all continue to inform each other, with all parts of the model requiring continual study. For example, if we neglect those I have described as 'Justify Field' we may find that we miss some of the basic developments, such as the ongoing discussion around film-induced tourism longevity, which remains important and somewhat controversial.

Concluding this Introduction to the Second Edition

I have taken the opportunity in this introduction to not only indicate what differences there are to this second edition but also to address points of methodology that were not as clearly articulated in the first edition, and to explain the Australasian focus of my work. While the approach has not changed, I suspect that many readers may not have adequately grasped the underlying theories and approaches that were embedded in the work. However, in order to retain a level of readability, and to not interrupt the flow of the arguments presented, I felt that it would be preferable to outline this here, in a separate, introductory discussion. Also, there are other publications to which I have referred (including some of my own) where the methodological material is discussed in more detail. I recommend that any prospective researcher looks to this literature, particularly in relation to Yin and his colleagues regarding the case study, and additional sources on ethnography and autoethnography.

Part 1

Introduction to Film-Induced Tourism

Global and local events, from terrorism through to disease, epidemics and political uncertainty, impact communities around the world in ways that have not always been foreseen. Changes have been felt socially as well as economically as the ground shifts beneath once-stable, predictable societies. Tourism, while being a victim of all these events, is also a protagonist, creating change while having a major role to play in community reconstruction. Tourism can exert political power, be a force for peace, an economic and social regenerator and diversifier, and can bring communities together (or tear them apart). The popular media also plays a major role in today's society, particularly the medium of film, be that through television, movies, DVDs or videos. The link between travel and popular media, particularly in terms of imaginative literature, has been long recognised, while the pervasiveness of film in today's globalised society has strengthened this link, and is the genesis of this book.

This publication considers the relationship between film and tourism, and, while the need to look at some aspects in detail has placed a certain focus on specific sites in Australia, the United Kingdom and New Zealand, film-induced tourism is given a global treatment. As the popularity of researching this phenomenon has increased, numerous international examples and cases are included. Ongoing, immersive visits to film tourism sites around the world also support the work presented here, resulting in a global approach, while still considering elements of film-induced tourism on a micro, local level.

Due to my own Westernised background and heritage, the primary focus in this publication is on developed nations, or 'first world countries'; however, there are many developing countries that are used as film sites in the hope also of attracting tourism. Where reliable information is available, such cases have been included, but it is outside the scope of this publication to detail the effect of film on developing countries, their communities and

1

tourism. This is a topic for further study and publications by others, and is starting to be addressed.

Countries such as Australia and New Zealand do not have such high population densities or tourist numbers as other parts of the world, yet tourism is extremely important to them. One of the consequences of this is that, while the impacts of tourism are not as evident, the effects can be just as powerful over time, both negatively and positively. Consequently, such nations need to be studied in their own right – they cannot rely solely on repeating international trends. This point is amply demonstrated when we look at film-induced tourism and the cases examined throughout this book.

1 Popular Media and Tourism

The popular media of the day influences the appeal of travel destinations and activities through constructing or reinforcing particular images of those destinations, and acting as 'markers' (MacCannell, 1976). In the past, media such as literature, music and poetry have been a major element, even more so than visual media such as art (Seaton, 1998). This first chapter sets the context by looking at the general influence of popular media, developing it to include film. Film-induced tourism is described and defined, along with a discussion of the two different elements of on-location and off-location film tourism. By the end of the chapter, some of the complexities of film-induced tourism are becoming evident, which are discussed in more detail in subsequent chapters.

Popular Media, the Picturesque and Tourism

Prior to the development of film and television, a mass audience had access primarily only to written works. From the early 20th century, film (and later television) became the main mass media outlet and has been particularly effective in affecting tourism, with moving images being intricately intertwined with travel, especially in terms of moving people, and exoticness since their inception in the 19th century (Beeton, 2015).

Anthropologists such as MacCannell (1976) view tourism attractions as requiring a marker that provides 'meaning' as well as signifying the attraction. Media such as literature and film can provide a wealth of meaning, real and imagined (Laing & Frost, 2012). In a rare, yet pertinent, comment on film's role as a tourism marker, MacCannell cites the case of a film site:

> As a sight, it amounts to no more than a patch of wild grass, but it was recently provided with an elaborate off-sight marker by the motion picture industry. The fortuitous acquisition of this new marker apparently caught the promoters of the area by surprise as the following information in the brochure is over-stamped in red ink: VISIT THE BONNIE AND CLYDE SHOOTOUT AREA. Also overprinted in red ink is a square box surrounding a site description that appeared in the original

printing of the brochure...They [visitors] do not arrive expecting to see anything and are content to be involved with the marker. (MacCannell, 1976: 114)

Time and again we see film-based tourists and fans being attracted to what, to an outsider, is completely nondescript, but is powerfully significant, often, but not always, marked by a small plaque or note on a movie database such as the Internet Movie Database (IMDb). Many of the sites in *The Lord of the Rings* and *The Hobbit* have even been identified by their global positioning system (GPS) coordinates in Ian Brodie's publications (Brodie, 2004, 2011, 2014). I discuss the rationale (even necessity) behind this elsewhere in the book, but primarily this was because many of the sites were not immediately recognisable due to significant use of computer-generated imagery (CGI) technology and as other sites were returned to their original states.

Since the late 19th century, cultural representations through literary associations have become increasingly important in tourist visitation and promotion throughout the world, from the New England town of Concord with its famous 19th-century residents Henry Thoreau, Louisa May Alcott and Nathaniel Hawthorne to the British Tourism Authority's (BTA) promotion of regions known as 'Burns Country' and 'Bronte Country'. The link between literature, film and tourism is examined further in Chapters 3 and 10 as well as incidentally throughout the book.

While books and the written word remain influential tourism influencers today, as evidenced in Laing and Frost's 2012 publication, *Books and Travel*, these touristic concepts have now expanded into other popular media, in particular, film. Various tourism and film authorities and even fans have developed *movie maps*, many of which are now available as interactive sites on the internet, such as the MovieMaps site at https://moviemaps.org, and as mobile apps, such as *Film Locate* with locations of over 150 films by map, satellite, hybrid, list or directions, while others such as the *MovieLoci* app show the locations of movie and television sites near your current location and can compare the current site with how it appears in the film.

Most of the world's great pilgrimage and tourist sites were established through the written media such as those literary associations noted above, well before the coming of film, limiting the effect that film had on actually establishing the iconic status of such sites. However, as mooted in the introduction this is not the case in countries such as Australia and New Zealand, where the majority of our tourist sites (including the ancient indigenous sites) are, in one way or another, products of the 20th century. In other words, they have developed in the age of film. For example, the Sydney Harbour Bridge and Opera House, the Outback and High Country (as generic Australian bush heritage sites as well as relating to specific legends) and even Uluru have reached iconic status through the influence of film, still photographs, documentaries and even science fiction movies. In fact, the early

European records of Ayers Rock (Uluru) had photographs and moving pictures associated with them. New Zealand's Maori culture and dramatic scenery (thermal in the North, glacial in the South) are achieving similar status through film. Consequently, by studying Australasian cases, we can see how film affects images and emotions, and how related tourism can develop. This in turn enables us to propose theoretical models and approaches to the study of film-induced tourism.

In spite of these modern influences, the Romantic movement of the 18th and 19th centuries maintains its influence on all areas of tourism. Romanticist writers such as Wordsworth, Keats, Shelley, Byron and Rousseau stimulated an interest in nature, scenery and mountains (Lickorish & Jenkins, 1997). Such literary movements grew up more or less concurrently in Scotland, Germany, Switzerland and England, followed by France, and worshipped 'nature as a benign, maternal goddess capable of renewing the spiritual batteries of jaded urbanites' (Seaton, 1998: 11). This longing for exotic and/or unspoiled landscapes brought the countryside to symbolise a 'golden place' that still exists in the psyche of urbanites today and has had a major impact on the development and imaging of tourism (Beeton, 2004).

By the turn of the 19th century, attitudes towards the countryside had emerged based primarily on the Romantic movement (Slee, 1998). Romantic pastoral images predominated during and after the Industrial Revolution, when the urbanisation of many countries underpinned a longing for the rural idyll. For example, in 1800 only a quarter of the population of England and Wales lived in cities, whereas by 1900 three-quarters did. Victorian families sought escape from their blackened cities to a romantic other world where nature was transcendent (Seaton, 1998). The influence of the imaginative literature of the Romantic period is particularly evident in Scotland, where tourists were attracted '...not just from England, but also Europe, particularly Germans – ardent devotees of Romanticism – many of whom wrote accounts of their visits which helped to popularise the country still further' (Seaton, 1998: 17).

Closely aligned with Romanticism and highly relevant to the development of modern tourism and film is the concept of 'picturesque'. This was an 'ideology of landscape as pretty pictures for consumers, to be enjoyed as a visual experience divorced from any concept of use value or human purpose except private enjoyment' (Seaton, 1998: 9). Picturesque views became a key component of the tourist gaze, with rough bridges, sunsets, moonlight, cattle (seen from a distance), hedgerows and winding, tree-lined lanes being some of the desired elements.

However, in Australia and North America, the predominant romantic rural idyll was not green fields and hedgerows, but revolved around a frontier, pioneering heritage, reflecting elements of the romantic notion of 'noble savagery' and 'otherness'. It was about man against nature and, at times, against the savage natives who formed part of that 'enemy of nature'. The rural idyll was one of achievement against adversity, rather than the gentler, rural idyll of Europe (Beeton, 2004). Such differences reflect the various needs of those who created them, such as in Europe where the move towards industrialisation and urbanisation had to be tempered by a contrasting rural peace, whereas in the new worlds of the Americas and Antipodes, pride in achievement against adversity, man against nature, had to be developed. This was particularly the case in Australia, which began as a penal colony – a place where heroism threatened to be non-existent. Hence, we see the development of the tough, resourceful Australian bushman who continues to represent Australia in the minds of others (particularly visitors), much as the Romantic rural idyll represents Europe.

The popularity of these romantic pastoral and pioneering images at the end of the 19th century may have been a nostalgic longing for a past already fleetingly gone, but it has remained in the popular subconscious up to today, despite (or because of) the suburban concentration of the population (Wallace-Crabbe, 1971).

The above discussion sets the context for the study of film and tourism. From the influence of literature and prose as well as the visual arts, the moving image has become the singular most influential form of creative art today, reaching mass populations never before envisaged or possible. As each generation becomes more and more familiar with filmic media, its influence grows exponentially.

The Influence of Film

The effect of film on human behaviour has long been debated, especially in terms of influencing acts of violence and effecting social change. When discussing film's power in influencing behaviour and effecting social change (or supporting the status quo), Slocum notes that many social scientists assume that '...Hollywood...serve[s] as both an agent of social control and change' (Slocum, 2000: 649). The 1955 movie, *Rebel Without a Cause*, was censored in the United States and Britain because of contemporary public anxiety over juvenile delinquency, as it was believed that offensive scenes or dialogue would influence teenagers (Simmons, 1995). However, it is the influence of media violence on children that has received the greatest attention. The American Academy of Paediatrics claims that media violence affects children by making them less sensitive to acts of violence, increasing their aggressiveness and antisocial behaviour, increasing their fear of becoming victims and increasing their appetite for violence in entertainment and real life (American Academy of Paediatrics, 2002). According to Huesmann and Moise, more than 100 studies in the past 40 years have supported the thesis that after being exposed to visual depictions of violence, some children behave more aggressively (Huesmann & Moise, 1996). What we are now witnessing is not only the influence of film on the behaviours outlined above, but also the recognition of the role that it plays in tourist motivation and behaviour. Just as extensive research has been undertaken on the negative behavioural influences of film, so must we develop our understanding of film's tourism motivational power and its consequences.

If we acknowledge such influences, the development of a country's modern identity, image and cultural representations can be traced through popular film and television series. Using Australia as an example, images including those in 1980s movies such as *Crocodile Dundee* and *The Man from Snowy River* through to film and television series such as *Sea Change*, Australia's most popular television drama series in 1999 and 2000 (*The Age Green Guide*, 1999) and the long-running soap opera *Neighbours* (1985–current), along with a range of movies including *Wolf Creek 1* and *2* (2005, 2011), *Kenny* (2006), *Australia* (2008), and *Oddball* (2015) have reflected and reinforced the cultural mores of the day. The television series *Sea Change* (1998–2000) reflects the late 20th century's desire for a simpler, 'community' experience, with its name mirroring its use in common vernacular. It depicts a high-flying city lawyer who has moved to a small seaside town with her children to take up the position of local magistrate in order to 'rediscover' herself and her children. The town is peppered with gentle, quirky, likeable characters and the obligatory male romantic lead. The storyline relies as much on the physical setting of the series as on the quaint characterisations and is examined in some detail in this book.

At the time of writing, Australia was commemorating the centenary of the World War I battle at Gallipoli. Not only did thousands of pilgrims/tourists gather in Turkey for the commemoration, a plethora of film and television programmes were presented or re-presented, including the iconic 1980s movie *Gallipoli* (1981) and television mini-series and documentaries such as *Deadline Gallipoli* (2015) and *Why Gallipoli?* (2015), starring well-known Australian actor Sam Neil. There is no doubt that this will increase tourism to specific (and general) World War I sties by Australians, and goes towards creating images and emotions connected to these places.

For some time now, persuasive economic arguments have been presented regarding the money and jobs brought to a town or region during the filming process, such as US$21 million and 183 full-time jobs brought to Illinois during the filming of *A Thousand Acres* (*Economist*, 1998a). There is ample anecdotal evidence that tourists soon follow, looking for the sites, people, experiences and even the fantasies portrayed by the film (see Chapter 2). However, film producers, in general, have little concern for the impacts of film-induced tourism as, once they have completed their on-location filming, they leave. There is little if any evidence of initial site selection being based on any long-term community impacts, positive or negative. An example of how such a lack of concern from the film industry can backfire is illustrated in the case of *Baywatch* (1989–2001), where the residents of the site chosen in Australia for filming a new series (Avalon Beach, north of Sydney) protested vehemently against it being filmed on their beach. Such widespread antagonism resulted in the producers filming the new series in Hawaii.

Yet this began to change towards the end of the 20th century, with the Hawaiian Tourism Authority, in its first ever Strategic Tourism Plan in 1999, identifying encouraging filming in the state as one of its key tourism promotion strategies (Hawaii Tourism Authority, 1999). However, in spite of the recent popularity of *Jurassic World* (2015), filmed on the island of Kauai, such focus has again shifted. Regardless, tourists remain interested in filming sites, and the development of Hawaiian-based film tour company, *MovieTours* is discussed in Chapter 5. Some other film commissions have engaged in funding film, such as the regional film funding body, *Film I Väst Trollhättan* in Sweden which will only provide funding for projects that use local expertise, preferring those that actually feature the region itself.

In the 1990s, Tooke and Baker (1996) noted that the average worldwide screen audience for a movie was 72 million, arguing that a film can provide significant exposure to a particular tourist attraction, town or region; subsequent research demonstrates that such an effect has the potential to last for decades (Beeton, 2015). Movies remain an important element of many people's lives, with global box office takings in 2014 valued at US$36.4 billion with growth being driven by the Asia-Pacific region, while more than two-thirds of North Americans attended a cinema at least once in 2014 (MPAA, 2015). Certainly, film and television are pervasive educators and persuaders, even when they are entertaining.

A somewhat perverse demonstration of the influence that film exerts in our society is the way it was used in rebuilding confidence in the United States post September 11 2001. The terrorism of September 11 2001 decimated tourism to both New York and Washington DC. The local tourism boards in each city produced a series of advertisements featuring well-known 'personalities' exhorting visitors to return, assuring them that it was safe to do so. People used in the New York advertisements included New York sports stars, film stars and the former Mayor, Rudolph Giuliani, while Washington employed fictional characters from *The West Wing*, a television series set (but not filmed) in Washington (Torchin, 2003). It would appear that the tourist authorities felt that fictional characters from a programme about life in the White House and at the Capitol are more believable, trustworthy and convincing than their real-life counterparts. While it can be argued that the New York stars are just as manufactured as any fictional characters, such a juxtaposition of the imagined world with the real world at a time of deep national mourning better demonstrates the power of the popular media in the 21st century than any academic research exercise does.

The popularity of certain movies and television series has not only increased tourist visitation to the sites featured (and been used to encourage the return of tourists), but has also created a range of niche tourism operations based on the storyline, notoriety and cultural aspects of such media representations.

Throughout this book, the importance and place of imaging in tourism and its construct in visual media such as film (which here refers both to movies and to television films such as mini-series and even soap operas) is considered, along with the effects of film on tourism, specific film-related business ventures in the form of film studio theme parks and local communities.

The reach of the 'small screen'

According to Schofield, 'TV viewing is probably the greatest single domestic pastime' (Schofield, 1996: 334), and the influence of visual media has increased through the development of cable and satellite television as well as VCRs and DVDs. This is important in terms of the decision-making process and influence of television, and popular programmes acting as 'pull' factors for tourism destinations. This is supported by Australia's television viewing habits, where in the late 1990s 98% of all Australians watched some television each day, with an average daily consumption of two to three hours (Papandrea, 1996). By 2015, Australians were watching an average of 89 hours and 28 minutes of broadcast television per month, with the proportion of time for playback viewing starting to increase (Regional TAM *et al.*, 2015). Even with the rise of the availability of other viewing devices such as computers and smartphones, the television screen still accounted for 88.4% of all viewing. The use of new technologies is discussed further in the final chapter.

Schofield (1996) also propounds the theory that many tourists (especially mass tourists) tend to experience the world through a series of framed images, from the brochure through to car/bus windows and the camera lens. The television screen is yet another frame through which tourists vicariously experience a destination/attraction. Through its image-creating potential, film can also provide strong motivation to actually visit the places.

Describing and Defining Film-Induced Tourism

It is generally accepted that the term 'movie-induced tourism' relates to on-location tourism that follows the success of a movie made (or set) in a particular region. By using the term 'film-induced tourism', I have expanded this to include television, video and DVD. Today, there are many terms used to describe what I still generally refer to as 'film-induced tourism', from Riley's movie-induced tourism (Riley, 1994), through to television tourism (Evans, 1997), film tourism (Hudson & Ritchie, 2006a, 2006b), cinematic tourism (Tzanelli, 2007), screen tourism (Connell & Meyer, 2009), and even set-jetting tourism (Grihault, 2007). However, such simplistic definitions belie the variety and complexity of film-induced tourism. In order to demonstrate this, a survey of the emerging themes on film and tourism is outlined in Table 1.1.

Table 1.1 Forms and characteristics of film tourism

Form	Characteristic	Example
On-Location		
Film tourism as primary travel motivator	The film site is an attraction in its own right – strong enough to motivate visitation	Isle of Mull (Balamory)
Film tourism as part of a holiday	Visiting film locations (or studios) as an activity within a larger holiday	
Film tourism pilgrimage	Visiting sites of films in order to 'pay homage' to the film; possible re-enactments	Doune Castle (Monty Python); Lord of the Rings sites
Celebrity film tourism	Homes of celebrities; film locations that have taken on celebrity status	Hollywood homes
Nostalgic film tourism	Visiting film locations that represent another era	The Andy Griffith Show (1950s era); Heartbeat (1960s era)
Commercial On-Location		
Constructed film tourism attraction	An attraction constructed after the filming purely to attract/serve tourists	Heartbeat Experience (Whitby, UK)
Film/movie tours	Tours developed to various film locations	On Location Tours, MovieTours
Guided tours at specific on-location set	Tours of specific sites, often on private land	Hobbiton
Mistaken Identities		
Film tourism to places where the filming is only believed to have taken place	Movies and television series that are filmed in one place that is created to look like another; often in other countries for financial reasons; known as 'runaway productions'	Deliverance, Clayburn County (movie filmed there, but set in Appalachia)
Film tourism to places where the film is set, but not filmed	The films have raised interest in a particular country, region or place, where the story is based, not where it was actually filmed	Braveheart, Scotland (movie filmed in Ireland)

	Description	Examples
Off-Location		
Film studio tours	Industrial tours of working film studios, where the actual filming process can be viewed.	Paramount Studios
Commercial Off-Location		
Film studio theme park	Usually adjacent to a studio, specifically built for tourism with no actual filming or production taking place	Universal Studios
Museums	Museums and centres especially built to celebrate film, and attracts tourists; can include special exhibitions at more general museums	Museum of Moving Image, London; Australian Centre for Moving Image; general museums
Constructed studios	Not a theme park, working studio or museum, but constructed as a place for fans to visit and have an experience	Studio Gibley, Japan
One-off or Recurring Events		
Movie premieres	Particularly those outside traditional sites such as Hollywood	Lord of the Rings: Return of the King (New Zealand); Mission Impossible II (Sydney)
Film festivals	Many cities hold film festivals that attract film buffs and fans for the event	Cannes, Edinburgh
Fan-based events	Often events where participants dress in character, meet the stars (both in and out of costume) and purchase memorabilia. Based at convention sites, not filming sites or studios	Comic Con
Armchair Travels		
Television travel programmes	The successor to travel guidebooks and written travelogues; can also be comedic/satirical	Getaway, Pilot Guides, An Idiot Abroad
Gastronomy programmes	Many cooking shows take the viewer to various places around the world, usually featuring the food of the region	Cook's Tour, Rick Stein's programmes
Documentaries (cultural and natural)	While not focused on selling travel (as with many travel programmes), these documentaries focus on the exotic and unusual in the world	National Geographic; David Attenborough programmes

Riley and Van Doren (1992) even liken movie-induced tourism to that of a hallmark event, defined by Ritchie (1984) as:

> Major one-time or recurring events of limited duration developed to primarily enhance the awareness, appeal and profitability of a destination in the short and/or long term. These events rely for their success on uniqueness, status, or timely significance to create interest and attract attention. (Ritchie, 1984: 9)

They argue that as a movie lasts for a limited duration, can be seen once or repeatedly (including on video or DVD) and relies on its uniqueness and status to create attention, it can be considered a hallmark event. However, there are some major flaws in their rationale, one being that films are not developed to primarily enhance the destination or bring tourists, which is a primary goal of hallmark events. Riley and Van Doren concede this point, but fail to adequately explain why it has been ignored in their proposition. They also fail to acknowledge that the film is rarely consumed at the destination, therefore its viewing is not part of any destination-based event, 'hallmark' or otherwise. Such spatial and temporal separation makes film more of a promotional vehicle akin to a brochure or television advertisement rather than a hallmark event.

That Riley and Van Doren's point has rarely been questioned or discussed in any of the subsequent literature indicates either a tacit acceptance of what they are offering as evidence of film's links to tourism and events, or else an inability to disaggregate and assess the variety of impacts that any individual film, and the entire genre, can have on a society. I also suspect that many of those researching film and tourism do not even read these source documents, let alone critically.

Cousins and Andereck see the recognition of a movie as a hallmark event to be central to maximising its tourism benefits. They took two cases of movies, one that was not seen as a hallmark event by the associated tourism agencies (*Bull Durham* (1988)) and another that was (*The Last of the Mohicans* (1992)), and compared their visitation numbers and interest after the release of each movie (Cousins & Andereck, 1993). They found that the movie that was treated as a hallmark event, *The Last of the Mohicans*, resulted in higher levels of tourist interest and visitation numbers than the other. However, they caution that aspects such as storyline and perception of the setting, as well as aggressive marketing, also contribute to the flow-on effects (or not) of tourism (Cousins & Andereck, 1993).

While I continue to argue that film tourism is not a hallmark event per se, types of film-induced tourism such as one-off events (movie premieres and film festivals, for example) are specifically related to events, and some do fit Ritchie's definition. In Chapter 8 this is looked at in more detail in terms of the world premiere of *The Lord of the Rings: The Return of the King* in Wellington, New Zealand.

In this publication, 'film-induced tourism' takes a broad brush, applying the term to visitation to sites where movies and television programmes have been filmed as well as to tours to production studios, including film-related theme parks. So, my use of the term 'film' is more reflective/representative of the filming process rather than the format or place of delivery (on disk, video, DVD, digitally, or at a cinema, on television or a mobile device 'anywhere'). What is of interest here is the tourist activity associated with the film industry, be it on-site in the field, or at (or near) the production studio.

Differences and Similarities between Movies and Television Series

Before introducing the overall concepts of on-location and off-location film tourism as previewed in Table 1.1, a discussion of the rationale for the choice of the field of study is central to understanding the approach in this publication. Most of the academic studies of film-induced tourism are focused on movies, whether they actually call it, 'movie-induced tourism' or one of the many other terms in use. While movies can be powerful cultural representations and motivators, they tend to be a one-off or limited experience, for both the producers and the majority of viewers (in spite of the availability of videos and television screenings), whereas television series have a longer screening and filming period, with a greater and more complex story arc. For example, Australian television series, *Neighbours* (1985–) celebrated 30 years of continuous screening, five nights a week, in 2015, while the United Kingdom (UK) series *Last of the Summer Wine* (1973–2010) was screened on British television for over 37 years. Consequently, the viewer's empathetic relationship with the story, characters and setting is developed and maintained over a period of time. This not only keeps the region where the series is filmed in people's minds, building on and reinforcing the desire to visit, but also sees the film crews spending extended periods of time at the on-location sites over many years.

Unless the movie proves enormously popular, television series tend to have more long-term impacts. *Crocodile Dundee* (1986, 2001) is arguably the only movie filmed in Australia to have an instant and broad-ranging recognition throughout the United States, even though others such as *The Man from Snowy River* (1982) and *Mad Max* (1979, 1981, 1985, 2015) have been popular, but to a more limited audience. Because of the evidence about the long-term impact of successful series, I have paid particular attention to a specific series site in Australia, namely the village of Barwon Heads, portrayed as Pearl Bay in the ABC television series *Sea Change* (1998–2000), and while the series is no longer screened, the region still experiences related tourism and, more importantly, a strong image primarily created by the series. I also look at the aforementioned series *Neighbours* along with television tours in other parts of the world. In addition, the English village of Goathland in the North

Yorkshire Moors, the site of Aidensfield in the BBC series, *Heartbeat* (1982–2009), is also a significant focus of this work, particularly as the programme has been aired on television since 1992 and has only recently been made available on DVD.

Movies are covered in more general terms, often in relation to destination marketing (see Chapter 3), but there is a focus on the *Lord of the Rings* (2001, 2002, 2003) and *The Hobbit* (2012, 2013, 2014) movies and their significance for tourism in New Zealand, along with some consideration of the community's response to the tourism potential of an Australian movie *Oddball* (2015).

On-Location: Film, Tourism and Country Town Development

Most of the reports that have been produced by local government agencies, tourism associations and film companies in relation to film-induced tourism tend to focus on the numbers of visitors that are attracted to an area and how much money they spend. This creates the distinct impression that economic gain is the first (and only) tourism performance indicator. However, one of the quandaries of tourism is that it carries with it the seeds of its own destruction, which may contribute to (or even cause) the deterioration of communities and the environment, leading to justified questioning of short-term economic rationalist justifications. This 'love it to death' dilemma has been well documented in terms of the natural environment and nature-based tourism, particularly in relation to ecotourism, where overcrowding and over-commercialisation may dramatically alter, if not destroy, those elements that people wish to experience (see Buckley & Pannell, 1990; Richardson, 1993; Harris & Leiper, 1995; Beeton, 1998a). Such losses can also adversely affect the local culture, particularly (but not exclusively) indigenous cultures that rely heavily on (and are intricately connected to) the environment. A case in point is Uluru in central Australia, where the pressure of visitors and their needs threatens to damage not only the environment of 'the Rock', but also the culture of the indigenous community.

The term *tourism development* has become over-simplified by the economic rationalist camp through equating it solely with economic growth, which continues to ignore, or even suppress, any social well-being and community benefits or drawbacks (see Murphy, 1985; Suzuki, 1993; Sofield, 2003). Economic development is important, but is only one aspect of the influence of tourism on an area. Intangible benefits are certainly more difficult to measure, but this in itself makes them even more important to the overall impact and influence of tourism development in small communities.

Consideration must be given to flow-on effects of such development, such as the impact of house price increases on the local rental market and low-income households. This is particularly relevant in communities such as

Barwon Heads (the real-life site for the Australian television series *Sea Change*) which has a proportion of residents who have 'done a *Sea Change*', and moved to the area for the relaxed, small-community lifestyle, taking a drop in income in exchange for a more modest seaside life. Consequently, these residents may not have as much income as they had prior to their move. These communities also tend to have a high proportion of retirees and people on a range of pensions who, unless they are owner-occupiers, stand to be affected by increased land and, as a consequence, rental prices. Of course, others may find increased rental prices to their benefit if they own their property and are able to rent it out during the peak holiday season.

Consequently, it is important to be concerned not merely with the immediate increase in visitors but also with the overall effects that occur within the community over time, particularly from the aspect of changing attitudes and social representations. The level of importance of the economic and social impacts to the Barwon Heads community will be relative to the social representations held by each community member, so it is important to identify the range of attitudes that are dominant in the town. Simply put, social representations theory (SRT) looks for similarities in the attitudes ('representations') that people have, then considers the similarities between such attitudes and those who hold them (Pearce *et al.*, 1996).

In their monograph, *Tourism Community Relationships*, Pearce *et al.* (1996) introduce the concept of social representation as a means to understand micro-community relationships regarding tourism. SRT was introduced by French social psychologist Moscovici (1972, 1984), who first mooted and then developed the SRT concept in the early 1970s. Relying heavily on Moscovici, Pearce *et al.* present their argument for the application of SRT to tourism community research in a most compelling manner, providing examples from their own research (in the form of case studies) as well as building on recognised earlier work.

The theory of social representations can provide the means with which to consider individual attitudes within communities, and to group them according to their similarities. This is the reverse of the commonly used process of identifying the groups and then looking for their attitudes, and provides a more comprehensive examination of communities at the micro level. Community attitudes and interactions are dynamic, requiring a dynamic, evolving vision from any researcher or student. As it is driven by the subjects, SRT is an emic form of study, giving the participants the opportunity to drive the research, rather than the researcher prescribing (and at times proscribing) the investigative path. In addition, in-depth analysis of small communities can provide a sound basis for the development of broader, more complex tourism models on a larger scale. This provides a sound methodological basis for tourism-related community research, which is preferable to more prescriptive social-research methods, and is applied in Chapters 5 and 6.

Increased tourism may improve the standard of living in the town by helping to maintain current levels of employment (against a possible regional decline) and possibly by creating jobs for the unemployed and welfare-dependent. Tourism may also lead to a greater level of pride in the town and a sense of belonging, in addition to the recognition amongst residents that they possess something that others desire – such as the tranquillity of a small fishing village. The imaging power of film can work constructively, providing residents with a positive view of their town, if they see the complementary film portrayal as realistic, evocative and desirable.

Many of the economic benefits of increased tourist visitation will go to those who rely on earning their living from the respective town, such as those directly involved in tourism, local traders and associated services (such as tradespeople), as well as rental and investment property owners. Those who make their living away from the town or are already on retirement incomes may have a stronger desire to resist the economic changes associated with tourism growth, as they are not dependent on the economic health of the area. Rather they choose to live in a small, non-urban community precisely because it is a slow, sleepy backwater. The adverse reaction of residents of Avalon Beach in Sydney towards the filming of *Baywatch* is a pertinent example. Even though Avalon Beach is far from 'slow and sleepy', a majority of its residents work away from the area.

Increased development has the potential to dramatically change the nature and visual landscape of the town, particularly if more motels, units, marinas or condominiums are built. For example, let's look at the Australian case of Barwon Heads and *Sea Change* where the visitor accommodation base of the town is heavily concentrated in caravan parks and holiday homes, and the visitor base is integrated into the town's local built environment. With a capacity for 2490 overnight visitors in holiday homes, 2620 in caravan parks and 60 in hotels, motels and units, totalling 6170 overnight beds, the town has a greater overnight visitor capacity than other higher-profile, long-established resort towns (City of Greater Geelong, 1998). However, the mix is very different from that of a standard resort-based town that boasts a preponderance of hotels, motels and units. The prevalence of holiday homes and caravan park spaces at Barwon Heads reflects the current nature of the town's overnight tourism market (including longer stays) which is predominantly families holidaying in the town regularly, especially annually. A change in the type of accommodation base usually alters the visitor demographic. If holiday rents go up, some families will be forced to choose lesser-known beachside locations, probably much further afield.

Increasing tourist numbers may not be entirely positive, even for a town that appears to be reliant on the tourism industry. This study considers places that are affected not only by increased tourist visitation, but also by changing visitor patterns as well as the potential alteration of the commercial focus of the town from servicing residents to providing for tourists. Those aspects that affect the main stakeholders in the town (the local community, traders, weekend residents and regular visitors) are considered in some depth.

Off-Location: Film Studios and Tourism

Taking the concept of tourists visiting the on-location sites of certain films to its next logical step has seen the creation of purpose-built tourist attractions at the movie studios themselves. Paramount Studios in Hollywood runs guided tours of its site, creating a workplace tourism site in the same vein as other industrial tourism enterprises (from chocolate factories to car plants). Other Hollywood studios (in particular Universal, Disney and Warner Brothers) have developed tourist-specific theme park entertainment based around their hit movies such as *Back To The Future* (1985, 1989, 1990), *Jurassic Park* (1993, 1997, 2001, 2015), *The Blues Brothers* (1980), *Superman* (2006), *Finding Nemo* (2003), *Brave* (2012), and *Harry Potter* (2001, 2002, 2004, 2005, 2007, 2009, 2010, 2011). Interestingly, most of these movies are part of a series or franchise, giving them greater longevity.

The notion of theme parks that represent a phenomenon that is in itself already a representation of something else (that is, in the film), leads us into the field of postmodernism and post-tourism. Notions of representation, simulacra, pastiche and hyper reality are central to this field. Postmodernism is introduced and outlined in Chapter 8, contextualised by the ensuing discussion of film studio theme parks and themed events in that chapter.

In the early 21st century, Fox Studios Australia attempted to produce a hybrid of the working studio/industrial tourism attraction and theme park, with its development of the Fox Studios Backlot and commercial precinct in inner Sydney. The studios have been used to film *Mission Impossible II* (2000), *Moulin Rouge* (2001), *Babe, Pig in the City* (1998), the *Star Wars* (1999, 2002, 2005) prequels, and *The Matrix* (1999, 2003) series. In spite of the box office success of such movies, the cost of production is high, hence the interest in developing other income-generating ventures at the site. The tourism theme park outlet developed at Fox Studios proved a dismal failure, with the Fox Studios Backlot closing within two years. Such a reversal of fortunes suggests that film-induced tourism is not as simple as it seems, in this case failing to attract enough paying visitors to a site based in one of the world's most recognisable cities, Sydney. The failure of the Fox Backlot is studied in detail in Chapters 8 and 9, where a model that goes some to towards explaining the failure is also presented.

Film as a Souvenir

As well as creating destination images and encouraging tourist visitation, films are often consumed after the visit, as (usually unacknowledged) souvenirs. They may be purchased or hired as videos or DVDs, or down-loaded digitally, to be consumed in private, or viewed at a public cinema or on television. Still pictures, publicity posters or even film 'cells' can be displayed much as other souvenirs, or presented as gifts.

Love and Sheldon (1998) defined souvenirs broadly as items purchased at the site of the tourism activity; however this somewhat basic definition ignores the complexity of souvenirs and memorabilia, especially in relation to filmic experiences. A common souvenir typology separates them into pictorial images (postcards, photos, books, etc.), pieces-of-the-rock (things from the natural environment), symbolic shorthand (manufactured miniatures), markers (souvenirs inscribed with words that locate them in place and time, such as tea towels), and local products (foods, crafts, etc.) (Gordon, 1986). MacCannell (1976), however, gives markers a broader role than Gordon, claiming that they are all pieces of information about a specific site, which in turn renders all souvenirs as forms of markers and vice versa.

MacCannell's description of souvenirs as markers relates to his widely accepted description of a tourist attraction, comprising three elements: a tourist, a site and a marker. Other markers include guidebooks, maps, travelogues and stories, all of which can return with the visitor as souvenirs (MacCannell, 1976). In a study of the meanings that tourists give their souvenirs, Love and Sheldon (1998: 174) found that the 'meanings that tourists imbue their souvenirs with are fluid, embracing experiences before, during and after the time souvenirs are acquired'. As with Graburn (1989), they suggest that souvenirs communicate meanings beyond tangible evidence, form and function, and bring back memories of the experience.

As inferred earlier, film adds yet another dimension, as it can actually take the specific attraction away from its site by being purchased after the experience, yet retain its travel meaning for the tourist. According to Graburn (1989: 34), tourism is rife with snobbery, with 'the next best thing to travelling is to know someone who did' through displaying souvenirs as gifts, such as placing postcards on a noticeboard, wearing a T-shirt, or sticking magnets on a refrigerator. There is also a certain snobbery attached to film and media, especially in terms of celebrity, as discussed in Chapter 2. However, the difference between film and other souvenirs is the increasingly complex, layered and emotional memories that it may hold, enabling the owner to construct an additional travel 'story' related to the film, which can be quite separate from the personal experience of that place. Often, it is this difference that becomes the story.

A movie may simply represent the scenery of a place, reflected in the picturesque, as described at the beginning of this chapter. However, storylines and today's obsession with celebrity (even that of a place) complicate even the simplest motive for purchasing film as a souvenir. For example, after riding a horse through Monument Valley, when I got back home I hired the 1935 John Wayne movie *Stagecoach*, not to view the scenery (which was poorly rendered in black and white), but to experience the story in the movie through my personal knowledge of the landscape, as well as the history of the production of that film, which is famous in its own right. I had not merely hired a horse and ridden through some spectacular scenery, but had been a part of the early development of the cult of the Western movie! However, this was not enough, and I have subsequently purchased a special edition DVD of the movie, now displayed prominently on my bookshelf.

The tourist may have experienced or witnessed only one minor element of a movie, yet that moment on film is powerful enough to evoke the entire holiday. Another personal example comes from the movie *The Firm* (1993), filmed in Memphis, Tennessee. While we were at BB King's Blues Club on Beale Street in 1999, a young man who 'flips' down the street for about 20 seconds in the film performed for us. We subsequently hired the movie and watched the whole film for a glimpse of the boy, representing and enabling us to re-live our experience on the famous street. While I did not purchase this movie, I have also seen it many times subsequently on television. During a recent visit in 2015, teenagers were flipping down Beale Street for tips from tourists in a very sophisticated set-up, and I was informed that the young man I saw over 15 years ago runs this enterprise, still trading on his movie fame.

Also, on returning home, tourists may develop an interest in a television series set in a place they visited, purely as a means to re-live or display their own experiences. Conversely, it can be argued that it is the site itself that becomes a souvenir of the film, but this is a topic for further anthropological/social study not covered here.

Longevity of Film-Induced Tourism

Such souvenir collection and the re-viewing of movies and television series can contribute to maintaining and developing interest and passion through the re-telling of re-living of the touristic experience. However, there are movies and television series that have also created long-term tourism, right from the early days of the moving image. In *Travel, Tourism and the Moving Image*, I argue that 'travel and tourism has been linked inextricably with the moving image since its 19th-century inception' (Beeton, 2015: 6) and illustrate the enduring nature of film-induced tourism through examples such as the 1930s westerns of John Ford which still attract tourists to Ford Point in Monument Valley. *The Sound of Music* (1965), referred to in later chapters, continues to attract tourists to Salzburg over 50 years later, while we see many other movies also influencing tourism long after their initial screening. While I cite many personal examples in *Travel, Tourism and the Moving Image*, one that stays with me is the Disney movie, *The Miracle of the White Stallions* (1963), which I saw back in the 1960s and influenced my visit to Vienna some 50 years later, to the extent that I had tears in my eyes.

Figure 1.1 Recycled houses built for *Kita no Kunikara (From a North Country)* (1981–2001) still receive high levels of visitation near Furano, Japan

As well as movies, many television series regularly attract tourists throughout their years of screening, such as the Australian series *Neighbours* (1985–) and the UK series *Heartbeat* (1992–2010); but it is not only a Western, European phenomenon, television series in Asia attract their own fan-based visitation, such as with the Japanese television series *Kita no Kunikara (From a North Country)* (1981–2001), which has its own museum in the town of Furano dedicated to the planning and filming of the series, while many of the houses in the series, which were built from local, found and recycled materials, have actually won environmental planning awards (Figure 1.1). One of the houses, known as The Recycled House, was listed as one of the top 100 ecological architectural structures in the world by the Public Style Institute at Ritsumeikan University College of Science and Engineering (Furano Tourism Association, 2012).

The Australian soap opera (or television series) *Neighbours* (1985–) has tours of the street where all the neighbours 'live' as well as the dedicated filming studio every day of the year, apart from Christmas Day and Good Friday. The tours are extremely popular with British backpackers, but fans of all ages and from around the world take the tours. The actual street, known as Ramsay Street in the series, is in a quiet non-descript suburban area of Melbourne, yet is so popular with fans that security guards are stationed there 24 hours a day (Figure 1.2).

Figure 1.2 The security guard watches *Neighbours* fans act out in suburban Melbourne

The Study of Film-Induced Tourism

The study of film-induced tourism is complex, incorporating aspects of disciplines such as sociology, psychology and communications, as well as industry-based sectors from film making through to destination marketing, community development and strategic planning. And, in spite of an increase in research into this area over the past 10 years, this remains a relatively untapped and little-understood field of tourism research.

While earlier exploratory studies such as Cohen's 1986 paper speculated on the nature of film-induced tourism and recommended further research into the field, progress up until the 21st century had been slow. Riley, Tooke, Baker and Van Doren took up the challenge in the 1990s, but, after publishing their interesting results in some four or so papers, moved on to other areas of study and research. Much of the academic literature of the later 1990s and early 2000s did not specifically add to the body of research, tending to focus on replicating (and supporting) these earlier studies, looking mainly at the promotional value of film in relation to tourism. While this has reinforced the results of earlier research, I have argued that little new material has been added to the literature on film-induced tourism, and much of the research has been conducted in a piecemeal, ad hoc manner. While there are some commendable examples that have taken us forward, including the work of Reijnders (2007, 2009), Tzanelli (2007, 2015), Frost (2006, 2008, 2010), Hudson and Ritchie (2006a, 2006b), Connell (2005, 2012), Kim (2010b, 2012), Kim *et al.* (2015), Roesch (2009), Sugawa-Shimada (2015) and Yamamura (2011), this statement remains valid. Each paper published concludes by stating the need for further research, but few have followed their own recommendations, leaving the impression that such statements are merely escape clauses for those undertaking short-term, one-off research projects.

I hope that the work presented in this book, plus other studies currently underway at doctoral level and some larger team-based projects in Europe and Asia, will actually progress our knowledge of film-induced tourism, which is far more complex than being merely a simple promotional tool. By adopting a mixed social sciences approach, the discussion is opening up to areas beyond merely the economic imperative of increasing visitor numbers and creating jobs.

Voice and Structure of the Book

All writing and all writers have a 'voice', which is a combination of the conscious application of a style and of personal elements. I have used an active voice here as much as possible, and where required have alternated between third person and first person. I have used the first person when referring to my first-hand experiences on site visits, which is often used in sociological research when the researcher is also a participant (Jennings, 2001) and is an essential element of autoethnographic studies. The very nature of tourism lends itself to participant observation research methodologies, as it is not always possible (or even desirable) for researchers to be impassively removed from their subjects. There were times when objective assessment or study of film sites became impossible, such as the visit to Doune Castle in Scotland, the site for *Monty Python and the Holy Grail* (1975) (Chapter 2). When Monty Python was at its peak in the mid-1970s, one either 'got it' and was an obsessed fan, or didn't. The bizarre humour left no middle ground. I was one of those who 'got it', spending too many hours at university listening to *Monty Python* tapes while reading *Phantom* comics. So, a visit to the site of the movie so many years later was a pilgrimage, and I was immersed in the experience. This does not make the study of Doune Castle any less relevant than if another research methodology had been used. All research contains elements of bias, and it is the recognition of the level and type of bias that is important.

The book is presented in four parts, with Part 1 incorporating a contextual introduction as well as introducing the various perspectives and ways of looking at film-induced tourism. Part 2 focuses on on-location film-induced tourism with chapters looking at film images in relation to destination marketing, followed by a consideration of community impacts and tourism impacts related to film. The findings of this section are brought together in a community tourism planning framework in Chapter 7. Part 3 examines off-location film studio tourism, utilising theme park theory to assist in the development of a film studio theme park model, which is applied to successful and failed film tourism theme park enterprises. In order to contextualise the theme park discussion, elements of the postmodern tourism discourse are outlined in Chapter 8. Part 4 concludes the study and leads into areas for further research that have become apparent throughout the course of this enquiry into the fascinating field of film-induced tourism.

This chapter has set the basic parameters for the context of this book. Chapter 2 provides that context by introducing the range and variety of perspectives and ways that film-induced tourism can be perceived and studied.

2 Perspectives on Film-Induced Tourism

As noted in Chapter 1, the significant effect of film on tourist behaviour is acknowledged, yet its complexities remain little understood. This chapter, in effect, goes back to the beginning of the studies of film-induced tourism, presenting evidence of the power of film as a motivational and image-making tool, through the pioneering work of Riley, Tooke, Baker and Van Doren, among others, before moving on to consider more recent research. The benefits and drawbacks of film-induced tourism that have been identified by these researchers are outlined, and this is followed by some discussion on the concept of 'celebrity' and its possible links with film-induced tourism. Connected to this concept of celebrity and tourism is the notion of pilgrimages to filming sites, which is introduced towards the end of the chapter. All of these perspectives are returned to and developed throughout the book as further information is uncovered.

The power of film to motivate travellers, create new images, alter negative images, strengthen weak images, and create and place icons has been recognised by many as a major factor in tourism promotion for some time. For example, James Alfred Wight (aka James Herriot, pen name of the author of *All Creatures Great and Small* that also became a popular television series screening from 1978–1990) won a special award in 1984 from the British Tourist Authority for '...making even more people aware of the delights of Yorkshire and Britain' (Tooke & Baker, 1996: 90), while the visitor attraction, The World of James Herriot, was awarded Gold in the Small Visitor Attraction category at the 2015 VisitEngland Awards for Excellence, demonstrating the longevity of this series. More recently, Academic Award winner, Sir Peter Jackson has received a number of acknowledgements for his contribution to New Zealand tourism, most recently in 2014 when he was awarded the Blake Medal for his outstanding leadership and contribution to tourism, his local Wellington community and the New Zealand and international film industry.

Over 20 years ago, Tooke and Baker (1996) suggested that the effect of film-induced tourism may be sufficient to warrant tourist destinations encouraging film producers as a formal policy. This has occurred in some parts of the world, including the US, where some tourism commissions are partnered with the local film commission, indicating that the connection is considered to be extremely important. For example, in the 1990s the film offices of Montana, Wisconsin, North Dakota and South Dakota were part of their state's tourism operations, funded through their respective tourism departments (Cobb, 1996). In an English Tourism Council publication on developing film tourism, the Head of Borough Liaison at the London Film Commission, Harvey Edgington, advised that '[i]f a film office exists in an area, I would advise all tourism intermediaries to make use of it…Even a scuzzy housing estate is of interest' (English Tourism Council, 2000).

While not all regions have such close relationships, an increasing number of tourism associations are working with their associated film offices by encouraging their regions to become 'film friendly', and at the same time recognising the ongoing tourism benefits. This recognition of the flow-on benefits of tourism has resulted in some cooperative ventures, such as publications that provide information for film producers as well as visitors. For example, VisitScotland and Scottish Screen developed a brochure, *Mansion Locations in Scotland*, covering 64 potential film locations in the country, supplementing a database of over 500 houses available for filming (Scottish Executive, 2002a). Another cooperative venture between Scottish Screen, VisitScotland, The British Council and the Highlands and Islands Film Commission has resulted in a further publication, *The Pocket Scottish Movie Book*. This is aimed at 'all Scots, tourists, film fans and film makers…' (Scottish Executive, 2002b). VisitScotland continues to tie together filming and tourism, being voted as the top destination for the silver screen by readers of *USA Today* and the travel website *10Best* in 2015.

However, there are still many instances where film corporations and individual organisations are not working so cooperatively, and this can create problems when the aims of the tourism organisation clash with those of the film office. Even with those who are supposedly working together, there is little evidence of any concern for the consequences of over-promoting a region due to film. In fact, it seems that the more cognisant of the power of film that people have become, the more they are blindly chasing it (especially destination marketing organisations (DMOs), local government, journalists and tourists) with little regard for the consequences. While I remain excited by the concept of film-related tourism, my concerns remain. In 2014 I spoke at a screening of the documentary *Gringo Trails* (2013) which, while not focusing on film-induced tourism per se, dramatically demonstrated the perils of popularity. Its focus was on young travellers, not the usual 'mass' tourist that many focus on, presenting powerful evidence of the ways that young people travel and communicate via all forms of media and the extensive damage this can bring. This is a serious issue, and is a theme that takes up much of this book.

Tooke and Baker (1996) also suggest that the producers themselves should consider approaching locations for financial investment or seed funding for their films. It has certainly been recognised that the value of promotional advertising provided by some films would be out of the price range of tourism offices (for example, Vieh, 1997). As far back as 1997, the creator of a new television variety show in Miami applied to the Miami Beach Visitors and Convention Authority for a grant, arguing that the programme would have positive tourism flow-ons, if successful (Levine, 1997). Unfortunately, the literature does not inform us as to the success of either the grant application or the series.

Many cities, states and even countries are touting themselves as 'filmworthy', and an interesting illustration of the extent to which some places will go is provided by those associated with the Hollywood film *A Thousand Acres* (1997). The script required a farm with '...a sea of corn as far as the eye can see' (*Economist*, 1998a: 28) and had specified Iowa, in the middle of America's Corn Belt, as the location. However, Illinois wanted the economic benefits of filming (which came to U$S21 million local economic benefit and 183 full-time jobs) in their region and also hoped for induced tourism in the future. Consequently, the Illinois Film Office provided the producers with pages of data on Illinois corn, and even suggested a range of hybrid varieties that could simulate an entire growing season in just six weeks. They were successful in their bid, and the movie was filmed in Illinois, just outside Chicago (*Economist*, 1998a: 29).

In a similar manner, an article from *Inside Tucson Business* exhorts the entire business community, not just tourism, to get behind its film office. The article claims that everyone has '...an obligation to aggressively campaign for Arizona as a good place to produce motion pictures and TV programmes' (*Inside Tucson Business*, 1998: 4), citing examples of the potential tourism value to the state as the most valuable aspect of filming in an area. The examples used include the notion that *Titanic* (1997) is helping the cruise industry to surge (an interesting example of selective adoption of parts of the storyline as a positive motivator, namely the romance, as opposed to the negative motivational aspect of the sinking of the ship) and that *Forrest Gump* (1994) provided a tourism boon to the Louisiana bayou (*Inside Tucson Business*, 1998).

Such intriguing suggestions beg further investigation into the imaging power of film and its relationship to tourism, so that it can be used effectively in tourism planning instead of in an ad hoc manner. This is reintroduced in more detail in the next chapter.

The Effect of Film on Tourism

While figures relating directly to the impact that films (both movies and television series) have had on tourism are limited, there is still some impressive data. In 1978, the year after *Close Encounters of the Third Kind* (1977) was released, visitation to Devil's Tower National Monument increased by a staggering 74%, while in a survey conducted 11 years after the film's premiere, one-fifth of respondents attributed their initial knowledge of the monument to the movie (Tooke & Baker, 1996). Lazarus noted that tourist interest in visiting the sites of the Western movie *Shane* (1953) was prevalent 40 years after it was filmed, and that when television programmes move to syndication and Pay TV, they enjoy extended periods of public exposure (Lazarus, 1999).

As discussed in Chapter 1, tourism boards have developed tourist precincts based on literary figures (such as Burns Country), and this has now been extended to incorporate themed products based on film and television. There are a number of examples from the UK where fiction has been incorporated into historic sites and events, including '*East Ender* Breaks', '*Last of the Summer Wine* Country', '*Coronation Street* Experience', and 'In the Footsteps of Brother Cadfael' (Schofield, 1996). In such instances of fiction being combined with fact, boundaries can become blurred between what is real and what is not. However, tourists are often more interested in experiencing what has been promoted through the powerful visual media than in gazing at so-called 'dead' history, which is even more pronounced in this era of the moving image.

Between 1981 and 1988 American tourists to Australia increased by 20.5% per annum. This remarkable increase has been attributed to a number of factors, not the least being the impact of Australian movies such as *Mad Max* (released in the US in 1980), *The Man from Snowy River* (1982) and *Crocodile Dundee* (1986). In 1987, tourism numbers increased more rapidly in Australia than in any other developed nation (O'Regan, 1988). Also, in 1985 the Australian soap opera *Neighbours* (1985–) was first screened, going on to success in the UK from 1986 where it has taken on a legendary, cult status, as well as over 50 other countries including New Zealand, the US, Belgium, Barbados and Kenya. The story of the popular *Neighbours* tour that still operates in Melbourne every day of the year (apart from Christmas Day and Good Friday) is described in Chapter 3.

Crocodile Dundee can be considered to be the first movie that consciously and simultaneously encouraged tourism to Australia. According to Crofts (1989), the drive to export film in the 1980s arose from a desire to develop foreign trade and tourism. Crofts goes on to explain that Paramount, the US distributor of *Crocodile Dundee*, introduced its promotional campaign for the US release of the movie after Paul Hogan's 'throw another shrimp on the barbie' television advertisements for the Australian Tourist Commission, when his face, if not his name, had become widely known (Crofts, 1989). There comes a point in that series of tourism advertisements, which were developed over a period of many years, where Hogan adopts his Crocodile Dundee persona, directly referencing the movie.

Increased horse- and adventure-related tourism activity grew extensively following the two *The Man from Snowy River* movies, particularly in the Mansfield district in Victoria where the movie was filmed (even though the story was actually set in-country further north-east, where the Snowy River really flows). These activities ranged from horseback tours through to restaurants such as the Snowy River Steakhouse, and canvas and saddlery suppliers such as the Snowy Mountain Rug Company (Beeton, 1998b). In addition, horseback tourism in Australia's High Country increased 10-fold in as many years, from three operators before the movie's release to more than 30 by 1996 (DNRE, 1996). The Hunt Club Hotel in the tiny village of Merrijig, where most of the cast and crew stayed and/or socialised, has decorated its walls with photographs and memorabilia from the movie, and locals still dine out on stories of the stars. Over 30 years later tourists still come to the region, as exemplified by a horseback tour I undertook in 2013, hosted by the star of the 1982 movie, Tom Burlinson. I recount my experience of this tour in Beeton (2015), but to summarise, young and old fans came from Australia, the US and Canada to be part of the experience, with some of the strongest fans barely born when the movie was first released. As we cantered up the mountains, the group hummed the appropriate theme music and re-enacted scenes with Tom. The Australian morning television programme *Sunrise* also joined us for three days, filming live each morning from the (sometimes remote) places made famous in the 1982 movie and interviewing the tourists as well as Tom Burlinson and the horseback operator who was also involved in the movie, Charlie Lovick.

However, film-induced tourism was not the sole driver for international tourism growth of the 1980s. During that decade there was a range of high-profile international events that influenced the growth of Australian tourism. These included the Commonwealth Games (Brisbane, 1982), America's Cup defence (Western Australia, 1986–1987), Australian Grand Prix (Adelaide, 1985 onwards), Australia's Bicentenary (especially Sydney, 1988) and World Expo (Brisbane, 1988), as well as the floating of the Australian dollar in 1985. The latter's subsequent drop in value against the US dollar made Australia even more attractive and affordable to North American and Japanese visitors. So, we do need to be careful when contributing simply one factor to human behaviour, such as film and tourism. That said, *Crocodile Dundee* remains a significant image-maker and attraction, with the new owner of the Walkabout Creek Hotel, Frank Wurst, explaining on Australian radio in 2015 that 90% of their business still comes from fans of the movie (http://blogs.abc.net.au/queensland/2015/06/are-you-a-television-tourist-.html).

Relationship between Tourist Attraction and Storyline

The physical environment or site of a film can relate to the storyline in varying degrees, from being a passive backdrop to the action (as in many of the older Westerns), right through to being an integral part of the storyline as in *The Man from Snowy River* (1982) where the specifically Australian 'High Country' played a major role as friend, protagonist and enemy. Riley and Van Doren note that the Australian movies that attracted interest in the US had three things in common. They used the natural environment as a backdrop to the action, there was interaction and struggle of man with that environment, and the lifestyles depicted were relatively uncomplicated (Riley & Van Doren, 1992). This correlates with my own experiences, particularly with the American Western, which I watched avidly as a child (and later), finding myself in middle-age riding through Monument Valley in the US on a horse, imagining myself as John Wayne and experiencing many powerful emotional reactions, which I still find today. As well as discussing this in more depth later in the book, I detail this experience and my ongoing fascination with the Western genre in Beeton, 2015. Tooke and Baker tended to see the storyline as providing a contextual package in which attractions and experiences for the tourist can be grounded, which supports earlier suggestions that many tourists are wanting to experience at least part of what was depicted in the film as opposed to merely gazing at the site/sight (Tooke & Baker, 1996).

Post-war Greece saw a rapid increase in the numbers of domestic and international tourists, with international tourism increasing five-fold from the 1950s to the 1960s – the era of the Greek film musical. During those decades, Greek living standards increased dramatically, followed by an increased interest in tourism and an ability to realise that interest becoming a 'new' consumer activity (Clogg, 1992). Papadimitriou (2000) considers this increase in tourism to be directly linked to the themes reflected in the Greek film musical, stating that 'the Greek musical deploys tourism itself as a fantasy of transformation...[addressing] its spectators as virtual tourists' (Papadimitriou, 2000: 98).

The Greek film musical is 'a cinema of spectacle, characteristically integrating a minimum of six song-and-dance numbers with a romantic narrative' (Papadimitriou, 2000: 97), pre-empting the Indian 'Bollywood' movies of the 1990s and 2000s. The Greek film musicals of the 1950s and 1960s share similar goals to those of tourism – providing entertainment and escapism. The Greek musicals made extensive use of tourism imagery such as sun, sea and food, along with culture surrounding classical Greek monuments. The storylines directly incorporated tourism into them, with the characters either being tourists themselves or working in the tourism industry.

However, as Riley *et al.* postulate, '...the locations need not be beautiful nor the storylines positive in order to attract visitors' (Riley *et al.*, 1998: 932). An excellent example of this is in the *Mad Max* movies where the desert is depicted as a hostile, barren, dangerous environment, yet tourism to, and interest in, the Broken Hill region in Australia increased markedly after *Mad Max II* (1981) (the first instalment being filmed in Melbourne) and Wolfe Creek Crater after *Wolf Creek* (2005), both of which did not possess beautiful scenery or positive storylines, even though Max did find his humanity at the end of Mad Max II (Frost, 2010). The movie *Titanic* saw the burgeoning cruise industry benefit from a movie about the disastrous sinking of the most famous passenger ship of all (*Inside Tucson Business*, 1998).

In his seminal 1975 work, *The Image: A Guide to Pseudo Events in America*, Boorstin believes that the public's interest in visiting sites depicted in film is based on curiosity about whether the depiction is 'real', postulating questions such as:

> Is the Trevi Fountain in Rome really like its portrayal in the movie *Three Coins in the Fountain*? Is Hong Kong really like *Love is a Many Splendored Thing*? Is it full of Suzie Wongs? We go not to test the image by the reality, but to test reality by the image. (Boorstin, 1972: 116)

Cohen considers the relationship of the setting with the storyline to be crucial to the magnitude of its touristic attraction, stating that '...the most basic issue is whether the setting must be in the foreground of the story to truly leave an impression on the viewer's mind' (Cohen, 1986: 232), and tentatively concludes that such is the case.

The relationship between storyline and tourism is examined further in the destination marketing discussion in Chapter 3, yet is an area little studied or adequately understood. Another aspect of the viewer's relationship with representations in the story can be found in the emerging field of semiotics, which is considered briefly in terms of film in the following literature review.

Representation and Semiotics in Film and Tourism

According to Hall (1997), culture is produced through shared meanings that can be represented by a variety of modern media, including film. Film, as a visual language, can create a 'meaning of place' in terms of the representational system shared by members of the same (or similar) culture. Such representations and meanings can be made to perform specific destination marketing roles by creating a desire in the viewer to experience the place in a less vicarious form (by visiting the site of the film).

The meaning and representational systems behind language and shared culture can also be examined through semiotics. First coined by the linguist Ferdinand de Saussure as 'a science that studies the life of signs within society' (Hall, 1997: 36), the theory of semiotics deals with the connection between meaning, experience and signification (code). In other words, it deals with the signs and codes of messages through the use of markers and signs (MacCannell, 1976; Tomaselli, 1985; Urry, 1990). Semiotic analysis has been applied to many areas of the arts, marketing and advertising in an attempt to explain and even predict consumer behaviour and cultural responses to certain signs. In relation to film and semiotics, Kindem states that:

> An understanding of the semiotic sources and possibilities of meaning based upon a semiotic, typological analysis can be of value to both the film maker and the film viewer, critic and theorist. (Kindem, 1979: 65)

Semiotics and the Tourist Gaze

In 1990, Urry presented us with the concept of the 'tourist gaze', applying it in representational terms, explaining that '[t]he gaze...presupposes a system of social activities and signs' (Urry, 1990: 2), noting that film and television are instrumental in constructing and sustaining the anticipation of the visitor. However, at that stage, there had not been any study of film-induced tourism for him to draw on. However, in *The Tourist Gaze 3.0* (2011), Urry and his co-author Larsen consider the *mediatised gaze*, as 'a collective gaze where particular sites famous for their "mediated" nature are viewed...so-called movie induced tourism' (Urry & Larsen, 2011: 20). Tourism markers in today's society are so prolific that they tend to overlap and reinforce each other, often as a result of media-related contributions, in particular, film. The extent of this is increasingly vast, with Urry and Larsen arguing that film landscapes are so pervasive for the tourist that the destinations themselves become *'fantasylands* or *mediaworlds'* (Urry & Larsen, 2011: 117). We revisit this concept in the discussion on postmodernism in Chapter 8.

Prior to the explosion of the mediatised gaze and use of film as a landscape signifier, Kindem (1979) felt that it was difficult to predict the popularity of a certain film simply through using semiotic analysis because factors such as economics, ideology and psychology come into play. As far back as the 1940s, analysts such as Rosten commented that '...more people lament the fact that reality does not reflect the movies' (Rosten, 1941), pre-empting the desire of viewers to visit the sites featured in film 'in real life'. Incorporating social science analytical approaches into an analysis of the popularity of film-induced tourism seems important when considering the significance (signs and codes) of the romantic rural idyll in terms of the popularity of recent television series such as *Heartbeat* and *Sea Change* and ongoing series including *Neighbours*. More researchers have expanded the study of semiotics into realms such as contents tourism discussed below and notions of the imagination, including Reijnders (2011, 2015) and colleagues (Reijnders *et al.,* 2015), along with my own attempts.

Contents Tourism

When we consider the reasons for the popularity of certain films (including television series) and the tourism to the sites ('on-location tourism') that follows some films, we find that markers, signs and meanings play an important role, not in only establishing motives for the visitation but also in presenting the site to the tourist. In Japan, the term 'contents (*kontentsu*) tourism' has come to represent tourism based around signs and meaning, with a particular focus on (but not exclusively) the role of anime in Japanese tourism. While a relatively new term in the English-language literature, contents tourism has been used in Japanese academic and business circles since the 1990s. The term refers to the various narrative and creative components of popular culture, including stories, characters, music, locations and, in particular, film.

Emerging in the 1990s, the concept of contents or narrative presented via pop culture was officially adopted in the Japanese government's 2005 tourism strategy (Masubuchi, 2010; Beeton *et al.*, 2013). The Ministry of Land, Infrastructure, Transport and Tourism (MLITT), the Ministry of Economy, Trade and Industry, and the Agency for Cultural Affairs defined the essence of contents tourism as

> the addition of a 'narrative quality' (*monogatarisei*) or 'theme' (*teemasei*) to a region – namely an atmosphere or image particular to the region generated by the contents – and the use of that narrative quality as a tourism resource. (MLITT, 2005: 49)

Table 2.1 summarises the various forms that contents tourism takes in Japan, and while there are many similarities with our Western concepts of film-induced tourism, it is interesting to note that this was developed independently from the Western literature by the Japanese government department, the MLITT (2005), where they encouraged local authorities to develop contents that are distinctive to their region as tourist resources.

Certainly there many striking cases in Japan where even visitors to the theme parks dress up, and Japanese anime films such as those produced by Oscar-winning director Miyazawa Hayao at Studio Ghibli (a site I visited and recount later in the book) have achieved a high level of global as well as local recognition. Along with this are the enormous domestic audiences of 10–20 million viewers of Japanese dramas such as the aforementioned *Kita no kuni kara (From the Northern Country)* (1981–2002) with its own dedicated museum as well as a park with the houses built for the series (including Goro's Stone House and the Recycled House), remaining strong tourist attractions around the Furano district today (Beeton *et al.*, 2013). Again, I recount the story of my site visit to this region later in the book.

Table 2.1 Forms of contents tourism

Type of contents

	Films, television dramas, novels	*Manga, Anime, Games*
Displays or exhibitions of the contents	– Museum about the writer – Exhibits of the sets or props used during production	– Museum about the writer or producer – Exhibits about the characters
Preservation or construction of sites that contribute to the use of contents	– Preserving locations – Preserving sets used in filming	– Erecting monuments in stations or high streets
Holding events related to the contents	– Film festivals – Talks by directors, actors and writers; accompanied tours – Cosplay events for fans and *otaku*	– Talks by directors, voice actors and writers; accompanied tours – Cosplay events for fans and *otaku*
Performances for enjoying the contents	– Accompanied tours with directors, actors and writers	– Putting anime characters on public transport
Sale of spin-off goods or product branding	– Using images from the contents on local products – Using the contents in local area branding strategies	
Information provision	– Publicity through various media: television, newspapers, magazines, etc. – Publicity on the internet – Local information provision through weblogs	
Human resources	– Training volunteer tour guides – Encouraging the participation of locals as extras during filming – Holding competitions to develop a new generation of creators – Supporting local people working in creative media	– Supporting the local people working in creative media

Source: Beeton *et al.* (2013: 147) from MLITT *et al.* (2005: 50). Translated by the authors.

The Japan National Tourism Organization has a series of movie/anime-based maps, and in 2012 their webpage had a link, 'Pilgrimages and Sites', leading to an interactive map covering anime and cinema. I was excited when on a recent walking tour in Japan we inadvertently came across one such site at Hikone Castle (rendering me an 'incidental' film tourist!; Figure 2.1).

Figure 2.1 Photos from Hikone Castle showing the filming and anime setting

However, sources of *content* do not only relate to film. They can be formal, as in recorded histories, popular culture (literature, art, music, theatre, film and television, gaming), fan-driven activities and events and informal in terms of shared memories and oral histories. Consequently, the notion of contents tourism takes us beyond a single notion of film and tourism into the realm of popular culture, enabling us to study the complexity of human nature and tourism in an inter-related manner.

Tourism Imaging and Imagining

It has been well-documented and taken as given that numerous elements motivate people to become tourists and to select particular destinations and activities. The social scientist John Urry (1990) postulates that one of the basic consumer motivations is the desire to experience, in reality, imaginary pleasures that have been developed in the consumer's mind. Tourism, by its very nature, involves daydreaming and the anticipation of different experiences, and this suggests that it is the image in a tourist's mind that is the most powerful motivator. Butler and Hall (1998) support this view, adding that mental images not only form the basis for selection of a destination, but are also used in post-experience evaluation. Reijnders (2011) has taken the concept of imagination and film to another level, considering this in terms of how we take material reference points from film to create our own imaginary world. This is an active and iterative process, with the artists themselves participating in this creative transformation of places which are appropriated by fans and tourists in their imagination and then in 'reality' through visiting these places.

While supporting the notion of imagination as a tourism motivator, Davidson and Spearritt (2000) conclude that society may be drifting from desiring authentic tourism experiences towards the staged authenticity of a society focused on infotainment. They note that the cost of producing the movie *Titanic*, which included the construction of an entire studio complex in Baja Mexico, was more than the inflation-adjusted cost of building the original ship. Furthermore, the 2012 centenary of the sinking of the *Titanic* provided even more tourism-related development such as a themed museum at the Belfast shipyard where the liner was built, complete with rides, animation and other special effects, not unlike a specialised theme park (see their website at www.titanicbelfast.com/The-Experience.aspx). In what was seen by many as an example of cynical opportunism, the movie was re-released that year in 3D, while cruise ships visited the site of the sinking.

Tourism images are developed from the stories of returning travellers as well as the media of the day. During the 19th century, novels, poetry and painting were the main sources of image-creation and reinforcement, while the growth of communication techniques and media sophistication in the 20th century has brought radio, film and television to the fore (Butler & Hall, 1998). For some time, authors and poets have influenced tourist visitation to certain areas to the extent that they have become synonymous with the destination, creating tourist destinations in their own right, as noted in Chapter 1 (Butler, 1990).

Central to ways that film constructs cultural representations and images is the manner in which we consume film. Where a film is viewed (the cinema, on video at home, on television) and with whom (friends, family, strangers, alone) can affect the viewer's relationship with the work. The viewer may identify with the subject or storyline from a personal or relative standpoint. Many times I find myself re-living the emotions of the time when I first experienced an influential movie, seen either on a first date or other special occasion, such as *Morning of the Earth* (1971), *Notting Hill* (1999) and even *The Killing Fields* (1984). Not only have I visited the film sites for the emotional response I have to the story, but also I have found myself re-experiencing those early emotions. These are not always romantic – while *The Killing Fields* was not directly connected to romance per se, it was more connected to a rite of passage, especially during my subsequent visit to Cambodia many years later.

Film as a Destination Marketing Tool

Many have noted (albeit often anecdotally) that numerous DMOs use the success of film-induced attractions to promote their regions to visitors. However, after the early work of Riley, Tooke, Baker and Van Doren, only limited literature that takes this concept any further has been published, apart from some work from Croy and Walker (2001), Hudson and Ritchie (2006a, 2006b) and Croy (2010). Certainly others have undertaken studies, but most of them tend simply to confirm what has already been noted rather than moving the theory on. They introduce this aspect of film-induced tourism, but rarely undertake detailed research into it. Nevertheless, as far back as 1986, Cohen mooted 'media fiction' as a tourism promotional tool. Cohen noted that '...no empirical research has been done on this subject...', theorising that '...media fiction [has] a definite effect on tourism – but not for all tourist markets' (Cohen, 1986: 229–300). There are, however, more recent academic researchers undertaking studies in this field and building on the work of their predecessors, particularly PhD and Masters' students, many of whom have grown up in a culture aware of the influence of multi-media on their decision-making patterns.

In a study of the effect of *The Sound of Music* on visitation to Salzburg, Austria, Im *et al.* (1999) found that over half of the respondents (who were on a *'Sound of Music* Tour') cited the movie as creating the desire to visit the film locations. Unfortunately, the report of the study is very brief, rendering it impossible to extract any further data with confidence.

In 2000, Croy and Walker (2001) initiated research into the importance and use of feature films in imaging destinations in New Zealand. After surveying New Zealand's local government offices and regional tourism organisations, they found that 71% of respondents believed that films produced in their area could be used as destination image promotion and that 58% considered the use of films produced in their area to be important in tourist promotions. Croy and Walker recognise the limitations of their research and the lack of other destination marketing research in this field, stating that 'research is needed at the destination level to assess the evaluative components of image and to measure the effect…film [has] on image' (Croy & Walker, 2001: CD-ROM). While such research is not the primary focus of this publication, some aspects of destination marketing came to light through aspects of my own research which are outlined in Chapter 3.

Hudson and Ritchie (2006a) surveyed 140 DMOs based in the UK and US on their perceived success in attracting film tourists, proposing a model that outlines ways in which DMOs can use a film to promote their destination, as reproduced in Figure 2.2.

They conclude that,

> …in an increasingly competitive and crowded marketplace, destination placement in films and TV shows is an attractive marketing vehicle that increases awareness, enhances destination image, and results in significant increases in tourism numbers, succeeding where traditional marketing efforts cannot. (Hudson & Ritchie, 2006b: 395)

Yet, they maintain that these elements were not being sufficiently leveraged by DMOs. However, while the academic research may lag behind in this area, many destinations are working to become 'film friendly' with some attempts to ultimately tie the destination in with tourism. According to Roger Grant (personal interview, 2001), long-time Executive Director of Geelong Otway Tourism (now Geelong Bellarine Tourism), their region took a proactive stance towards encouraging filming in the region by developing relationships with the major film studios, international and local public relations (PR) companies and advertising agencies. Activities include providing relevant filming

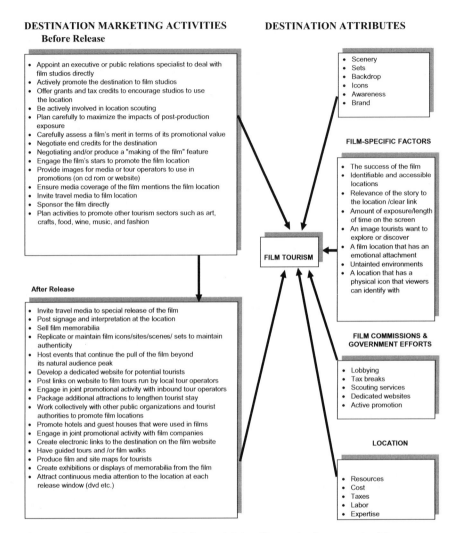

Figure 2.2 Film tourism: A model for exploiting film marketing opportunities
Source: Hudson and Ritchie (2006b: 390)

information regarding sites, tides, legal requirements and so on. Grant comments that much of this work is time-consuming and not always successful, but it is nevertheless crucial to attracting film activity, explaining that often film is considered 'free footage' in similar terms to 'free ink', but that the effort required to encourage film can be costly and time consuming. Nevertheless, Grant recognises that such free footage has a far higher credibility than a tourism body promotion has and needs to be pursued.

A recent case that is incorporated into this second edition regarding the 2015 Australian movie *Oddball* (2015) presents us with clear evidence that

DMOs as well as the local tourism and residential community are aware of the potential for film tourism. Due to the timing of the release of *Oddball* (literally as we go to press), I studied residential attitudes prior and up to the release. It is certainly in marked contrast to the community attitudes towards *Sea Change* (1998–2000), where most residents failed to understand the link between the television series and future tourism. These points and the outcomes of the research are outlined and discussed in future chapters.

Film-induced tourism does not merely occur at the external, on-location locations, it can also exist off-location. The production studios and sets provide opportunities for industrial-style tourism activities such as tours of the working studios and hands-on experiences with the technology. Even places further removed from the film itself, such as the homes of the stars and tourist constructs such as Hollywood Boulevard play a strong role in the tourism industry. These phenomena have not been studied at all in terms of film-induced tourism, hence the literature is even less forthcoming than in other areas of this field of study. The most relevant area of literature in terms of film studio tourism is that relating generally to industrial tourism and theme parks, which is covered in Chapter 8. The creation of Hollywood Boulevard and its current re-development and re-imaging as a major tourist precinct, and the appeal of gazing at the homes of movie stars as well as the fascination with other minutiae of their lives, is outside the boundaries of this publication, but is being considered in future work.

The Benefits and Drawbacks of Film-Induced Tourism

Researchers looking at this phenomenon have identified a range of benefits. However, because of the limited work carried out in this area to date, these have not been adequately quantified. Schofield (1996) comments that because of their association with fame, buildings and streets that were formerly considered commonplace and ordinary suddenly acquire interest, status and ambience. This could also be said of some aspects of the natural environment and of people, as discussed in the next section. Riley *et al.* (1998) identify numerous tourism benefits flowing on from filming, including the introduction of organised tours, expansion of community festivals, new use of sites, memorabilia sales, and the exposure received by the hotels and guest houses that were used as film locations.

One of the major economic benefits and factors of film-induced tourism is that viewing past locations can be an all-year, all-weather attraction, thus spreading out the seasonality inherent in so many tourist attractions. Also, both movies and television programmes have a wide socio-economic appeal, potentially broadening the base of the visitor market (Schofield, 1996). According to the Executive Director of the Madison County Chamber of

Commerce, Doug Hawley, the tourism generated from the movie, *Bridges of Madison County* (1995) kept the region alive, creating an international market for their covered bridges (Edgington, 1996). The Scottish Tourism Board (STB) recognised the promotional benefits of such Hollywood movies as *Rob Roy* (1995) and *Braveheart*, and worked hard to capitalise on the images that were being presented to the world. Derek Reid, the Chief Executive of the STB, persuaded MGM to run, free of charge, a Scottish travel advertisement before each screening of *Rob Roy* in the US (*Economist*, 1995a). This also provided them with the opportunity to diversify their market beyond their mainstay English visitors.

Bringing new businesspeople into the tourism industry, and encouraging them to take it seriously is a major challenge facing the industry worldwide, and film-induced tourism provides some opportunities in this area by introducing other members of the business community to the flow-on benefits of film-induced tourism. Tom Kershaw, the owner of the Bull and Finch hotel in Boston, has become extremely active in both the local and national tourism industry ever since his hotel was used as the site of the bar in the long-running television series *Cheers*, and in 1994 he was appointed by President Clinton to the US Travel and Tourism Administration's advisory board (Neale, 1994). (The direct economic benefits of *Cheers* that Kershaw has realised include around 500,000 visitors to his pub per annum, an annual food and beverage turnover of US$6 million and *Cheers* merchandising sales of around US$7 million.)

As always however, there is a range of potentially negative attributes or drawbacks of film-induced tourism, mainly in the less-quantifiable areas of social and environmental impacts. Tooke and Baker (1996) consider the (usually limited) carrying capacity of a site to be a major concern for an area that gains sudden tourist significance, particularly in relation to increased vehicle traffic and pedestrian congestion. Riley *et al.* (1998) have identified the drawbacks of main concern as the exploitation of locals and visitors, increasing prices, lack of preparedness from locals when dealing with the tourist influx, the way the location differs from the way it is portrayed on film, resulting in a loss of visitor satisfaction, and the various effects of souvenir hunters, especially those that seek highway and street signs. The first three elements relate to any increased tourist visitation regardless of the reason, whereas the remainder are related specifically to film-induced tourism.

In 2006, Hudson and Ritchie summarised the research to date, finding that there was significant evidence 'that film and television can have a very positive impact on tourism visits' (Hudson & Ritchie, 2006b: 388), while noting some of the work regarding the drawbacks, including my own comments regarding the change in visitor profiles, which is discussed in Chapter 5. Nevertheless, much of the subsequent literature remains primarily focused on economic benefits with still far too little consideration of the negative aspects of film-induced tourism, in particular the social costs of the aforementioned change in visitor profile (see also Beeton, 2001c). A notable exception to this is the work of Cohen (2005) and Higgins-Desbiolles (2001) relating to the movie *The Beach* (2000) which not only outlines the environmental issues during filming, but also the attempts to control subsequent tourism to the site, which, as noted in the documentary *Gringo Trails* (2013), has failed, with thousands of visitors flocking to this fragile area. It appears that the beach being used for the film was bulldozed and widened, and much of the native vegetation was removed. On the other hand, Fox claims that they removed three tons of rubbish from the isolated beach and posted a US$150,000 bond, promising to return the beach to its former state (Gritten, 1999). Nevertheless, such was the concern about the destruction of the natural environment that North Americans were asked by conservationists such as Professor Paul Eagles, the Chair of the Task Force on Tourism and Protected Areas, World Conservation Union, to boycott the film, sign a petition or write to the producer (Bushell, 1999). In a study of the controversy, Higgins-Desbiolles (2001) found that the effect of the conflict regarding the environmental and community issues surrounding the filming occurred on a series of diverse 'fronts':

> It tarnished the Thai government and its new Constitution; it bruised the Thai activist movement; it damages the image of Twentieth Century Fox; it sparked a desire for travel in its young fan base; it opened up a marketing for opportunities of companies...to promote themselves; it gave the Tourism Authority of Thailand a cheap promotions campaign (ignoring environmental and socio-political costs); and it caused academia to debate the context in which tourism operates in a more lively and heated manner. (Higgins-Desbiolles, 2001: 132)

A poignant example of the drawbacks of film-induced tourism can be found in Juffure, the African village on which Alex Haley based his book and mini-series, *Roots*. Tourists are visiting the town, and Gambia's tourist trade is now its number two industry after agriculture, largely due to the success of *Roots*. However, the villagers are disillusioned, poor and resentful of the promises of a lucrative future that did not eventuate for them. They feel that Haley and others made fortunes out of them, but that they received too little in return, both financially and socially, resulting in resentment towards tourists and the *Roots* phenomenon (Jet, 1995).

After the success of the TV series, *Pride and Prejudice*, the Friends of the Lake District (1996) expressed concern over what they termed the 'Darcy effect', which included negative social and environmental impacts. They were concerned that money would have to be diverted from other community projects to repair wear and tear and provide additional infrastructure and services for tourists, which they saw as more than mere opportunity cost. However, they failed to recognise any additional benefits that increased tourist numbers would bring. This suggests a lack of community consultation and education in this area, which is not surprising when one considers who would be responsible for such consultation – the filmmakers who will be long gone by the time the impacts become evident, or the tourist association who probably had little to do with the filming or choice of location. Perhaps the local councils, who have to approve certain aspects of the filming, such as closing public areas, need to take a more proactive role here. The Friends of the Lake District suggested, somewhat naively, that the producers and film companies consider the effects and costs to the community of the success of their projects. As I discuss in many of the cases that I have studied and presented here as well as elsewhere, most of the time this just does not figure in the thinking of most film makers, unless they are seeking funding for their production.

In addition to this range of issues, an important, potentially ambiguous, aspect to be considered when attempting to maximise the benefits of film-induced tourism, is that of the actual versus the imagined (as created by the film). Butler (1990) reminds us that films are often not shot at the locations they purport to be. For example, the Philippines was used to depict Vietnam in *Platoon* (1986), and Canada is often used to stand in for the US, as in the case of the sequel to the movie *The Blues Brothers* (1980), *Blues Brothers 2000* (1998) and many cowboy/Western films such as *Brokeback Mountain* (2005) and *The Assassination of Jesse James by the Coward Robert Ford* (2007). This can create a situation where people are basing their knowledge on false information as well as developing false expectations of sites they choose to visit, resulting in dissatisfaction with the experience. This notion is supported by Hall (1998), who sees the appeal of tourist attractions as relating directly to the image that the tourists have brought with them.

To illustrate the above point, journalist Jim Keeble relates his pilgrimage to Normandy to visit the sites from the film *Saving Private Ryan* (1998). Keeble (1999) found that 'unfortunately, most of the film was shot on the coast of Ireland...Spielberg only spent one day in France...I spent two days cursing Spielberg...'.

However, many of the findings outlined in this publication suggest that tourists are quite aware of the 'inauthenticity' of film and accept that places may not be where or what they are depicted to be. For example, Seaton and Hay (1998) found that visitors were coming to Scotland to visit the places depicted in the movie *Braveheart* (1995), even though most of it was filmed in Ireland and were not disappointed. In fact, they also go to Ireland to look at the 'fake' historical places (but 'real' filming sites) (see Chapter 3). The tourism potential of 'runaway production' is under-investigated and noted again in the concluding chapter of this book. However, the notion of visitors' views on authenticity and film is investigated further in the chapters on film studio theme parks.

The Cult of Celebrity

Fascination with the famous and infamous is not new – tourism itself has been based around visiting famous (or 'sacred') sites since it first appeared in the form of the pilgrimages of the 11th century and the Grand Tours of the 18th century (Leiper, 2002). Furthermore, there is evidence of even earlier tourism and guidebooks from Roman times (Beeton, 2015). However, the concurrent development of mass travel and mass media propelled the 20th century into the era of celebrity tourism. Consequently, popular culture of the late 20th and early 21st century has been deemed a culture of fame (or 'cult of celebrity'), where contact with famous people in turn makes the individual more worthy. According to Collins, '…Hollywood's special glamour came from concentrating so many [stars] in one place' (1987: 173). Collins suggests that, while the growth of mass media was central to the cultivation of celebrity, the worship of movie stars filled a psychological or even spiritual need in a century where religion was declining and heroism was becoming more difficult to identify. This is a particularly interesting concept, which I continue to consider and explore, both on a personal as well as external level.

The continued popularity of 'reality TV' since the late 1990s, along with the consequent fame that follows the 'ordinary' people from these programmes is symptomatic of society's obsession with fame, especially fame that is seemingly created overnight. Such shows foster the belief that we can all be famous, even if it is only for the '15 minutes' proposed by Andy Warhol (1968).

The power of the famous to add celebrity status to all they touch is reflected in the Hollywood tours of the homes of the stars (most of whom no longer live there), the fascination of tourists in the names of stars embedded in Hollywood Boulevard (after all, it is simply a list of celebrities), and their footprints outside Grauman's Chinese Theatre – an edifying 1920s representation of the Hollywood view of China, with its 'authentic replica' of the facade of a Buddhist temple that has become the spiritual repository of the celebrity. In a delightful take on the culture of celebrity that defines Hollywood, a public access television presenter developed a programme, *Driveways of the Rich and Famous*, that is now available on the internet (www.driveways.com), where it has gained attention from European and Japanese media (Craig, 1998). What started as a humorous, even satiric, take on the cult of celebrity has become what it started out deriding. Having their driveway featured on the programme has become a status symbol amongst celebrities. In a delightful case of inversion, the programme's presenter and creator, John Cunningham, has himself been followed by news crews, once again slipping effortlessly into the realm of hyper reality.

By interviewing the staff of the rich and famous, Cunningham extended celebrity status to those who have some contact with a famous person, then on to himself. This is not unlike the fascination that visitors to film studios

have with the production and ancillary staff – it is a case of 'celebrity transference' through proximity. According to Cunningham '...it was great getting Frank Sinatra's mailman, who admits that delivering his mail every day
adds a thrill to an otherwise boring job' (Craig, 1998). While his tour and
website is no longer available, another was developed by Debbie Burton, a
'virtual' online realtor, with YouTube images of the driveways of the homes
of Nicholas Cage (previously Tom Jones' home), Marilyn Monroe's last home,
and the homes of Antonio Banderas, Kurt Russell and Goldie Hawn, and so
on (www.stardriveways.com). Along with her realtor enterprise, the site is
sponsored by Burton's husband's company that sells granite bench sealant.

One way to uncover the link between the cult of celebrity, film and tourism, is to examine it in the context of personality types. Maltby *et al.* (2001,
2003) have been studying personality and celebrity worship – an approach
that tourism researchers may adopt. The low levels of celebrity worship that
tend to have an entertainment–social value may also relate to a general attraction for visiting and gazing at celebrities' homes and various filming sites.
However, higher levels of celebrity worship may be detrimental to the development of back-stage tourism experiences, owing to the link between this and
Borderline-pathological personality types. Such types, Maltby *et al.* argue, are
exemplified by items such as 'If I were lucky enough to meet my favourite
celebrity, and he/she asked me to do something illegal as a favour I would probably do it' (Maltby *et al.*, 2003: 7). Maltby and Day (2011) have also looked at
the link between the increasing incidences and acceptance of elective cosmetic
surgery and celebrity worship, suggesting that the power of celebrity can alter
what is acceptable behaviour and what is not. While they have not looked
specifically at tourism, their work reflects the power of celebrity.

As Powers (2001) argues, the famous do not merely add status to all they
touch – they can also add 'content' and interest to light media stories, refuting
the adage that 'celebrity is the enemy of content'. Powers argues that the role
of celebrities featured in a story (that is not about them) where the content
may be too light, is to add their own story, giving some depth or additional
interest to, for example, a predictable story on Yoga or the Information Age.

The Planet Hollywood chain of restaurants not only celebrates celebrity,
it is also owned by celebrities, giving 'content' to what is in effect just
another restaurant chain. The aim of most themed restaurants is not merely
to provide entertainment and sustenance, but also to sell merchandise items
enabling customers, for example, to sport the logos of Planet Hollywoods
around the world. The bars based on the television series *Cheers* (1982–1993)
also play to the cult of celebrity by providing an environment similar to the
set as well as special menus and memorabilia. According to Frost (1997: 18),
'[t]here is also a significant element in most themes – the "cult of personality"...Planet Hollywood has the movies and their stars...'.

As demonstrated by themed restaurants, the obsession with fame goes
beyond people to places and artefacts, both real and created, and has been

maximised in the film studio theme park. The possibility of encounters with famous people, in this case actors, is an added, powerful attraction of the film studio theme park within its various levels of authenticity, interaction and control, ranging from the frontstage to the backstage regions.

Visitors to Warner Brothers Movie World on the Australian Gold Coast can experience a frontstage encounter with famous-actor look-alikes from Marilyn Monroe through to fictional characters such as Batman, Superman and Beetlejuice. Tales from staff about the stars they saw wandering through the frontstage region 'just the other day' are eaten up by visitors, always hoping for such luck. Midstage experiences tend to focus more on ancillaries to fame – placing visitors into simulated sets and films. Fox Studios gave people the opportunity to be an extra on the *Titanic* in their '*Titanic* Experience' and to appear on video in a *Simpsons* cartoon through the application of motion capture technology (Emmons, 1999). Personal encounters in the midstage region are restricted to encounters with staff associated with fame, such as make-up and sound (in particular Foley) artists. Backstage encounters tend more towards the voyeuristic experience of watching actors working on films from a controlled environment, usually behind soundproof glass windows. Other backstage encounters are with original sets and props that provide a link with fame.

It has been suggested that the cult of celebrity has become so significant because it distracts people from their growing sense of disconnection from their local communities (Fyfe, 2000). The theme park concept – described elsewhere as 'Fantasy City' – provides clear boundaries – externally between the rest of the world and the park, but also those clearly defined regions that can be the physical substitution for a community. The film studio theme park, with its resident celebrities adds the personal ingredient into the community – visitors know more about the intimate details of the stars or the characters they represent than they do about their neighbours 'on the outside'.

The relationship between the need to belong and the disenfranchisement of so many from their communities has led to a gap, and the concept that film studio theme parks may create a sense of community, be it brief, certainly has some resonance. Another means of recreating the sense of belonging to a community can be looked at in terms of pseudo-religious experiences such as secular pilgrimages, another perspective of film-induced tourism.

Fans, Film and Pilgrimage

Numerous researchers and commentators consider tourism to have elements of, and to perform a similar role to, a religious pilgrimage (see Graburn, 1989; Lickorish & Jenkins, 1997; Davidson & Spearritt, 2000; Fullagar *et al.*, 2012). Brown (2015) considers tourism to the graves of writers as a form of pilgrimage, not unlike some film tourism experiences, while Okamoto

(2015) discusses the role of pilgrimage to sacred anime sites in Japanese contents tourism. MacCannell (1976) sees the modern traveller, searching for authenticity, as similar to pilgrims, searching for reaffirmations of their beliefs. While the motivation of medieval pilgrims to go on a pilgrimage was purportedly religious, there was also a social focus and pilgrims often travelled in groups, not only for safety, a desire for adventure and a break from home were significant motivators (Finucane, 1977). By the 13th and 14th centuries, the pilgrimage had become a mass phenomenon with a tourism infrastructure that included package tours from Venice to the Holy Land, supported by guidebooks and tales (Cohen, 2002). Relics and souvenirs (bones and badges) of religious figures (saints) were viewed and collected and representations taken back home, raising the pilgrims up in the view of their peers. Lickorish and Jenkins (1997: 14) note that '[p]ilgrims were distinguished by the scallop shell badge of achievement, perhaps the earliest travel award'.

Pilgrimage itself is a feature of all religions, not just Christianity, connected to the worship of ancestors as well as to so-called 'holy places'. According to Vukonic:

> ...the most regular travellers in ancient times were pilgrims who gathered in great numbers at well-known shrines or oracles on religious holidays...The holiday in honour of Zeus was celebrated every fourth year (the Olympic Games) starting from the 8th century BC. (Vukonic, 1996: 118)

Treks have also been an integral part of pilgrimage up to the current day, and the close link with creative works such as song, art and poetry is a common factor in both pilgrimage and tourism (Gupta, 1999). Lennon and Foley (2000: 4) consider pilgrimage to have 'a religious or, at least, mystical significance...which contains both a personal physical as well as often a psychological journey for participants'.

Film-induced tourism has strong overtones of pilgrimage, with the tourist travelling (trekking) to sites considered sacred through their connection with fame and notions of fantasy. Film tourists collect memorabilia of places, actors and characters, taking them home along with stories of fame that raise them up in the view of their peers. The intimate reaction of visitors to many sites can be highly emotionally charged, verging on the spiritual and mystical. Supporting this, Cohen states that:

> [m]odern tourists are sometimes perceived as secular pilgrims in search of authentic experiences, a secular surrogate of the sacred, which they hope to encounter in the course of sightseeing trips...Tourists, like pilgrims, often mix a serious quest with recreation, play and fun... (Cohen, 2000: 438)

Film fans as pilgrims

Matt Hills has been studying the concept of fans and fandom for some years, and while he has not directly focused on the tourism aspect of fandom, his works show that there is an intimate relationship at play, such as in Hills (2002). In a more recent paper on the BBC television series *Doctor Who* (1963–1989, 1996, 2005–) he looks at the manner in which today's fans are creating their own reflective, commemorative writing on the series, which he has called, *fanfac*. In these examples, the fans are relating their personal experiences as related to the television series, '…drawing on a sense of shared recognition' (Hills, 2014: 35).

We also see fans parodying and re-creating scenes on YouTube as well as simply acting out at the film sites, as discussed by Roesch (2007, 2009) and Buchmann *et al.* (2010). Some fans even go to the extent of re-creating opening title scenes of programmes, such as with the iconic *Andy Griffith Show* (1960–1968), where childhood fans re-created them as adults (Beeton, 2015). I also recount my own 're-enacting' on horseback at Monument Valley, the site for many Western movies starring John Wayne, where I rode around this remarkable site pretending to be Wayne (Beeton, 2015), while I also present a number of other examples throughout this book.

Film fans often take what can only be seen as a pilgrimage to the sites, sets and studios related with their passion. As Hills (2014) so aptly notes, fans often wish to commemorate the programme they love through their own creations and, I would argue, touristic pilgrimages. Below, I relate one of my own pilgrimages, inadvertently in the style of Hills' *fanfac*, where I narrate an account of my own memories and experiences, while witnessing others re-creating and re-enacting.

A personal pilgrimage: *Monty Python and the Holy Grail*

In many cases, the decision to film at certain sites has often been serendipitous (or not, depending on the tourism outcomes). Such was the case of Doune Castle, near Stirling in Scotland, the site for the 1975 cult movie *Monty Python and The Holy Grail*. Two weeks before filming, the Monty Python team was informed that they could not use any publicly owned castles in Scotland, so they chose the privately owned Doune Castle to play two castles in the movie, 'Anthrax' and 'Swamp' (Diary, 2000; Whipp, 2001). This would not have happened today – tourism destination marketing organisations such as VisitScotland now work closely with the film industry, hoping to encourage the filming of movies and television series and their concomitant tourism, as discussed earlier in this chapter. Yet, the castle makes a wonderful pilgrimage site, close to the township of Stirling and within an hour or so of Edinburgh and Glasgow.

A trip to Doune Castle is certainly in the realm of pilgrimage, complete with a sense of place, history and fame. Among the many personal pilgrimages taken while researching the film-induced tourism phenomenon, the one I undertook to Doune Castle stands out. Over 25 years since *Monty Python and the Holy Grail* was filmed, the site has taken on mythical, spiritual connotations that continue to attract media attention as the site of the movie (for example, Petty, 2003; *Scottish Daily Record*, 2003; *The Independent* (London), 2002; Dancis, 2001; Whipp, 2001). In terms of pilgrimage to a 'sacred' site, it is not merely the humour of the movie that attracts, but more importantly the stage in one's life that it represents – for me it was a coming-of-age experience, being accepted into an 'elite' group (of Python fans – or those who 'got' it). The movie and the site become representations or simulacra of something else, as do many religious pilgrimage sites.

As I walked up to the castle, it looked eerily familiar, evoking an excited emotional response, tinged with awe at the actual age of the structure itself (it was built in the 14th century). However, the sense of familiarity provided a link with something else, something arcane, known to a special few (Monty Python fans!), other than the obvious heritage of the site.

This publication is not the forum for an in-depth examination of the humour of Monty Python, but the movie not only marks an era (the 1970s), it also has elements of mystique, esoteric and even arcane symbolism as it is set way back in the Dark Ages of the Arthurian legend. However, the arcane refers not to the heritage of the castle, but to elements of the movie, along with what this represents in one's life – when a visitor asks at the information desk for the coconuts, all those 'in the know' smile and laugh as coconuts are handed over. There are no signs advertising the existence of such an unusual phenomenon in a Scottish castle, but within three minutes of my first visit, I had requested (and used) them, and every page of the visitors' book has a comment on them.

Why the coconuts? They formed an important prop in the movie, and were part of a discussion in an opening scene that set the tone for the rest of the film. According to the staff at Doune Castle, visitors from the UK, the US, Australia and other parts of the world quote this and many other parts of the movie verbatim, with great enthusiasm and reverence. Of the 23,000 annual visitors, it has been estimated that over a third are visiting on a Monty Python pilgrimage (Petty, 2003). As well as the official Monty Python movie website (www.sonypictures.com/cthe/montypython), George McMillan, the manager of Doune Castle, established his own website at www.holygrailcastle.com, which includes photos of visitors using the coconuts as well as stills from the movie.

The screenplay, along with Holy Grail Ale ('tempered over burning witches'), replicas of the catapult that sent dead animals over the castle walls, the grail, and other items can be purchased at the castle (see Figure 2.3). Some of the costumes used by the cast, hand made by locals, are on display, and I was privileged to be shown others that are currently kept in bags in the

Figure 2.3 Souvenirs for a pilgrim: Monty Python's 'Holy Grail Ale' and *Heartbeat's* Greengrass 'Old Rogue Ale' take the humour and quirkiness of characters and story to another level

back room! My visit also prompted a (most enjoyable) reading of the screenplay, necessitating a second pilgrimage to Doune Castle.

As noted elsewhere, the re-release of movies on video and now DVD has given them an added 'life', and this is certainly the case for *Monty Python and the Holy Grail*. The movie was re-released in the US in 2001 with an additional 23 seconds and stereo soundtrack (the original was recorded in mono) (Whipp, 2001). To celebrate 25 years since the movie's release, a DVD was released, complete with a documentary, *The Quest of the Holy Grail Locations*, in which Michael Palin and Terry Jones revisit sites such as Doune Castle. On their visit to Doune Castle, Palin and Jones actually discover that many of the visitors 'are Python fans on a pilgrimage' (Dancis, 2001). This confirmation of the status of the movie and the castle no doubt raised the pilgrimage profile of the castle. Even though the 25th anniversary DVD was subtitled 'the ultimate, definitive, final special edition' (Dancis, 2001), the movie was re-released yet again on DVD in 2003 (Sony Pictures, 2003). Included in this edition are a cell of a film frame from the movie and a paperback of the movie script. Doune Castle has been used in film as far back as the 1920s, when it was used in the movie *Young Lochinvar* (McKenzie & McKenzie, 1988), but it was not until it received 'the Monty Python treatment' that it became a film-tourism pilgrimage site.

Packaging film tourism as pilgrimage

Just as pilgrimages have been organised as package tours, so film-induced tourism is being packaged as pilgrimage and near-religious experience. New York-based On Location Tours started in June 1999, after the proprietor, Georgette Blau became aware of the interest in film in New York, a city used in hundreds of movies and television series. She began with a *Sex and the City Tour* that appealed primarily to 30-something women, going to many of the glamorous sites used in the popular television programme. The business now runs tours that include *Celebrity Homes Tour, Manhattan Movie Tour, Manhattan TV Tour, Central Park Movie Tour* and *Sopranos Tour* as well as its original *Sex and the City Tour*. Participants range from their late teens to their fifties, looking for a different representation of New York – one that for many people verges on a pilgrimage.

Blau's tours have been studied in terms of Boorstin's pseudo-events, MacCannell's authenticity and Eco's hyper reality (see Torchin, 2003; and Chapter 8 of this volume for an overview of the postmodern tourism discourse). However, they have not been considered in terms of pilgrimage, which certainly appears to be a powerful motive for participants.

According to Blau's website, the aim of On Location Tours is to create tours that allow people the opportunity to straddle fiction and reality, letting them feel as though they are part of the television show or movie, ultimately bringing them closer to the characters themselves (www.onlocation.com). I found that the appeal is far more, and it is evident from the structure of the tours and commentary that Blau also recognises this. On my own visit, I did not experience the personal reverence and level of pilgrimage I had at Doune Castle, but there were certainly others on the tour for whom the site of the apartment in the television show *Friends*, or the Soup Kitchen from *Seinfeld* performed similar roles, and all the participants took photos of themselves actually at the sites, or 'in' the series. Anecdotal reports from Blau and numerous media reports also support this perception (for example, Peyser &

Gordon, 2001; Espinosa & Herbst, 2002; Quiglen, 2002; Sloan, 2002). In Chapter 5, I look at On Location Tours again in terms of it being a film-tourism business in a major city.

Conclusion

This chapter has built on the introductory notes in Chapter 1, introducing some of the perspectives and themes that are returned to throughout the book. In many ways, this book is like a journey, starting off with an outline of the current state of knowledge (similar to pre-trip research), then further developing and teasing out the issues as the journey progresses.

The significant relationships that have been introduced, such as that between film offices and production companies and tourism offices and businesses is central to any consideration of film-induced tourism, and is the basis of much of the research outlined in later chapters. The relationship between the storyline of a film and tourist attractiveness as well as imaging and destination marketing are also introduced and taken up in more detail later. In the same way, the benefits and drawbacks of film-induced tourism have been briefly outlined in terms of research undertaken by others, and this theme is developed throughout as we uncover more and increase our knowledge and understanding of film-induced tourism.

The two very interesting notions presented towards the end of the chapter, that of 'celebrity' and 'pilgrimage', are both elements of film-induced tourism that require further study and as such are discussed again in the concluding chapter, along with ways that we can take the Japanese concept of contents tourism into the world.

Part 2

Film-Induced Tourism on Location

This second part of the book looks at film-induced tourism on location – that is, at the places where particular scenes or elements of movies and television series are filmed. The various elements that provide the framework for on-location tourism consist of image creation, destination marketing and place promotion, along with the effects on tourism itself and host communities. In turn they support the over-arching concept of community development – something that is far easier to 'say' than to 'do'.

With the shift from predominantly manufacturing to information-based economies, developed and developing countries and their communities are transforming themselves into 'sellers of goods and services...proactive marketer[s] of [their] products and place value' (Kotler *et al.*, 1993: 10). Places have become products ('destinations') that must be strategically designed and marketed, and those that fail face the risk of economic decline. Such destinations are 'places with some form of actual or perceived boundaries – physical, political or market created' (McCabe *et al.*, 2000: 213) and can include villages, geographic regions, whole cities or parts of those cities, or they can be bounded by non-physical boundaries such as culture, language or habit. Taking this concept of place as destination sees certain tourist enterprises being termed 'destinations' in their own right, in particular the larger theme park developments such as Disneyland and Universal Studios, and clustered theme parks such as those on the Gold Coast, Australia and in Florida as well as regionally-based heritage parks such as Sovereign Hill in Australia.

3 Film Images and Destination Marketing

Destination (or 'place') marketing relates to strategic planning and the conscious use of publicity and marketing to promote business investment, visitation or in-migration to a particular country, state, region or town as well as using it to increase exports (Nielsen, 2001). Often seen as purely economically driven, the health of a destination must also be measured against other goals such as community well-being and lifestyle which, while closely linked with economic fortune, are also quite separate. Therefore, in an ideal situation, destination marketing (unlike business marketing) requires cooperation and input from all sectors of the community – the government, businesses, interest groups, residents and even visitors. However, issues of community power relations and politics tend to undermine any idealistic notions of cooperation. This is an important issue that is addressed a little towards the end of this section and in more detail in Chapter 7. This is particularly the case in terms of a destination's image, which is not solely in the control of the destination marketing organisation (DMO). In their seminal work on destination management, Ritchie and Crouch (2003) see image as being an intrinsic, often unconscious and less controllable element of the destination marketing process than the more conscious activity of destination branding.

While planning tourism development, conscious destination strategies that aim to create positive images of the destinations and cement them in potential visitors' imaginations are usually developed. According to Hall and Jenkins (1995), such strategies have four main aims, namely to attract tourism expenditure, to generate tourism employment, to provide positive images for potential investors and to attract professional workers to the area – all of which are central to the economic and social development of an area or region. Hall maintains that imaging processes are characterised by a combination (of some or all) of the development of visitor attractions and/or facilities, the introduction of hallmark events, the development of leisure and cultural services and projects and also the development of tourism strategies and policies. An additional process that could be added to this list is the powerful role played by visual media in the imaging process in terms of education and entertainment in film (television programmes and movies) as opposed to direct advertising. In support of this comment, in their paper 'Movie induced tourism' Riley *et al.* conclude that 'the visual media of today appear to construct anticipation and allure that induces people to travel' (1998: 932). Urry and Larsen (2011) go further by acknowledging the subsequent literature in this field that has focused on the concept of film as a 'marker' of tourism, where tourist destinations can become fantasylands. They acknowledge that movies and television programmes 'often cause tourist flows where few roamed before...' (Urry & Larsen, 2011: 177), creating new destinations and enhancing others.

While destination marketing also targets business investment and in-migration, it appears that tourism receives the greatest benefit from destination-marketing initiatives. Consequently, destination marketing has been criticised by promoters of business as an ineffective means for increasing economic development in relation to industries such as manufacturing, mining and processing. Illustrating this point, Young and Kaczmarek (1999) question the effectiveness of place promotion activities in Lodz, Poland in terms of attracting new business to the town, citing commentators who feel that such external promotion is a costly and time-consuming way to achieve such a goal. However, in their study, Young and Kaczmarek tended to ignore the tourism aspects of destination marketing and the subsequent flow-on business development opportunities, which might have provided them with a better understanding of the significance of destination imaging and marketing to the wider community.

Yet, Young and Kaczmarek have fallen for the convenience of equating place promotion with place (destination) marketing, which is an all-too-common error. Effective destination marketing provides a framework not only for a place's promotion but also for planning and development, with a long-term vision (Kotler *et al.*, 1993; Ashworth & Kavaratzis, 2010; Gartner, 2014; Pike & Page, 2014), which we need to remember as we look at destination marketing and the role of destination image.

The image of a destination has been shown to be a significant tourist motivator, playing an important role in travel decision-making. It is also well-documented and accepted that increased tourism affects a wide range of businesses, from transport and accommodation to suppliers of products and services, as well as tourism businesses themselves. Such widespread benefits support the case for government-assisted/endorsed tourism destination promotion. As a function of the wide dispersion of tourism economic benefits, destination marketing is generally coordinated through public-sector-based DMOs, predominantly at government level (federal, state and local). Supporting and reflecting this position, much of the general academic literature on destination marketing has tended to focus on the larger DMOs and visitor services sector (see Ritchie & Crouch, 2000, 2003; Goeldner *et al.*, 2000; Sirgy & Su, 2000; Anholt, 2010), often neglecting the role of individual operators and principals in promoting a destination. For example, Ritchie and Crouch (2000) developed a model of 'destination competitiveness and sustainability', yet relegated individual tourism and hospitality businesses to merely a supporting role, and did not include them as direct contributors to destination marketing. However, as stated earlier (and supported by Kotler *et al.*, 1993), destination marketing requires active support from all community sectors, including individual operators who often wield great influence. This becomes even more pertinent as our destinations move into the 'new economy' that is characterised not only by globalisation but also by small, flexible businesses working cooperatively with government and each other.

Despite the limited academic recognition of the role of individuals in marketing their destination, it has been recognised by many actually out in the field that it is in their own interest to also take on some of the responsibility for promoting their destination. Such a notion of competitive cooperation has been refuted by some academic observers, including Weaver and Oppermann (2000), who believe that individual tourism businesses will not promote their destination as this would benefit their competitors as well as themselves. While there are those who take this stance, further research indicates that those operators who promote their destinations first and their product second are among the most successful, also termed by Edgell and Haenisch (1995) as 'coopetition' (Bramwell & Lane, 2000a; Edgell, 2013; Kylänen & Mariani, 2014).

This notion of coopetition is particularly pertinent for destinations such as regional centres and communities that can often have an overriding single image with a comparatively limited diversity and number of tourist products. Large, major cities and destinations such as the countries themselves that are promoted on a broad scale have a variety of products and markets and require a more diverse destination image. In order to maintain some continuity of marketing image, such promotion must also be coordinated cooperatively by the DMOs. As destination marketing is now pursued by local trade and tourism associations and individual operators as well as by the government-based DMOs, the issue of maintaining a consistent marketing image has become complicated and nebulous. Nevertheless, any study of destination marketing should consider those aspects that are used by individual operations, particularly in small towns and regions that are often overlooked by the larger DMOs. In support of this proposition, Buhalis notes that:

> [t]ourists' overall experience is composed of numerous small encounters with a variety of tourism principals, such as taxi drivers, hoteliers, waiters as well as with elements of the local attractions. Their overall impression develops the image of a destination after their visitation. As a consequence there is much overlapping between strategic marketing of the destination as a whole and of each individual supplier of the region. (Buhalis, 2000: 99)

One of the problems that can be addressed through a cooperative approach to destination marketing is the tendency for individual concerns (whether in the public or private sector) to take a non-strategic approach to planning. Often with minimal consultation and consideration, action is undertaken on the assumption that if something works in place A, then it is likely to work in place B (Beeton, 2006b). Such assumptions are evident in the development (and subsequent failure) of Fox Studios Backlot and are discussed in the following chapters. Generally, if all stakeholders are included in planning for a destination, the consequences of such ad hoc development can be considered from a more holistic aspect.

Destination marketing planning (along with other tourism planning) has been criticised as lacking 'true' inclusive community consultation (Hall, 2003), yet, as noted throughout this and the following chapters, destination marketing requires cooperation from all sectors and stakeholders. Hall (2003) argues that cooperative community consultation and decision-making is power-based, questioning 'the processes that occur within communities [and] participation with respect to which stakeholders have the greatest ability to achieve their aims and why' (Hall, 2003: 100). Hall maintains that a belief that every person in a community and any tourism stakeholder (which includes the tourists themselves) can have equal access to representation in destination decision-making is naive and impractical. Power issues have been discussed in some community-based tourism work (see Hall & Jenkins, 1995; Hall, 2003; Sofield, 2003; Beeton, 2006b; Marzano & Scott, 2009; Nunkoo & Ramkissoon, 2012; Ooi et al., 2015), with growing interest in power relations in China from scholars such as Zhao and Timothy (2015), but are generally given little attention in the overall literature (Beritelli & Laesser, 2011). This is of some concern due to the clear imbalances in community consultation and decision-making. In a study on tourism and international film businesses I note that many collaborative or public-private partnerships assume 'that all parties have equal access to processes and have similar levels of power, which is rarely the case' (Beeton, 2008c: 262), often failing in the process. Such issues of power tend to reduce the complexity of tourism down to one or two elements, often those of the powerful economic interests, neglecting the true nature of the tourism experience, in spite of Pine and Gilmore's oft-cited work on *The Experience Economy* published at the end of the 20th century (Pine & Gilmore, 1999).

The development of destination branding can potentially further reduce the richness of communities' cultures and environments. In order to create a generalised, marketable destination image or brand, the richness and complexity of a place and its people (predominantly its culture and heritage) tends to be 'flattened', narrowed and simplified. In some cases, the predominant image that has been imposed on a place (by tourists, operators or DMOs) can cause problems with the host community and overall economy. Taking the development of Monterey as a tourist destination as a case in point, Hall (2003: 108) comments that, the 'narratives of labour, class and ethnicity are typically replaced by romance and nostalgia' as reinterpreted by the local elite who have the power in the community. Singh *et al.* (2003b: 8) support this criticism, stating that 'this concept [of easily-defined communities]…is put to good use by the tourism industry to sell quaint destination irrespective of the locale'. Baptista (2012) goes on to argue that niche tourism products such as slum tourism are negatively affected by simplistic tourists' perceptions, where the tourists' expectations of poverty as a one-dimensional way of being influence not only their reality, but also that of the community. While such simplification is tempting when marketing a destination, this homogenising of our communities will ultimately affect tourist visitation to and interest in many of these destinations.

Promoting this singular focus as a necessary element of destination marketing, Ritchie and Crouch (2003: 198) maintain that 'a challenge facing destination managers is to decide which aspect of the destination experience should provide the basis for a brand'. Notwithstanding, a community is more than a collection of buildings, and this provides enormous challenges for DMOs, and may go some way to explaining the almost pathological desire for a film to provide a significant fillip to tourism by presenting more complex and intangible images, with seemingly no effort from the DMOs.

In 2004, Tourism Australia launched an innovative re-branding of Australia. It signified an attempt to move away from iconic built and natural formations towards a more complex, experiential brand. They developed the proposition of 'Life in a Different Light', based on the notion that the light in Australia is different from that in other countries, which in turn affects the tourism experience. Such a brand opens up many more experiential avenues for destination marketing and imaging. This was one of the most complex destination branding efforts to date, and signals a greater proactive and conscious use of visual tools such as film. Subsequent promotions include the 2010 'There's Nothing Like Australia' campaign focused more on the experiences of local Australians, who sent in photos of their favourite places which were then mapped on to an interactive map of Australia. The campaign was introduced into China in 2012, and in 2013 encompassed food and wine experiences, continuing this focus on 'experience' as famously introduced by Pine and Gilmore some 15 years prior (Pine & Gilmore, 1998, 1999).

An even longer-term successful tourism branding campaign was developed for the Australian state tourism body, Tourism Victoria, known as the Jigsaw campaign. As Victoria did not have any single iconic image such as the Sydney Opera House or Uluru in central Australia, the campaign's developers came up with the concept of pieces of a jigsaw fitting in to each other, with the tagline 'you'll love every piece of Victoria'. This campaign has been running since 1992, demonstrating the power of a flexible, creative brand that can be applied in many different ways, rather than a single iconic brand (Rinaldi & Beeton, 2015).

Tourists' Destination Selection Process

According to Weaver and Oppermann (2000), most consumers decide on a destination after considering only three to five options, demonstrating the importance of a powerful destination image and marketing process. Yet, the actual process involved in a person selecting a holiday destination is extremely complex, relying on the physical needs and psychological wants of the consumer as well as on complex images, preconceptions and biases that person (or people) may hold.

Weaver and Oppermann's model outlines the process from the intrinsic push factors matching with the differentiating pull factors of the destination through to image development and the decision to travel to a particular destination. While they list the push and pull factors as the first stage, it can be argued that at the beginning only the push factors are involved, with the pull factors coming in between the stages of need recognition and primary destination image. Nevertheless, the model serves to illustrate the subjectivity, complexity and circularity of the destination decision-making process.

Destination Promotion Techniques

When promoting the need to simplify destination branding, Ritchie and Crouch (2003: 245) note the complexity of destination imaging and promotion, stating that '...awareness and image are usually a function of such a wide variety of sources and forms of information about a place and its people that explicit efforts by a destination marketing organisation in this regard normally play only a minor role'. Consequently, DMOs rely on a mix of four main strategies to attract visitors, residents and business and to increase exports, namely image, attractions, infrastructure and people marketing (Kotler *et al.*, 1993) – some of these are in their control, others are not. When considering tourism development, promotion of image and attractions are among the most predominant in the mix, even though all four strategies ultimately need to be incorporated.

While published over 20 years ago, Perdue and Pitegoff's (1994) list of the most commonly utilised promotional activities by DMOs to encourage tourism provides a good basis (shown in Table 3.1). I have modified it in light of the rapid growth and popularity of travel and lifestyle television programmes (many of which are sponsored by the DMOs themselves, especially at the state and federal levels), the internet and tourist signage, as well as promotions from individual operators, mainly in the form of brochures and souvenirs. Also, the effect of creative media such as film on tourism promotion has been included, particularly in light of the enormous push by DMOs to have their regions featured in film (both television and movies). Postcards and souvenirs complete the circuit, being sent back to the homes of others. All these additions are shown in *italics*.

Table 3.1 Common destination promotional methods

Timing of promotion	Promotional technique
At home, prior to trip	Media advertising. Familiarisation trips. Sales blitz and trade mission. Travel writer tours. Consumer shows. Direct mail. Travel and lifestyle programmes. *Internet.* *Individual operators' brochures.* *Creative media (film and television, books).* *Maps.*
While en route to the destination	Interstate welcome centres *(Visitor Information Centres).* Outdoor advertising. Visitor centres. Creative media (film and television, books). Tourist signage. Maps.
After arriving at the destination	Media programmes. Hospitality training. *Tourist signage.* *Maps.*
At the homes of friends and family	*Postcards and souvenirs.* *Creative media (film and television, books).* *Photos.*

Source: Adapted from Perdue and Pitegoff (1994); author's additions are in *italics*.

This list is used later in this book as a reference point and basis for the examination both of destination marketing activities in Australia and of the use of *Sea Change* imagery at Barwon Heads.

Understanding the Role of Destination Image in Destination Marketing

Image is central to marketing, even more so in tourism destination marketing, which promotes an intangible product. As Ritchie and Crouch (2000: 1) point out, 'the fundamental product in tourism is the destination experience' – an intangible, image-laden creation that relies on individual operators as much as on the funded marketing organisations. Destination imaging is multi-dimensional, comprising both symbolic and tangible features (MacKay & Fesenmaier, 2000). 'Image' has long been acknowledged as a primary decision-making and motivational factor in holiday travel, and it has been a long-standing area of interest for tourism researchers such as Crompton (1979), Pearce (1982a), Chon (1991), Reilly (1990), Echtner and Ritchie (1993). The power of film in relation to creating, changing or reinforcing a destination's image has been considered in previous chapters. As already noted, agreeing on and maintaining a consistent image throughout individual promotions has become an issue because of such an uptake of destination marketing by individuals, which requires DMOs to effectively consult with these stakeholders in order to develop a destination image that is owned and therefore utilised by all groups.

The image a (potential) visitor may have of a destination is developed through a combination of factors and processes, from an initial cognitive perception to the effective translation of that perception into an attitude or 'mental map'. Such attitudes are pivotal to the evaluative aspects of image assessment, which is crucial in the design of effective place marketing strategies (Reilly, 1990). According to Walmsley and Young:

> Evaluative images are important because of their influence on discretionary trip-making behaviour…[and]…they can serve as a basis for marketing places. (Walmsley & Young, 1998: 65)

Walmsley and Jenkins (1992) also recognise that places evoke an entire range of emotional experiences and evaluations. In an attempt to measure such diversity, they utilised personal construct theory in a study of evaluative images in travel behaviour in Australia. They identified two principal evaluative components of the emotional meaning that people attach to environments, namely arousing–sleepy and pleasant–unpleasant. Kim (2010a) explores the way in which viewing experiences of film tourists can create personal memories and attachment to the filming location, with visitors re-creating through re-enacting key scenes with 'an emphasis on action, fantasy, nostalgia, memory and emotion' (Kim, 2010a: 72). Such components are positively reflected in the comments and actions of visitors to and residents of Barwon Heads and the story line of *Sea Change* outlined in Chapters 4 and 5, remaining pertinent today.

The Role of Destination Image in Travel Behaviour

As with other service-based products that cannot be sampled before use, the purchasing decision process of a tourism product calls for subjective judgements based on the formation of an impression of that product prior to purchase/consumption, and is heavily reliant on word-of-mouth. The importance of the role of destination image in the travel decision-making process has long been accepted in tourism marketing, as noted by LaPage and Cormier almost 40 years ago. They stated that, 'in many cases, it is probably the image more than the factual information that produces a tourist's decision on where to travel' (LaPage & Cormier, 1977: 21), while Croy (2010: 27) notes that 'the importance of destination image to destination mangers is not to be underestimated'. An accepted maxim is that a beneficial image would tend to increase desire to visit a destination, whereas a negative image would deter visitation.

Most tourist places already have an overall image that was formed prior to any decision to strategically develop an image. Some will have a positive image that can be built on to attract visitors, while others may have a weak, negative, mixed, contradictory or even overly picturesque image (Kotler et al., 1993). Each type of image requires different strategies to either capitalise on or ameliorate the problems associated with the fit of the image with the target consumer groups. The process of developing a destination marketing strategy follows basic marketing principles and is well-documented by Kotler and others, and will not be discussed in detail here (see Kotler et al., 1993; Heath & Wall, 1992; Kelly & Nankervis, 2001; Pike & Page, 2014; Zhang, 2014; Heeley, 2015).

Some places appear to focus almost exclusively on finding a clever slogan, then using it in a consistent, if somewhat blanket, manner, from tourist promotions through to vehicle registration plates. While having a widely adopted slogan may be important, it alone cannot successfully market a place. As stated by Kotler et al. (1993: 37), '[a] place's image must be valid and communicated in many ways through several channels if it is to succeed and take root'.

Consequently, a major goal of many tourism marketing researchers is to determine which image attributes influence the decision-making process, and the extent of such stimuli. Determining the relative importance of various attributes of image is a significant field of study, and Tapachi and Waryszak (2000) synthesised much of the research in this field undertaken prior to the turn of the century. They produced a *beneficial image model* based on the work of Seth, Newman and Gross on the multiple decision-making values of functional, social, emotional, epistemic and conditional values that remains relevant today. Assuming a holistic approach not unlike that posited by Walmsley and Young (1998), Tapachi and Waryszak propose a theory of the formation of a beneficial image of a destination as:

> perceptions or impressions of a destination held by tourists with respect to the expected benefit or consumption values including functional, social, emotional, epistemic, and conditional benefits of a destination. These perceptions/impressions in turn lead to the decision to visit a country [region or town] as a vacation destination. (Tapachi & Waryszak, 2000: 38)

Testing their theory, Tapachi and Waryszak studied the perceptions of potential visitors regarding the US and Thailand. While the sample was small and non-representative, being exploratory in manner, they found that there were differing levels of importance attached to the five values (functional, social, emotional, epistemic and conditional). Their results relating to the US are of more relevance to this study as it is a developed, democratic, Western society, similar in many regards to Australia. They found that the emotional value rated highly, between 60.3% and 65.5%, which is of interest to film-induced tourism, which tends to rely on and emphasise an emotional response in visitors.

In a paper titled, 'Destination image, self-congruity, and travel behavior: Toward an integrative model', Sirgy and Su posit a series of proposals, the most relevant to this discussion being that:

> ...travel behaviour is affected by self-congruity. That is, the greater the match between the destination visitor image and the tourist's self-concept (actual, ideal, social, and/or ideal social self-image), the more likely that this tourist will be motivated to visit that destination. (Sirgy & Su, 2000: 343)

Sirgy and Su explain that the match between a tourist's ideal self-image and the destination image is a powerful motivator, as visitors will tend to select a destination that allows them to experience their ideal self-image (which is usually different from their actual self-image). For example, a person who sees him/herself as working hard to make ends meet may choose to go to a resort with an up-market image in order to emulate the lifestyle 'of the rich and famous', even for a few days. By recognising such a desired (or ideal) self-image, a destination can tailor its imaging to attract this market, if so desired. This concept of self-image and its relationship to tourism destination marketing is widely supported by DMOs and other researchers (Goh & Litvin, 2000; Usakli & Baloglu, 2011; Zhang, 2014), but actually identifying self-image and then matching it to the destination is an intricate and often difficult process, with many of the so-called success stories being more serendipitous than conscious marketing efforts. In fact, they often relate to the popular media of the day, such as film, art or even literature.

Literary Tourism and Destination Marketing

Mention was made in Chapter 1 of the widely recognised influence of literature on tourism destinations. Watson (2009: 4) affirms the significance of literature in relation to imaging and tourism, noting that '[r]esearchers with interests in the history of travel, travel-writing, and imaginary national geography have some-times remarked on the leverage of the literary upon the tourist imagination', yet she argues that literary tourism has received limited attention from the literature field itself. Her statement reasserts the notion that, in certain academic fields, 'tourism' has been considered not worthy of serious study. Fortunately, with the work of Watson and others, this is changing. As she eloquently notes,

Literary tourism has recently become more interesting to the academic eye in part simply because of the astonishing acceleration over the last 20 years of all forms of travel and tourism worldwide and a related desire to develop and memorialise places and localities as unique in a post-modern world in which they may otherwise appear to be becoming so many interchangeable provinces of Planet Global. (Watson, 2009: 5)

The main difference between literary and film tourism is that, in relation to the former, visitors often go to the regions that relate personally to the writer (such as places of birth and death), whereas film tourists visit the places portrayed or the homes of the film stars and even hotels where they may have stayed (Laing & Frost, 2012). Possibly the interest in the actors' personal lives is marginally similar to the interest in authors' lives, but a screenwriter is rarely viewed as a source of interest or tourism. As further evidence to support this premise, Herbert (2001) identified the reasons for visiting a literary site as being to satisfy interest in the writer's life and work, to recall childhood memories (of reading the story), to visit a place imbued with special (additional) meaning, and to visit places that refer to events in the writer's life. Watson (2006) presents the extent of literary tourism sites as ranging from where the stories are set, from where they were actually written (author's home, a hotel or boarding house) to where the author 'was born, grew up, courted, lived or died' (Watson, 2006: 3). From Herbert's and Watson's reasoning, it can be seen that literary tourism has more to do with the creator of the work, not least because the author produces the prose, the only product of a book, whereas film-induced tourism has a number of progenitors.

To demonstrate the relevance of literature as a tourist generator, Müller looked at Leiper's model of a tourism attraction, comprising a sight, marker and visitor, explaining that:

> ...the site is formed by a place mentioned in the literature or in some way connected to the author's life. The marker that attaches meaning to the place can appear in various forms. In the case of literary tourism the literature itself plays a significant role as a powerful marker...simply by naming them, by attaching meaning to them, and by exposing them for readership. (Müller, 2001: CD-ROM)

Müller's comments support the agreed influence that literature has had (and still has) on tourism. Slee (1998) sees literary tourism as a form of pilgrimage, a concept with which Robertson and Radford (2009: 206) agree, further explaining that these so-called pilgrims are searching for 'a physical body to enable their senses to connect with objects read'.

There are many guidebooks and internet references regarding where these sites are, including the eponymous *Oxford Guide to Literary Britain and Ireland* by Hahn and Robins (2008). First published in 1977, it is now in its third edition, including an online version published in 2009 by Oxford

Reference. The guide includes over 2000 places, with hundreds of illustrations of writers, their homes and the landscapes that inspired them. While literary tourism is a global phenomenon, the UK has been a major destination for literary tourism, with places connected to literature used to promote destinations, including *Shakespeare's Stratford, Wordsworth's Lake District, Dickens's London* and so on (Hoppen *et al.*, 2014). As Seaton reinforces, '...the importance of the printed word to tourism development in Scotland cannot be over-estimated' (1998: 16).

Since the inception of the internet there are now countless online guides, including the extensive LiteraryTourist.com which includes bookshops as well as literary destinations. The site, founded in 2010, has links to literary places in the Americas, Asia Pacific and Africa as well as Europe, and details everything from literary events to writers' homes and the aforementioned bookshops along with maps, a trip planner and a blog as well as offering consulting services to places who wish to attract literary tourists.

Laing and Frost (2012) looked at different genres in light of how travel is conceptualised. They considered historical novels, crime stories, children's books, science fiction and the Western, finding that 'travel is conceptualised in a remarkably similar way throughout different eras and cultural contexts' (Laing & Frost, 2012: 192). Importantly, they note that the fact that travel as related in stories is usually presented as transformative (either metaphorically or literally) may create expectations in tourists that cannot be realised. This is not unlike some of the arguments against film-induced tourism, which are addressed throughout this book.

While I have noted that much of the focus on literary tourism has tended to been in the UK, Europe and North America, LiteraryTourism.com demonstrates that there are an increasing number of destinations in other regions identifying with their literary ties. For example, South Korea has adopted many literary sites, particularly since the introduction of *Hallyu*, or the Korean Wave, which celebrates Korean popular culture, including historical novels and literature. Popular novelist Kim Yujeong's home village has been named as the Literary Village of Kim Yujeong, with Lee and Weaver (2012: 181) referring to this as a 'hyper destination'. An article on the VisitKorea website asks whether 'K-Lit' is the next Korean Wave, supporting its argument with details of many literary tourist sites, including bookshop cafes and literary houses (Kelly, 2011).

A study by Hilty (1996) that examined the manner in which tourism is induced through the promotion of literary locations remains relevant today, concluding that authorities need to take steps to minimise the social and cultural negative impacts of increased literary tourism. Such steps include evaluating the existing infrastructure to ensure it is capable of coping with any tourist influx, preparing residents to deal with changes, and determining at what point residents and visitors will perceive the location as overcrowded.

Books and film tourism success

One interesting outcome from studying the successes and failures of movies for inducing tourism is that most of the popular film tourism sites have come from movies (and some television series, such as *Game of Thrones*) that were popular books in the first instance. *The Lord of the Rings*, often cited as a great example of film-induced tourism and partly studied in this book, already had a strong and passionate fan base from the book series by Tolkien, as does Dan Brown's *The Da Vinci Code* and the *Harry Potter* movies and books.

A further example of a book generating enormous tourism can be seen in the television series *Game of Thrones* (2011–), which is based on a series of books by American author George R.R. Martin (first published in 1996) and filmed in Northern Ireland, Iceland, Croatia, Morocco, Malta, Spain and Scotland. While fans are flocking to all of the sites, the Northern Ireland tourist board in particular has embraced the imaging, marketing and tourism opportunities.

On their industry website, under a section on 'Screen Tourism', the tourist board is actively encouraging businesses to consider not only film-induced tourism in general, but in particular *Game of Thrones*, stating that:

> Northern Ireland is the principal filming location using various studios as well as many spectacular locations across Northern Ireland. There is an international appetite to visit Game of Thrones filming locations providing a huge tourism opportunity for Northern Ireland. Many of these locations that are accessible to the public have been the catalyst for the development of new visitor experiences. (Tourism Northern Ireland, 2016: www.tourismni.com/BusinessSupport)

They also address some of the copyright issues that I outline in Chapter 4, producing *Tour Operator Guidelines* (c.2015) in conjunction with the producers, HBO. While tours to sites featured in the series are permitted, the operator is not allowed to use any imagery from the series, the logo, or similar typefaces in their printed material. They also need to produce a disclaimer that removes any liability from HBO. This is similar to the movie cases outlined in Chapter 4, where the production companies are highly protective of their creative material.

In a most interesting nod to *The Lord of the Rings*, the trivia section of the Internet Movie Database (IMDb) informs us that, 'A replica of Gandalf's sword, Glamdring, from the Lord of the Rings trilogy and Hobbit trilogy, is forged inside the Iron Throne' (IMDb, 2015). Such minutiae are grist for fans and further add to both the series' and the movie's touristic appeal.

This notion is inherent in many of the research cases in this book, and as such can be seen as one of the success factors for film-induced tourism;

yet most of the focus on film-induced tourism success is on the post-screening marketing to potential tourists (see Hudson & Ritchie, 2006a, 2006b; Young & Young, 2008; O'Connor *et al.*, 2008; Croy, 2010; Vagionis & Loumioti, 2010; Yoon *et al.*, 2015 and so on). Volo and Irimais (2015) consider this aspect in a longitudinal study of films based in the Sicilian town of Cefalù and on how it exploits films in relation to tourism marketing. An interesting study in itself, once again research fails to investigate why certain films were more attractive in encouraging tourism than others. While the Oscar winning film *Nuovo Cinema Paradiso (Cinema Paradiso)* (1988) was not published as a book until the 1990s, movies such as *Tutti i SantiGiorni (Every Blessed Day)* (2012) are certainly based on novels, and, according to the authors, are considered to have had significant tourism impacts (Table 3.2).

Table 3.2 Tourism-inducing movies and television series based on books (a selection)

Movies	Year/s of release	Tourism examples
Gone with the Wind	1939	The movie was filmed on a now defunct studio backlot, yet the romanticized Southern lifestyle has encouraged tours to Antebellum homes, including the house from the novel, Tara, near Jonesboro, Georgia. The old mill that appears at the beginning of the film is in a park in Little Rock Arkansas and clearly marked.
Breakfast at Tiffany's	1961	Presented what has become a romanticized view of New York and raised the profile of Tiffany's which has become a site of pilgrimage for fans of the movie.
James Bond Films	1962–	The many exotic locations, particularly in Europe have spawned numerous feature tours (particularly of London) as well as general interest. 'James Bond Island' (Phang Nga Island) in Phuket has many guided tours as well as touring the Swiss Alps by Aston Martin. There are also film studio tours of Pinewood Studios in the UK.
The Sound of Music	1965	In spite of the Austrian government's concern over their representation in the movie, over 300,000 fans continue to visit sites, re-enacting their favourite scenes. Alongside the more standard bus tours, sites can be visited by horse and carriage or rickshaw and even with a singing tour guide.
Jurassic Park	1993, 1997 2001, 2015	Limited commercial tours to Kualoa Ranch in Kuaui, yet is regularly noted in many Hawaiian tours, along with Jurassic Park hiking and helicopter tours.

(Continued)

Table 3.2 (*Continued*)

Movies	Year/s of release	Tourism examples
Forrest Gump	1994	The seat where Forrest Gump sat is at Universal Studios in Los Angeles and is a highly popular site for tourists to take photos while on a formal tour of the studio.
The Beach	2000	Extremely popular with backpackers and young film tourists. Overcrowding of film tourists at the site, Maya Bay on Phi Phi island overshadows the dark storyline of the movie.
The Da Vinci Code	2006	There are self-guided trails, walking tours, commercial tours of many of the sites in the UK and France. In particular, the small Rosslyn Chapel in Scotland has been affected by film tourism, as there was little tourism to the chapel prior, unlike most of the other sites.
Slumdog Millionaire	2008	Tours of Mumbai slums have created a great deal of controversy – some provide support to the residents and restrict invasive tourist behaviour, while others tend to romanticize poverty.
Eat Pray Love	2010	Tours of Italy, India and Bali have been developed covering all three countries, while others specialize in moments from the film. Many other tours focus more on the 'theme' of spirituality rather than the actual film sites.
Wild	2014	Adventure based walking tours that follow the protagonist's journey along the Pacific Crest Trail in the US. Limited mass tourism, but presents a niche opportunity for fans and the more adventurous.
Television Series		
Midsomer Murders	1997–	Self-guided (Midsomer Murders Trail maps available for download) and formal tours (walking, day trips and overnight stays) of various shires including Buckinghamshire and Oxfordshire under the title of VisitMidsomer www.visitmidsomer.com/guided-tours/
Sex in the City	1998–2004	Manhattan TV Tours has specific Sex in the City Tours as well as including it in their general commentaries.
Game of Thrones	2011–	Formal tours and destination support for setting up such tours to Belfast, Northern Ireland, Reykjavík, Iceland and Dubrovnik, Croatia as well as fan events and individual visitors.

Many of these examples illustrate the longevity of film-induced tourism, with their popularity seemingly increasing over the years and as the tourism industry has recognised their potential, as in *The Sound of Music* (1965), where tourism was initially discouraged. In fact, there are few recently released movies or television series listed here as the tourism outcome is often not clear for a year or so after release, particularly if it is an international destination that may take some planning. However, one needs to remain cautious when looking at such factors, as not all movies made from books generate tourism, and at times the book actually comes from the movie, such as with *Nuovo Cinema Paradiso (Cinema Paradiso)* (1988). Nevertheless, it certainly seems that a high percentage of those movies that are strong tourism generators found their origins (and strong fan base) in literature.

From Reading to Looking: Art-Induced Tourism

In his inspiring travel-themed publication, *The Art of Travel*, Alain de Botton eloquently applies his love of art as well as literature to travel, using the works of Vincent van Gogh to guide him through Provence and to assist him to see places in a more nuanced way – 'a successful work will draw out the features capable of exciting a sense of beauty and interest in a spectator' (de Botton, 2002: 187). He is particularly interested in the relationship between the anticipation and reality of travel, especially as created through literature and art, explaining that, while he travels, he is often tempted to enjoy a more internal journey of his imagination than the banal reality of the experience.

De Botton (2002) uses artworks to present ways that may encourage consideration of *why* and *how* we travel as opposed to simply *where* we travel to. He argues that a work of art can draw our eyes towards certain aspects of a place that we may not otherwise notice, as well as imbuing it with emotional content and context. This visual resonance continues on to the current art forms of today, including movies and television programmes, where we are presented with emotional keys and links to places that we otherwise may simply pass over.

As Busby and Klug (2001) point out (and as considered in the opening chapters of this work), by the beginning of the 21st century film has become so pervasive that its influence and effect outstrips that of literature as well as art. Film is to literary tourism what the Boeing 747 was to mainstream tourism – a major booster for mass tourism. We have moved from small, niche-based personal pilgrimage literary tours to the mass (and at times over-full) visitation of film sites. As the popularity and use of film and television have grown rapidly as major ways of obtaining information to gain knowledge as well as entertainment, the influence of movies, videos, DVDs and television is becoming even more important and pervasive, with fewer people relying on written information. The rise of social media and the internet have dramatically changed the way in which we source information and view content, yet the television remains a powerful medium, along with cinema. Consequently, television programmes, documentaries, movies and so on still play a significant role in creating our image of destinations, as discussed in the following section.

The Role of Film in Destination Imaging and Marketing

Place (or destination) marketing, a central aspect of any tourism strategy, is aimed at either reinforcing the existing image in the potential visitor's mind, or constructing a new image to replace vague or negative images (Holcomb, 1993). Once again, visual media are considered to be the most powerful image-creators rather than marketing, especially when their effect is subtler, when they have not been primarily developed to achieve this goal. In other words, a movie set in a particular destination may appeal to the audience as a place to visit, but it was a secondary (or later) motivation for them to actually see the film. This makes the promotional process more subtle and akin to word-of-mouth, as opposed to direct destination advertising. The natural scenery, exciting/exotic locations, storyline themes and human relationships portrayed in the film are recognised motivators for people to visit certain locations, and many movies present the backdrop of the setting of the film as more than mere 'scenery', producing icons that are central to the storyline. A much-cited early example of this is Devil's Tower National Monument in the science fiction movie *Close Encounters of the Third Kind* (1977), in which the monument played a pivotal role.

As such, movie icons can be recurrent, or single, climatic events with which viewers (and later as visitors to the site) identify. The icons do not necessarily have to be visual, but can be embedded in the storyline or character themes (Riley *et al.*, 1998). Riley and Van Doren (1992) also include the motivations of pilgrimage, nostalgia and escape as tourist attractions inherent in certain film and television programmes. Table 3.3 illustrates some of the locations and iconic attractions from a selection of Australian movies and television programmes.

As shown in Table 3.3, the iconic attractions for many popular Australian programmes include straight visual backdrops and those inherent to the storyline, as well as emotional relationships between the place and characters. For example, *The Man from Snowy River* (1982) incorporates the Australian countryside as a visual backdrop, while at the same time presenting it as a final frontier to be overcome through the application of the bush culture and the symbiotic relationship between man and horse. *Sea Change* (1998–2000) tends to use lifestyle change and the small, caring community as its main drawcard, with the scenery providing aspects of the storyline, but tending to be more of a peaceful backdrop to the small community's foibles and machinations. Australians recognise familiarity, even when it is to an imagined past or culture as in *The Man from Snowy River* and *Crocodile Dundee* (1986), while the predominant international appeal is the reinforcement of a certain level of safety combined with adventure. Such a combination is a powerful tourism motivator.

Table 3.3 Iconic attractions of Australian film

Movie/TV Programme	Location	Iconic attraction	Australian vs international appeal/legibility
The Man from Snowy River	Alpine National Park, Victoria	Australian bush culture – The land as nurturer and protagonist. Final frontier adventure. Man and horse striving together.	Reinforcement of an imagined bush heritage. International appeal of final frontier in a 'safe' visitor destination.
Crocodile Dundee	Kakadu National Park, Northern Territory	Australian bush culture – humour. Laconic Australian identity.	Supporting an imagined outback culture experienced by few Australians. International appeal of final frontier in a destination that Americans can travel through safely.
Neighbours	Melbourne, Victoria	Australian suburban culture. Gender relations in the suburbs.	Appeals to a predominantly urban-based Australia as local, able to relate to. International appeal of a clean, safe Australian culture.
Home and Away		Australian coastal lifestyle (sun, sand, surf and sex). Youthful characters. Small, caring community.	Appeals to a predominantly coastal-based Australian culture as local, able to relate to. Reinforces international image of sun, sand, surf and sex.
Mad Max	Silverton, New South Wales	Futuristic, post-nuclear world. Land as enemy. Foreign, barren landscape.	Landscape not perceived as Australian by either locals or internationals.
Sea Change	Barwon Heads, Victoria	Change of lifestyle (competitive urban vs cooperative rural). Small, caring community.	Appeals to Australian 'baby-boomers' longing for their own 'sea change.' International reinforcement of a friendly, quirky Australia.

Furthermore, many of the movie studios have become so closely linked to a destination that they are also used to market the destination. For example, Los Angeles often uses its built movie heritage sites such as the recognisable entry portals of Paramount and Universal Studios as destination images. While not related to a specific film, these studios are strong image-makers in their own right, with their own stories of celebrity-making that at times have also been immortalised in film.

Tooke and Baker (1996) postulate that a movie can fit Ritchie's definition of a hallmark event in that it is of limited duration and enhances awareness, appeal and profitability of the destination, which is supported by the discussion above. However, visiting the site of a movie or other film (such as a television series) relates more to a pilgrimage than to an event, particularly where visitors are motivated by the thematic contents rather than the environmental attractions. Examples of such pilgrimages include visits to Arches National Monument in Moab as featured in the movie *Thelma and Louise*, and even to Kakadu National Park, looking for the Paul Hogan character from *Crocodile Dundee*, Mick Dundee (and possible romance!).

When considering Sirgy and Su's proposition that the match between a tourist's self-image and destination imaging is a motivator, film becomes a powerful means of developing an image that supports a commonly held ideal self-image. In their efforts to be successful, many television series look to their predominantly urban audience's desires and ideal self-images, and often portray communities of friendly, caring people who still have time for each other in contrast to the self-interest of those in large cities. Such series are numerous and include the English shows *All Creatures Great and Small* (1978–1990), *Heartbeat* (1992–2008), *Doc Martin* (2004–), the Scottish *Hamish Macbeth* (1995–1997) and the Irish *Ballykissangel* (1996–2001) as well as the more recent *Game of Thrones* (2011–), along with Australian series such as *Blue Heelers* (1994–2006), *Home and Away* (1988–), *Neighbours* (1985–) and *Sea Change* (1998–2000). This is a common dream (or ideal self-image) of many people in industrialised societies, for whom the small-town rural idyll is 'still out there somewhere'. Therefore, the aims of film producers can be seen in many cases to be congruent with those of the DMOs – that of using the medium of film to develop an image that is desired by their market. As discussed in Chapter 2, this has resulted in numerous cases of tourism marketing organisations working closely with their film office, with some regions offering attractive incentives to film producers for on-location filming. An excellent example of this has been the New Zealand government's appointment of a so-called 'Minister of the Rings' to leverage the international profile of the country through the publicity brought by *The Lord of the Rings* movies. The Minister worked with the government tourism, trade and film commissions in order to achieve this, and more than NZ$6 million over three years was allocated to the task (*New Zealand Herald*, 2001b).

Filming a television series or movie in a region or town has been seen to have a dramatic effect on tourist visitation and expectations (as discussed in Chapters 2, 4 and 5). Those destinations and operations that have capitalised on the images portrayed in film have met with mixed and at times significant results. The interesting aspect of this is that often community members have not been party to the decision to film certain sites, nor have they any control over the image presented, and this results in often unrealistic and, at the extreme end of the scale, negative images. However, if the image is desirable, it stands to reason that tourism operators and DMOs alike will take advantage of this boon of 'free' publicity, even to the point of re-imaging the destination to bring it into harmony with the film-generated imagery.

That said, the promotional capability of films is not equal, and some television programmes and movies have little impact, while others may be both influential and memorable – it may be the plot, the characters, the setting or all three that combine to create a film experience of lasting importance. While the level of importance and influence of a film depends upon its popularity, the size of the production company also plays a role in reaching a wide audience – a Fox Studios production has far greater reach than a production from a smaller independent studio. Therefore, it is not merely the level of empathy and self-congruity with the storyline that creates a film tourism destination, rather a range of (sometimes competing) factors. Global factors also play a role in shaping a population's choice of film; for example, in times of war or other hardship more positive, 'happy' and even patriotic films seem to abound. When considering the range of emerging issues and aspects that affect destination marketing, Buhalis concludes that:

> Consumers are increasingly following special interests and regard their trips as both recreational and educational experiences. Therefore, destination themes and their interpretation become more important for the future. (Buhalis, 2000: 114)

Such a statement augurs well for the application of film imagery as a cohesive destination image, providing that the image is congruent with the desired self-image of the community and tourism businesses of that destination and with the level of reach of the film itself. Portegies (2010) points out that, as the film maker is expert in using film images and storylines to convey a sense of place, they may well be far more powerful and successful than the DMO. Furthermore, film may also be 'a credible tool to modify people's image of place'. (Croy, 2010: 27)

Braveheart: Destination marketing through film

Historically, the town of Stirling in Scotland has been an economic and politically strategic site, and many celebrated victories against the English occurred there. One such success was the Battle of Stirling Bridge, won by

William Wallace ('Scotland's liberator') in 1297. After decades of heated public debate regarding the site for erecting a national monument to William Wallace, in 1869 the National Wallace Monument was completed on the Abbey Craig in Stirling, a steep hill overlooking the site of the Battle of Stirling Bridge. The monument, a 220-feet-high stone tower with a spiral staircase of some 246 steps to the top of the monument, was financed through public fundraising and overseen by a building committee headed by a local minister, Reverend Charles Roger.

On completion, the monument was leased to private individuals living on the site to run it as a public facility. In order to provide income for the lessees, a tea room was deemed essential and was certainly welcomed by those who made the steep climb up Abbey Craig to the foot of the monument. In 1995 a small bus was introduced to take people up the steep climb to the monument (King, 1997).

In an indictment of the current push to privatise public amenities, the Wallace Monument was not an economically successful tourist attraction, in spite of the importance of Wallace and the Battle of Stirling Bridge to the Scots. Management of the site was taken over by the local council in the 1990s. It was not until the 1995 release of the Hollywood blockbuster, *Braveheart*, starring and directed by Australian actor Mel Gibson, that the monument took on true iconic tourism status and turned a profit.

Notwithstanding the fact that much of the movie was filmed in Ireland and other parts of Scotland, and none of it was filmed anywhere near Stirling, let alone the monument, and that an Australian played the part of the great Scottish liberator, visitor numbers to the National Wallace Monument increased immediately after the release of the film – up to three-fold (Argyll and the Isles, Loch Lomond, Stirling and Trossachs Tourist Board, 2001). In 1996 a statue of Wallace was erected near the visitors' centre and carpark at the base of Abbey Craig, directly below the monument. The statue bears an uncanny resemblance to Gibson and is by far the most popular photographic site at the Wallace Monument (see Figure 3.1).

In a most pragmatic, postmodern take on reality, film and authenticity, Elspeth King, the author of a book about William Wallace available from the visitors' centre at the National Wallace Monument explains the use of an Australian actor's image in the following manner:

> In the late 20th century, the face of William Wallace, known and recognised worldwide is that of Mel Gibson from the film *Braveheart*. As many of the episodes in the film are suffused with the spirit of, and closely based on the tales of Wallace's biographer Blind Harry, it is entirely appropriate. (King, 1997: 13)

Consequently, Mel Gibson and the film *Braveheart* are used openly (and successfully) to promote Stirling as a destination, not only at Abbey Craig and

Figure 3.1 *Braveheart* the movie meets *Braveheart* the monument. Modelled on a movie star, this sculpture has pride of place at the Wallace monument near Stirling in Scotland. While none of the movie was filmed here, tourists flocked to the site after the release of *Braveheart*, essentially turning a losing public monument into a profitable enterprise

in so-called 'historical' publications, but also on the website for the tourism region of the Scottish Heartlands (Argyll and the Isles, Loch Lomond, Stirling and Trossachs Tourist Board, 2001). By titling the webpage, 'Hollywood Legends', the DMO has also been able to access some of the 'magic' and glamour associated with Hollywood, which is rarely associated with Scotland! The success of the marketing of the Stirling Monument and consequently the town itself is also remarkable in that it was not used as a site during the filming of *Braveheart*, indicating that with the 'right' promotion, places referred to, but not seen, in film can capitalise on the film's imaging power.

Around the time of the release of the movies *Braveheart*, *Rob Roy* and *The Bruce*, all around 1995, the Scottish Tourist Board undertook a study to quantify the volume and value of the publicity that these movies generated. Much to their delight they found that, between April 1995 and June 1996, a total of 213 articles and 37 broadcasts in 12 countries had been produced, with a retail advertising value of £11,454,879 (Seaton & Hay, 1998). While the study did not attempt to quantify the actual tourist visitation influence, a study by the Stirling Council and Forth Valley Enterprise found that the films were influential in exerting a greater influence on trip decisions once overseas visitors were already in Scotland (System Three, 1997). Seaton and Hay (1998) point out that this study assessed only the immediate influence of the films, suggesting that their influence may be activated later, and this is supported by the communication theory of 'sleeper effect'.

However, they also warn that there is no guarantee of a film's success, and that the message of a feature film will not always conform to the strategic objectives set by a destination agency. For example, the traditional 'tartan' image projected by *Braveheart* and *Rob Roy* was consistent with the Scottish Tourist Board's image for its overseas markets, but not with its image for the UK market. Films such as *Trainspotting* (1996) and *Young Adam* (2003), depicting Scottish cities as an urban jungle of crime and drugs, are even less consistent with this image, but little (if any) research has been done to assess such influences.

The Andy Griffith Show: Destination creation through television

In a thought-provoking postmodernist monograph on the culture of festivals in the American South, *Ghost Dancing on the Cracker Circuit*, anthropologist R.L. Brown (1997) visits the 'Mayberry Days Festival' at Mount Airy in North Carolina. This festival is based on *The Andy Griffith Show* (1960–1968), a popular television programme set in the 1950s screened in the 1960s whose author and main protagonist, Andy Griffith, grew up in Mount Airy. According to the IMDb, '[w]idower Sheriff Andy and his son Opie live with Andy's Aunt Bee in Mayberry NC. With virtually no crimes to solve, most of Andy's time is spent philosophizing and calming down his cousin Deputy Barney' (IMDb, 2015). At times Griffith incorporated the names of people and places from Mount Airy into fictional Mayberry, the town depicted in his show. The series itself celebrated an era of emblematic middle-class America not unlike a 1950s' *Sea Change* (1998–2000), with quirky, friendly small-town characters and goings on. Re-runs of the series are still being shown on American television, resplendent in their original, untouched black-and-white format.

Mount Airy is typical in that it has experienced flagging economic fortunes, with a downtown that has dried up, like main streets in many small towns. The streets are quiet, not because of any conscious decision to retain the 'good old days', but because the shopping 'centre' has moved from the town centre to the large department stores and malls on the highways out of town. Brown (1997) argues that the town is attempting to revive its flagging economy by assuming the identity of an idealised media representation.

Mount Airy promotes itself as 'the real Mayberry', wearing its ordinariness as something extraordinary via the television series – if it were not for *The Andy Griffith Show*, it may well have become another declining mid-American small town. Even though the programme was written and first screened in the 1960s, it is still being shown in the US on free-to-air television as well as cable channels, and the town has been able to ride on its back for over 40 years. In his book, *A Cuban in Mayberry: Looking Back at America's*

Hometown, Firmat (2014) reports that a high percentage (over half) of his students at Columbia University are aware of this series even today. He expresses some surprise, but also sees this as evidence of the longevity of the small town America dream, where '...a generation of texters and tweeters are still drawn to Mayberry' (Firmat, 2014: 17).

In 1990, the annual Mayberry Days Festival was first held. Visitors can view back-to-back re-runs of some of the 249 episodes, see concerts hosted by character look-alikes, attend a tea party and other such 'small town' activities (Surry Arts Council, 2003). 'Mount Airy is doing its best to imitate an imitation of itself and become America's official make-believe town' (Brown, 1997: 181). Brown (1997) relates this to a form of the romantic pastoral impulse, where the town leaders even considered changing Mount Airy's name to Mayberry, or building a theme park on the edge of town. While this did not happen, the simple fact that it was even considered is instructive, with Benjamin *et al.* (2012: 141) observing that 'portions of the town have been (re)designed to reference, and at times re-create, fictional characters, places, and experiences from the show'.

Brown (1997) sees festivals such as Mayberry Days (and by inference, the films connected with them) as an attempt to return to and/or resurrect a past. However, the past of *The Andy Griffith Show* celebrated by the festival never existed. Brown compares this with the Native American Ghost Dancing movement of the late 19th century, where it was believed that the dead could be summoned to return and avenge the social and cultural deprivations experienced by the native people. The celebrations at Mount Airy express a similar desire – a 'postmodern ghost dancing...[presented by] the public performance by pop simulacra of a simulated golden age' (Brown, 1997: 180). Affirming this, Benjamin *et al.* (2012: 144) found that 'some devoted fan tourists approach the representation of Mount Airy as Mayberry with a sense of "emergent" or negotiated authenticity...and thus blur the lines between "reel" and "real" places, but this potentially creates locational dissonance as well as broader social tensions'. The world portrayed in the television series is significantly different from reality, with the emerging issues of civil rights receiving no acknowledgement in this all-white constructed Mayberry, yet African-Americans were living in Mount Airy. A few years after the initial screening of *The Andy Griffith Show* in 1963, a black teenager was arrested for refusing to leave a drug store where he had been denied service (Alderman *et al.*, 2012).

Brown's discussion on postmodern ghost dancing and additional research into the television series and the town on which it is based resonates with many of the popular movies and television series that have supported (or even at times created) a tourism industry. Holidays are the ultimate form of escape, and experiencing simulacra such as the friendly morality offered in Mount Airy, or playing adventure roles aka *Man from Snowy River* begin to make sense.

Enduring Imagery? Longevity of Film-induced Tourism

During the early days of film tourism research, many argued that such tourism would be short-lived, as films and television programmes come in and out of style (Riley & Van Doren, 1992; Riley *et al.*, 1998). Connell (2005) found that the tourism enterprises themselves were not willing to invest in developing film-related tourism due to their belief that it would be short-lived. Yet, the example above of *The Andy Griffith Show*, along with my own experience in Australia with the movie *The Man from Snowy River* (1982), lead me to think about this a little more. When we see many DMOs changing their marketing strategies every few years, the 55+ years of film tourism to Mayberry, along with over 25 years of the Mayberry Days Festival, puts paid to such simplistic criticisms, yet they are often repeated by inexperienced or unaware researchers and industry professionals.

In 2015, the Australian television programme *Neighbours* (1985–) celebrated 30 years of the show. Every day of the year, apart from Christmas Day and Good Friday tours of primarily British fans head out to Pinoak Court, the site for the street in which all of the 'neighbours' reside, Ramsay Street, and the film studios solely dedicated to the show, or a meeting with one of the actors from the series. I have participated in a number of tours over the past few years, and relate the experience as well as more about the operation in the following chapter.

Movie Maps and Guidebooks as Significant Destination Marketing Tools

Maps indicating the sites of film and television series have become a major destination promotional tool, especially in the UK and the US, with interactive versions provided on the internet as well as hard copies available for potential visitors and film and television buffs. The map produced by the British Tourist Authority (BTA, 2001b) in the early 1990s is now available as an interactive map on the internet as well as a hard-copy brochure and has television as well as movie sites indicated on it. The hard copy of the map lists some 67 movies and television programmes in England, Scotland, Wales and Ireland, while in 2001 the internet site listed more than 107 films in England, Scotland and Wales (BTA, 2001b). The internet site also presented a special 'Bollywood' map for fans of Indian-produced films and a site specifically devoted to the places featured in the *Harry Potter* movies (BTA, 2001a). At the time of writing, this responsibility is now that of VisitBritain, which provides a 'Top Ten' list of movies, which includes the *Harry Potter* and *James Bond* films along with specific popular movies such as *Braveheart* (1995), *Pride and*

Prejudice (1995), *Four Weddings and a Funeral* (1994), with hyperlinks to a vast range of film sites (VisitBritain, 2015). They also have a stand-alone site for the popular television series *Downton Abbey* (2010–) and the 'top' stately homes shown on film as well as an updated list of and links to Bollywood filming sites. These maps perform a dual purpose of promoting the films and television series themselves as well as the destinations at which they were filmed, and is interesting to note that many of them are over 20 years old.

According to Busby and Klug (2001), the main purpose of the BTA movie map was to even out the seasonal spread of visitors and was promoted only to overseas visitors. Such limited market targeting may have had little effect on reducing seasonal variations. It has been shown by Croy and Walker (2001), as well as in the research outlined in this book, that visiting a film site is rarely a primary motivator. Consequently, it may have little effect on encouraging international visitation at off-peak times. However, domestic tourists may have been encouraged to visit the sites, as they have with Barwon Heads in Australia. Unfortunately, it has not been possible to assess the success of BTA's target marketing due to limited available data. However, they claim it has been successful because of the extent of media coverage ('free ink') received and the overall increase in visitors to some of the sites featured (Busby & Klug, 2001). There is no available data as to whether visitors were international or domestic, or what time of year they were visiting.

Following the success of the movie maps in the UK and the US, Denise Corrigan developed a movie map of Australia in 1996, with support from Tourism New South Wales, the Australian Film Commission, the New South Wales Film and TV Office, the Museum of Contemporary Art, Village Roadshow, the Australian Centenary of Cinema, the National Film and Sound Archive and Film Victoria. The map includes information on movies from *The Story of the Kelly Gang*, the world's first feature film in 1906, through to *Babe* in 1996. The *Map* also includes information on the National Film and Sound Archive and a treatise on 'The Australian Land in Australian Films' (Routt, 1996).

The map itself was recognised by BTA as a competitor to their own movie map (Busby & Klug, 2001), however it has not had the longevity of the BTA version. The financial support given was for a one-off production and, despite the growing popularity of film-induced tourism, Corrigan was unable to obtain further funding to produce an updated version, hence the films featured finish at 1996, just as Australia was once again making major inroads on the international film and television scene. The map also seemed to be distributed spasmodically and was difficult (if not impossible) to find at Tourist Information Centres – in order to obtain some copies to pass on to interested visitors it was necessary to approach Corrigan directly. An opportunity to capitalise on the lucrative international tourism spin-off from popular Australian films was lost as destinations in other countries developed and updated their own movie maps.

Nevertheless, the publication of movie maps, both in hard copy and on the internet, as well as on smaller devices such as smartphones, has become a significant marketing tool in the arsenal of many DMOs, and appears to be one way to build on the growing interest in visiting film sites. Other interactive sites are available from the US, especially in California and Hollywood, with extensive links and interaction. The California film and television map, *Hollywood on Location*, lists some 240 films and television programmes (California Tourism, 2001), while Australia is 'catching up', with a movie map for South Australia produced by the South Australian Tourist Commission in 2002. Smartphone apps that I have found to be great fun when travelling include location-based apps such as *The Reelist*, *The MovieMap.com* and more specific destination-focused apps such as *Times Square Movie and TV Locations*, *ParisHugo* and *AnimeTrakr* in Japan. Many are supported by film commissions instead of DMOs. However, many are either in development, not updated, have limited information or have been superseded, such as one of my old favourites, *The Location Scout*, which was associated with the IMDb.

New Zealand published maps identifying the country as the 'home of Middle Earth', encouraging road trips to the sites, and included a pictorial journey of the key movie locations on its tourism websites. In the week after the release in 2001 of the first *Lord of the Rings* movie, *The Fellowship of the Ring*, the number of visitors to the Tourism New Zealand website doubled. The Chief Executive of Tourism New Zealand, George Hickton, summarises the hopes that he has for film-induced tourism, saying that:

> The *Lord of the Rings* trilogy will be a very exciting event for New Zealand…and we are hoping through the destination work that has been done that it will be a major driver for visitors to this country from some of our most important markets. (Tourism New Zealand, 2001a)

Whereas movie maps are generally funded publicly through regional and national tourism organisations, most of the film-related guidebooks are privately/commercially produced, often by fans. The commercial success of some of these publications has surprised authors and publishers alike. *The Lord of the Rings Location Guidebook* was reprinted twice in 2002 and five times in 2003 prior to the release of an updated guide that year. This is no mean feat, considering that little built evidence of the sets remains, and even some of the most significant 'natural' locations (such as the 'Pillars of the Kings') were computer enhanced. In addition, in 2003, the travel guidebook publisher Rough Guides released a *Rough Guide to The Lord of the Rings*. It will be interesting to see how many visitors to New Zealand use this as an information source, and how many have purchased it as fans to add to their Tolkien collections.

While not meeting quite the same sales figures, many guidebooks have been published in the UK on visiting film sites. These include *Filming On and Around the North Yorkshire Moors Railway*, *Classic Heartbeat Country*, *TV and*

Film Locations Guide – Northern England and *Southern England*, and *TV Country Favourites from the BBC and Yorkshire TV*, which includes programmes from Scotland and Ireland as well as England.

Travel guide publishers such as Lonely Planet and Rough Guides, while not producing any specific film tourism books, do take advantage of their market's fascination with film. The Rough Guide has produced a small booklet on cult television programmes, *The Rough Guide to Cult TV, The Good, the Bad and the Strangely Compelling*. However, this has not linked any of the programmes with actual sites, which is an oversight (to say the least), as the booklet itself is 'un-putdown-able' and would enhance and cross-promote their travel guides.

Animation and Tourism

Animated films have, until recently, received little attention as opportunities for place and product placement and have not been recognised in any published academic tourism studies of film-induced tourism. However, the enormous and growing popularity of animation in its various forms has prompted some tourism organisations to use them to leverage their destinations.

In 2002, the Hawaii Visitors and Conventions Bureau (HVCB) negotiated a US$3.9 million three-year marketing contract with the Walt Disney Company to promote Hawaii through the animated film *Lilo & Stitch* (Ryan, 2002). Hawaii was keen to reposition itself as a family destination, and an animated film set in Hawaii with a storyline all about 'family' was considered to be ideal, and Disney's market reach and penetration was seen to be significant. This became particularly pertinent in the wake of the September 11 2001 downturn in tourism and concomitant return to family values. The trailer of the film was altered to specifically mention Hawaii, while a web link to the HVCB was included on the official *Lilo & Stitch* website. Other product tie-ins include commercials about Hawaii on the ABC television broadcast of the film's Los Angeles launch and messages about the islands on the DVD release of the film (Nichols, 2002; Wu, 2003).

However, the Hawaii Tourism Authority (HTA) who subcontracts (and funds) the HVCB to promote Hawaii, withdrew support for the Disney deal after only 12 months, even though they were quoted as being 'happy with the first year results...' (Ryan, 2003); they stressed that box-office success does not directly correspond to successful tourism marketing outcomes. The HTA also claimed that it was shifting its marketing efforts away from families to higher-yield tourist markets such as golfers.

After being 'burnt' by the *Lilo & Stitch* deal, Disney executives stated that they were 'unlikely to offer a similar agreement again to anyone' (Ryan, 2003). So it was interesting to see that the Australian Tourist Commission

(ATC) and Disney formed an agreement regarding the 2004 animated movie *Finding Nemo*, which is set in Australia. While actual reports on any agreements are commercial-in-confidence, tie-ins similar to those in Hawaii are evident. In the build-up to the movie's release in the UK, a promotional CD-ROM was included in *The Mail on Sunday* newspaper, which included a competition to win a trip to Australia, supported by the ATC. Similar competitions were run in the US, where the movie was the most popular animated film of all time, and noted as 'the most attractive advertisement for Australia tourism since *Crocodile Dundee*' (Bodey, 2003).

Finding Nemo was released in Japan after being screened at the 2003 Tokyo International Film Festival. Tie-ins between the ATC and regional tourism associations and the Film Festival included the development of special summer Sydney and coral reef tours related to *Nemo*, specifically for the Japanese market. *Finding Nemo*'s Swiss release included a private premiere screening of the movie for more than 400 travel agents, hosted by the ATC in conjunction with its partners, Disney, Qantas and Tourism Queensland (ATC, 2003a). In conjunction with the launch of *Finding Nemo*, the ATC and partners ran an online competition on australia.com to win a return trip to Tropical North Queensland, and free ATC/*Finding Nemo* postcards featuring information about the competition were also distributed to record shops throughout Switzerland (ATC, 2003a).

These cases are not exhaustive, and are presented as an indication of the type of tie-ins that the ATC has been working on in terms of a relatively 'new' form of film-induced tourism. At the time of writing, the success of such initiatives has not been ascertained; however, there are very strong positive indications of increased interest in visiting Australia from the regions noted above. A new movie, *Finding Dory*, was released in June 2016, and the lead actor, Ellen DeGeneres weighed into a current debate on Australia's Great Barrier Reef, seen by some as a publicity stunt, but also this reflects on the focus such films bring to major tourist destinations.

Japanese anime maps

In Chapter 2 I introduced the concept of contents tourism and the role of anime in this form of Japanese tourism. At the risk of repetition, I will make a few more comments here to bring this into the discussion on animation and tourism. For many with a more Western perspective, the place of animation is more of a fantasy than reality. However, many of the Japanese anime films and stories are based in real places that are carefully rendered in minute detail. Consequently, tourists go to visit these places, often imbuing them with a form of sacredness. The *Japan Anime Map* (subtitled, *Sacred Places Pilgrimage*) from the Japan National Tourism Organisation (JNTO), presents a range of powerful examples from this genre. For example, the classic movie from film maker Hayao Miyazaki, *Princess Mononoke* (1997), featured the Shirikami Mountains and Yakshima Island, which attract thousands of fans; while *Spirited Away* (2001) features many Onsen (Japanese hot springs), with the Dogo Hot Spring again becoming a place for anime fans, tourists and pilgrims (JNTO, 2015).

One anime website, *Anime Pilgrimage*, claims to have listed up to 348 titles and 10,125 locations of anime, manga, gaming and pilgrimage sites, both in English and Japanese, but with only a rudimentary coverage in English (Anime Pilgrimage, 2015).

Some Comments on Destination Marketing, Image and Film

This chapter has introduced the principal concepts of destination marketing, including some of the criticisms surrounding the simplification of a destination's complex culture through conscious imaging and branding exercises. This has been linked to film and its power to create (and change) images that may be out of the control of a DMO. The contribution of all types of films plays a significant role, yet we still do not fully understand all elements of this phenomenon, particularly in terms of how significant empathy towards a story line may be. Furthermore, there seems to have been limited research into the fact that many popular movies are based on popular novels, which in many ways gives them the longevity of a television series.

Product tie-ins between film and television and DMOs as well as individual businesses provide opportunities to increase exposure and broaden the market base, but it must be part of a coordinated marketing strategy. The Hawaii Tourist Board and the HVCB appear to have failed in this by changing their marketing strategies from being family-based to high-yield, with little consultation, resulting in the cancellation of a contract with Disney two years early, as well as distancing its film office from its tourism office. This is not sound business practice, and may impact on Hawaiian film-induced tourism.

However, we can see that film-related tourism can continue for many years, and even with my concerns regarding Hawaii's approach, the movie tours on the island of Kauai, where many movies and television series have been filmed, including *Blue Hawaii* (1961) and *Jurassic Park* (1993) as well as *Jurassic World* (2015), remain popular. The background of the MovieTours enterprise is discussed in Chapter 5.

Certainly, as Portegies (2010: 57) reminds us, there is a need for more attention to be paid to 'this complexity and hybridity of tourism experiences and how they are related – through potential visitors' attribution of meaning'.

The following chapters look at film tourism at various locations as well as off-location in film studios, being continually underpinned by notions of imaging and the various consequences of promotion.

4 Film and Place Promotion

In this chapter, we consider three main examples of film-induced destination marketing: a seaside village in Australia (Barwon Heads), an English village within a national park (Goathland), and the entire country of New Zealand, which is considered in terms of the *Lord of the Rings* movies. While I began studying these cases in the late 1990s, they remain relevant today, with all of them, to some extent or other, still influencing tourism and the image of their respective places. Nevertheless, I am including a new Australian case in the study, which is looking at community attitudes prior to the release of what looks to be a strong movie for tourism. My reason for this is to compare the ways in which communities now consider film-induced tourism with the attitudes they had when relating to *Sea Change* (1998–2000), and to further understand how this affects destination marketing, image and place promotion. I will introduce the movie *Oddball* (2015) in the appropriate section. Furthermore, New Zealand producer Peter Jackson has created and released a further Tolkien trilogy in the form of a prequel to *The Lord of the Rings* (2001, 2002, 2003): *The Hobbit* (2012, 2013, 2014). This has had a strong effect on many places and their promotion (particularly Matamata and Hobbiton), which is also noted where appropriate.

While Australia and New Zealand are geographic neighbours settled (from a colonial perspective) by the English, sharing a similar Western culture, there are differences between the countries, not least in their indigenous and environmental heritage. However, what is at issue most in these case studies is the approach taken (or not) by small villages, national parks and an entire nation. In other words, how can (and does) film-induced tourism work at a local, environmental and national level? The structure of destination marketing for each site is outlined where relevant, and is followed by an examination of how the elements of film-induced tourism have been applied. The cases then serve to inform the section on destination marketing recommendations for film-induced tourism, and this is followed by a brief discussion of copyright and confidentiality issues that can affect the type and level of film-induced promotion.

At the national level in Australia, the federally funded national tourism organisation, the Australian Tourist Commission (ATC; now renamed Tourism Australia), operates as the country's tourism destination marketing organisation (DMO), with other DMO activities undertaken by the federal immigration and business portfolios. However, at the state and regional levels, such differentiations blur, with tourism destination marketing being an integral part of (and often driving) the overall destination marketing process. The majority of tourism organisations at the local level operate under the auspices of their respective economic development units (EDUs), where the responsibility for attracting investment and migration also lies. Generally, most of the destination marketing is undertaken by the tourism organisations, whether in conjunction with the EDUs or separately.

This can create some problems, as promoting a destination by tourism agencies for purposes other than tourism is fraught with conflicting imagery and needs. Tourism marketing is subjective, and tourism promotion tends to present images of the past and reinforce the images that outsiders (the potential tourists) have of the area. Objective reality is not the aim in tourism destination marketing, but rather reinforcement of the potential visitor's subjective needs, where image is paramount. For example, much of Australia's tourism marketing by the ATC relates to the frontier, pioneering idyll of the outback and remote areas (such as nominating 2002 the 'Year of the Outback'), whereas Australia is one of the most highly urbanised societies in the world. While visitors may wish to see koalas and crocodiles, potential business investors and professional migrants may not. Even if they do, they are receiving an unrealistic perception of the major population and business centres, underlying the need for such destination marketing to be handled by other agencies. Unfortunately, when dealing at the local level, such differentiation is not always possible because of resource limitations. Consequently, small towns and regions wanting to simultaneously increase tourism, investment and industry face issues of representation and 'appropriate' imagery.

By looking at the television series *Sea Change* and the seaside village of Barwon Heads, where much of it was filmed, as the local destination marketing case, the main activities undertaken at each destination marketing level and the extent to which film is utilised can be illustrated. Table 4.1 combines the promotional techniques listed in the previous chapter (Table 3.1), identifying the appropriate DMO agency. For the purposes of analytical comparability in this chapter, we consider the tourism destination marketing organisations as the DMO, as they carry out all the activities identified by Perdue and Pitegoff (1994) previously in the chapter, and as already discussed, are most prevalent in the smaller regional areas and towns.

In order to illustrate the similarities and differences between various countries and types of film-induced tourism, the exercise is repeated for the UK series *Heartbeat* and the North Yorkshire Moors town of Goathland later in the chapter, and this is followed by an analysis of New Zealand and *The Lord of the Rings*.

The television series *Sea Change* provides a range of positive and ideal self-images, tangible and intangible, that may be captured and utilised by

Table 4.1 Destination place marketing in Australia

Level	Tourism destination marketing agency	Promotional activities
International	Tourism Australia (ex Australian Tourist Commission)	• Media advertising. • Familiarisation trips. • Sales blitz and trade mission. • Visiting journalists programme. • Aussie specialists programme. • Internet.
National	See Australia	• Media advertising. • Consumer shows. • Direct mail. • Travel and lifestyle programmes. • Internet.
State	Tourism Victoria	• Media advertising. • Consumer shows. • Direct mail. • Travel and lifestyle programmes. • Internet. • Signage. • Hospitality training.
Regional	Bays and Peninsulas	• Media advertising. • Direct mail. • Travel and lifestyle programmes. • Internet. • Brochure development.
Shire	City of Greater Geelong – Geelong Otway Tourism	• Media advertising. • Visitor Information Centres. • Direct mail. • Travel and lifestyle programmes. • Internet. • Signage. • Brochures, maps, posters, etc.
Local	Barwon Heads Traders and Tourism Association	• Signage. • Brochures, fliers.
Individual	Barwon Heads Tourism and Hospitality businesses	• Brochures, maps, posters, etc. • Internet. • Business signage. • Souvenirs and postcards. • Art and craft. • Hospitality.
	Independent	• Movie map.

Barwon Heads and the wider region. The tangible images include sites such as Laura's cottage, Diver Dan's shed and the views of the Barwon River, bridge and ocean. In a study conducted at Barwon Heads, 40% of those surveyed stated that the appeal of the series was its location and scenery, and this provides an excellent opportunity to promote these aspects of Barwon Heads. The logos and promotional material such as videos and CDs of the soundtrack are also tangible products from the series that can provide additional destination marketing material.

The more intangible aspects of *Sea Change* are those that come out of the storyline, such as the small-town ambience, the personalities and quirks of the characters, and even the nod to Shakespeare, with the use of lines from *The Tempest* (where the term 'sea change' originates), as 'something rich and strange' (*The Tempest*, Act 1, Scene 1), as the subtitle of the series. Such intangible, almost subliminal, aspects can be seen as powerful travel decision-making motivators as they are among the main appeal of the series and support a common ideal self-image. Once again, of those surveyed at Barwon Heads, 40% stated that the appeal of the series was its friendliness, quaintness and quirkiness.

Making a Sea Change for Barwon Heads?

Considering the potential that film has to attract visitors to a site (as discussed in Chapters 1 and 2), the interest in the series *Sea Change* and the overall beneficial imaging possibilities outlined above, it is apt to consider whether Barwon Heads and the surrounding region have capitalised on the popularity of *Sea Change* as a destination promotional tool.

Barwon Heads is on the Bellarine Peninsula, part of the Victorian State Government's Bays and Peninsula's tourism region. It is also part of the City of Greater Geelong, coordinated through the DMO, Geelong Otway Tourism, and is included as part of the Great Ocean Road tourism region. Table 4.2 lists a range of promotional collateral gathered from these groups as well as from businesses in the village itself. Sources that also contribute to the promotion of the destination are media articles and reports that focus on Barwon Heads as the site of *Sea Change*. These have been considered as being 'tourism and destination independent' in that they are not primarily concerned with the development or promotion of either. Media reports are also time-sensitive, tending to lose their impact and efficacy soon after publication or broadcasting. A content analysis of the material is included in order to assess the level of use of the imagery created by the *Sea Change* series.

According to Roger Grant, Executive Director of Geelong Otway Tourism, filming (including advertisements as well as television and movies) is an important aspect of their destination marketing in terms of positioning, branding and adding a new dimension to a destination. He also recognises the power of

Table 4.2 Level of destination marketing material relating to Sea Change and Barwon Heads

	Shire	Local (Barwon Heads)	Traders & Tourism	Individual	Media
	Geelong Otway Tourism/ Great Ocean Road	Township	Association	Barwon Heads Operators	Local, state, national
Articles & Reports	Geelong Advertiser	Bellarine Paper			The Age; The Herald Sun; Royal Auto; ABC Radio; ABC TV
Brochures & fliers	Double page on 'Sea Change now showing on the Peninsula'		Flier with list of traders with a note on Sea Change	Map of Sea Change sites; Campground brochures	
Internet		Barwon Heads site comments on Sea Change			ABC; Sea Change fan sites
Books/Miscellaneous					Melways Street Directory – Barwon Heads noted as the site of Sea Change
Posters	'Discover Sea Change at Barwon Heads'				
Souvenirs				Stickers; Mugs; Postcards	
Signage		Directional: to the Sea Change Cottages		Entry to campground (Home of Sea Change); This is a Sea Change shop (one shop only)	
Creative media (e.g. film)					Barwon Heads noted in Sea Change credits

film-induced tourism, commenting that wherever he travels in the world he is shown 'famous' film sites, yet sees it not as a primary tourism motivator, but rather as something that adds another layer (Grant, personal interview, 2001).

Site visits to Barwon Heads in 1999, at the height of *Sea Change's* popularity, indicated a limited use of the series as a promotional tool, either by local businesses or by the destination. The only business that had taken advantage of this was the take-away food shop at the beginning of the bridge, across from the main locational focus of the series. This establishment had taken a rather quaint stance, which also gained it much publicity from visiting journalists. Its activities included running a series of blackboards outside the shop with captions such as 'Have Coffee and Cake like Sigrid' and repackaging its range of lollies as 'Diver Dan Liquorice' and 'Bob Jelly Babies'. The owners took the friendly small-town appeal of the series and applied it to their business, creating the image for which visitors were searching. While some traders considered such simple promotion as rather 'twee', it created a sense of fun and simple excitement from the series, and provided the business and town with some valuable promotion (Figure 4.1).

By 2000, the camping ground had a sign welcoming people to 'Barwon Heads, the home of *Sea Change'*, which remains today, yet few other

Figure 4.1 What's in a name? In the small town of Barwon Heads, Nanette Cribbes utilises the fictional name, Pearl Bay, to sell her coffee and cake

businesses were taking direct advantage of the popularity of the series and its instantly recognisable title. The Barwon Heads Park had also developed a map and walking trail of *Sea Change* sites, which were all on public land managed by the Barwon Coast Committee of Management. This free, one-colour cheaply-produced map is an example of a movie map produced on an individual, local level and has met with some success even though its distribution was limited to the town itself and it is not used as a pre-trip tool in the decision-making process.

In 2000, ABC added information on the actual sites to its *Sea Change* webpage and also constructed a map of 'Pearl Bay', based heavily on the layout of Barwon Heads, even for the sites that were not filmed there. The basic geographic outline on this map is the same as the Barwon Heads/*Sea Change* walk map shown earlier. However, additional 'fictional' sites that were not filmed in Barwon Heads have been incorporated, such as the Tropical Star Hotel, Courthouse, Pearl Bay Coop, Police and Jelly House.

During a field trip to Barwon Heads in July 2001, I was particularly interested to note any additional destination marketing that used *Sea Change*. The first destination marketing tool I found was a poster on the wall of the cabin in which I was staying. Produced by Geelong Otway Tourism and entitled 'Discover *Sea Change*, Barwon Heads', this includes an inset photo of Diver Dan, complete with the little ferry the character used in the first series. While there are no other captions, the *Sea Change* references are certainly there – at an almost subliminal, subtle level. Geelong Otway Tourism continues to use *Sea Change* to promote Barwon Heads and the Bellarine Peninsula through the brochure mentioned in Table 4.2, and sees the *Sea Change* image as compatible with the positioning of the region, celebrating the coastal lifestyle (Grant, personal interview, 2001).

Other promotional materials from individual accommodation and restaurants make mention of *Sea Change*, but have not taken on the promotional tags or logos to any great extent. This could in part be due to licensing issues for commercial operations (Grant, personal interview, 2001). It is also interesting to note that in all tourist literature (including the service directory in my cabin), the *Sea Change* sites were not listed as tourist attractions. In one of the few examples of utilising *Sea Change*, Geelong Otway Tourism's destination brochure for the Great Ocean Road has a double page featuring the star of the series, Sigrid Thornton, promoting the Bellarine Peninsula (as noted previously). In another case of taking advantage of *Sea Change* without open acknowledgement, two local photographers produced a series of postcards focusing on Diver Dan's shed (past and present), without naming the actual site. The local bookshop had artistic models of 'Diver Dan's' for sale, and labelled them as such. The corner take-away food shop still has its signs in the window denoting it as a '*Sea Change* store', but the blackboards out front no longer invite people to 'have coffee and cake like Sigrid'.

When asked if *Sea Change* should be used more to promote Barwon Heads and the region, the key personnel interviewed gave a mixed response. Roger Grant (personal interview, 2001) from Geelong Otway Tourism believes that, as the *Sea Change* image is compatible with the positioning of the region, it should be taken advantage of. This is in direct contrast to the attitude of the residents, who do not recognise any similarities between Barwon Heads and Pearl Bay, and this may cause some community issues if the *Sea Change* image is taken on without due consultation/education. This comes back to the community planning process outlined in Chapter 7. Tim Caithness (personal interview, 2001), from the restaurant *At The Heads*, was surprised that more local people have not cashed in on the *Sea Change* phenomenon, especially as it has broadened the visitor base and given people a reason to visit at other times of the year. Bob Jordan (personal interview, 2001), manager of the Barwon Coast Management Committee, tended to agree that *Sea Change* should be used to promote the town more, but felt that it would not happen because of those residents who did not see the town as similar to the series, and this is also supported by the surveys. President of the Traders and Tourism Association, Bernard Napthene (personal interview, 2001), did not think that it should be used to promote the town because of the lack of tourism infrastructure that would be required to support the increased visitation, especially in relation to mid- to up-market accommodation. While Napthene was not aware of the problems Goathland has experienced in the UK, he expressed similar concerns.

If we accept that the *Sea Change* image is an appropriate destination marketing image for Barwon Heads, the question that needs to be addressed is, 'how long will the *Sea Change* image be relevant to visitors to Barwon Heads?' According to Uysal *et al.* (2000), there is a general belief that images and perceptions of a place do not change quickly (unless there is a natural or political disaster), which supports the use of the imagery for at least a few more years. If there are re-runs of the show or a further series is filmed (not entirely unlikely), the image will remain longer.

Subsequent visits to Barwon Heads, culminating while writing this in 2015 demonstrated that there is some *Sea Change* legacy evident in spite of not being re-screened and its limited international exposure due to the failure of the producers to secure the hoped-for distribution in the UK. This was no fault of theirs, but was due to changing local content laws in the UK, which also threatened the highly popular *Neighbours* (1985–) and *Home and Away* (1988–), both of which did continue, and remain popular in the UK today.

As mentioned at the beginning of this chapter, however, there is a forthcoming movie that can demonstrate to us how communities now envisage the potential of such tourism. The movie *Oddball* (2015) was inspired by a true story, but also has significant fictional elements included in the final telling, including a rapacious developer. It is a family oriented movie starring Shane Jacobson, who came to fame in *Kenny* (2006), and other well-known

Australian actors including Deborah Mailman. The synopsis on Jacobson's website states, '[t]o save his daughter's job and keep her from moving away, an eccentric chicken farmer teams with his granddaughter to implement his controversial idea – to protect an endangered penguin colony using a troublemaking dog' (www.shanejacobson.com.au/oddball/). At the time of writing, the movie is about to premiere, which is discussed later in this publication. In a most interesting co-promotion, and further blurring the lines between fact and fiction, *National Geographic* has also taken to this story and the movie, producing a five-part documentary, *Oddball: The Nature of a Movie*, based around issues raised in the film, which went to air in the week prior to the movie's premiere. The topics covered in the series are, *Real Oddball, Little Penguins, The Maremma, Predators* and finally *Warrnambool*, which looks at the touristic elements of the film, interviewing myself as well as locals. They also ran a competition to win tickets to see the movie.

Overall, community support for the movie and the tourism potential has been strong, and I look in more detail at the attitudes of this community in comparison with the Barwon Heads community in the following chapter.

Goathland, a Village in a National Park

National parks were not established in England until halfway through the 20th century. However, the driving philosophy was similar to that of the US, New Zealand and Australia, namely to provide a recreation resource (Beeton, 1998b). The preservation of nature for its own sake did not become a driving force until later in the 20th century. In 1931, the Addison Committee expressed a vision of national parks in England as being '…a resource and a refuge for those whose lives were timed by factory sirens six days a week' (Breakell, 2002). National parks would provide for the health of the soul as well as the body, and were to be available for all.

National parks in the UK consist of public land, private land (farmland) and even villages, which creates a different (and more complex) management environment than in countries such as Australia, New Zealand, the US and Canada, where national parks have been established in primarily natural environments. Some may contain evidence of past human occupation, but current occupation is rare.

The North York Moors National Park was the sixth national park to be established in the UK. However, this was not until 1952, and the first park (Peak District) had been designated only a year earlier. Such recent national park designation has led to a very different structure and management regime from that in North America, New Zealand and Australia, where the parks exist on public-owned land. As a consequence of thousands of years of settlement, a significant proportion of private land falls into national parks in the UK. Close to 250,000 people live in the national parks of England and

Wales, and the North York Moors National Park has a resident population of 25,406 (ANPA, 2003). The term 'national park' does not in this case signify national ownership, and private owners such as farmers hold much of the land. Development is permitted in national parks; however it must be demonstrated to 'be in the public interest' (DEFRA, 2003).

According the Association of National Park Authorities (ANPA, 2003), '[t]he Parks are made up of countryside which has been shaped over 5000 years by people at work'. The UK notion of 'freedom to roam' across rural landscapes was a major factor in the development/creation of the UK national park system, with the North York Moors having some 2200 kilometres of public rights of way (NYMNPA, 2003).

Public bodies such as the National Park Authorities manage the national parks under the auspices of the Department of Environment, Food and Rural Affairs (DEFRA) according to the National Parks and Access to the Countryside Act of 1949. The National Park Authorities are free-standing (with separate funding from central government) within the local government framework and are the sole planning authorities for their areas. The North York Moors National Park Authority (NYMNPA) is the planning authority that oversees Goathland, and plays a major role in local recreation management. It appointed a Tourism Officer in 1990 (the first such post in any UK national park), which was extended to Tourism and Transport Officer in 1994 to recognise the critical relationship between the two (Breakell, personal interview, 2003).

The park's guiding principles are set out in the Environment Act 1995, Section 61 (1) as:

(1) conserving and enhancing the natural beauty, wildlife and cultural heritage;
(2) promoting opportunities for the understanding and enjoyment of the special qualities of those areas by the public (DEFRA, 2002).

The second of these principles confers an obligation on the park to encourage a wide range of visitors, reflecting the founding principles that national parks are for all, not merely for a wealthy or educated elite. This is important when looking at those attracted to Goathland by *Heartbeat* and the community's responses described in Chapter 5. Under Section 65 of the Act, the National Park Authorities have the power to do anything that they believe will help to accomplish those purposes.

North Yorkshire, Goathland and Film-Induced Tourism

The Yorkshire Moors have featured in numerous media of the day, including the poetry of Wordsworth, books by James Herriot, television series such as *Heartbeat* and movies like *Calendar Girls* (2003). The television series *Heartbeat* embodies all that is good and bad about film-induced tourism, and is studied over the next three chapters. Based on the 'Constable' books by Yorkshire resident Nicholas Rhea, *Heartbeat* follows the fortunes of a small community in the 1960s, and revolves around the local police force. Filming of the series began in the North Yorkshire region in 1991, with the first episodes being aired in 1992. The series is still being shown on television stations around the world, and much of it was still filmed on-site some 12 years later. The small village of Goathland in the North Yorkshire Moors National Park was chosen as the site for Aidensfield, the main town in *Heartbeat*.

Tourist visitation to the village of 450 residents has soared from a steady 200,000 before 1991 to more than 1.2 million (Mordue, 2001). *Heartbeat* is considered to be the primary reason for such a dramatic increase. Issues relating to this and the local community are discussed in Chapter 6.

Unlike most villages in the region, which are nestled into small dales, Goathland is spread out, sitting on a broad spur of the moors. The village centre consists of a post office, gift shop, tearooms, and a general store combined with an outdoor pursuits shop and a World War II memorial. A hall and service station are also nearby. The church is on the way out of the village towards Pickering, with a pub, guesthouse and popular walking track opposite, as well as significant common land, creating another town 'centre'. At the other end of the town (going towards Whitby) is the historic railway station, used not only in *Heartbeat* but also in the *Harry Potter* movies as well as in *Carrington*, a film set in World War I (Idle, 2003). The pub, the Aidensfield Arms from *Heartbeat*, is located between the railway station and the shops in the village's centre.

While Goathland is in the North York Moors National Park, as explained above, there are still private landowners, such as farmers and homeowners, in the village. The Duchy of Lancaster (that is, the Queen) is the main single landowner in the area, and has ownership over all common land in Goathland. Residents pay a fee to the Duchy for access to their properties over the commons and to graze stock on the commons. While the NYMNPA is responsible for all planning issues, planning permission is not necessary for events/activities of less than 28 days per year, which can include filming in the park.

Table 4.3 outlines the main tourism promotional activities undertaken by the various agencies as well as by the businesses involved in marketing North Yorkshire, with a focus on filming as well as general tourism promotion. As with Table 4.1, the list moves from international down to individual businesses, in this case in Goathland. However, unlike Australia, there are no state bodies in England, as there are no states as such, and the 'regional' section incorporates the various counties as it is the regions that are most involved in tourism destination marketing at that level.

Information about the moors in general is plentiful, with Goathland being mentioned in the promotional literature as one of the villages in the

Table 4.3 Destination/place marketing in North Yorkshire

Level	Tourism destination marketing agency	Promotional activities
International and national	VisitBritain (ex British Tourist Authority – BTA)	• Media advertising. • Visitor information network. • BTA *Movie Map* brochures. • Internet – *Movie Map* website.
Regional	Yorkshire Tourism Board	• Visitor information network. • Internet. • *On-Screen Guide to Yorkshire* (brochure). • Media releases (e.g. *Calendar Girls*).
Local	North York Moors National Park Authority (NYMNPA)	• Visitor information network. • Internet.
Individual	Goathland businesses	• Brochures. • Internet sites, esp. booking services.
	Independent	• Guidebooks, esp. film-related: *TV Country Favourites, TV & Film Locations*.

moors, particularly in terms of accommodation. However, its profile in the general destination marketing literature is quite small, which is not surprising for a village of 450 residents, though its high level of visitation and its high profile as the township of Aidensfield belies this. The film-related guidebooks focus much more on Goathland, due in no small measure to the willingness of Yorkshire TV, the producers, to allow use of images and photos of the actors.

Table 4.4 lists the range of promotional activities in the form of destination marketing material that come directly from the *Heartbeat* series. While such material is being used to promote Goathland and provoke a nostalgic image of the village, the majority is only available in the township itself. Nevertheless, taking gifts and souvenirs back to friends and relatives moves such material outside of the destination.

The list of newspapers that have featured articles on Goathland and *Heartbeat* is not limited to those listed in Table 4.4 (which were the ones that I noted personally), and also fairly regularly ran such stories. Since *Heartbeat*'s first screening in 1992, many papers around the world have covered the series and the village.

Of particular interest, however, is the phenomenon of various commercial premises retaining at least part of their *Heartbeat* signage. They do not refer to being 'the home of *Heartbeat*' as the caravan park at Barwon Heads has done with *Sea Change*, nor do they refer to themselves as '*Heartbeat* Stores', but even the shops that have not kept any television series signage prominently display *Heartbeat* souvenirs. This is a little more subtle, but an

Film and Place Promotion   95

Table 4.4 Level of destination marketing material relating to Heartbeat and Goathland

	National	Regional	Local (Goathland) NYMNPA	Local (Goathland) Township	Individual Tourism operators	Media
Articles & reports	VisitBritain (ex BTA)	YTB; Numerous press releases on leveraging the tourism potential of filming (e.g. Calendar Girls)				Local, state, national; Yorkshire Post; Yorkshire Evening Press; Scarborough Evening News; Evening Press; The Gazette; The Herald; The Times
Brochures & maps	BTA Movie Map	On-Screen Guide:- Yorkshire				
Internet	Interactive Movie Map					Yorkshire TV; Heartbeat fan sites
Books					Guidebooks produced by private authors: Greengrass's Guide to Goathland; Filming on the North Yorkshire Moors Railway; Classic Heartbeat Country	
Souvenirs					Stickers; Mugs; Sweets; Handcuffs; Small items (erasers, etc.); Postcards	
Themed attractions					The Heartbeat Experience in Whitby	
Naming		'Heartbeat Country'				
Signage					Goathland Hotel retains one Aidensfield Arms; One shop retains the Aidensfield Stores sign; Garage retains name change (Mostyn's Garage)	

extremely effective destination marketing exercise on that individual level – a passing visitor not aware that the television series was filmed in Goathland would soon become aware of the fact if they watched the series themselves. In this way the commercial operators are 'enhancing' the destination purely for *Heartbeat* fans rather than for those who may be attracted through some form of celebrity worship or desire to connect with 'fame' (see Chapter 2 for a brief discussion on the cult of celebrity).

The range of souvenirs available is extensive, with plenty of police-related items, such as plastic handcuffs and bobby's hats. Virtually anything that could have the words '*Heartbeat*' or 'Aidensfield' fitted on it was a likely target, including fudge, chocolates, tea towels, jigsaws, magnets, pencils and erasers, miniature police, and even a walking stick badge. Some indicated their relationship to Goathland with some sort of acknowledgement, while others, such as a fridge magnet with a map of Aidensfield noted that it was in the North Yorkshire Moors. I wonder how many have tried to locate the fictitious Aidensfield in the real North Yorkshire Moors.

Much of the *Heartbeat* information, such as the guidebooks, was prominently displayed in Goathland, but was not evident at the Yorkshire Tourist Board information centres in the entry towns such as Whitby, which tends to go against their statements in the next section regarding *Calendar Girls* and tourism. However, Whitby is now home to *The Heartbeat Experience*, a themed attraction focusing very much on the series and the era it is set in. Established in Goathland in 1995 by a local landowner as a general heritage attraction, the *Goathland Exhibition Centre* had limited success owing to its location, which was not on the route of the *Heartbeat* tourists. Consequently, the proprietor relocated the centre to the seaside town of Whitby where it became more focused on the television series itself. While it has a strong *Heartbeat* theme, the attraction includes non-specific material, playing on the 1960s nostalgia theme of the series, with memorabilia and recreations of 'typical houses' of the time. One of its displays relates to Goathland, and there is a section presented by the NYMNPA on experiencing and enjoying the moors. This indicates some interest from the National Park Authority in capitalising on the visitors being attracted to the region by providing some environmental education.

The North York Moors National Park website does not have any comments regarding *Heartbeat* per se, but it does provide information (including accommodation) on Goathland. Both of these situations could reflect some subconscious de-marketing efforts as discussed in Chapter 7.

As with many other countries, tourist promotion in England falls under the remit of the DMOs, in particular the tourism organisations, with little, if any, formal recognition or official link with those who have to manage the tourists once they arrive – the actual land management agencies. According to the Yorkshire Tourist Board (YTB, 2001), tourist promotion in England is organised outside the National Parks Authority as illustrated in

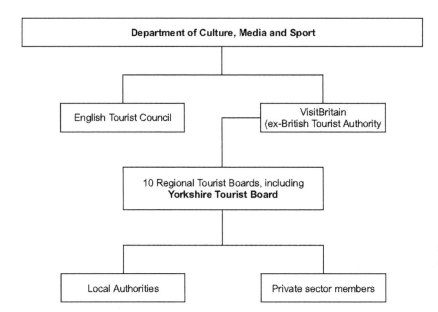

Figure 4.2 Tourist promotion in England
Source: YTB (2001).

Figure 4.2, even though much of Yorkshire falls under national park management. The 'local authorities' shown here do not officially incorporate the NYMNPA in this model, as it refers to those that are under the remit of the Yorkshire Tourism Board (YTB). See Beeton (2003) for a discussion on the consequences of excluding the land management agencies such as the NYMNPA.

The NYMNPA recognises that film is a strong image-maker and welcomes the broadening of its visitor base to include more working-class visitors (see the next chapter for more detail on the implications of this); however, as the primary management agency it has had to deal with many issues, social and environmental (outlined in the following chapters). Consequently, the authority has tended to refrain from extensive destination imaging via *Heartbeat*.

In direct contrast, the YTB focuses on the benefits of film-induced tourism and is committed to maximising them. In a media release marking the world premiere of the movie *Calendar Girls* (filmed in Yorkshire), the chief executive of the YTB stated that:

> Posters and adverts for the film carry Yorkshire branding and details for more information to encourage potential visitors to come and try Yorkshire for themselves. Already, we are receiving request from the public for details of 'Calendar Girls' Yorkshire. (YTB, 2003)

The YTB also planned to leverage film-induced tourism effects of the movie internationally, stating that:

> …the impact the film will have in the international market is considerable and already YTB is working closely with VisitBritain to ensure maximum exploitation of coverage abroad over the coming months as *Calendar Girls* releases in the rest of Europe, USA, Australia and Asia. (YTB, 2003)

In 2010 the *Heartbeat* DVDs were at last released in the UK, while Australia still had to wait until 2012 – as I discuss elsewhere, there were many issues with getting copyright permission for all of the music that is so central to the series. Ultimately, some of the music had to be partly changed, but, after waiting some 20 years for them, this has not detracted from the ultimate re-viewing of the series.

The Lord of the Rings and New Zealand

In what may be considered an action of great foresight, when the filming in New Zealand of *The Lord of the Rings* trilogy was announced, the New Zealand government appointed a 'Minister of the Rings' (*New Zealand Herald*, 2001b). The Minister's remit was to maximise the benefits from the trilogy for the entire country, both in terms of filming employment and film-induced tourism. For a country the size of New Zealand (population 4.6 million), the resources committed to leveraging the effect of *The Lord of the Rings* is unprecedented.

Interestingly, this is not the first time that New Zealand can claim fore-sight in terms of developing and promoting tourism. As far back as 1901, a government tourism department, Department of Tourist and Health Resorts, was established – arguably the first in the world (Tourism New Zealand, 2003a). However, the country did not have a global brand marketing campaign until the launch of the *100% Pure New Zealand* campaign in 1999. Tourism New Zealand currently promotes the country overseas, much in the same manner as the ATC does for Australia, but with a lower level of funding. Annual funding for 2003 for the ATC was A$90 million (with an additional $100 million over four years committed from 2004), while for Tourism New Zealand it was NZ$55 million.

Being a relatively small country, particularly in terms of population and economy, New Zealand has generally taken a whole-of-country approach to promoting inbound tourism. While there are distinct differences between the North and South Islands, with the North having thermal activities such as pools and geysers and the South with glacial formations and an Antarctic climate, tourism promotion has primarily been handled nationally. New Zealand does not have the equivalent of the Australian states and territories as an additional level of government with their own funds for destination marketing and tourism promotion. At a more local level, various regions market their differences, and city and district councils have a more local remit in terms of destination marketing. Many such city councils have to deal with their surrounding rural areas owing to some unusual zoning, with the southern university town of Dunedin incorporating 3350 square kilometres within its city boundaries. Table 4.5 lists the various regional councils and tourism organisations.

In addition, some 30% of New Zealand is protected in parks and reserves, with significant use of its hiking trails, which has contributed to the outdoors adventure image of the country. While the Department of Conservation (DOC) conducts some visitor promotion of its parks (mainly through websites), its remit is primarily conservation, leaving much of its promotion to the primary destination marketing groups. DOC's mission is 'to conserve New Zealand's natural and historic heritage for all to enjoy now and in the future' (DOC, 2003).

The only references to visitor use of the parks is in terms of basic activities such as walking, and there is no *Lord of the Rings* information on its website, which indicates a conscious decision not to promote tourism per se. Where DOC previously had its own separate visitor information areas in its offices, most of their promotional material, such as maps and camping guides, is now distributed via the tourist Visitor Information Network.

Table 4.6 outlines the basic destination marketing responsibilities and activities undertaken at various levels, as introduced above.

The national air carriers of many countries are their country's primary international DMOs because of the clear economic benefit they receive from encouraging people to travel to that country. New Zealand's carrier, Air New Zealand, promotes New Zealand both domestically and internationally. The methods undertaken by Air New Zealand are outlined later in this section.

Table 4.5 New Zealand regional councils and tourism organisations

	Regional councils	Regional tourism organisations
North Island	Northland, Auckland, Waikato, Bay of Plenty, Gisborne, Hawkes Bay, Taranaki, Manawatu/ Wanganui, Wellington	Northland, Auckland, Waikato, Coromandel, Lake Taupo, Bay of Plenty, Eastland, Taranaki, Ruapehu, River Region, Hawkes Bay, Wellington, Wairarapa
South Island	Marlborough, Nelson/ Tasman, West Coast, Canterbury, Otago, Southland	Marlborough, Nelson/Tasman, West Coast, Canterbury, Mackenzie, Central South Island, Hurunui, Central Otago, Dunedin, Lake Wanaka, Queenstown, Southland

Table 4.6 Destination/place marketing in New Zealand

Level	Tourism destination marketing agency	Promotional activities
International and National	Tourism New Zealand	• Media advertising. • International media programme. • Media releases. • Travel trade training (offshore). • Internet.
International, national, regional and local	Department of Conservation (through the visitor information network)	• Internet. • Maps. • Guides.
Regional	Regions such as Northland, Marlborough	• Visitor information network. • Internet. • Media releases.
Local	City/District Councils such as Wellington, Dunedin	• Visitor information network. • Internet. • Media releases.
Individual	New Zealand tour businesses	• Brochures. • Internet sites, esp. booking services. • Air New Zealand.
	Independent	• Guidebooks. • Posters. • Brochures. • Internet. • Business signage. • Souvenirs and postcards. • Art and craft. • Hospitality.

As noted earlier, the New Zealand government has committed significant funds to leveraging the effects of film on tourism. While it is difficult to accurately extract the funding related specifically to film-induced tourism, Table 4.7 outlines the funds committed as stated in government reports and media releases.

There are varying reports on the use of these funds in the period from 2001 to 2003, as the government linked the promotional campaigns for the film with that for the 2003 defence of the America's Cup in Auckland. However, the government has itemised the NZ$4 million that it has committed to *The Lord of the Rings* world premiere over 2003 and 2004 as shown in Table 4.7. Nevertheless, it is still difficult to isolate all tourism-related expenditure as any imaging process will effect tourism, as discussed in the introduction to destination marketing in Chapter 3.

Table 4.7 National government money spent on *The Lord of the Rings*

Date	Purpose	Tourism related	Actual
2001/2	Promotional campaign for America's Cup 2003 & LOTR*	✓✓	6,000,000
2002/3	Various initiatives around America's Cup 2003 & LOTR**	✓✓	10,395,000
2003/4	Various initiatives around LOTR World Premiere:#		Total: 4,000,000
	World Premiere event support & visiting media	✓	2,000,000
	Offshore premieres/openings	✓	240,000
	Promotional goods	✓✓	80,000
	Pre-Oscar Events	✓	150,000
	Promotional Video/DVD	✓	60,000
	Film NZ Internet Portal LOTR Refresh	✓	30,000
	Film Trade Magazine Advertising	✓	180,000
	Film Trade Markets		250,000
	Inward Mission from the US & Canada	✓	160,000
	Australia Inward Film Mission		50,000
	LOTR Marketing & Production Guides		100,000
	LOTR Te Papa Touring Exhibition	✓✓	100,000
	Research on LOTR effect on tourism in key markets	✓✓✓	20,000
	Tourism NZ video: NZ & *The Return of the King*	✓✓✓	30,000
	Post 2004 Oscars advertising for *The Return of the King*	✓✓	350,000
	Film and Music Initiative		120,000
	Postproduction Group Initiative		160,000

Notes: *Ministry of Economic Development (2004a); **Ministry of Economic Development (2004b); # Hodgson (2003).

In Chapter 8, some questions are raised as to the justification for the expenditure on the world premiere. It is not easy to quantify the returns on film and film-induced tourism owing to the long-term effect that imaging may have, and the power (positive and negative) that inadvertent media may also play. Trying to ascertain the economic benefits of film-induced tourism such as *The Lord of the Rings* on a national level is fraught with complexities. Not the least of these is ascertaining whether the money that international tourists bring in to the country is 'new' money, or merely money that they would have brought in anyway. The issue here is that, if visitors were coming anyway, but merely changed the time when they were visiting and where they were going, the overall national benefit is unchanged. However, visitors may extend their stay in order to undertake additional activities, and this is a direct benefit. If there is a significant shift in visitation to a film site from another site, then there can be significant local effects, including the failure of some businesses at the expense of others. The individual economic contribution of these businesses can also differ, particularly in terms of induced expenditure and leakages.

From a domestic point of view, shifts from one local destination to another are common; however, there may be those who choose to holiday in New Zealand instead of overseas, retaining money that would have been lost. This is rarely considered in economic analyses, yet in some cases there is sufficient anecdotal evidence to suggest that we need to include this element in our economic studies.

Concern has also been voiced over the tax breaks that the New Zealand government (as in other countries) has given film makers in order to lure them to the country. Such revenue losses need to be balanced against all of the economic benefits of filming, including tourism-related benefits. They also need to be considered in terms of opportunity costs – the money that the government spends on supporting filming (or the taxes it foregoes) cannot be spent in other areas, raising issues of public good. Once again, these analyses are complex exercises, and no such comprehensive and transparent reports are available publicly, in any country.

Finally, measuring the non-economic benefits of all tourism, not just film-induced tourism, is extremely difficult – what value do we give to increased pride and the associated flow-on effects? Visitors to cities, towns, regions or sites where the residents are proud of what they have report far higher levels of satisfaction with their experience, which in turn increases the community's pride. All these issues raise questions as to who should be promoting tourism and to what extent. The methods used to promote/image New Zealand through *The Lord of the Rings* movies are outlined in Table 4.8.

Interestingly, all of the film sites apart from Hobbiton, which is on private land, have been returned to their original state, primarily because this was a requirement of filming in national parks and reserves as well as a commercial decision by the film company, New Line Cinema. In order to provide a more tangible access to *The Lord of the Rings*, some of the costumes and sets from the earlier movies were on display at Wellington airport during the world premiere in 2003, and a series of postage stamps was released. In addition to the stamps, 40 large street banners were made using the artwork, which decorated the main streets of towns throughout New Zealand from a month prior to the world premiere and for three months afterwards.

Air New Zealand promoted the country through the movie not only by utilising the traditional form of media advertisements including a clever poster series with captions such as 'The movie is fictional. The location isn't. Middle Earth is New Zealand' (Air New Zealand, 2003a: 87), but also through their travel centres, in-flight media, their internet site (www. airnewzealand.co.nz) and also to the general media through media kits, press

Table 4.8 Level of destination marketing material relating to *The Lord of the Rings* (LOTR) and New Zealand

	National		Local	Individual	Media
	Tourism New Zealand	*Air New Zealand*	*City/district councils*	*Tourism operators & commercial businesses*	*Local, state, national*
Articles & reports	Numerous press releases on leveraging the tourism potential of filming.	Press releases & media kits.			Reports on events (e.g. World Premiere). Articles on tour sites, etc.
Brochures & posters		*LOTR* poster series 'The film is fictional, the location isn't'.		Specialised tour brochures. Air New Zealand poster series in all travel agents.	
Internet	Special *LOTR* tourism site. Link to the movie site. Link to *LOTR* tour operators.	*LOTR* material and links on the company's website.		Air New Zealand. *Lord of the Rings* official movie site. Fan sites.	
Books & magazines		In-flight magazine for Dec features *LOTR* stories.		Guidebooks produced by private authors: *LOTR Location guide. Rough Guide to LOTR.*	Stories on locations in various magazines.
Souvenirs	NZ stamp series.			Film-related (but not locational).	

(*Continued*)

Table 4.8 (*Continued*)

	National	Local	Individual	Media
Film sets & costumes		LOTR costumes & sets at Wellington airport. Enormous Gollum over the Wellington airport terminal. Dragons and black riders on buildings in Wellington.	Hobbiton near Matamata.	
Shop displays	Window displays at Air New Zealand offices around the country & internationally. Air New Zealand posters & related images at travel agents.	Competition in Wellington for the 'best shop window display'.	Window paintings in Matamata shops.	
Naming	The Real Middle Earth.	'Airline to Middle Earth.'		
Signage banners & billboards	Four Air New Zealand jets painted with LOTR scenes 'Flying billboards'.	'Welcome to Middle Earth' signs at Wellington airport.	Hobbiton sign at Matamata. Banners produced by NZ Post.	

releases and the like. More specifically, for the duration of the premiere celebrations, the airline took on the sobriquet, 'Airline to Middle-Earth', with the pilots welcoming passengers to Middle Earth when they land in Wellington. In addition, the company has taken to using its aircraft as promotional vehicles by decorating them not just with national emblems, but also in this instance with *Lord of the Rings* characters and scenes. Touted as 'the world's largest collection of flying billboards' (Air New Zealand, 2003c), the two Boeing 747-400s and two Airbuses were part of a four-month promotion linked to the screening of the final episode, and flew to some 22 international gateways (Air New Zealand, 2003d). In addition, the artwork was replicated on the Air New Zealand letterhead and other material.

The sole remaining 'authentic' *Lord of the Rings* site (Hobbiton) is in private hands; however, there has been a positive flow-on to the community of the nearby town of Matamata (population 6000). The Matamata public relations and business association has subsidised the costs of painting the shop windows in the town with Hobbit themes, particularly 'Hobbit holes' through which the shop's traditional merchandise is displayed. The window displays have differentiated the town from its neighbours in this primarily agricultural region. On my visit to the town in 2003, not only were more than 60 of the shop windows painted, but there was also a sign as one enters the central shopping area saying, 'Welcome to Hobbiton, Matamata'. The small visitor information centre has one of its two counters dedicated solely to booking tours of Hobbiton and selling related merchandise. Since then, the Information Centre has been re-developed with a strong Hobbit theme and doubled in size (Figure 4.3).

With the release of *The Hobbit* (2012, 2013, 2014), Matamata retained its place as a stop-over for those travelling to Rotorua from Auckland (and vice versa) along with having the added attraction of a fully redeveloped Hobbiton village set. While the window displays are not prominent any longer, even though I visited during the release of the final instalment *The Hobbit: The Battle of the Five Armies* (2014), the town clearly leverages its connection. The

Figure 4.3 Matamata Information Centre

'Welcome to Hobbiton' sign remains and is a site for many photos, along with statues and other related items that see people using them as their own personal markers, most likely posting their evidence of 'being there' on Facebook and other social media sites. The business aspects of the Hobbiton village site are discussed in the next chapter.

There was a palpable sense of pride in the town, with many shopkeepers offering to assist in taking photos of the windows and very happy to talk about what the movie has done for them, particularly since the Hobbiton tours began in December 2002. During my most recent visit in late 2014, many remain positive, stating that they could not exist without the additional visitors to the region, particularly the newer cafes and bars. The tour and some of the issues the operators have had to deal with prior to the re-construction of the site for filming *The Hobbit* is discussed later in the chapter in the section on 'Film Promotional Images and Copyright'. The story continues in the next chapter.

The limited remaining tangible evidence of filming is a challenge to destination marketers, and is a common element of film-induced tourism, especially with movies. This has had to be addressed in the two relevant guidebooks, *The Lord of the Rings Location Guidebook* by Brodie (2002) and *The Rough Guide to The Lord of the Rings* by Errigo (2003). The first edition of Brodie's publication sold more than 70,000 copies (Tourism New Zealand, 2003b), while the second edition, which includes sites from the final movie, *The Return of the King*, was heavily promoted in bookstores and as prizes associated with the movie's world premiere in Wellington in December 2003.

The *Lord of the Rings Locations Guidebook* is not like the television film site publications in the UK, which allow specific built sites to be located, as it has had to deal with the fact that most of the sites have been returned to their natural state, and/or were enhanced through computer imaging. Consequently, most of the information is about travelling in and around the sites featured, with information on other activities and sites of interest to tourists. Many of the locations are so similar to the surrounding countryside that Brodie has provided global positioning system coordinates to enable fans to find the exact sites. The challenge to describe sites that either could not be seen or no longer exist has been met in the book by providing many stills from the movies, and much additional, non-film-related touring information about each region. Brodie refers to the surrounding area as 'looking like' where certain activities could have taken place.

It is primarily because many of the sites are unrecognisable to the casual visitor that such a guidebook has been so popular (Brodie, 2002). Without it, the fans will not know whether or not they are in the right spot. The book is heavily illustrated with scenes from the movies, which for many will be the closest they get to any sense of 'reality' (in terms of the movies) with the sites themselves.

With a 126-page 'Extended Edition' published in 2011, and a separate 176-page book for the destinations featured in *The Hobbit* movies, this is a great publishing success story (Brodie, 2011, 2014). Where many of these guides become merely quaint souvenirs for fans, these books have become major publications, produced as high-quality coffee-table books with many stills from the movies as well as quotes from the director, actors, production staff and so on, but still providing the location detail required by fans.

While using many of the shots from the movies to augment its information, the Rough Guide publication is more rounded in terms of *The Lord of the Rings* information. A brief look at the table of contents illustrates this, with chapters on The Origins, The Books, The Motion Picture Trilogy, The Characters, Middle-Earth, The Locations, Ephemera, and The Context. With only 32 pages out of a total of 304 actually dedicated to various Tolkien locations, including his birthplace in South Africa and the place in England where he grew up, not just the sites used in the movie trilogy (which takes up fewer than 15 pages), the book is far more than a location guide.

Rough Guides are extremely popular around the world, and in many ways their publication will appeal to a different audience than Brodie's publication, which is primarily a New Zealand guidebook. They may not encourage direct visitation to the same extent as Brodie's publication does, but they may encourage the more literary-based enthusiast to visit New Zealand, which in effect may be an entirely new market.

Destination Marketing Recommendations

The preceding cases illustrate some of the differences in the approaches taken, depending very much on the marketing responsibilities and imperatives at each destination. A further difference is the actual structure of the film sites in terms of being in a national park or on other types of public land compared with private land. We can, however, develop some generic and specialised destination marketing strategies for film-induced tourism. The following recommendations are not exhaustive, neither should each film site take them all on.

Film-induced tourism can be used to support (or even develop) the community's vision for the region, to broaden the visitor base and to even out seasonal peaks and troughs. Destination marketing strategies that film-induced tourism could contribute to include areas such as community visioning, festivals and tangible representations of the film.

For example, research at Barwon Heads found that the most commonly held community vision for Barwon Heads was that of retaining its village atmosphere and managing development. As the *Sea Change* image is one of a small community (or village), with storylines often opposing unplanned development, as well as having high levels of self-congruity with visitors and the majority of residents, this image can be used as a visioning image for the town.

Themed festivals

In this era of festivals, one based on the television series or movie/s in the region could reaffirm the community's vision as well as bring visitors in off-peak times. However, when Croy and Walker (2001) surveyed local government and film offices in New Zealand they found that some 71% of respondents did not consider festivals and facilities to celebrate films to be of great importance. One of the benefits of running a festival that would have a community base through its film-induced tourism is that it provides the opportunity to bring people together under a common theme/banner/image and to improve the negative community attitudes towards filming. Wellington, New Zealand, conducted a successful, and in many ways unusual, movie premiere event, which is discussed in more detail in Chapter 8, along with the concept of film festivals per se.

An outstanding example of the success of a television-series-themed festival can be found at Mount Airy, which has been happy to present itself as a fantasy town from a time that never existed. What is so interesting about the example of *The Andy Griffith Show* is that the town of Mount Airy has not had to change dramatically, as visitors tend to focus on the main street, and the festival runs for only two days of the year – in the (even) slower tourist month of September.

Social media representations

With the increase in the use of social media and individual filming technology, fans themselves are now creating 'content' which destinations can themselves also access and use, as well as developing their own on these platforms. This can include re-enactments on-location as well as parodies such as *AVATAR II: My Big Fat Pandora Vs The Deathly Hallows Striking Back At Muriel's Lethal Weapon: Reloaded*, available via YouTube: www.youtube.com/watch?v=MjFknbCqXio. As we note in Beeton *et al.* (2013), fans are not only uploading their home-made videos to YouTube, but also producing online guidebooks and blogs about the locations of film sites; there are those who also establish events where they gather together in character (cosplay) and even develop their own fanzines. In this sense they are both the producer and consumer, becoming 'prosumers' as described by Yamamura (2011) in relation to Japanese anime tourism. This relationship completes its cycle when the fans' work becomes part of the tourist attraction alongside the formal movie or series.

Tangible representations

Another possibility is to encourage visitation by providing a tangible representation of the series, such as the *Braveheart* statue in Stirling. While this may sound far-fetched, such a representation provides a focal point for visitors and can move them to (and keep them in) a specific area. In Wellington, New Zealand, not only were some sets and costumes displayed at the airport, but also many giant-sized characters adorned the buildings around the town, from the character, Gollum with the Ring at the airport terminal to dragons, orcs and arrows on the roofs and walls of city buildings. These were to be temporary installations, but they provided outstanding opportunities for the images themselves to be used in the future. Yet a return visit in late 2014 saw that Gollum is still at the airport terminal and continues to create interest.

Film memorabilia such as used in the 'Heartbeat Experience' may be a little less dramatic than a statue, but could well produce the desired effect and fit better with the community's cultural sensibilities – just because something is tourism related, it does not have to be 'tacky'. Statues, signage, museums, interpretation centres and even individual collections could all be utilised.

A less intrusive form of tangible representations, and one that appears to be extremely successful, is the publication of guidebooks. Independent travellers use guidebooks extensively and, as many film tourism sites are not on any current tourist trails, it is often the independent traveller who seeks them out. The style of book can vary, and some focus primarily on the sites (if there are sufficient numbers of them), while others focus on the story of the film and its background (particularly if it was based on a book), or on the history associated with the subject matter in the film, or even on the other things that can be done while visiting the region. The success of *The Lord of the Rings Location Guidebook* is testament to the popularity of a publication that meets what the visitor is looking for or needs.

By providing the opportunity to go into more depth and either support or reduce the effect of some of the other imaging efforts, guidebooks have significant influence on the image of a destination. As they are generally produced independently of the DMOs, local community and tourist ventures, it is important that a close relationship is developed between the various interest groups and the guidebook writers and publishers.

Nomenclature

Another somewhat dramatic destination marketing tool that has been suggested at all the sites studied, is changing the actual names of the towns. For example, from Barwon Heads to 'Pearly Bay' and Goathland to Aidensfield. While such suggestions met with considerable resistance from many in the local communities, New Zealand managed to re-name the region around Wellington as Middle Earth, at least for the duration of the world premiere. 'Welcome to Middle Earth' signage at the main entry points to the city as well as verbal announcements from pilots on Air New Zealand when touching down at Wellington created a sense of actually 'being there' and added an element of excitement and playfulness.

A further way to leverage the imaging power of film without actually changing the name of the towns is to develop a regional title, such as 'Heartbeat Country', which has been done in many regions. However, such nomenclature must be supported by product and other promotional activities, otherwise it will fail.

Tourist precincts

While for many regions, increasing visitor numbers is a high priority, community concerns regarding crowding and loss of privacy are considerable, and must be considered alongside any marketing decisions. Education and awareness-raising programmes to demonstrate that it is possible to have certain levels and types of tourism alongside local privacy are absolutely necessary. One way to approach this issue is to create tourist precincts that focus the visitors into specific primarily non-residential areas. In the case of *Sea Change*, this is feasible as all the film sites are on hardened public land that could be modified to cope with increased visitation. This may not be so easy for other areas that involve fragile environments such as in New Zealand's national parks. However, New Zealand has certainly made use of its hardened sites, such as the city of Wellington, which was the 'headquarters' for *The Lord of the Rings* movies. A marketing planning model that incorporates these issues is introduced in Chapter 7.

A warning

Previously in this chapter I have noted that Barwon Heads has not taken advantage of the promotional opportunities that film can offer, and recommend that it should. However, after studying and visiting the Yorkshire Moors, I am becoming increasingly concerned that some agencies such as the YTB are over-promoting their region through film-induced tourism, which is a powerful image-maker and motivator in the UK. This in turn may result in significant social and environmental problems that the NYMNPA will have to deal with. This is a classic case of tourism authorities chasing increasing numbers of visitors, while not working closely enough with the management agencies who have to deal with their 'success' (see Beeton, 2003). These issues are considered in more detail in the following chapters.

Also, the effects of *The Lord of the Rings* movies are spread throughout the entire country, thanks to the foresight of New Zealand producer, Peter

Jackson, who used sites from many different regions. The production base was a major city, Wellington, the capital of New Zealand, which can cope far more easily with increased visitation than small, rural communities and national parks.

The issue of who controls the destination image will also affect the relevance, effectiveness and even the possibility of enacting some of the above recommendations. As noted in Chapter 3, 'image development' is a complex, multifaceted phenomenon that relates to increasingly complex and multifaceted communities. Simplifying these into manageable destination marketing elements is problematic and can tend to flatten rather than deepen the tourism experiences and the communities they depend on (see Hall, 2003).

Film Promotional Images, Copyright and Confidentiality

Posters used to promote movies and other film, advertisements for movies and movie trailers often use images of sites from the film as well as featuring the stars and/or lead characters. While there has been some study of images used in historical tourism posters and postcards (see Davidson & Spearritt, 2000), there has been little examination of contemporary film promotional images and their link with tourism. This is yet another example of 'free ink' as far as destination marketing goes and, owing to the collectability of movie posters, stands to have a significant long-term effect on tourism imaging.

An issue that has repeatedly presented itself throughout my study of film-induced tourism is that of the need for the film company to protect its own product, which is in itself an image. This is achieved through copyright law in addition to the use of confidentiality contracts. *The Lord of the Rings* makes an interesting study, as all three movies were filmed at the same time, then released over a period of two years (2001, 2002 and 2003). This meant that many of the filming 'secrets' had to be kept from the time of pre-production in 1998 until the release of the final movie in December 2003.

The site for the village of Hobbiton was chosen in 1998 during an aerial search for suitable sites. The main reason for the selection of the site was a large, established pine tree in front of a lake, along with the fact that the surrounding rolling countryside had little if any evidence of the 20th century (Rings Scenic Tours, 2002). The site was constructed some 1.5 kilometres into the property, with gardens planted, hedges and trees brought in as well as the construction of 37 Hobbit holes from timber and polystyrene. Filming at the site took place over a three-month period, and included filming scenes for the first and final episodes of the trilogy.

From the very beginning, the owners of the property, the Alexander family, recognised the commercial potential of being able to run tours to the site after filming. A good access road had been constructed to get to the set that would be suitable for tour buses and it was out of sight from casual visitors, giving the property owner financial as well as physical control over visitation. However, the overall policy of New Line Cinema was to return every site to its original state, so permission was denied. Also, all those involved in the movies, from catering staff to extras as well as the stars, had to sign confidentiality agreements, which meant they could not take photos of any of the filming, sets or costumes for over three years (until the final episode was screened). This policy was endorsed so firmly that it was not until some of the costumes were displayed at Wellington airport around the time of the world premiere of the final episode that those who had worked on the film were able to photograph their own costumes.

The Alexanders did not give up on their requests, however, and in the end it was nature that came to their aid. The set of Hobbiton had been partly bulldozed when hit by severe rainstorms that halted its demolition, giving them one final opportunity. New Line Cinema relented, but placed severe restrictions on the operation. Tours were not permitted to commence until December 2002 and were tightly scripted by the cinema company. When the owners were permitted to commence their tours in December 2002, New Line Cinema provided photo boards along with instructions as to what they could show and say. In addition, no re-working of the Hobbit holes or restoration/renovation of the site was permitted – they had to stay as they were. As the holes were built from untreated wood and polystyrene, their collapse was inevitable. Finally, in late 2003, the family was given permission to maintain the site, but not to enhance it.

In spite of the state of the set, tours have been highly successful. The operator has turned the copyright and confidentiality issues and restrictions into a benefit by taking them as the main theme of the tour, which may disappoint young visitors looking for a theme park style recreation. During my own visit, however, all the visitors were adults and were quite fascinated with the issues.

With the development, filming and release of *The Hobbit* trilogy, Hobbiton had to be reconstructed and so Peter Jackson and the Alexanders' relationship dramatically altered, with Peter Jackson taking an active role in the tourist venture which is now a significant enterprise, as discussed in the next chapter.

Issues of copyright through Warner Brothers for the *Harry Potter* movies have gone as far as restricting any tourism promotion of Goathland, where the historic railway was used as Hogwarts Station (Idle, 2003). The town has a 'witches and wizards day', but is not permitted to refer to *Harry Potter* in any way.

However, producers of television series seem happier to allow the use of images, and there are many occasions where the actors (either in character or as themselves) are used to promote these areas (for example, the Bellarine Peninsula in Australia and *Sea Change* star Sigrid Thornton). This could be due to the need to develop/build relationships that will enable ongoing filming in the region and the difficulty of maintaining copyright over such a diverse product. A television series generally has some 13 programmes, and over 10 years or more that adds up to a lot of filming time and product to protect, which could end up to be more costly and time-consuming than working with the various DMOs on cooperative promotional and community ventures. Also, merchandising is not as intense with television series as it is with movies, possibly because of the longevity of a series – most movie merchandising deals are aimed at a short-term, maximum impact before the market tires of them.

Conclusion

The range of views, opinions, legalities and applications outlined in this chapter illustrates that, even from those who stand to benefit most from increased tourism, there are difficulties inherent in obtaining community consensus for imaging a destination, and may go some way to explaining some of the insipid, commonplace, generic destination images and marketing campaigns evident around the world. Film can provide us with alternative, powerful images, but communities need the courage to follow up on such images, and the cohesion to make sure that they maximise the benefits while minimising the problems related to the (often unasked for) boon of film-induced tourism. These issues are discussed further in Chapter 7 on Community Planning.

Audiences do not always appreciate that even a locality-based television series does not necessarily use many existing structures, let alone construct sets that will last. For example, the major sites for *The Lord of the Rings* movie in New Zealand are in protected national parks, requiring the built sets (including entire villages) to be removed and the natural environment restored to its original state. Such restrictions and regulations may be to the detriment of the much-touted tourism benefits of *The Lord of the Rings* to New Zealand. With councils and governments becoming more aware of the benefits of film-induced tourism, we could even see instances where producers and directors are encouraged to leave grander built legacies.

The different history management approach towards national parks in the UK has resulted in a quite different scenario. Because occupied villages are incorporated into national parks, often with an already strong domestic visitation and previous imaging through literary associations, imaging through film may exacerbate already high levels of visitor impact. On the other hand, imaging through popular television series may provide access to the parks for a broader range of visitor. Such complexities are developed and illustrated by the Goathland study in the next chapter.

5   Effects on Tourism

The early chapters of this book have referred to the potential effects that film has on tourism, such as increased visitation and economic development. While there are many cases today along with anecdotal data in the popular media supporting this notion, research and academic study has, at the same time, given further insight and depth to such claims, as well as uncovering some unforeseen issues. This chapter focuses on the effects that film-induced tourism has on destinations that already have a tourist base, from small towns to entire countries. In actual fact, there are very few places that do not have some tourist visitation.

After detailing an Australian study on the effects of the television series *Sea Change* (1998–2000), we look at film-induced tourism in the Yorkshire Moors in England. The effects of these two series on the visitor markets are compared and discussed, followed by further findings from the *Sea Change* study on the social representations that visitors have. Finally, rural small-town tourism is contrasted with film-induced tourism opportunities in a large city, namely New York, along with the effect on an entire country, New Zealand.

One of the issues in studying film-induced tourism is that it is often not until after the series or movie attracts significant numbers of tourists to a site that it comes to the attention of tourism marketers and others. In the past, tourism has rarely been thought of when a film is screened, let alone during filming. However, if we wish to understand the phenomenon more fully, we need to study the process over time, not simply at one point after it has been aired. In an attempt to achieve this and to make comparisons with film-induced tourism in other parts of the world, research into the impact of *Sea Change* was conducted in Australia over a three-year period from November 1998 to December 2001 at Barwon Heads. This study tracked the influence of a popular television series on tourism to the village from shortly after the series first screened to some 18 months after it finished. Furthermore, I visited the village some 15 years later, providing a truly longitudinal case study.

The findings are included in the next three chapters, as appropriate. The commercial changes that occurred in the town are outlined in the first section of this chapter, followed by the results of visitor surveys and a discussion on the potential impact of the early changes noted in Barwon Heads on the main group of visitors to the town, the budget (or family) holidaymaker.

Following chapters consider the effect of the series on the local community and its implications for community planning. Also, the upcoming movie *Oddball* (2015) is included where relevant to illustrate the changes in the overall understanding of film-induced tourism over the last 10–15 years, particularly regarding the local community.

An initial demographic survey was undertaken in 1998 to obtain some baseline data on visitors to Barwon Heads as well as a photographic study of the town. Those coming to the area purely because of *Sea Change* tended to arrive later in the study period, particularly in the period from September 1999, after the airing of the second series, reflecting the growth in popularity of the series as well as recognition of where it was filmed. In addition, the *Sea Change* visitors tended to come from further afield than the regular visitors, indicating a broadening of the visitor market due to the television series.

In order to assess the impact of the series on visitation over a period of time, the attitudes and opinions of visitors to the *Sea Change* sites were surveyed at Easter, 2000, and in the September school holidays in 2001. The results of the surveys are augmented with the observed changes to the town during that period (as illustrated below), as well as interviews with key players in the Barwon Heads community. Each site visit traces the changes and provides an in-depth picture of those changes to the village, with a follow-up of what, if any, effect remains more than 10 years since these earlier studies and 15 years after the final screening of the series.

From 'Village by the Sea' to 'Pearl Bay'

The main street shopping strip altered dramatically in the 12 months after the commencement of the *Sea Change* series. In 1998 there were vacant shops and others in the process of closing down, in particular basic services such as the greengrocer, butcher and baker. These shops have not reopened to provide the same service, but as of January 2000 all shops were occupied, with the main shopping precinct now boasting a predominance of tourist services as opposed to general residential and product services. There were four cafés, a bar and restaurant, a second-hand bookshop, gift shop, Indonesian import shop, two fish-and-chip shops, a takeaway chicken shop, two surf shops and an art gallery. Of these, one of the surf shops, two of the coffee shops, the gift shop, book shop, chicken shop, bar and restaurant all opened in the 12 months since the screening of the *Sea Change* series.

Seven months since *Sea Change* last aired on television, the main street boasted another up-market restaurant, a further restaurant due to open and an application for yet another before council, a new bakery and café, a homewares store and an art gallery. On a winter's day, the town was alive with people partaking of the café culture. The local supermarket remained remarkably inadequate and no butcher or greengrocer had replaced those that closed some years ago.

By 2015, the shopping centre has expanded to cater for the current café culture trend, with many new cafés, bakeries, restaurants and wine bars. While the direct *Sea Change* effect may have passed, the region is one of the prime areas for those wanting to make a 'sea change'…

Furthermore, the Barwon Coast committee that manages the range of caravan parks in the region still promotes the *Sea Change* connection, with various references throughout their website, such as '[a]n easy stroll across the bridge brings you to Barwon Heads, the town made famous by the ABC TV series, "Sea Change"'(www.barwoncoast.com.au/riverview-family-caravan-park/1001/, accessed September 2015).

A visit to the real estate agent in 2001 showed an enormous increase in property values in those early years post *Sea Change*. Two years prior to my initial study, the agent was looking forward to his first A$500,000 sale – at the time of the study in 2001, there were numerous houses in this range, going up as high as A$900,000, with nothing advertised below A$180,000. By 2015 the median house price was A$760,000 and for units A$615,000, with four properties being sold in the first half of 2015 for between A$1.2 million and A$1.52 million (realestate.com.au; yourinvestmentpropertymag.com.au, accessed August 2015). However, the changes observed in 2001 cannot be totally attributable to *Sea Change* per se. According to local real estate agents, the buoyant economy, recovery from a major regional investment failure with the Geelong-based Pyramid Building Society and low interest rates create a favourable buying environment throughout the region (Bodey, 1999). Nevertheless, it is recognised that the high prices now being asked for residences in Barwon Heads have been augmented by the *Sea Change* syndrome, with cheaper houses disappearing (Keenan, 1999). This phenomenon has occurred in hundreds of near-metropolitan coastal locations (say, within three hours of a capital city) throughout Australia, and the term *sea change* has come to refer to this phenomenon.

The impact of *Sea Change*

In the initial visitor survey, the largest motivator for new visitors was to see the *Sea Change* sites, with visiting friends and relatives (usually the highest motivator in domestic tourism) at less than one-quarter. These findings raised concerns about the possible impact of the needs of the 'new' visitor on the traditional budget holidaymaker so prevalent in the town, prompting additional visitor interviews in Easter 2000 and September 2001. The following discussion of the potential social issues that such changes may bring is based on a series of participant-observer site visits.

High-yield tourism displacing traditional holidaymakers?

When the Victorian state tourism body, Tourism Victoria, released its initial strategic business plan in 1993, a key objective was to position the state as a significant tourism destination, through the development of regional tourism development plans for the 13 regions of the state. The reports were released throughout 1997–1998 in conjunction with Tourism Victoria's second business plan for 1997–2001, which gave a clear direction for regional tourism bodies to target high-yield market segments – reinforced by the main strategies in each of the regional tourism plans (Tourism Victoria, 1993). What we began to see was the squeezing out of the budget holidaymaker in the rush for the limited number of high-yield socio-economic groups, which continues today.

Barwon Heads has certainly benefited from the series in terms of a higher profile and altered demographic of visitors (evidenced by the increase in 'café culture' types), in turn affecting land prices. The series' timing was absolutely perfect for the town, as it gave it a profile at a time when people were looking for somewhere to spend their holidays as well as to purchase a second home. However, there are other factors at stake here, with people now turning to Barwon Heads as a cheaper alternative to the Mornington Peninsula. Prior to *Sea Change*, this demographic would have been less likely to consider Barwon Heads as a place to visit and stay, as it then had only two very plain cafés, fish-and-chip shops and no book or gift shops.

The Barwon Heads Park and camping ground is the site of the most recognisable aspects of *Sea Change*, namely the residences of the main romantic leads, now known as Laura's Beach House and Diver Dan's shed. Also, the images of fishing boats, the bridge (which is central to the narrative) and the tidal views feature significantly in the series, providing more than merely a visual backdrop to much of the action. The light and changes due to the tidal flows in the area provide some of the most beautiful images in the series and are also among the main attractions for campers and other recreational visitors to the park.

Staying in the serviced cottage used as Laura's residence has become extremely popular, with the cottage booking up for over six months in advance. However, issues of privacy arose, with tourists taking photos and peering through windows. Park management expressed concern over the privacy invasions that were being experienced, and suggested that the site may need to be fenced off, which would restrict public access to the foreshore walk. Instead, they took a more basic approach, erecting signs that read, 'Visitors are requested to respect the privacy of the beach house residents'. The increasing number of visitors wishing to view and photograph the cottage and its surroundings was also imposing on campers adjacent to the cottage. In order to gain some privacy for guests, earthworks and vegetation plantings were added to discourage people from walking right up to the cottages as shown in Figure 5.1.

Figure 5.1 Laura's residence

By 2015, three beach houses had been built in line with Laura's cottage, totalling four cottages located in the prime position in the park. The Barwon Heads Caravan Park still promotes the primary cottage as Laura's cottage from *Sea Change* (www.barwoncoast.com.au/barwon-heads-caravan-park/102/). However, while there are more cottages, many new powered caravan sites have been opened up along the cliff, providing more people with these million dollar views. So, while the 'budget' holidaymaker has been catered to, the prices for these sites have increased significantly, while at the same time removing native vegetation.

A bitter argument raged regarding the development of the Fisherman's Cooperative (the site of Diver Dan's home) into a restaurant. Each side of the development debate appropriated the *Sea Change* effect to support its stance, with opponents to the restaurant development claiming that the sheds and jetty provide 'an environmentally sound, sustainable and growing attraction for visitors...' while also stating that 'in Britain, governments are...protecting the charming local sights of TV series...' (Oberin/Trayling & Flick, 1999: 13). On the other hand, supporters of the development claim that it is needed and that:

> *Sea Change* (1998–2000) has certainly livened up Barwon Heads...a couple of local young men were enterprising enough to set up a make-shift outdoor café near...Diver Dan's...The café was so successful, the young men...are about to convert the Fisherman's co-op into a restaurant. (Ryllis Clarke, 1999: 4)

In fact, the restaurant development did not come out of the popularity of the series. For a number of years, park management plans had recommended developing a restaurant on the site and when the contract was granted to the restaurateurs, they could not commence immediately due to the fact that filming of the series was underway at the site. Consequently, they began by opening a small café on the first day of filming the second series of *Sea Change*, intending to commence the restaurant development on the completion of filming by Easter 1999. The story had been altered to support a particular perspective.

However, with the increasing popularity and demand for the more up-market serviced cottages such as Laura's cottage, the prime campsites on the foreshore were phased out to make room for more cottages. Families who had been camping at the same site for generations were relocated to less prestigious sites, effectively being squeezed out from an affordable, enjoyable holiday experience. In addition to the campsite squeeze, the increased housing prices also raised the rents for other traditional family groups who have rented homes for their summer holiday.

While tourism bodies remain focused on the high-yielding sectors of the tourism industry, disenfranchisement of the budget holidaymaker is a real issue. Until the prevailing economic–rationalist attitude is tempered with recognition of the value of intangible aspects that make up the quality of life, such a focus will remain, with potentially dangerous results. The need for recreation and relaxation is recognised as central to a healthy, happy, productive life, but while the tourism industry is preoccupied with the apparently lucrative high-yield market segments, the health of the Australian community is compromised. This situation does not appear to have altered, with Barwon Heads services catering to a highly cashed-up demographic, particularly in the retail area.

Tourism and Film in the Yorkshire Moors: *Heartbeat* and *Harry Potter*

In contrast to the high- versus low-yield visitor noted at Barwon Heads, other tourist sites featured in film have seen a downward shift in certain types of visitor and visitation to a lower socio-economic demographic, or 'lower class'. Demetriadi (1996) found that hoteliers in Goathland (the town portrayed as Aidensfield in the British television series *Heartbeat* (1992–2010)) were experiencing lower occupancy levels after the success of the series, even though the town of 300 residents experiences upwards of 1.1 million annual visitors. He claimed that the sheer number of visitors, increased traffic and loss of privacy have repositioned the town as a day visitor attraction in contrast to its earlier role as a quiet location from which to explore the moors. Consequently, according to Demetriadi, the economic benefits of *Heartbeat*'s popularity were being experienced in the neighbouring towns where the day-trippers are staying, with the traditional, up-market visitor staying elsewhere. The issues surrounding the management of this day-visitor effect are addressed in Chapter 7, which focuses on community planning.

However, a site visit in 2003 did not find any evidence to support this effect, even though there were very mixed views from the resident population regarding the pros and cons of film-induced tourism. Many of the B&Bs and guesthouses reported that their traditional customer base of nature-lovers continued, and that while guests commented on the *Heartbeat* visitors, they tended to avoid them by visiting the moors. It may be that some businesses experienced changes in their visitation during the initial phase of *Heartbeat* tourism, but that over time their original customers have returned, even though television-related visitation to Goathland is still high. Nevertheless, I found some guesthouse owners bemoaning the fact that such visitors were now coming to the area, in effect changing the ambience of the place in which they had chosen to live. As with the attitudes of the residents of Barwon Heads outlined later, it was those who had moved to the area themselves relatively recently who were most resistant to these changes.

According to Mordue (2001), the overriding impression is that *Heartbeat* visitors are day-trippers who primarily focus on the area in the village from the railway station to the shops. This was the case during my own site visits, which coincided with a few days of filming in the town. When the actual filming of the series was away from the town centre, it attracted only a handful of onlookers, whereas the filming in the centre of town attracted over 100 people, even though the visual element was less exciting than at the less-attended site. The filming on the edge of the village was of action scenes, with a lot 'going on' for people to watch, whereas the filming opposite the shops entailed a person knocking on a door.

Demetriadi (1996) also commented on a fundamental change in the nature of the relationship between the village and its visitors, which had become more resentful owing to crowding and the loss of opportunities for the local community to use the village's own facilities. While it may not be evident to the casual visitor, many residents have altered their living arrangements to retain their privacy. For example, residents of houses facing the Common, where many visitors walk and park, now live in the rear of their homes, in effect 'turning their backs on the visual and physical intrusion' (Mordue, 1999: 640). Also, Mordue (2001) found that there was a feeling that the *Heartbeat* day-trippers participated in unwelcome behaviour, bringing their own food and picnicking outside the guesthouses, playing their loud transistor radios and sporting games; and not contributing in any way to the economy or ambience of the village. Such community responses are discussed in more detail in the next chapter.

Goathland has experienced further film fame via the *Harry Potter* movies, as the town's historic railway station has been used as Hogwarts Station in the movies. This is now encouraging a new, younger, family market to the town; however, they tend to focus around the steam railway, travelling on it and stopping only briefly at Goathland. During a series of site visits in 2003 and 2007, I witnessed most of the visitors interested in *Harry Potter* photographing the station and train and then moving on, not venturing much further into the village.

A new kind of visitor

While we were concerned that the budget, family visitor was being forced out at Barwon Heads, it appears that the opposite occurred at Goathland. From a predominantly middle-class visitor base, the film-induced tourism effects of *Heartbeat* have attracted a different ('lower') class of visitor to Goathland and the North Yorkshire Moors.

In spite of the integrating effects of increasing globalisation, England remains a class-based society. The concept of the 'rural idyll' in England has been developed and maintained by its middle class. Mordue (1999) supports this, commenting that, '[a]s both a large and privileged group in terms of numbers as well as material and cultural capital, the middle classes can appropriate and read the countryside more widely and intensively than other social groups' (Mordue, 1999: 634). According to Urry (1995), developing an interest in exploring nature seems to require a large amount of cultural capital, commensurate with a level of education more common in the middle classes.

In discussions with the Goathland Residents' Association and the Goathland Parish Council, Mordue noted the resentment towards the shift in the majority of visitors, combined with a 'sense of loss...of the predominantly middle-class tourists who can afford to stay in the village hotels and guest houses and who have traditionally come for the scenery and peacefulness of the place' (Mordue, 1999: 637). On my own visit to Goathland, guesthouse and B&B providers lamented the loss of ambience and the 'wrong type' of visitor now coming to Goathland.

These studies are supported by research undertaken by the Yorkshire Tourism Board (YTB) and the North York Moors National Park Authority (NYMNPA) in 1997, which found that '[m]any residents feel that the traditional walking tourists are now put off by the crowds of visitors to Goathland' (YTB and NYMNPA, 1997: 61). Over one-quarter of those residents surveyed commented on the different type of tourist now coming to Goathland because it is a film location.

In fact, this so-called 'lower class' of visitor is supported by the second guiding principle of the NYMNPA, which is to encourage greater use (and understanding) of the park (see Chapter 4). A 2002 review of the National Park Authorities found that they 'could do more to encourage social inclusion, particularly through the second purpose of promoting enjoyment and understanding' (DEFRA, 2002). Also reflecting the nature of being part of a National Park and the English attitudes of the rights of access, were the attitudes expressed by many of the lower-class visitors to Goathland. In a series of interviews, Mordue noted that visitors saw the village and its surrounding countryside as a public good to be shared with the local residents. Mordue quotes a respondent from Newcastle upon Tyne, forcefully summing up the issue from the visitor's perspective:

I don't know who lives here. Is it some tycoon from the London stock markets who has decided to buy a house here and has decided he's not going to let us Geordies or Yorkshire lads and lasses in here as he thinks he owns it? Well, it's not his. *It's as much ours as it is his, only I can't afford the house.* I can, and should be able to walk around the road, and I mean that truly from me heart. (Mordue, 1999: 643)

Goathland continues to attract both classes and type of visitor; however, the friction remains, even to a casual observer. Ironically, it is the rural idyll presented in *Heartbeat* that is now encouraging the new, lower-class tourist to the region, who may in turn squeeze out the traditional, middle-class nature tourist.

In the cases of *Sea Change* and *Heartbeat*, film-induced tourism can be seen to either broaden the visitor base or squeeze out traditional visitors, who can be from either end of the socio-economic scale. The challenge is to market and manage tourism in such a way that the positive outcomes are achieved. However, just as not all members of a community are the same, not all film-induced tourists to a site are looking for or expecting the same experience.

Expectations of Visitors to Film Locations

There is anecdotal evidence, supported to an extent by the writings of MacCannell (1976) in relation to tourists' search for authenticity; that visitors to filming sites are disappointed when they do not see exactly what was portrayed on the screen. For such film-induced tourists, this presents an 'inauthentic' experience, as, to them, what was on the screen was the 'reality' they wanted to experience. Mordue found that some visitors to Goathland reported this, and one person commented, 'I expected to come here and see it how you see it on the TV...but things look different, there's lots missing. It should be more sixties-like really...' (Mordue, 1999: 643).

However, this is not the entire picture. Today's film and television viewers have become familiar with the make-believe of filming, due in no small part to the number of 'how the movie was filmed' documentaries used as pre-publicity for many movies and also the subsequent DVD sales. In addition, the popularity of 'blooper' programmes has resulted in many comedy programmes broadcasting their bloopers at the end of each programme, which breaks down the myth of filming. For many visitors to film sites, seeing how the fantasy was created from the raw materials of the site is a powerful motivator. Certainly, on my first visit to Goathland I was surprised how close the area was to what I saw on television, blurting out to my taxi driver 'It's exactly like Heartbeat – they really DO have those sheep wandering around!'

as we came around the bend and down into the village and laid out before me was 'Aidensfield' and typical small-town rural England.

Also, the rise in 'prosuming' discussed in Chapter 4, where fans are producing their own homages to and parodies of film, brings further understanding of the filming process into the public realm. One that particularly appealed to me was a re-enactment of the opening credits of *The Andy Griffith Show* (1960–1968), where the 'actors' are fans who are now adults, playing the role of a young Ron Howard throwing sticks into a pond for the film website, OVguide.com, as well as a family re-creating and presenting their version on YouTube with the description:

> This is a video featuring Myers Lake used in 'The Andy Griffith Show'. The real lake sits in a secluded canyon near Beverly Hills. It is called the Franklin Canyon Reservoir. We reenacted the opening credits in the same spot that they filmed the original. As you can see in the video, the water that Opie throws his rock into is no longer visible. Now it is overgrown with reeds, plants and trees. The water is still there but much further away as the lake is at a much lower level than it was 53 years ago. My family loves this show! We hope you enjoyed watching this little video. (Published May 12, 2013, www.youtube.com/watch?v=FjXsfFNN204, accessed August 2015)

Such differing expectations and understandings are evident at all film sites, and, in order to better understand the different types of film-induced tourists, a study of *Sea Change* visitors was undertaken. In order to identify any distinct groups among the respondents, social representations theory (SRT) was applied (see Pearce *et al.*, 1996), and this distinguished three groups, which are outlined and discussed below.

Groups of visitors to Barwon Heads that held similar social representations were identified as Café Society, Visual Aestheticists and Familiar Comfort Seekers. These three representations are illustrated Figure 5.2 as quite distinct entities by using the differentiators of age group, development stance (whether due to filming or not) and residence. The attitudes of each group towards *Sea Change* and what they were looking for in relation to the series and Barwon Heads are clearly differentiated.

The Café Society was identified through respondents' additional comments about the improved nature of Barwon Heads in terms of cafés, restaurants and town revival. This group of one-fifth of overall respondents can exert a great deal of economic influence on the town. The age range indicated is the predominant grouping of those who have spearheaded the exponential rise in and patronage of cafés and restaurants, in particular in Melbourne, whose tourism agencies have used the café culture as their core destination image. In addition, the Melbourne residents in this group hail from the more upper-class suburbs – once again among the main consumers of café culture.

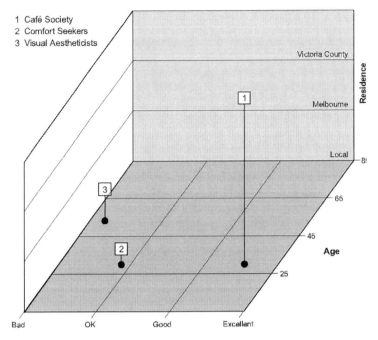

1 Café Society
2 Comfort Seekers
3 Visual Aestheticists

Figure 5.2 Social representations of *Sea Change* (1998–2000) visitors at Barwon Heads

This is not a group that traditionally stayed or even stopped at Barwon Heads, yet their influence is evident in the cultural development of the main street as well as in the increase in housing prices. The Geelong residents represent a more local group (being a short 20 minutes' drive away) who also appreciate the increased gastronomic opportunities so close to home. *Sea Change* was the primary vehicle for raising the profile of the town for those coming from further afield.

The Familiar Comfort Seekers are not looking for change from their daily lives. They rate *Sea Change* in terms of familiarity and relatedness and are predominantly from the local region. That they can relate to the series indicates a certain agreement between the nature of the programme and the town itself, which is not evident from the responses overall. Segregating visitors through using SRT has teased out this significant group and attitude.

Visual Aestheticists were initially identified through their positive comments on the scenery and location of Barwon Heads and *Sea Change*. These constitute the largest group, and consist of a predominance of urban dwellers for whom the location and scenery at Barwon Heads (and in *Sea Change*) rates highly, indicating a longing for, or interest in, places that are aesthetically different from an urban centre. In other words, these people appear to appreciate and to be looking for an ideal self-image along the lines of the rural idyll with its open landscapes, slower lifestyle and cohesive community.

In terms of each group's attitudes towards the effects of *Sea Change* and its relationship to Barwon Heads, the Visual Aestheticists appear to be the most receptive, not only to the series but also to the changes it has brought to the town. The Familiar Comfort Seekers would be the most concerned about 'authenticity' in terms of not seeing what was presented on the screen, while the Café Society visitors are mainly interested in the hedonistic developments of the town, and less in the *Sea Change* storyline and its representation in the town.

As well as looking at this in terms of social representations, it is worth noting the overall shifts in opinions and attitudes of visitors. During the 2001 spring school holiday break in September, further interviews were conducted with visitors to Barwon Heads. The questions were similar to those posed some 16 months earlier, with a little more focus on the impacts of *Sea Change* on the town. The most commonly cited similarities between Barwon Heads and the fictional town of Pearl Bay centred on the small coastal town and people and personalities, as shown in Table 5.1.

When we compare the visitors' attitudes with those from the 2000 survey, we see a dramatic shift in their belief that the location and scenery were similar to that shown series, from 50% to only 4%. The comment that rated consistently in both surveys (at around 15%) was that the people and personalities were similar. It appears that it is the characters portrayed in *Sea Change* who have created the most lingering and consistent impression of the series. This suggests that it is the characters, not the Australian scenery that holds the greatest key to film-induced tourism for this type of programme. Quirky series like this tend to be character-driven, and these results support that notion, compared with the power of the Australian countryside as seen in movies such as *The Man from Snowy River* and *Crocodile Dundee*, which tended to use the uniqueness of the bush as a character in its own right.

The power of images and their varying relationship to the storyline have become apparent in the course of this study, and are discussed in other chapters. Questions relating to perceived similarities to the series and its appeal provide some information, such as in Table 5.1, where visitors and residents saw links between the characters in the series and the people and personalities in the town. General series appeal was also strong due to familiarity and being easy to relate to – aspects that featured in the 2000 survey.

Table 5.1 Similarities between Barwon Heads and Pearl Bay (September 2001)

Similarities	Percentage
None	13
People, personalities	14
Small coastal town	11
Location, scenery	4

Table 5.2 Perceived effects of Sea Change (1998–2000) on Barwon Heads (September 2001)

Effect of Sea Change (1998–2000)	Percentage
Positive	
Raised awareness	18
Real estate increases – good	11
More people year round	20
Good for the economy	5
Good for tourism	7
Improved shops, cafes	18
Neutral	
No effect	2
Negative	
Loss of small town atmosphere	0
Price increases	7
Real estate increases – bad	4
Too much Sea Change signage & promotion	2
Crowds, lack of parking	2

Table 5.2 outlines the interviewees' comments regarding the impact that the series has had on the town. Regardless of whether they felt that Barwon Heads was similar to Pearl Bay as depicted in the series (27% overall saw no similarities), all those interviewed believed that it had an effect on the town. This is important, as it indicates the range of changes that can be brought about by film-induced tourism. Comments were more favourable than negative, indicating that Barwon Heads was not suffering the negative effects seen at towns in the UK such as at Goathland, where the class difference has become problematic, at least in terms of visitor attitudes.

As well as cafés and restaurants benefitting serendipitously from film-induced tourism we are seeing the development of dedicated film tourism enterprises, some of which are discussed below as well as later in the book.

Serving the Visitors: The Business of Film-Induced Tourism

While there are now many examples of businesses that have developed around the tourism interest generated by movies and television series, including theme parks and events which are discussed in subsequent chapters, in this section we focus on two significant enterprises, namely the Hobbiton site in New Zealand (introduced in the previous chapter) and the Hawaiian-based MovieTours, arguably the first registered film tour enterprise.

Hobbiton

As noted in the previous chapter, Hobbiton had to be reconstructed some years later due to the decision to film *The Hobbit* trilogy. By then the touristic appeal of the village had become clear, so it was decided to make some of the hobbit holes more permanent as well as building a fully operational tavern, The Green Dragon. Peter Jackson joined the Alexanders in a partnership to develop the post-filming tourist attraction, which provides the visitor with a dramatically altered experience from the initial tours.

I was able to visit Hobbiton on a number of occasions in 2014, both during the day and in the evening, as a general tourist and conference attendee. Both times we were guided around a fully 'functioning' hobbit village with maintained houses and gardens. All visitors had to be part of a guided tour, whether with a pre-arranged tour group, or from the Information Centre in Matamata or the souvenir shop and café outside the property. This souvenir shop is extensive, with fans and tourists able to purchase everything from small souvenirs to expensive woven wraps and limited edition items. On my visits, the queues at the cash registers were substantial, and there were back-to-back tour groups being marshalled in and around Hobbiton. Clearly, people were enjoying themselves, but I felt that the site had lost its movie-set feel and become a rather boring static theme park.

Below is a series of photos from 'before and after' *The Hobbit* re-development, forming a photo-essay, visually representing my experiences over the years.

On my most recent visit I found that I was not required to use my imagination or even 'think' about the story and remarkable creation and transformation that had taken place. To me, this is no longer a place for film fans, supported by some of the comments on TripAdvisor (even though many were extremely positive, as it is a well-constructed, if controlled, experience).

Some TripAdvisor comments, including my own, which is the first one:

'Little left for the Imagination'
Reviewed 12 January 2015
I have now visited Hobbiton four times, twice when the landowners were not allowed to do any work on the property, and twice last December when the site had been re-made for The Hobbit trilogy, clearly with future tourism in mind. Previously, one had to imagine the site as it looked during filming and in the movie – the hobbit holes were unpainted, with some collapsing under the weight of the earth (as they were only plywood and polystyrene), while elements such as the Green Dragon Inn and the bridges and lanes were non-existent. Today, the gardens are planted, flowers bloom and one can have a cider at the Green Dragon Inn. Three gardeners are employed to keep Hobbiton as it should look for the tourists. While I had a good time, I confess I felt flat after leaving, and more than a little overwhelmed (or was

it underwhelmed) by the sheer number of tourists and the crush in the souvenir shop. For me, there was no longer any 'movie magic' there, simply a theme park.
Visited December 2014
www.tripadvisor.com.au/ShowUserReviews-g3395240-d1382525-
r248915663-Hobbiton_Movie_Set_Tours-Hinuera_Waikato_Region_
North_Island.html#

Hobbiton 2003 (starting from the left)

- Tour Guide with story board explaining how it looked in the movie
- Un-adorned hobbit holes
- Bilbo's cottage, no longer painted or with any garden

Hobbiton 2006 (clockwise from the left)

- Tour Guide still using story board
- Collapsing hobbit holes
- Bilbo's cottage, painted white with grass and a storyboard, but no garden
- The general appearance of the site

Hobbiton 2014 (clockwise from the left)

- Tour Guide no longer needs a story board
- Bilbo's cottage completely restored, but no public access
- The village now has a tended garden
- The hobbit holes each have specific items relating to the profession of inhabitants
- Tourists
- The Green Dragon Inn
- The gift shop

'Managing the masses well.'
Reviewed 12 January 2015
What to say about this? It is a business with *lots* of visitors. They had tours of 40 people leaving every ten minutes. So it needs to be well organised in order to work well. And it is and did. ....

The tour guides tell you a bit about the filming and what they did, but their job is mostly shepherding people through and take their pictures. I would've liked to learn a bit more about the filming itself. The hobbit holes have been created with wonderful attention to detail and are very, very well maintained. The gardens of the hobbit holes are beautiful in their own right.

There is, of course, a shop with lots of Hobbiton memorabilia. Prices are somewhat exaggerated but not overly so (e.g. t-shirt 40$) but some are a bit over the top ($13 for a bottle of beer, t-shirt $40 if you take the set of 3, postcards $2).

If you are interested in movies it is a must do.
Visited December 2014
www.tripadvisor.com.au/ShowUserReviews-g3395240-d1382525-
r248915663-Hobbiton_Movie_Set_Tours-Hinuera_Waikato_Region_
North_Island.html#

'Entry fee not worth the experience'
Reviewed 5 September 2015 NEW
Drove over to Hobbiton with some time to kill before handing my car back in. I was alone and expected to be able to just have a walk around the place. I was a bit disappointed when I found that the only way to get on site was to pay NZ $75.00 for the tour. Figuring there wasn't much more to do around and wanting to stretch my legs anyway I went ahead and splashed out on the 90 min. guided walkabout.

The place itself is very well maintained and actually pretty magical to step into. Certainly more impressive than I expected. Our guide however was quite young and not half the LOTR geek I was hoping to get. She also seemed quickly agitated with group members walking about. There is a constant stream of tours going around the property and I got the feeling we were just one of today's many groups in the way information and jokes were delivered. This in its turn made people lose interest, wander around more and test our guides patience futher.

Did not leave disappointed, but found $75.00 a lot of money to put up with a guide that was not able to bring Hollywood magic to live.
Visited September 2015
www.tripadvisor.com.au/ShowUserReviews-g3395240-d1382525-
r307377433-Hobbiton_Movie_Set_Tours-Hinuera_Waikato_Region_
North_Island.html#

MovieTours

In a series of interviews and meetings, founder of Hawaii-based MovieTours, Bob Jasper outlined the MovieTours story for me. He came about the concept in 1994, some 18 months after Hurricane Iniki hit Kauai in 1992, virtually destroying their current livelihood, necessitating Bob and his wife Jerri to leave the island. They returned in 1993, photographing the exotic birds for tourists at Wailua Falls, where Bob found he was fielding many questions regarding the movies filmed in the area, particularly the television series *Fantasy Island* (1977–1984), as the opening sequence features the Falls.

The hurricane also seriously damaged the iconic resort, Coco Palms, where many stars, including Elvis Presley, stayed and where the famous wedding scene from *Blue Hawaii* (1961) was filmed. Bob was aware that many popular movies and television series had been filmed on Kauai, including *Jurassic Park* (1993), *South Pacific* (1958) and *Blue Hawaii* (1961) as well as the pilot for *Gilligan's Island* (1992) which was actually filmed in 1963, but not seen on our screens until 1992, some time after the series itself, which was ultimately filmed elsewhere. He and his wife Jerri believed that people could be interested in discovering this aspect of Hawaii, in particular Kauai, so undertook around eight months of exploratory market research. Once they decided this was feasible, they spent another 16 months researching film and television programmes, script writing and acquiring equipment. After a series of test runs, the first official tour was held on 11 September 1996, exactly four years to the day after Hurricane Iniki.

The tours are conducted on mini buses with a television screen where clips can be shown while travelling to the various sites around the island. Stories such as the aforementioned *Gilligan's Island* pilot are of particular interest as they provide an insider's perspective. While tightly scripted, on all of the tours I have participated in I found the guides and drivers to be extremely knowledgeable and welcoming, providing a very personalised experience. On one tour we were treated to home-grown fruit from the driver's garden, which was a delicious treat. This is not an easy feat for a tour guide and also requires a level of trust from the business owner which is not always apparent, as I note on the tour I took in New York where the guide 'blamed' the script for any bad jokes or other things she was required to say.

One of the challenges Bob faced was to sort out the licensing costs with the Hollywood studios, so that he could show extracts from the relevant movies during the tour. Initially the studios charged $1,000 per minute, but eventually Bob was able to negotiate a broad licence covering the use of the films. This has been an issue confronted by many people running such tours, including On Location Tours in New York and even the *Neighbours* tour in Australia, both of which were able to negotiate a reasonable outcome, but there are those who could not. To this end, Georgette Blau of On Location Tours established a network of film tour companies to represent each other to the studios, which is outlined in the next section.

After trademarking the name MovieTours in 1999, Bob and Jerri were able to promote the concept to other places in the US, with licences to use the trademarks currently in Monterey, San Francisco, Hollywood, New Orleans and Atlanta. There were also licensees in Portland, which at the time was not successful, and Boston which was bought out by New York movie touring company On Location Tours and re-named the TV and Movie Tour Company. As well as participating in a number of the tours on Kauai, I have also experienced the New Orleans MovieTour as well as Georgette's tours in New York, which I recount later.

In 2007, Bob Jasper also became the property manager of Coco Palms Resort which had not been repaired since it was seriously damaged by Iniki due to a number of legal and financial issues, keeping this iconic resort in ruins until today. On a side note, the resort now seems likely to be restored in the next year or two. At the time, due to the dilapidated nature of the buildings and the hundreds of coconut palms with seriously large coconuts that have a tendency to drop, the site was closed to the general public. However, Hawaii MovieTours had permission to take groups there from the early days of their tours, becoming a true highlight of the experience, not the least because there was no other way to visit (Figure 5.3).

Figure 5.3 Coco Palms and tour

Why was this so important? Coco Palms resort did not only host many celebrities, but also was a pioneer in developing what we recognise now as the Hawaiian resort experience. Many activities that the tourist may consider 'authentically Hawaiian' were developed by Grace Guslander, the manager from its opening in 1953 until 1985, including the lighting of torches at sunset by young Hawaiian men calling people to meals. She also popularised (appropriated?) the use of the conch shell blowing greeting on arrival at the resort, which also became the resort's logo. She also introduced the practice of celebrities planting a palm tree, with many of the plaques recently coming to light.

In 2011, the Jaspers sold Hawaii MovieTours to the long-standing Hawaiian tour company Roberts, where the tours continue with the same itinerary, script and staff as before. Bob Jasper welcomes the tour group to the Coco Palms resort where they may also be entertained by the famous Kauai musician Larry Rivera who talks proudly about playing with Elvis and travelling to the US with him. Both the movie tours overall and additional tours of Coco Palms remain financially viable, particularly with the growing media interest in the re-development of the resort fuelling visitation and the filming in Kauai of more blockbuster films such as *Jurassic World* (2015).

Film-Induced Tourism in the Big City

Many of the effects of film-induced tourism described in this chapter are evident in small rural communities, but have received little attention in larger urban centres. Generally speaking, tourism in cities does not create the same level of impact (positive as well as negative) owing to their existing population size, infrastructure and site hardening. In addition, visitors are not as obvious, with many integrating into the resident community, even if only visiting for a few days. Nevertheless, film-induced tourists' desire to gaze on private sites where current residents live and work potentially infringes privacy as well as creating a traffic nuisance to both pedestrians and vehicles.

While many urban centres are currently being revitalised and developed to encourage a stronger residential population base in the central business district (CBD), New York has traditionally been a city with a high number of inner-urban apartment dwellers, from the wealthy areas around Central Park to the struggling boroughs of Harlem and the West Village. Such areas are now receiving the attention of those who cannot afford a Central Park address, resulting in a gentrification of many of the poorer areas of New York. Tourism has traditionally been strong in New York, with attractions such as the Statue of Liberty and the Empire State Building ensuring it has a place in the hearts of the millions of Americans, migrants and native-born alike. The theatres of Broadway, the hundreds of movies, musicals, television programmes and songs about New York have given the city a predominant place in the minds, not only of Americans, but other nationalities, resulting in a strong domestic and international tourism market.

On Location Tours is a film tour business operating in New York, running film-based tours to various sites around the city. Starting out initially with a *Sex in the City Tour*, the one-person business established and run by Georgette Blau in 1999 soon expanded to encompass other themed tours such as *The Sopranos Tour* and a generic *TV Tour*.

According to Blau, New York has more exterior film sites than anywhere else in the world – she estimates that there are around half a million (Torchin, 2003). Many visitors taking the tours see them as a less traditional way to see the town, and this appeals to independent travellers who are not interested in a 'normal' tour with bored tour guides narrating the same facts and figures day in, day out. As Torchin notes:

> [t]he everyday world of New York City is reconfigured as interesting as apartment buildings, parks, non-celebrity chef restaurants become exhibits in an open-air museum of fictive worlds. (Torchin, 2003: 248)

My own immersive participant-observer New York site visits and interest in the tours concurs with much of Torchin's (2003) description, allowing a comparison between the tour guided by the proprietor Blau (as experienced by Torchin) and by other guides (my own experience). It was clear that Blau had tightly scripted the tour narrative, to the extent where our guide commented (after a rather poor joke), 'Don't blame me, I just say what they tell me to...' while waving a sheet for us all to see. This is in contrast to many of the tour companies that I have either worked with or had a professional relationship with, where the guides are encouraged to develop their own 'scripts' and put their own personalities into them. Even MovieTours in Hawaii, while scripting their tours, appears to give the guides a little more leeway; however, this was only one experience some years ago and many not be common.

The tour provides not only information on the filming aspects of a site, but also other historical, cultural or popular snippets of information that visitors find engaging, with one telling me that this was a 'better way to see New York than on a traditional tour'. For example, the New York Public Library is noted not just because of its use in the movie *Ghostbusters* (1984) and the television series *Mad About You* (1992–1999), but also because of the history of its roots as a private library. This varied information allows the tour guides to 'animate multiple locations in single sites: historical New York, New York's lived reality, the production history, and the fictive worlds' (Torchin, 2003: 259). Table 5.3 outlines some of the tour sites and the historical information provided, along with the fictional narrative of the films in which they were utilised.

As can be seen from Table 5.3, the majority of the sites are filmed for their exteriors only, being used for establishing shots in the television series and movies, while the interior filming is primarily studio-bound, often in

Table 5.3 On Location Tours' scripted on-location information

Current New York site	Historical/cultural references from tour	New York film background from tour
Jacqueline Kennedy Onassis High School	High School of the Performing Arts	High School of the Performing Arts in *Fame*. Interiors shot in Hollywood. Students from actual school sent to Hollywood to play the New York City students.
Flatiron Building	Most photographed building in New York City	Houses the fictional offices of *Veronica's Closet*, a television show about an upscale lingerie company set in New York, but shot in Hollywood.
West Village apartment block	Apartments renting for $US3000–5000 per month	Apartment block where the characters from *Friends* live. Much shorter than it appears on *Friends* and the neighbouring buildings are further away than shown in specific episodes. The internal apartments are much smaller than shown in *Friends*. The coffee shop from the series is not in the building.
West Village brownstone terrace style home	Four apartments renting at $US2000 per month	Brooklyn home to the Huxtable family on the *Cosby Show*. The exterior is reversed in order to fit the interior set. Filmed in studios in Brooklyn and then Queens.
Al's Soup Kitchen International	Very popular soup restaurant with tyrannical owner. Favourite lunch spot of the writers of *Seinfeld*.	Real-life basis for the fictional 'Soup Nazi' on *Seinfeld*. Not used for any establishing shots.

another city such as Hollywood. Pointing out such dissonance is a recurring theme of the tours, which revel in drawing out the make-believe elements of film. This is significant in that it supports my own belief that many visitors to film sites and sets do not expect to see exactly what they viewed on the screen, rather they share a fascination for the 'inauthenticity' of the film media. They can now return home, 'knowing how it's done', and brag about possessing an insider's knowledge. As Torchin (2003: 250) also notes, 'the tourist is not duped by a "thicket of unreality", but rather, remaps a terrain in a way that enhances the landscape'. This concept and its significance in the study of film-induced tourism is revisited in the concluding chapter.

However, even though urban centres do not face the same level of issues that rural towns and villages may, elements of privacy invasion are evident. During the tours, groups of up to 40 gather outside people's homes taking photos (such as at the brownstone home from the *Cosby Show*) and blocking the narrow, crowded New York sidewalks (at the 'Soup Nazi' kitchen). The tour company has permission from the owner for people to sit on the stoop and take photos of the fictional Huxtables' house, however the tenants of the four apartments in the building have to step around these people to get into their own homes (Figure 5.4).

Tour participants also undertook somewhat 'insensitive' and dangerous tourist behaviour when photographing the building that 'plays' the role of the *Friends* apartment block, standing in the middle of an intersection to get a better shot (Figure 5.5). While the owners of the buildings receive substantial payments for the use of their building facades (and interiors when used), as with many of the rural sites, there is no undertaking from production companies in terms of the flow-on tourism impacts. Such issues do not appear to have been addressed by the tour company, and may present commercial difficulties

Figure 5.4 Tourists at the fictional home of the *Cosby Show's* Huxtable family

Figure 5.5 Dangerous tourist behaviour at the *Friends* apartment block

in the future as the residents (who are renting and rarely benefit from the financial incentives from the film companies) become weary of the exposure.

Blau has also established the Association for Tours of TV and Movies (attam) with a primary goal of providing a united way to approach movie studios in relation to gaining access and permission to show clips as well as representing the group internationally. As of September 2015, membership included Flat Earth NZ Experiences, Salzburg Panorama Tours, Red Carpet Tours: Lord of the Rings/Hobbit Tours, San Francisco Movie Tours, Miami Movie Tours, Liverpool Film Tours, Set in Paris, Love Rome – Tours in Motion (Rome, Italy). While not a complete list of enterprises, this range of organisations illustrates the development of film tourism over the past 10 years.

Over the last decade, On Location Tours has expanded significantly, making it arguably the largest and most successful dedicated film tour company.

The Effect of Film-Induced Tourism on a National Scale

Since the screening of *The Fellowship of the Ring*, the first movie in *The Lord of the Rings* trilogy, New Zealand claims to have experienced an increase in international tourism as a direct result of the movies. As noted in other parts of the book, when we measure tourist behaviour and changes on a large scale such as that of a nation, the effects of film-induced tourism may not be as pronounced as on a local level, especially if it is a long-haul destination such as New Zealand. This is due primarily to the simple fact that most international visitors plan to visit the country anyway, and while the film provides another activity of interest, it is not necessarily a prime motivator. This issue has been noted in a report to the New Zealand Film Commission on the long-term effects of *The Lord of the Rings* (Yeabsley & Duncan, 2002). However, only one page out of the 59-page report was dedicated to film-induced tourism, which is an indication of the past dearth of research and information on the topic.

When initially looking at film-induced tourism, research and studies into the subject were scattered and not easy to bring together to create a clear picture of the phenomenon. For example, research undertaken in 2003 by NFO New Zealand (2003) with current and potential international visitors found that some 72% of current international visitors had seen at least one of the first two *Lord of the Rings* movies, as had 75% of so-called 'potential visitors' (those visiting the Tourism New Zealand website and choosing to complete the survey). This is a very high figure, and while it does not indicate motivation, such findings need to be considered, especially in terms of leveraging this exposure and converting it into visits. Supporting this is the evidence that a large majority of both groups were aware that the movies were filmed in New Zealand, and such recognition is vital for film-induced tourism. However, the actual motivational strength of the movies was not significant, with only 0.3% of international visitors saying that the movies were the main reason for visiting New Zealand, and only 9% noting it as 'one reason, but not the main one' (NFO New Zealand, 2003).

Nevertheless, the power of film to raise the profile of New Zealand to potential travellers is evident, with close to two-thirds of potential travellers agreeing that they were more likely to visit New Zealand as a result of the movies. A separate report on the effect of the movies on tourism to Wellington in 2002 estimated that an additional 9200 international tourists a year could be expected to visit New Zealand over the next three years to 2006, spending NZ$5 million annually (Wellington Regional Council, 2002). However, it was not possible to examine the rationale behind these figures, which tend to contradict the NFO results, and is a common problem faced by tourism researchers.

One indicator of the economic benefits from media exposure of a place (often referred to as 'free ink'), such as through movies, is the value of that exposure in terms of its cost if it had been done through commercial advertising. Tourism New Zealand has estimated the value of the country's exposure in the first movie of the trilogy, *The Fellowship of the Ring* (Table 5.4).

Tourism destination marketing organisations seem to like using such data, and the numbers are certainly impressive. Also, it is relatively easy to

Table 5.4 The estimated value of New Zealand's exposure in *The Fellowship of the Ring*

Country	Audience	Cinema weeks	Equivalent adverts	Total adverts/ cinema week	NZ$/advert/ cinema week	Total value US$
USA	50,989,397	4,856	15	74,784	300	22,435,335
Japan	5,499,006	170	15	2,625	590	4,758,473
UK	13,771,517	1,312	15	20,198	580	11,714,970
Australia	4,962,725	473	15	7,279	125	909,833
Germany	1,066,180	102	15	1,564	260	406,570
Korea	3,864,447	368	15	5,668	300	1,700,357
Total	76,443,824	7280	92	112,118		41,925,538

quantify. However, is such exposure going to the places where the destination marketer would have spent its promotional funds? If we compare the data with Tourism New Zealand's primary international tourism markets of Australia, the US and Japan, the 'value' of New Zealand's exposure to countries such as Korea and Germany through film becomes a little less grand (Tourism Research Council, New Zealand, 2004).

The value of exposure from the movie in Australia, by far New Zealand's largest market and one with further potential for film-induced tourism due to its proximity, does not reflect this significance in the table. Where such comparisons become very murky is that, while the films may actually present the country to a new audience, if this audience does not have the desire, time, money and access to travel, this will not have any effect.

One of the key elements of encouraging tourism is the role of a 'champion' who can influence communities and decision-makers. New Zealand director Peter Jackson stands out as an exemplar of how this can work on a local and national level. His continued passion for New Zealand's film industry and the place itself has not only built a strong film industry with a cluster of innovative studios and workshops based in Wellington, such as his own Weta Studios, Camperdown Studios, post-production house Park Road Post, and Stone Street Studios, but also film-based tourism. Jackson takes every opportunity to promote New Zealand's tourism assets as well as its growing technological and creative capacities, which has proved highly successful. He has also invested in both the film and tourism industries via his Weta Studios and the Hobbiton site as outlined earlier.

The Games the Media Play

Relying on the media for 'free ink' does not always produce favourable or appropriate destination marketing initiatives owing to the (sometimes conflicting) aims of the media. While the example described here is a few years old, it remains a pertinent case and one that, at the time, I found rather surprising. In a stunning role-reversal, ABC TV appropriated a local tourism-related development controversy to promote the *Sea Change* series through a report on its television current affairs programme, *The 7.30 Report.* The anchor, Maxine McKew, introduced the report stating that '...some ambitious locals want to develop a $500,000 restaurant on the site where Diver Dan dallied with Laura Gibson' (ABC TV, 1999). The report was heavily peppered with references to the series (which is shown on ABC TV), and with inferences of some real-life connection between the fictional characters of Pearl Bay and those living in Barwon Heads. It also featured cuts to selected clips of the series featuring the fictional real estate agent Bob Jelly interspersed with comment from the real-life Barwon Heads agent Rodger Bodey. Discussion with some of those interviewed revealed a high level of dissatisfaction with the selective and inaccurate nature of the report. Supporting this stance, resentment towards being compared with characters in the series was evident in the findings of the residents' survey discussed in Chapter 4, in which over one-third commented, 'Barwon Heads is not Pearl Bay'.

Such blatant self-promotion from Australia's publicly owned national broadcaster in the guise of 'current affairs' is misleading at the very least, demonstrating the temptation for even investigative reporters to confuse fantasy with reality. *The 7.30 Report* is generally considered to be 'above' the cross-promotional antics of the commercial networks, with this particular current affairs programme considered among the most balanced programmes of its kind in Australia. The use of this reputation to promote a series that has been the station's most successful to date, and present a false 'angle' on the report, brings into question the reliability and potential bias of all of the station's current affairs reports.

Where the case above illustrates the use of different forms of media under the same ownership (even when it is government/public ownership) promoting each other, there are other benefits that certain types of reporting can bring to the media, such as increased readership. It is well-documented that the news media thrive on controversy and 'bad news' stories, so by reinforcing (if not creating) controversies such as that at Barwon Heads, good news can be turned into bad news.

When we look at a series of newspaper headlines about *Heartbeat* and the effect of film-induced tourism on Goathland, we also see a theme of conflict emerging. Table 5.5 lists a representative selection of the headlines over a five-year period from 1991 to 1996.

The relationship between the headlines and community attitudes is considered in the next chapter. While the issues reported on certainly existed, according to the NYMNPA Transport and Tourism Officer, Bill Breakell (personal interview, 2003), in many cases the reporting was biased and not representative of all the views (or even the presiding view) of the residents of

Table 5.5 News headlines regarding the effects of film tourism on Goathland

Year	Headline
1991	• Village Row Over TV Series Plan. • TV Dream Off Air. • Village Anger as TV is Forced Out. • TV Intruders Win Praise at Goathland. • Cameras Roll at Goathland.
1992	• Cars Ban to Protect Moors Heartbeat Village. • Cars May be Banned at Village. • Heartache as Visitors Choke Village. • Heartache Over Traffic Jams. • Heartbeat of Tourism. • TV Village Fury. • Bid to Ease TV Village Jams. • TV Village Blocks Car Park Plan. • Heartbeat Meeting Anger. • Talking Tourism at Heartbeat Village.
1993	• Heartbeat Heartache. • TV Village Feeling the Pressure. • Dilemma as Fame Draws in TV Fans. • Heartache Over Coaches Beating a Trail to Village. • Fears for Village Which Beats with Nostalgia. • Heartbeat Mania Must be Controlled. • Heartbeat Putting Strain on Arteries. • Assurance on Future of Favourite TV Show.
1994	• TV Firm Asked to Save Village. • Heartbeat Breathes Life Into Village Store. • Heartbeat Heartache. • Influx of Fans Angers Villagers. • TV Crews Not a Problem. • Have a Heart – Townies Leave us Alone. • Trippers Drive Heartbeat Family Out. • Easing Strain on Goathland. • Village Divides Over Parking.
1995	• Rebellion by Heartbeat Villagers. • Villagers Backlash at Heartbeat Fame. • Real Drama as Village Rebels. • 'Friendly' Goathland Tackles Parking. • Heartbeat Influx Puts Strain on Village. • Heartbeat Boosts Crime.

(Continued)

Table 5.5 *(Continued)*

Year	Headline
1996	• Yellow Peril heads for TV Village.*
	• Parking Blow for TV Village.
	• We Don't Want Your Yellow Lines.*
	• Village with a Big Heart.
	• TV Fame Brings Car Chaos to the Village.
	• Congestion Misery Ends – 'At a Price'.
	• Heartbeat Blamed for Traffic Invasion.
	• Heartbeat Villagers in Row Over Parking
	• Cars Banned from Heartbeat Village
	• The Price of Fame.
	• Car Park Curbs for Heartbeat Headache.
	• Parking Ban will End Heartbeat Misery.
	• Easing Parking Chaos at the Heartbeat Village.

Source: Breakell (1996).
Notes: *Refers to the painting of yellow 'no parking' lines down the side of the roads.

Goathland. Some reports on the same topic were conflicting, while others seemed to find a catchy headline and then write the story to fit. In some instances, the media reports actually caused internal community altercations and divisiveness, particularly when they reported the opinions of a vocal minority (sometimes of only one person) as an overall community attitude. In particular, the reports that housing prices had actually depreciated due to tourism (the reverse is more often the case, as in Barwon Heads) has been challenged as a 'media beat-up' (see Chapter 6). While prices did fall, this was common across the region, not just at Goathland (Breakell, personal interview, 2003).

This is not the forum for an in-depth discussion on media ethics, influence and responsibilities; however, it is important to recognise that, as tourism can provoke a range of reactions, relying on the media to report such reactions impartially must be treated with caution.

The Legacy of Film-Induced Tourism on Existing Tourism

As noted at the beginning of this chapter, there are few places today that do not experience any tourism, so when we consider the effects of a 'new' type of tourism or tourist on an area, we must consider the effect not only on the community, but also on the existing tourism base. The cases and research outlined also warn against assuming that the film-induced tourist will be an up-market tourist displacing the traditional, budget-oriented visitors. While there is evidence of such a situation occurring at Barwon Heads in the camping reserve, the opposite situation exists at Goathland in the UK. In addition, such changes may not be 'all bad', as a broadening of the visitor base can be desirable. It is the unforeseen issue of displacement (whether it be of residents or regular visitors) that is of most concern, particularly from a societal perspective.

The potentially negative effects of crowding and displacement of locals and regular visitors, while evident, did not occur to any great extent at Barwon Heads, despite the enormous popularity of *Sea Change* in Australia. This is most likely due to the dispersed nature of domestic tourism in Australia, as well as to the country's limited neighbouring tourism-generating regions. New Zealand is Australia's closest neighbour and one of its main inbound tourism markets; however New Zealand is predominantly a short-break urban tourist market for Australia. Also, for most international visitors Australia is a long-haul destination with the major tourism icons attracting the bulk of visitors. The Great Ocean Road has become a significant international tourism destination, but most visitors tend to by-pass the Bellarine Peninsula and Barwon Heads. Because of the problems of selling Australian television series overseas (a consequence of local product rulings in many countries), *Sea Change* did not achieve its anticipated international profile, in particular in the UK.

With the Australian movie *Oddball* (2015) being set and filmed in Warrnambool, a Great Ocean Road destination, the effect there can be expected to be significantly different to the *Sea Change* experience, not in the least due to international distribution deals that can be expected to induce a broader range of international visitors to the region. The producers have been able to secure distribution via Global Screen, which should give the movie strong international exposure.

Film-induced tourism in the UK presents quite a different picture – one where the influence of 'class' on certain tourist activities and attitudes predominates, along with a large population and many neighbouring countries. Domestic tourism numbers are high compared with countries such as Australia and New Zealand, and have impacted significantly on the environment and social fabric of rural communities.

While some of the figures being cited regarding the national benefits of *The Lord of the Rings* (2000, 2001, 2002) to New Zealand are questionable, the movie and books do have an enormous number of enthusiasts and the championing of New Zealand by Peter Jackson, along with *The Hobbit* (2012, 2013, 2014), has basically re-imaged the country. While there are criticisms that New Zealand is more than a hobbit hole, overall the connection has enabled a broader image to be presented. The strength of this motivator has not yet been adequately quantified and has primarily been the basis of much conjecture and guesswork, which is surprising considering the high levels of government funding committed to leveraging the effect of the movies, as outlined in Chapter 4.

We have seen that the media manipulate stories for their own benefit, either in terms of cross-promotion or sensationalisation. This is important not only in terms of the film-induced tourism cases discussed here, but also when conducting research that may rely on media reports that may be serving a different agenda. For example, the study of Fox Studios Backlot featured in Chapter 9 had to rely on media reports owing to lack of access to commercial-in-confidence data. However, where possible, the media reports were tested against relevant Australian Stock Exchange data, and were not used if there was any discrepancy. This approach also enabled me to develop an understanding of some of the journalists' attitudes towards the partners in Fox Studios (Newscorp and the Lend Lease Corporation) and also to see the various news publications in terms of their overall editorial stance and self-interest. Even the most impartial of people and media (and researchers) do at times reflect their personal attitudes.

This chapter has looked at the changes to existing tourism patterns, types of visitors and their interests, along with some visitor services and related enterprises. While there is strong evidence that film-induced tourism does often bring in new tourist markets, the issues surrounding their differences from the current visitor base can be seen. The following chapter considers many of the elements raised in this chapter in terms of the host communities themselves, from the effects on small rural villages and seaside communities, through to the effects on entire nations.

6   Effects on Community

Where the previous chapter looked at the effect of film-induced tourism on existing tourism, this chapter moves on to consider its effects on the communities that support and host the tourists. Due to the extensive use of the term, such a discussion needs to begin with an outline of what 'community' means, and how the term is being used in this book. After an outline of the concepts of communities and community tourism, the effects of film-induced tourism on small, local communities is considered in some detail from the original Barwon Heads and Goathland studies along with some additional notes from Warrnambool, the site of the new movie, *Oddball* (2015). These in-depth examinations allow the significant differences between the English and Australian sites to be highlighted. Finally, the effect of film-induced tourism on a broader community is examined by looking at the country of New Zealand and *The Lord of the Rings* movies. These cases continue to serve as illuminative studies, with many of their features being transferrable to other situations around the world, including some Asian situations. In the end, we tend to respond to the effects of tourism on and in our own communities in similar, yet complex ways.

Agreeing on what is actually meant by 'community' is fraught with complications, arising from the assumption that we are talking about the same thing, without actually articulating or explaining the term. The term 'community', is in such common and constant use today that we must consider what we really mean by it. Communities can be defined spatially by the limits of a town, for example, politically by a shire or state, geographically by the type of countryside (the valley region), by land use (a farming community), or psychologically by fields of interest (such as the artistic community, or the globally geographic virtual communities linked via the internet) (Beeton, 2006b). We are primarily concerned here with spatially-defined communities, but there are some differences between them. For example, among the many examples and cases of film-induced tourism, we look at a small seaside holiday village (or town) in Australia (Barwon Heads), a quaint well-established English village in an English national park (Goathland) and an entire country (New Zealand). They all have similarities and differences, as becomes apparent in this and the following chapters. Another 'community' that underpins film-induced tourism is that of the film fan, enthusiast or buff. Such a community type is not discussed separately here, but underpins the work, and its potential as a field of research is noted in Chapter 10, and being explored in Europe by Reijnders, Bolderman, van Es and Waysdorf, along with Yamamura, Sugawa-Shimada and Seaton in Japan and, in a small way, myself, primarily in collaboration with these researchers (Yamamura, 2011; Beeton *et al.*, 2013; Reijnders *et al.*, 2015; Sugawa-Shimada, 2015; Seaton, 2015).

The impacts of tourism on local communities have been well documented over the past 35 years (see Murphy, 1981, 1985; Krippendorf, 1987; Pearce *et al.*, 1996; Robinson & Boniface, 1997; Bramwell & Lane, 2000a, 2000b; Murphy & Murphy, 2001; Singh *et al.*, 2003a; Beeton, 2004, 2006b). However, it is pertinent to outline the range of social impact issues that have been reported over that period. Table 6.1 summarises these in terms of tourism development, tourist–host interactions and cultural impacts.

The list is not exhaustive, and does not judge whether the impacts are good or bad, which often depends upon an individual's perspective, perceptions and values, while the level of impacts also depends on the pace of community change, which tourism tends to accelerate. Film-induced tourism has the potential to increase that pace even more. In order to demonstrate this, the following work includes an assessment of attitudes from the residents'

Table 6.1 Reported social impacts of tourism

	Social impact
Tourism development	Modifies the internal structure of the community
	Divides the community into those who have/do not have relationships with tourists
	Has colonialist characteristics
	Employment in tourism offers more opportunities for women
	Instigates social change
	Improves quality of life through infrastructure development
	Increased pressure on existing infrastructure
Tourist–host interactions	The nature of contact influences attitudes/behaviour/values relating to tourism
	Young locals are most susceptible to the demonstration effect
	Cultural exchange/increased understanding and tolerance
	Increased social interaction increases communication skills
	Hosts adopt foreign languages through necessity
	Hosts develop coping behaviour and avoid unnecessary contact
Cultural impacts	Arts, crafts and local culture revitalised
	Acculturation process likely to occur
	Assumed negative effects of commodification of culture
	Meaning/authenticity not necessarily lost

survey undertaken in 2000, at the height of *Sea Change*'s (1998–2000) popularity. Groups with similar social representations have been identified and the potential effects of these groups on the future of the community and tourism are outlined.

Goathland in the United Kingdom (UK) and the entire country of New Zealand are also looked at in terms of their particular communities and their relationship with film-induced tourism. Goathland has been experiencing film tourists for some years and is exhibiting some classic stages along Doxey's Irridex model (Doxey, 1975), whereas New Zealand in the early 2000s was very much in the honeymoon stage of its relationship with film-induced tourism. Table 6.2 demonstrates these positions on the scale.

The positions that the three film studies have been given in the table are somewhat arbitrary, representing an overall impression of community

Table 6.2 Film-induced tourism on Doxey's Irridex model of host irritation

	Social relationships	*Power relationships*	*Possible position of film-induced tourism*
Euphoria	Visitors and investors welcome.	Little planning or formalised control. Greater potential for influence to be exerted by locals (not often taken).	Lord of the Rings (New Zealand)
Apathy	Visitors taken for granted. More formal relationships between hosts and guests.	Marketing is the prime focus of plans. Tourism industry lobby grows in power.	Sea Change (Barwon Heads, Australia)
Annoyance	Resident misgivings about tourism. Range of saturation points approached.	Planners attempt to control by increasing infrastructure rather than limiting growth. Local protest groups develop to challenge institutionalised tourism power.	Heartbeat (Goathland, UK)
Antagonism	Irritations openly expressed. Residents perceive tourists as the cause of the problems.	Remedial planning fighting against pressures of increased promotion to offset declining reputation of destination. Power struggle between interest groups.	

Source: Adapted from Doxey (1975).

attitudes towards visitors from a visitor's viewpoint. They are not static or homogenous, nor do all community members necessarily hold them. For example, there are residents in Goathland who range from being antagonistic towards visitors, moving right along the scale back to enthusiasm. The very nature of the communities being studied adds complexity to Doxey's simple model, introduced in 1975. Since then, community planning has become a field in its own right, and has developed in terms of community consultation and empowerment. This point is examined further in the following chapter on community planning. Unfortunately, at times, those studying such phenomena fail to recognise such developments, a criticism supported by researchers such as Bramwell (2003).

A chronology of community meetings at Goathland, outlined later in this chapter, and the topics or issues they have attempted to address provides an enlightening insight into the complexities of communities and tourism, particularly something as amorphous as film-induced tourism.

The Effect of a Television Series on Local Communities: Barwon Heads and *Sea Change*

As demonstrated in earlier chapters, much of the information on film-induced tourism is anecdotal, and has been examined in countries with high population densities and correspondingly high numbers of domestic and international visitation, such as in the US and the UK. As noted in the introduction, in order to understand the phenomenon of film-induced tourism, it is important to compare this data with countries such as Australia and New Zealand that have lower population and tourist densities.

Research amongst residents of Barwon Heads (Australia) was undertaken using a mail-back questionnaire in March 2000, after the busy summer holiday season of late December to February, as well as numerous participant-observation site visits.

Community's perceived value of tourism

Three questions related to tourism in the region, covering the number of visitors that could stay at Barwon Heads at any one time (that is, the number of visitor beds), the average time visitors spend in the region, and individual expenditure for a single overnight stay. The aim of these questions was to probe the community's understanding of the scope of local tourism. This is particularly important as it is the residents who deal with visitors on a long-term basis. The results showed that the residents of Barwon Heads believe that fewer tourists stay longer and spend more in their town than actually do.

The 'people in the street' appear to have adopted similar measures of community and personal well-being as the economic rationalists (particularly all levels of government), ignoring aspects of civic engagement, community pride and a sense of achievement as community strength indicators. Nevertheless, it is precisely the more intangible community indicators that are being considered by social researchers and planners who have recognised the limitations of assessing communities purely on economic grounds. An example of this is the broad range of benchmarks established by the Oregon Progress Board for their *Oregon Shines Project* which is being used extensively in Australia as a basis for establishing community indicators (Oregon Progress Board, 1999). These include economic performance, education, civic engagement, social support, public safety, community development and environment, and are taken up in Chapter 7. This aspect is also noted when analysing social representations in the next section.

Residents' attitudes to *Sea Change*: Some common social representations

One of the main aims of this research project was to identify the various attributes of those within the Barwon Heads community who hold similar attitudes and representations towards film-induced tourism, represented by the television series *Sea Change*. In this way, various groups or stakeholders can be identified that may be otherwise overlooked using a more traditional segmentation method. Social representations have been distinguished by identifying recurring themes, as outlined in Tables 6.4 to 6.7. The variables of age, gender, average length of residency in the town, whether coming from a city or not, home ownership status and whether tourism featured in the respondents' top three preferred industries for the town were found to define groups within a range of representations.

It should be noted that the same person might have a range of different and at times contradictory social representations. For example, parents who have invested in a holiday house may see the increased tourism and higher profile of Barwon Heads as advantageous from the investment point of view, but detrimental to the future aspirations of their children (who may be trying to save a deposit to purchase their own property). This is a common flaw in the analysis of much psychographic-related material, where it is assumed that people belong to only one psychographic group at a time, though this is rarely the case.

To illustrate this point, take Plog's (1974) well-accepted psychographic typology of allocentric and psychocentric personalities, which he describes as segments of a population bell-curve. Such a model does not allow for simultaneous, multiple representations from each extreme of the curve. For example, as a tourism academic, I am personally interested in interacting with local communities and immersion in their cultures while travelling (allocentric). Yet, as a professional who works long hours, I would love to relax in a resort where I do not have to even make a decision (very psychocentric). Such interests and desires exist simultaneously, and while I might therefore be considered to belong in Plog's 'midcentric' group of those who want some cultural immersion along with comfortable hotels at the end of the day (for example), this is not the case. We are still referring to the desire for total cultural immersion and safe comfortable travel coexisting in one person. This is not a desire for a compromise between the two, but two separate, seemingly contradictory, yet valid, desires.

A more appropriate diagrammatic illustration of Plog's typology would have some version of a reverse overlay that allows for concurrent conflicting desires and needs. Such complexities do not lend themselves well to traditional models, such as those of Plog (1974) and Doxey (1975), so we need to develop models that can encompass developments in tourism planning and understanding over the past 40 years. Some of these models are presented in this book, while researchers such as Butler and Hall (1998), Jamal and Getz (2000), Bramwell and Lane (2000a), Hall (2003), Leiper (2002), Timothy and Tosun (2003) and Sofield (2003) continue to build on current knowledge, and strive to further explain the complex field of tourism.

Social representation theory (see Pearce *et al.*, 1996) is a flexible, emic-oriented theory that can incorporate these 'anomalies' because it does not set rigid parameters for each social representation group, but merely describes them, perceiving them to be fluid. It recognises that conflicting representations can coexist, allowing them to be. This is the theoretical framework for the Barwon Heads' study outlined in the following sections.

Representation clusters

Nine groupings of Barwon Heads' residents with similar social representations and concurring aspects have been identified. They have been labelled according to their overriding stance, namely 'Good for Traders' (economic benefits), 'Good for Tourism', 'Raises Profile and Pride', 'Good for Property Sales', 'Bad for Property Purchase', 'Flash in the Pan' (fiction – Barwon Heads is not Pearl Bay, so will not last), 'Don't Crowd Me', 'Steady as She Goes!' (the need for careful planning) and 'Retain Village Atmosphere'. The model in Figure 6.1 takes these stances and posits their social representation on a three-dimensional axis of average length of residency, ex-city dweller and listing tourism as a top three preferred industry, which are the main variables that differentiate them from the entire sample and population.

The model shows that two groups of representations, A (4 and 6) and B (1, 8 and 9), are clustered in a common region on all three axes. The proximity of the members in these clusters could have rendered them invisible to standard research methods, yet they exist as quite separate representations and can certainly influence and impact on the Barwon Heads community. The differences between the actual social representations in the

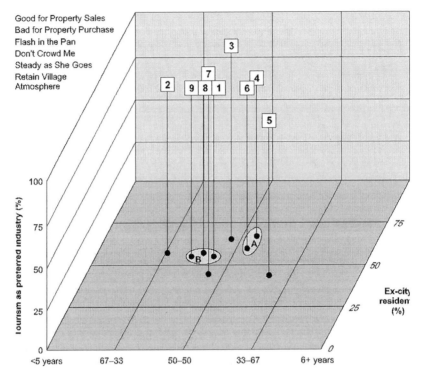

Figure 6.1 Social representations regarding film-induced tourism within clusters of the Barwon Heads residential community

clusters suggests that we are seeing evidence of contradictory representations held by the same people or person, which supports the aforementioned concept that a person can hold contradictory beliefs or attitudes. In particular, cluster A represents one positive and one negative attitude, suggesting that while this group recognises some benefits from *Sea Change* in terms of property prices, they are limited, short-term and temporary (a 'flash in the pan').

Cluster B is a little more complex, with three representations in this group, indicating that they see tourism as important (at least for the traders), yet desire to retain the town's village atmosphere. This is contradictory in so far as the benefits to traders go; however, the third representation – careful planning for tourism and other development – can be seen as a proposed solution from this group. It is tempting to read a lot into this cluster, and while it is speculative, the stance outlined here has been found to exist in the town through the findings of three years of participant observation. Around 60% come from a major city and are slightly shorter-term residents. Consequently, we have a group who may have first come across Barwon

Heads as a visitor, recognising the role that traders play for visitors and tourists (and vice versa).

The stances represented by numbers 2, 3, 5 and 7 are not clustered, being quite separate social representation groups. Numbers 3 and 5 are of particular interest because of their differing preferences for tourism in the town. Number 3, 'Raises Profile and Pride' has an extremely positive view of tourism, with the highest response rate of all the representations and has a higher female representation of 73% compared with 66% of the entire sample, and 52% of the population, as well as those who more recently lived in an urban centre. Recognition of the importance of intangible aspects of a community's well-being (such as pride) is often attributed to women, who tend to view such aspects more favourably. However, these intangibles have now been accepted by community planners as crucial. This is taken up in the community planning section in Chapter 7.

The other group that rates tourism highly is the group (number 2) that sees *Sea Change* as being 'Good for Tourism'. This is an identifiable representation group that stands out because just over half are from a major city, more recently arrived residents with slightly less than 75% support for tourism as an important, viable industry for the town. In contrast, those with the attitude/belief that *Sea Change* has a negative effect on home purchase can be distinctly grouped (representation number 5) as longer-term residents, the majority of whom previously lived outside major cities. This group has a relatively low view of tourism for the town. This group also has a lower home-ownership rate than the entire sample (78% compared with 83%), even though it is still high. The predominance of home ownership in the town reflects the ability, prior to the prices escalating, of residents in towns such as Barwon Heads to embrace the 'Great Australian Dream' of owning their own homes. Australian Bureau of Statistics figures show 74% owning or buying in the town, with the percentage of permanent tenants well below the national average of 32% (La Trobe University, 2001).

The final representation, number 7, relates to concerns about crowding and congestion in the town. This group comprises slightly more recent residents, with more than 50% coming previously from a rural or small town environment. Even though they are concerned about crowds, they still prefer tourism to many other industries – another group with contradictory attitudes.

So, what do these representations 'mean' in terms of film-induced tourism and community planning? These results have identified representations that may not have been obvious until it was too late, resulting in a fragmented, hostile community, as occurred to some extent at Barwon Heads, especially in relation to development issues. This issue is partly addressed below when looking for a common vision, and is considered in more detail in the next chapter.

The retail community: Local traders

In 2002, the traders remained ambivalent about the impact of *Sea Change*, but agreed that it had 'put Barwon Heads on the map' and that more people were stopping in the town rather than just passing through (or bypassing it). Locals generally appeared tolerant and even happy with the increased numbers of visitors; however, one commented that she hated the extra noise in summer.

In 2015, the general feeling of the traders, as outlined by Bernard Napthine, longstanding President of the Barwon Heads Traders Association was that there was a sense that, while *Sea Change* had provided a much needed focus and image for the town, the effect was no longer as evident as it had been. Napthine commented that it was rare for anyone to refer to the series when visiting (personal interview, 2015). One reason for this may be that, if one is a fan, it is now easy to access information via the internet, which was not as prevalent 15 years ago. Sites such as the Internet Movie Database (IMDb) list the filming locations, while review sites such as TripAdvisor and even personal blogs are easily accessible, often providing greater detail, information and insight for a fan than previously. The following extracts from TripAdvisor illustrate this and relate to visits in 2013, 2014 and 2015:

> *'Perfect location for "Sea change" nuts'*
> Reviewed 17 April 2015
> My wife and I are 'Sea Change' nuts so it was a particular pleasure to spend four nights in Barwon Heads. We watched ten episodes of 'Sea Change' while we were there! Even if we hadn't been 'Sea Change' fans, a beach house next to the beach at the Barwon Heads Caravan Park is a very peaceful place to spend a few days holiday. ...
> Stayed April 2015
> TripAdvisor http://www.tripadvisor.com.au/Hotel_Review-g552135-d2627208-Reviews-Barwon_Heads_Caravan_Park-Barwon_Heads_Victoria.html

> *'Feeling like Laura Gibson'*
> Reviewed 11 October 2014
> As my title indicates, I am a massive Sea Change fan. So finally in late September I stayed in one of the beach houses at Barwon Heads Caravan Park. It was exactly how I imagine it would be. Walks along the beach, sitting on the veranda, enjoying the views, relaxing, reading and just being. It was just magic.
> Stayed September 2014, travelled as a couple
> http://www.tripadvisor.com.au/ShowUserReviews-g552135-d2627208-r233703525-Barwon_Heads_Caravan_Park-Barwon_Heads_Victoria.html#

'Not "Laura's Cottage" but "The Boathouse" was a better choice in the end.'
Reviewed 14 May 2013
On a 'Sea Change' nostalgia trip, dearly wanted to stay in two-bedroom
Laura's Cottage. We were encouraged to take 'The Boathouse' next door
as we needed only one bedroom. Disappointed at first but after day one,
no such feeling. A superb view of the river, Bob Jelly Bridge across to Port
Deakin and Diver Dan's boat shed, now a wonderful restaurant.
Stayed April 2013, travelled as a couple
http://www.tripadvisor.com.au/ShowUserReviews-g552135-d2627208-
r160640675-Barwon_Heads_Caravan_Park-Barwon_Heads_Victoria.html#

Consequently, there is not such a need to discuss it with traders who
may not necessarily have been there when the series was being screened.
Certainly the caravan park's signage still notes that it is the 'home of Sea
Change' and as can be seen from the comments above, it still attracts fans.

A common vision?

Two representations in particular indicate a strong view held by many
people in the town, namely representations 8 and 9, 'Retain Village
Atmosphere' and 'Steady as She Goes!' These representations, when combined, comprise 54% of the entire sample, which is highly significant considering that the actual representations have been obtained from the open-ended
questions only. The other characteristics of this combined representation are
evenly spread along the entire sample, with a few minor differences, such as
older people and women being more highly represented. Even so, the differences are not significant, so it can be assumed that this could form a common
vision for the town.

Such a vision is essential when community planning processes are
applied, and is discussed in more detail in Chapter 7, where the findings
outlined in the preceding chapters are combined to assist and illuminate the
process. It is interesting to note that *Sea Change* itself celebrates such a village
atmosphere and community and condemns unsympathetic development,
and much of the storyline is devoted to the prevention of inappropriate
development, such as tunnels, theme parks, marinas and shopping malls.
This vision and its reflection in the storyline are taken up in the discussion
of destination marketing.

During the course of the three-year investigation into film-induced tourism at Barwon Heads, leaders in the community who had particular professional and personal interests in the phenomenon (as well as representing
their respective groups) were identified and spoken to on numerous occasions in an informal manner, as well as being formally interviewed. Those
interviewed included the executive director of Geelong Otway Tourism, the
president of the Barwon Heads Traders and Tourism Association, the

manager of the Barwon Coast Committee of Management, and one of the proprietors of At The Heads restaurant. Many have been contacted again in 2015 for an update on their professional opinions, with their comments noted where relevant.

Of interest in this section are the comments made and opinions expressed regarding the community and its response to tourism in general and film-induced tourism in particular, as well as the effect of *Sea Change* on Barwon Heads and current community issues. All of the groups represented believe that the series placed Barwon Heads 'on the map', and that the series actually gave the town an identity. They all also noted the increase of visitors all year round, crediting *Sea Change* for creating the interest, and expressing the belief that people were initially encouraged by *Sea Change* to visit Barwon Heads (usually on a day trip), then returned for a longer visit as they recognised the extent of things to do in the region. The importance of such awareness-raising should not be underestimated (yet often is).

All of those interviewed noted the revitalisation of the Barwon Heads shopping area into a tourism-focused area, and the Traders Association acknowledged that this has reversed the business flow from Barwon Heads to nearby Ocean Grove, with people from there now coming over to visit the restaurants and cafés. This is a pertinent observation, as much has been said (especially by residents) about the lack of basic services at Barwon Heads, such as banks, a butcher and a greengrocer, yet few have noted the significance of the Ocean Grove visitors. This is not surprising as it impacts dramatically only on the traders, not on the residents. On the negative side, petty thieves now come over from Ocean Grove owing to the lack of a police presence in Barwon Heads. An equally plausible or additional explanation for the petty thieving is that there is more to steal in houses and cars at Barwon Heads because of the increasing sociocultural demographic of the town.

Residents also commented on the need for beautification of the main street and the lack of parking as current community concerns, and the Traders Association explained that the nature of the businesses (cafés) means that people are staying longer in the on-street parking places, which results in lower turnover of vehicles and fewer free spaces. Issues regarding the cost of housing and rate of development were also mentioned, especially the preponderance of medium-density dwellings now being built close to the river.

While a few of the interviewees commented that the limited range of accommodation available in the town places limitations on the development of tourism, especially the mid- to up-market range, the Geelong-Otways Tourism Association noted that this was consistent with the *Sea Change* image, stating that people could stay on other parts of the Peninsula, such as in Queenscliff, which is only a 15-minute drive from Barwon Heads.

While *Sea Change* has not been the sole influence on the town, it is evident that it arrived at a serendipitous moment, when Barwon Heads was 'ready to take off', and appears to have facilitated and accelerated its development.

Developments in Community Responses to Film: Warrnambool and *Oddball*

The filming of the movie *Oddball* (2015), based on a true local story and briefly outlined in Chapter 4, reflects a shift in support for film and tourism in a slightly larger coastal town not far from Barwon Heads – the community is highly supportive and very excited about future tourism opportunities. Even so, there are those who remain sceptical. Many are considering how to deal with increased visitation, especially in terms of the impact on the local environment and the real-life work of the Maremma dogs on which the movie is based. As they need to 'embed' with the creatures they protect, they rarely bond with humans, yet these dogs have had a great deal of contact with humans during the filming as well as in terms of educational programmes they also assist with.

Peter Abbott, the Tourism Manager and Maremma dog handler, has expressed some concern regarding people wanting these dogs as pets, and is at pains when introducing people to them to stress that they are working dogs and do not make good pets. When I met Eudy and Tula (not their working names) while they were 'resting' on a local farm, they were overjoyed to see Peter, who commented that they were expecting some food; nevertheless, one of them continued to patrol the fence line rather than engage with us after the initial excitement.

As well as the movie, National Geographic filmed a five-part documentary that focuses on issues raised in the film, screening it on television the week before the movie's premiere. The five documentaries are themed around issues brought up by the movie, namely *Real Oddball*, *Little Penguins*, *The Maremma*, *Predators* and *Warrnambool*, the final one including a discussion on the impacts of film on tourism. My concerns regarding this becoming too popular for Warrnambool were shown in an interview I did for the series, and after seeing the movie (which I hadn't seen at the time of being interviewed) one that I remain primarily concerned with.

When a small group of Warrnambool residents were surveyed in relation to their attitudes towards the tourism potential and possible impacts of the movie *Oddball*, some interesting comparisons and contrasts soon became evident. While the sample size was too small to compare with the Barwon Heads *Sea Change* survey on which it was based, some of the additional comments are worth noting here. I am not going to draw conclusions from these comments and this survey; however, there are some good comments and indications that will be studied further in a long-term research project.

Supporting my overall impression that there is a greater understanding of the potential and role of film-induced tourism, one respondent noted:

> We rely on tourism. While we would continue to survive without the increased tourism the movie will create, we would be foolish not to take advantage of what it generates.

However, there remain those who do not see any longevity, illustrating that some opinions have not changed in the 15 years since the *Sea Change* study:

> I see the film a short term impact but not long term…

One respondent who volunteers at the penguin count noted:

> The island holds a special place in my heart so I hope that if *Oddball* is successful, which I hope it will be, that the preservation of the island, the penguins and the dogs remains the number one priority over the tourism trade.

This was a common sentiment reflected in comments from other respondents about the need to protect the beaches and natural environment and not have tourism development in these areas. However, what I increasingly find is that when those directly affected (in this case, the local community) by tourism are involved, they can often provide excellent, workable suggestions on dealing with some of the issues that may arise:

> Perhaps have people who have been involved in the program be scheduled to give a talk or something along those lines at Flagstaff Hill on particular days so that those interested in *Oddball*, particularly tourists, can gain unique insight in the 'behind the scenes' of the project without going to the island.

This comment about 'behind the scenes' experiences reflects elements of the theme park model introduced in Chapter 8, reinforcing the desire to experience something 'backstage' that cannot be easily experienced by the casual visitor. However, as with many communities, there is a sense of frustration with tourism planning at the local government level:

> Plan, implement, check and re-plan. Don't do the usual Warrnambool thing and just plan it once and let it run.

This is a key point, and one not just seen in Warrnambool – time and again researchers have noted this issue. Keeping the above comments in mind, I was very interested to visit Warrnambool again for some participant observation research, which I was able to do at the time of the pre-release screening of the movie.

Community screening at Warrnambool (13 September 2015)

I was fortunate to be invited to attend the pre-release screening of *Oddball* at Warrnambool, which gave me the chance to get a feeling for those most closely involved with the movie and its legacy.

On the highway coming in to Warrnambool, there is a large sign 'Welcome to Warrnambool, the Home of *Oddball*' with photos of the dogs and the movie. It struck me as a proud statement and announcement that film tourists are welcome, particularly as the signs were up before the movie was released. For the past few weeks, media reports had been everywhere, from commercial television slots on at least two of our four free to air television channels, commercial as well us national public radio interviews, the National Geographic documentary series, and many online previews. After such a build-up, I was relieved to find that I thoroughly enjoyed the movie and can see families in particular really enjoying it.

On the evening of the local screening, the local cinema was booked out, with a little over 400 people attending, complete with red carpet and local media. The leading actor, Shane Jacobson, the director, Stuart McDonald, and the writer, Peter Ivan, introduced the movie and had a long discussion afterwards, welcoming the inspiration for the movie, the real-life Swampy Marsh. The feeling in the cinema was one of great warmth and a high sense of pride. I sat next to two volunteers from the Flagstaff Hill Maritime Village where the Maremma dogs live and where much of the filming was done. They were delightful women who were looking forward to welcoming *Oddball* visitors to town. As long-time residents (one is 92 years old), they definitely could see the benefits of film tourism to the town and the lives of many, much like the longer-term residents in the Barwon Heads study.

The manager of my hotel, which is close to the film sites, supports the tourism potential, but also agrees that a major issue could be the problem of people trying to get over to Middle Island. When walking around there, many people were swimming near to the island (but not trying to get over there). There were also some tourists from Japan, and again I expect this movie to do particularly well in the Asian markets; Asian tourists already visit the region to see the iconic Great Ocean Road (featured in the movie), but rarely stay overnight. What this movie has the potential to do is encourage them to stay overnight in Warrnambool to have a more in-depth experience, with the opportunity to 'meet the Maremmas' and possibly take a guided visit to Middle Island. However, this will add to the potential of people trying to get on to the island itself. This will need careful monitoring, but, as Peter Abbott explained, the local community is passionately engaged with the island and its true story, not only volunteering to monitor the penguins, but also informing the authorities if they see people on the island. This engagement could enable a potentially disastrous situation (for the penguins and tourists) to be appropriately patrolled.

In an attempt to reduce the impact and demand for people to visit Middle Island, Peter Abbott has developed a range of Maremma and penguin-based experiences and activities that visitors can have at the maritime village rather than go to the island.

Some thoughts on the tourism potential of *Oddball*

In the National Geographic documentary, I made the point that a true story does not really impact tourist interest any more than fiction, as it is the emotional story that has the greatest effect; but on further consideration, and after experiencing the manner in which the true and fictional stories have been used, there are some aspects of having a true story that do help with tourism, namely:

- Being a true story, there are already 'sites' for tourists to visit – they do not have to be constructed;
- Also there are opportunities for extended and 'cross' promotion with other activities, such as penguin and other native wildlife protection, the Maremma (and other) protector dogs; these opportunities provide a wider public relations effect (such as celebrity vets on television, and the National Geographic documentaries).

Furthermore, in previous studies I have noted a series of success factors for film-induced tourism, which the movie seems to meet, as outlined in Table 6.3.

At this early stage, and with the limited research I have done, I do feel that *Oddball* has met all of these elements, so I expect that there will be a strong tourism effect here, and one that will be primarily positive. Anecdotally, after the first few days of screening, people were contacting Flagstaff Hill Maritime Village in Warrnambool wanting to come and visit to meet the Maremmas.

Longevity will be the next question, and while there is not the ongoing exposure that a television series such as *Heartbeat* (1992–2010) had, there are plans to keep leveraging the film for some time. The stuffed toy Maremma dogs are a great Christmas gift, along with other approved merchandising items as will the DVD be when it is released.

Table 6.3 Film-induced tourism success factors and their status in Warrnambool

Success factors	Status
Matching the markets for film and tourism	Families and Asians are both markets for the region, and while the movie is primarily aimed at the 'Western' family market, it will also gain the interests of many Asian pop culture fans who love 'cute things'.
Support from the film company	The three production companies, Kmunications, The Film Company and WTFN Entertainment (who produced the National Geographic documentaries) appear to be supporting the tourism potential by enabling merchandising and promotional tie-ins to the Maremma project and tourism to occur.
Engagement with community	This was apparent at the pre-release screening, illustrating strong engagement during filming as most people there had been directly involved. When the extensive thank-you credits rolled, there was applause and thanks from the audience.
Local government support	The Maremma project is funded by the local government-funded tourism group, so there has been clear support. They also eased many of the issues encountered when filming, including the loss of business of traders when a main street had to be closed for filming.
Understanding of film tourism	It seems that there is a broad acknowledgement and understanding of the pros and cons of film-induced tourism throughout much of the community and local government. This will need to be monitored.
International distribution of the film	The movie secured a large global distribution agreement some months prior to release, which will enable it to get out to many international markets, unlike *Sea Change*.
Opening at an optimum time of year for maximum exposure to correct market	The movie opened in Australia a few days before a two-week spring school holiday break – perfect for the film and also for families who may look to visit the town during these or the summer holidays.

The Effect of a Long-Term Television Series on Local Communities: Goathland and *Heartbeat*

While *Oddball* tourism is yet to commence (at the time of writing), the effect of *Heartbeat* tourism on the residential community of Goathland has been continuing for over 25 years, receiving an enormous amount of media attention, as illustrated in the table of newspaper headlines in Chapter 5 (Table 5.5). As noted there, at times the media inflamed community attitudes by inflating the opinions of a minority. To illustrate this, a selection of the newspaper headlines from 1991 to 1996 along with the actual

Table 6.4 News headlines with a chronology of community meetings prior to the screening of the *Heartbeat* series

Year	Theme	Community response	Headline
1991			
October	Conservatism/ opposition/fear of change	Parish council agrees with complainants (later changes mind)	Village Row over TV Series Plan.
November	Positive social and economic benefits: Local pride at being 'chosen' as location	Original complainants (one couple) continue to raise concerns. YTV agrees to move the main location nearer Leeds. Some locals complain at loss of revenue. Parish supports idea of filming	TV Dream Off Air. Village Anger as TV is Forced Out.
December		Filming of first series – locals appear as extras	TV Intruders win Praise at Goathland.

community reaction from various public meetings convened by the North York Moors National Park Authority (NYMNPA) is shown in Tables 6.4 to 6.7. The tables and much of the ensuing discussion are based on the working notes and interviews with Bill Breakell, the NYMNPA Transport and Tourism Officer; they have also been confirmed by other studies, as discussed further at the end of this section.

In September 1991, the NYMNPA Transport and Tourism Officer received a phone call from a couple from Goathland expressing concern over the negative impacts of a proposal from Yorkshire TV (YTV) to film a five-part programme called *Aidensfield*. As the filming was on private land, used public rights of way and had support from neighbours, the NYMNPA had no power to intervene (Breakell, 1996). This marked the beginning of what was to become known as *Heartbeat*. The accompanying media reports are illustrated in Table 6.4.

Even at such an early stage, some residents were concerned about the filming, even though such concerns were publicly expressed by only one household. As noted later, YTV did not have plans for a long-term series, so the concerns may not have received the attention that, with hindsight, they possibly deserved. However, challenging the legality of filming in the national park was shown to be an ineffective strategy when the same complainants tried again in 1995.

The first *Heartbeat* series screened from April to June 1992, with some 13.5 million viewers. At that time, annual visitation to Goathland was estimated at 320,000 (Breakell, 1996). The figures were obtained through the use of an automatic traffic counter situated on the main route through the village.

Table 6.5 News headlines with a chronology of community meetings in the first two years of screening *Heartbeat*

Year	Theme	Community response	Headline
1992			
April	Finding problems: seeking solutions	NYMNPA asked to take action: Attended Parish Council meeting • concern over possible visitor pressure leads to additional meeting. Park looks at range of options: • extension of existing carpark • one-way system • additional carpark.	
June		No decisions made.	Cars Ban to Protect Moors Heartbeat Village
		Open meeting planned by NYMNPA: To take the form of community-led ideas being expressed and discussed by the community. Over 60 villagers turn up. Some unhappy with the 'process'.	Heartache as Visitors Choke Village
July	Search for a scapegoat	Some villagers walked out of a further community meeting – expected a more confrontational meeting; Others found 'no problems'.	TV Village Fury
September		Meeting format still attempting to empower all villagers – showed comments from first meeting to consider what would be best for the village. Some villagers (2) walked out 'expecting a real meeting'.	Heartbeat Meeting Anger Talking Tourism at Heartbeat Village
1993			
February		Plans for kerbing parts of the Common to combat erosion – concern expressed at 'urbanising' village.	
October	Moving together: identification of common needs and goals	NYMNPA proposed 4 coach bays as part of carpark improvements. New signposts more in keeping with the village ambience.	

Source: Breakell (1996).

Table 6.6 News headlines with a chronology of community meetings during 1994

Year	Theme	Community response	Headline
1994			
January	Pragmatism: recognition of limitation of resources and powers	YTV asked for financial assistance to alleviate traffic problems. Reports of positive economic and employment impacts to counter negative stories.	TV Firm Asked to Save Village. Heartbeat Breathes Life into Village Store
June		Continuing rival views regarding impact.	TV Crews not a Problem
July		Field carpark opened at other end of village. 'No Parking' signs placed on Common. Carpark opposed by neighbours and some traders. Welcomed by others as returning the Common to the sheep (who traditionally graze there).	Have a Heart – Townies Leave Us Alone
September		Parish Council meeting – police suggest that yellow lines are the only way to resolve parking problems.* Some residents claimed that there had been a depreciation of house prices due to tourism.	
December		Proposal to consider additional carpark at church end receives hostile reception from some neighbours.	Village Divides Over Parking

Notes: *Refers to painting of yellow, 'no parking' lines down the side of the roads.
Source: Breakell (1996).

By the second quarter of 1992, the effect of the popularity of the series was starting to become apparent, with the community generally expressing some concern and requesting help from the NYMNPA, as noted in the first line of Table 6.5.

The reactions of some villagers to the community meetings convened by NYMNPA indicate the level of frustration being experienced by some. As noted in the June and July notes in Table 6.5, many were looking for a scapegoat, and while the NYMNPA continued to consult and work towards consensus, it was difficult to 'blame' them. This is a common situation in the community planning process, and reflects not only frustration but also a general misunderstanding of the empowerment process of community planning as outlined further in Chapter 7.

Table 6.7 News headlines with a chronology of community meetings during 1995 and 1996

Year	Theme	Community response	Headline
1995			
January	Community tries to regain control	Objections to coach parking plans and yellow lines. Residents association formed on the 'no coach park and yellow lines' platform.	Rebellion by Heartbeat Villagers
April		Coach operators leaflet produced by NYMNPA and police.	
June		Carpark works commence – no provision for coaches at the Parish Council's request (NYMNPA plans allow for future change of heart!).	
July		Coach bay proposed by NYMNPA, but village cannot agree on location – hostile letters.	
		Parish Council asks for NYMNPA to reinstate plans for coach area in carpark.	
		Kerbing works becoming more accepted – may restrict spread of winter salt and saline run-off.	
		Request for parking restrictions (yellow lines) in village. Proposals agreed and detailed scheme drawn up.	
September		Parking restriction proposals agreed by Parish Council, Duchy, NYMNPA, police and Highways.	
	Back to basics? Opposition groups re-form	One resident questions the 'legality' of filming in the village without sanction from NYMNPA, who responds that it is legal. Residents claim their freedom of movement is curtailed when filming is taking place.	
1996			
January		Some residents oppose parking restrictions as a blot on the village and drive traditional visitors away – campaign launched.	We Don't Want Your Yellow Lines*
February		County Highways receives petitions and letters re parking. Three distinct views: (1) Parking restrictions opposed; (2) Parking restrictions too lenient; (3) Proposals meet village requirements.	

(*Continued*)

Table 6.7 (*Continued*)

Year	Theme	Community response	Headline
1996			
April		Tensions heighten between village and YTV with concern expressed over their use of the carpark.	
May		Parking on main road deterred by new kerbing – many using side roads.	
		Local opinion appears to be shifting away from support for Heartbeat.	
September		Residents surveyed by YTB and NYMNPA to establish local views.	

*Refers to painting of yellow, 'no parking' lines down the side of the roads.
Source: Breakell (1996)

The filming of the second series of *Heartbeat* began at Goathland in October 1992, and by October 1993 visitation had reached 480,000 per annum.

By 1994, while crowding in general is mentioned, it is the car parking issue that attracts most attention and contention. Villagers want more car-parks, but 'not in my backyard', consequently they are unable to come to an agreement. Eventually the existing carpark managed by the NYMNPA is redeveloped. There are also meetings and proposals for 'no parking' signs to be erected on the Common, which traditionally has sheep roaming and graz-ing on it – a strong element of the rural idyll.

The claim that housing prices had actually depreciated due to tourism (the reverse is more often the case, as in Barwon Heads) has been challenged as a 'media beat-up' (see Chapter 5). While prices did fall, this was common across the region, not just at Goathland, and the sample used was very small (Breakell, personal interview, 2003).

The fourth series screened on television in September 1994 and filming of the fifth series began in January 1995. In October 1995, the annual visitor figure was initially put at 700,000 but, after the automatic traffic counter data was analysed, this figure was revised to 1.1 million visitor days per annum. While the term 'visitor days' and 'visitors' are quite different, this represents a significant increase, and was supported with December's data, which came in at 1.19 annual visitors. As can be seen, these figures are a little fuzzy but, unlike at Barwon Heads where there are no traffic counts, the use of the automatic traffic counter provides some comparative data. With an increase from an estimate of 320,000 visitors in 1991 to 1.19 million in December 1995, the growth has been exponential. Interestingly, from 1973 to 1994, the actual number of parked cars on peak days (such as Sundays in August) dropped slightly, as shown in Figure 6.2 (Breakell, 1994). The gaps in the data outlined in the figure are due to inconsistent collection times.

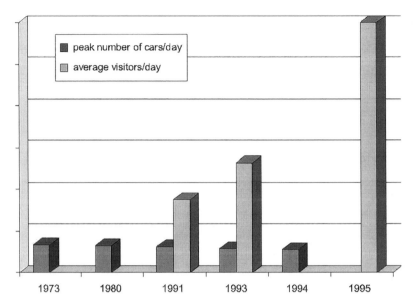

Figure 6.2 Number of cars and visitors to Goathland

When the number of parked cars on the busiest days is compared with the average visitor numbers (which assumes an equal number of visitors every day of the year), the results raise questions regarding the methods visitors use to get to Goathland, and demonstrate the significance of public transport such as the railway and bus network. In 1995 the North Yorkshire Moors Railway, a volunteer-operated tourist railway, carried 276,000 passengers (YTB, 2001). The numbers would be even more startling if actual visitor numbers were available for the days the parked cars were monitored, as they would be higher than the averages used here. Nevertheless, Figure 6.2 does illustrate that either people are crowding into their vehicles or using other forms of transport to get to Goathland.

In March 1996 the Goathland Exhibition Centre was opened at the 'church end' of the town – one of the sites mooted for an additional car park. As noted in Chapter 5, this attraction was eventually moved to the nearby seaside resort town of Whitby and renamed the *Heartbeat* Experience. This was mainly for commercial reasons, as there was insufficient passing trade without the car park at that end of the village, even though 3465 vehicles passed over the automatic traffic counter in the village on Easter Sunday! The car parking issue remains the most significant and divisive issue in the village.

Time was lost waiting for residents to 'come around' and agree to many of the parking restrictions, such as the yellow lines, and raises the question as to whether community consultation is the best process in the long term. Once again, this issue is discussed further in Chapter 7.

The Goathland community and film-induced tourism: A never-ending story

It is often lamented that a community is 'fragmented', but Breakell makes a strong point in support of such fragmentation when he notes that the:

> cohesion of community implies static community; there are many different sectors within the community, some families showing allegiance to more than one side, and some switching allegiance on different issues with the passage of time. (Breakell, 1996: 10)

This point about community dynamism is not only valid, but also extremely important – by seeing a 'community' as a single identity we run the risk of ignoring important sectors, opinions and priorities. This point is noted and reinforced by experienced community and tourism planning commentators such as Prentice (1993) Jamal and Getz (1995, 2000), Jopp (1996) and Singh *et al.* (2003b).

A survey of resident attitudes undertaken by the Yorkshire Tourism Board and NYMNPA in late 1996 did little to raise any additional issues to those identified in Breakell's working notes, the source for the preceding tables and much of the discussion, which were still evident during my site visit seven years later in 2003. Research and focus group studies undertaken by Mordue (1999, 2001) also support Breakell's notes. Confirmation from a more structured research process, other research and the site visit serve to triangulate and verify those notes. Not surprisingly, the YTB/NYMNPA survey found that

> [i]t was almost universally agreed that the actual technical process of filming was not a major problem. The main problems were the sheer volume of visitors attracted to the village and the issues related to this. (YTB & NYMNPA, 1997)

The stated aim of that survey was to ascertain community opinions and attitudes, and it did not attempt to come up with any proposals or recommendations. This is disappointing, as it has become clear that the community needs and wants some direction.

The wide-ranging views of the community demonstrate that models such as Doxey's Irridex (1975) are too simple to apply to real-life, dynamic communities that consist of real-life, dynamic people with dynamic opinions. Whilst some residents' attitudes followed the model from enthusiasm to resentment, others were 'anti' from the start and stayed that way. Still others became supportive of film tourism as some of the measures to cope with the parking issues were implemented.

Post *Heartbeat*...

Since the series stopped filming any new episodes in 2009 it has had continual re-runs on cable and free-to-air television around the world. However, as noted in Chapter 4, it was not possible to purchase any DVDs (or videos) of the series until after that time, which was primarily due to music copyright issues. So, not being able to view the 1992 episodes until some 20 years later (I was not able to get the DVDs in Australia until 2012) potentially reduced the ongoing impact of the series; however, it has now provided an additional fillip to its popularity, giving the series and film sites additional longevity. It is not unreasonable to expect another 20 years of interest in Goathland from *Heartbeat* fans; furthermore as the residents have become somewhat resigned to the phenomenon, and many actually came to the region because of the series, we can see a further, more positive shift in their understanding and acceptance of this form of tourism.

The Effect of Film on a National Community: New Zealanders, *The Lord of the Rings* and *The Hobbit*

As already noted, the majority of the sites used for *The Lord of the Rings* movies are in national parks which, unlike the UK national parks, do not have any current residential properties or villages in them, which makes the effects of the series on the host community quite different. With host communities outside many of the actual areas that film fans are visiting, they are not as easily recognisable, and interactions are not as clear-cut. When considered at a national level, issues of pride and economic development are predominant. Even if there were some crowding at certain sites, this would be averaged out when taking an overall, national view.

As noted and discussed in Chapters 4 and 5, the only significant *The Lord of the Rings* site that has not been returned to its natural state is the village of Hobbiton, which was built on private farmland in the rich agricultural region of Waikato in the North Island, a few hours' drive south of Auckland. The nearest town, Matamata, demonstrates enthusiasm towards capitalising on this commercial link, with many of the shops decorated with *Hobbit* memorabilia. The local community of the town also appears to welcome this, and on my visit demonstrated a high level of pride. This is a region that has not previously experienced high levels of tourist visitation, nor have they (yet) had to deal with issues of loss of privacy and crowding. Owing to the relatively lower levels of tourism in New Zealand, this may not be a significant issue. However as this is the only tangible site for *Lord of the Rings* fans, it may well be the current infrastructure and accommodation cannot support increased tourism. Local planning authorities need to consider these issues before they become evident, as illustrated by the case of Goathland.

Chapter 8 describes the event of the world premiere in Wellington for the final film in the *Lord of the Rings* trilogy, *The Return of the King* in 2003. What was most evident during the days leading up to and during the premiere was the enormous sense of pride felt by a town that may be the country's capital, but has always run second to Auckland in terms of image and visitation.

As with Australia, New Zealand has traditionally seen itself through the gaze of others, and it is still evident that the country desires to be recognised by those others as being part of their world. This is particularly reflected in the way the media presented its stories on the world premiere, continually referring (and deferring) to international opinion (and praise) on its success. In order to demonstrate to New Zealanders that they were being recognised on a world stage, New Zealand television news even presented media reports from Australia and the US.

There were hundreds of local New Zealand media reports about the movie premiere, with all of the country's newspapers and television news running *Lord of the Rings* stories in their premiere positions (front page, lead stories and so on). A very rough, quick internet search with Google.com produced 3710 New Zealand websites with *Lord of the Rings* reports on the premiere, and a total of 94,000 globally. Table 6.8 outlines the headings of a representative selection of New Zealand media reports leading up to and just after the world premiere of *The Return of the King*. Their relevance to tourism is illustrated by a tick (☑), with the strength of the tie-in shown by the increasing number of ticks. However, all of the reports contribute to presenting an image of New Zealand to itself and to rest of the world. There do not seem to be media reports on any negative elements of *Lord of the Rings* tourists or tourism, which indicates that New Zealand remains in the 'euphoria' stage on Doxey's Irridex, as proposed at the beginning of this chapter. A concerted long-term community planning effort is required to make sure that this is how it stays, which seems to have been realised when *The Hobbit* was proposed, developed, filmed and screened.

During my 2014 site visit, when the final of the three *Hobbit* movies was released, I found that the traders and others I spoke informally to at Matamata were very happy with the added services and facilities that tourism has brought to the town, including some funky bars and cafés, which were not there on my earlier visits. In some ways, the town is removed from the intrusive aspects of film-induced tourism that Goathland experienced, as the filming was actually done on a private property some 15 minutes' drive outside the town.

Table 6.8 New Zealand media reports November–December 2003

News headline	Tourism	News headline	Tourism
Fans give full navel salute as stars fly off		Peter Jackson up there with Steven Spielberg	✓
Orlando's mother blooms with pride		World premiere frenzy	
Dominion Post premiere day pictures for sale		Mortensen gives something back to Wellington at Rings premiere	
Rings party shows off the best of both worlds	✓✓	Unknown actor plays role as security guard	
Rings fans swoop on Net offerings		Tourists visit Rivendell set	✓✓✓
Hail saint Peter, lord of the ringing tills	✓✓	Wellington catches the fever and the tills are ringing	✓✓
Premiere planners 'deserve an Oscar'		The end of a journey	
Preciousss moments with Serkis		Rings concert reaches fever pitch	
Nonstop gushing on the red carpet		Rings star turns fans on to poetry	
Teenage soprano wows Rings composer		Inauspicious beginning leads to Rings partnership	
Don't give up your day job – Jackson's workmates		Hobbit actors share special Rings brotherhood	
Capital basks in Rings success	✓✓	Jackson nervous as premiere looms	
The night of their lives		Red carpet show goes rolling on	
Lord of the Rings just the beginning	✓	Academy Award written all over it	
Rings day 'one out of the box'	✓	Stars arrive for premiere screening	
Bigger, bolder and more breath¬taking		Gollum seen at last in Return of the King	✓
Jumbo salute	✓✓	Hobbiton emerges from paint pot	✓✓✓
PM gives thumbs-up	✓✓✓	'Rings' finale set to cast spell	✓
Party fare fit for a king	✓	Double Trouble	

Some Concluding Comments on the Effect of Tourism on Communities

While *Sea Change* was extremely popular and attracted increased interest in Barwon Heads, it did not result in an unsupportable increase in tourism per se. Rather than a tool for evening out the town's seasonality, when

Heartbeat was first planned, it was to be a single, ten-part series and as such extremely unlikely to generate much (if any) tourism to the area (YTB & NYMNPA, 1997). It would not have been viable for YTV to invest in constructing costly sets for just one series. By the time the popularity and longevity of the series was recognised, the sites (and sights) of Goathland were too entrenched in the whole series. Some attempt was made to reduce some of the impacts, for example, a set was made of the interior of the hotel (a direct replica of the Goathland Hotel/Aidensfield Arms) for later episodes. However, the external filming had to remain.

The situation in New Zealand with *The Lord of the Rings* is different yet again, primarily owing to the national nature of the filming of the movie. The costs and benefits have been spread throughout the country. The effects have been primarily positive and continue to be reflected in the tremendous boost to the country's pride. The ensuing years have shown that there is longevity in such film-induced tourism, particularly if there is ongoing related filming and strong community support, along with an influential, enthusiastic champion in the form of Sir Peter Jackson, as discussed in Chapter 5.

One of the main problems facing planners when dealing with the prospect of film-induced tourism that is amply demonstrated in this chapter is that it is difficult to know how popular a film will be, and for how long. However, we now have increased evidence of the longevity of a number of film tourism enterprises and sites as well as identify a possible range of success factors through studying the successes and failures of film-induced tourism. To test this, I have applied them to the movie *Oddball*, and by the time this book is published and read, we may know if I have been correct in predicting its success.

Nevertheless, it remains important to consider the different level and type of effects, as in many ways they underline the need to define what 'community' we are referring to, as they are all quite different from one another, yet all fall under the umbrella of 'film-induced tourism sites' and can be seen around the world. In the next chapter, the issues introduced here are incorporated into the field of community tourism planning.

7 Film-Induced Tourism and Community Planning

Planning has traditionally taken a top-down approach, particularly where governments (which tend to be hierarchically structured) are concerned. Those in power, at the top (notionally, with significant influence), have tended to direct what others should be doing, which filters right down to the community level. As evidenced in the previous chapter, it is the local community that can bear the brunt of such planning, and is often left to find its own solutions. Such a situation creates not only resentment, but also fosters a culture of blaming others as well as a form of learned helplessness. This chapter looks at some developments in community planning that are working towards the notion of empowering community members, away from the traditional top-down approaches. Any consideration of community planning brings up issue of power (in terms of who actually possesses it) and power relations between the various actors. These developments are linked here with community *tourism* planning, with an in-depth look at community attitudes and representations relating to Barwon Heads and *Sea Change* (1998–2000). By comparing a range of cases I am able to present a model that looks at power relations between film makers and destinations.

Regardless of whatever community planning approach is adopted, there will be unexpected outcomes, such as those associated with the popularity of film-induced tourism. I suggest some solutions to being too popular, supported by examples from numerous communities that have had to deal with film-induced tourism.

Destination planners and tourism marketers work within a fragmented, multi-faceted industry that, in spite of over 30 years of academic exhortation for cooperation and integration, remains contentious and problematic. Murphy (1985), Gunn (1988) and Prentice (1993) supported the concept of integrated tourism, social and economic planning, proposing integrated planning models in a similar vein to the 1970s participatory planning movement in urban planning. Nevertheless, as pointed out by Jamal and Getz (1995: 87), '[a]chieving coordination among the government agencies, between the public and the private sector, and among private enterprises is a challenging task', which is supported in numerous more recent studies, including Dredge

(2006), Spenceley and Meyer (2012), Boley *et al.* (2014) and Gustafsson *et al.* (2014). Singh *et al.* support the concept of planning for community tourism, while recognising the sometimes-impossible expectations:

> Despite the prevailing trends, and considering the noble side of tourism, it is unlikely that tourism itself is bad, it is simply badly planned and managed. Although it is clear that tourism is not the root of global crises, its practitioners and researchers have been called upon, time and again, for collective action to revive its lost charm and vitality. (Singh *et al.*, 2003b: 4)

The term *community* is so widely used today that it has almost lost any true meaning, simply referring to an amorphous, generalised group of people, particularly when the term 'community consultation' is used. While communities can simply be a group of 'interested' people, if we look at the Latin root of them term, *communitas*, we get a better sense of what community really means. As explained in my book on community development, it 'refers to the very spirit of community' (Beeton, 2006a: iv), allowing us to have communities described by a common interest, belief, birth (as in families) or heritage, or by a certain level of authority as well as geographically (such as a valley or mountain range) or politically (towns and countries). Nevertheless, community planning generally refers to spatially defined communities of towns and regions, yet such prescriptive notions often ignore those who may not reside in these areas, but have a high level of connection to the place, such as regular (or even occasional) tourists. These people can also wield a high level of influence and must not be ignored in the planning process (Beeton, 2006a).

So, 'community' planning should be inclusive and participatory, aiming to incorporate the needs and wants of all actors – Murphy and Murphy (2001: 168) refer to it as a 'round table planning strategy'. According to the United Nations, community planning and development is a 'process designed to create conditions of economic and social progress for the whole community with its active participation' (cited in Moser, 1989: 81). Ife (1995: 137) describes the process of planning as 'the people of the community defining their needs and working out what has to happen to have them met, as well as how the existing services and resources can be coordinated and utilised to best effect'. Of course, applying such principles is far from 'simple'. Without such inclusiveness and active participation, the results could well disenfranchise members and disrupt community cohesion. Few communities are truly 'cohesive', hence the enormous extent and range of study being done in this field in order to develop a model that goes beyond describing what should happen in a perfect world. The central tenet of community planning and development is self-sufficiency and local control over change, with the actual process itself considered to be more important than the outcome (Jopp, 1996; Beeton, 2006a).

Kotler *et al.* follow the shift from the Keynesian community of the mid-20th century to a new economic era brought about, in part, by global competitive pressures, contrasting the key differences between the old and new economic eras. They claim that '[p]laces whose industries and firms operate according to the old economic era concepts are headed for hard times' (Kotler *et al.*, 1993: 10). The new era is reflected in the move towards inclusive community planning and development such as that proposed by Wilkinson (1991), who identifies four basic attributes of community development:

- purposive action;
- having a positive purpose;
- focus on efforts;
- being structure oriented.

Understanding the elemental bond of interaction among people in a community results in aims and objectives that become the purpose of community development. Such purpose is expressed in positive ways, in that the participants believe they are improving their lives and contributing to community well-being. Wilkinson reinforces the tenet that many of the benefits of community development are gained from participation, not just from the outcomes (Wilkinson, 1991).

The concept that 'trying' is more important than succeeding is embedded in the complexity of community development – by coming together with a positive purpose, Wilkinson believes that community well-being is enhanced, even if there is no conclusive 'success'. The final attribute, being structure oriented, reflects the development *of* the community as opposed to development *in* the community. This final point may seem anathema in the new economic era; however, 'structure' does not necessarily mean 'stricture' and can still be fluid and responsive to community needs.

This concept of structure and purposiveness is reflected in Rogers' (2001) identification of optimal community development actions that can be taken to increase community well-being. The first of these is to build community capacity to respond to changing needs through strengthening networks and community-based learning. The second option is to improve participation through cultural development; the third is to develop community-based indicators of progress; and the final one is triple bottom line auditing of community performance (Rogers, 2001).

Triple bottom line auditing is increasingly used in many corporate and government areas, but has only recently been adopted by the community planning field. The process takes an integrative approach that evaluates performance based on economic, social and environmental factors, in contrast to the prevalence of economic-rationalist assessments of the late 20th century economic era. Inherent in triple bottom line auditing is the concept of sustainability, which requires the community to:

> ...utilise nature's ability to provide for human needs without undermining its ability to function over time; ensure the well-being of its

members...empower people with shared responsibility, equal opportunity, access to expertise and knowledge, and the capacity to affect decisions which affect them; and consist of businesses, industries and institutions...which invest in the local community in a variety of ways. (Rogers, 2001: 137)

As part of being inclusive and participatory, commentators stress that effective community development and planning must be a bottom-up process. Bottom-up planning is central to any truly 'community' based programme, and has led to the growing interest in community-based performance indicators developed by the community itself through public meetings, focus groups and other inclusive methods. This is seen as part of the inclusive process that has already been noted as being of particular significance – spurring the community to create new visions and working relationships (Rogers, 2001).

Five stages can be identified in the development of community strategies, starting with establishing a vision for the future of the community, as illustrated in Figure 7.1. This is followed by a community stocktake of human, natural and built resources as well as cash flows, leading on to the community audit that examines and measures performance, and may result in a re-defining of the vision. Following this, goals and strategies can be developed, finishing with performance indicators, both internal and external. While many models include an implementation stage at the end of the cycle, in the model outlined in Table 7.1 aspects of 'implementation' are assumed to be integral to each stage of the process.

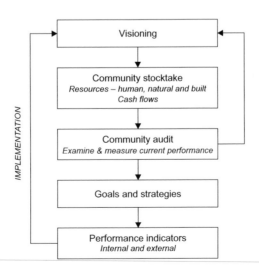

Figure 7.1 Overview of the stages in community planning

Table 7.1 Summary of issues and responses to film-induced tourism

United States

Intercourse *Witness*	Not sure what was meant – people do want to see the farm, but it's privately owned and doesn't look, like in the film.	Nearly 20 years ago. Many Amish not happy with the filming.		No!	State film commission agreed not to promote movies on the Amish. Some of the costumes used in the Amish Experience Theatre.		Most promotional material reminds visitors of privacy issues, especially not taking photos of the Amish people.
Mt Airy *Andy Griffith Show*	'The questions do not apply to Mt Airy'... (quote from respondent). *Questions were re-worded – no further response*						
Dyersville *Field of Dreams*	*No response*						

Australia

Barwon Heads *Sea Change*	More visitors in off-peak seasons.	Increased property prices & rents; Benefits only for traders, not for others who want to retain quiet, village atmosphere.	Increased sense of pride – put the town on the map.	No, resident resist such comparison.	Desire to increase parking in main street.	Public areas not possible.	Hardening and maintenance of tracks to sites in the caravan park.

In an ideal world, the process is cyclical, with regular reviews, audits and examination of the vision; however, maintaining the interest and limiting burnout of members remains a major practical issue. Embedded in each of these stages is the overriding requirement for community participation and consultation (see Ife, 1995; Jopp, 1996; Rogers, 2001; Murphy & Murphy, 2001).

When comparing community development and community *tourism* development, Jopp (1996) notes a significant difference in that many of the tourism initiatives have been driven by government through funding and facilitation expertise, rather than by the community. Not only was Jopp's article published over eight years ago (in a field that has seen much progress in the intervening years, as the new economic era has gained currency), her work has a particularly North American perspective that may be of limited relevance to Australia. Nevertheless, it is an important point to consider and keep in mind, especially in the current climate in Australia of limited and reducing government funding and focus on 'can do' communities – if community tourism development is reliant on government support, the realities of reduced funding may require a different approach. Jopp also notes that many community economic development projects arise from a crisis such as a factory closure, whereas community tourism projects arise from a perceived opportunity that presents itself, rendering community tourism development as having a particularly positive purpose.

Jopp is critical of a tendency towards the top-down, old economic era approach in community tourism development and also criticises it for being '...non-inclusive, focussing on business interests and mainstream historical, cultural and environmental groups, with no attempt to incorporate the disenfranchised groups in a community, in spite of such rhetoric' (Jopp, 1996: 477). Such criticism has been heeded by many initiators of the current community tourism planning schemes, where conscious attempts are being made to address such concerns. Jopp concedes that this has been the case in many areas where there are '...some excellent prescriptive community tourism models [but] they only focus on the visible and, to some extent, measurable aspects of the process...There is an assumption that all parties have an equal opportunity to participate' (Jopp, 1996: 478). This is another concern of today's community planners, yet in tourism major stakeholders are often excluded, particularly the tourists themselves. It has been argued in previous chapters that visitors, especially regular ones, are also members of the community they visit – partly because of the economic, social and environmental influence they can exert and partly because they possess a psychological sense of ownership.

The tendency of local government organisations to institute a community planning process then take an 'arms-length' approach may provide participants with a greater sense of ownership. However this can also reduce the chances of the policies developed by the community actually being accepted by local government (Jamal & Getz, 2000). In fact, local government is also a community member, and needs to be involved as such. These complexities and contradictions must be recognised and dealt with when moving from a top-down to a community-driven planning approach.

There is also a body of literature on 'collaborative tourism planning', which can be applied to community tourism planning. In essence, collaborative planning can be between two or more groups or stakeholders (as in partnerships), but there is general agreement that true collaboration must be inclusive of all relevant parties and interest groups (Bramwell & Lane, 2000a, 2000b), which is the basis of community planning. At times, the group instituting the collaborative process may not be the most appropriate to attain inclusion. For example, the politics of a conservation group may have a history of exclusion and confrontation with tourism operators. This was the case when the World Wide Fund for Nature (WWF) attempted to collaborate in the development of the Arctic Tourism Program, with some operators taking issue at the politics of the WWF and passively resisting through non-participation (Mason *et al.*, 2000).

While inclusion and equal representation are central to community and collaborative tourism planning, this is not an easy state to achieve. A shortfall in many community tourism publications (particularly 'how to' guides) has been the tendency to implicitly assume that people will have equal access to the process, which they do not (Reed, 1997; Hall, 2003; Ritchie & Crouch, 2003). Issues of power relations within a community, strength of voice, equity and identification of interest groups and differing social representations all contribute to the complexity of achieving a community consensus that can be acted on (Bramwell & Lane, 2000a, 2000b).

Hall considers calls for collaboration to be a response to the conflict among community members. 'Indeed, much of the recent burst of activity in the tourism literature regarding cooperation and collaboration in tourism destinations is a direct response to the need to find mechanisms to accommodate the various interests that exist in tourism development' (Hall, 2003: 100).

It is also taken as a given that an individual does not have sufficient power, and must cooperate with others, in order to influence the tourism process. While successful cooperative arrangements from the global alliances (such as airlines and hotels) down to politically-based community groups can wield enormous power, the power of the individual must also be acknowledged. Reed (1997) suggests that certain individuals can exert a great deal of power and influence, such as 'champions' of tourism like Tom Kershaw of *Cheers* fame, referred to in Chapter 2. Walt Disney himself, and now his entire corporation, is another example of the influence of individuals or companies. This influence often relates to power relations within a community that have been set long before tourism was considered.

Community-Based Tourism Strategies

Timothy and Tosun (2003) have summarised the main theories and paradigms of community and tourism planning, proposing a model that they refer to as the PIC (Participatory, Incremental, Collaborative/Cooperative) Planning Model. The model is process-oriented, and assumes that a sustainable product will be developed if adopted by destination communities and planners. The authors recognise that there are major obstacles to the model, noting that few advocates of community tourism planning highlight the very real implementation issues. Issues noted include inadequate representation, the varying traditions of power in communities (as reiterated by Hall, 2003), lack of awareness, time and money to undertake the process, and issues of peripherality. Many of these issues have been evident in the cases outlined in this book, in particular with the Barwon Heads research discussed in the previous two chapters.

Even though much of the community tourism development literature warns against communities relying on tourism as an economic saviour, analysts recognise that tourism can also benefit the community in other ways, such as conservation and community pride, and suggest methods to maximise this. What is disappointing is that some community development commentators regard tourism as solely an economic benefit that will automatically damage other facets of community well-being through commodification and loss of community control, without recognising the positive social effects (Ife, 1995). While the economic positivist stance of some promoters of tourism needs to be countered, and potential negative aspects recognised and dealt with, such blithe damnations demonstrate a lack of understanding of tourism and the community tourism planning processes that are gaining momentum, empowering communities to decide on their level and type of tourism. Two such cases are outlined below – one from Australia and the other from North America.

Kangaroo Island, off the southern coast of Australia, and the continent's third largest island, is popular as a wildlife-viewing destination for both international and domestic tourists. The island's economy is reliant on tourism and agriculture, with the former expected to grow at a rate between 8% and 10% per annum (Manidis Roberts Consultants, 1997). In response to residents' concerns over uncontrolled tourism development, a *Sustainable Tourism Development Strategy* was developed in 1995 by the Kangaroo Island Development Board. As part of the implementation of the strategy, consultants Manidis Roberts were contracted by the South Australian Tourism Commission to develop a tourism model for the island, which was to consider not merely ways to limit tourism impacts, but also ways to optimise tourism in a sustainable manner. The name for the model was itself carefully chosen, as it was recognised that the tourism industry had responded

adversely to models that might infer anti-growth and antibusiness senti-
ments merely through their names (such as Limits of Acceptable Change)
(Newsome *et al.*, 2002: 171). Consequently, the name chosen was the Tourism
Optimisation Management Model (TOMM). While this project was
prompted in a top-down manner from a government department, the
approach required holistic treatment of tourism and the community, establishing optimal conditions across economic, ecological and sociocultural factors as well as a series of benchmarks to measure the optimal conditions
identified by the community (Jack, 2000). There was understandable scepticism from certain areas of the community who saw the model as just another
expensive strategy, but there was overall support for the concept.
Complications arose when trying to establish a shared set of values (which
at the time of writing was still to be resolved) – a common problem experienced in vibrant communities.

The project was presented to the community as a form of long-term
'island insurance' in which they all played a role. As previously noted, the
process is as important as the outcome, and one of the recognised achieve-
ments of the TOMM process is that, in spite of the pockets of scepticism, it
made the residents and community groups consider the long-term future of
tourism as well as their own short-term needs. The outcomes of the project,
which is still in its formative years, include acknowledgement of the need to
articulate a set of values for the island, the establishment of core data-
collecting and monitoring programmes, sharing of information across agencies and a commitment from local agencies and groups to build a sustainable
funding source for the project (Jack, 2000). Once the project was established,
the South Australian Tourism Commission wanted to hand over funding
support to the community. This crucial transition phase is where such top-
down initiatives can fail, unless the community truly has ownership of the
scheme and is convinced of its benefits. Local funding has been found, but it
needs to be maintained for the long term.

One of the issues that islanders face is the cost of transport to their
island. In the case of Kangaroo Island, access is limited to expensive light
aircraft, an irregular passenger service and a regular vehicular ferry that, at
the time of writing, cost A\$202 return, with residents receiving a 20% dis-
count. Such a cost is formidable for day-trippers, automatically forcing the
length of stay to be at least two days, and often more. This places pressure
on the sensitive environment of the island, yet creates more opportunities to
gain economic and social benefits from visitors staying overnight, which can
ameliorate such environmental concerns.

Since 2002, visitor exit surveys have assessed the tourism experience on
Kangaroo Island against the indicators that were developed for the model.
The 2014 report of the model was able to identify which indicators were in
the range accepted by the community, along with those outside these levels.
For example, some of the economic indicators were not met, such as total

expenditure, which was below desired levels, but the number of visitors was within the optimum range. While the indicators relating to delivering an authentic and credible experience were met, the visitor satisfaction indicators were not, which is interesting in itself, but we do not have the space to consider the implications here, except to acknowledge that this knowledge enables the community, tourism operators and public managers to make decisions based on what the community sees as desirable (Climent, 2014).

The Kangaroo Island example deals with relatively high levels of established tourism, whereas other community tourism development programmes address the issues of introducing tourism to a region as a viable economic and social alternative. Of course, it is rare to find an area without any tourism; the case of Kangaroo Island is relevant for communities with low tourism levels and the potential to increase them. The simple fact that TOMM is still operational is credit to the commitment of all parties and ongoing funding of the project, demonstrating that, while challenging, effective and realistic community planning is possible.

The case of the Iowa Community Tourism Assessment model is one of many similar models being implemented around the world. What makes the Iowa one so interesting is that the process began in the 1980s, pre-empting the 'new economic era' of management and community development, and has the benefit of many years of development and refining.

In 1988, a community tourism conference concluded that a process was required for communities to realistically assess their tourism potential and determine associated costs and benefits (Western Rural Development Centre, c.1995). At the time, most tourism development 'guides' took a positivist, often boosterist stance, promoting tourism as the single most important community development option to pursue. As discussed throughout this book, tourism is not always the best option for a community, but is one of a range of options, and this was recognised by the multi-agency team formed to develop this community tourism assessment model. The model was tested over a two-year period by the community of Choteau in Montana, modified and then made widely available to other communities in the states of Alaska, Arizona and Nevada as well as Utah.

The process that was developed is in nine steps: Community Organisation, Visitor and Economic Profiles, Resident Attitude Survey, Visioning and Goal Setting, Tourism Marketing Basics, Attraction and Facility Inventory, Potential Project Identification, Initial Project Scoping and Impact Analysis (Western Rural Development Centre, c.1995). The process has been described in the *Community Tourism Assessment Handbook* published by the Western Rural Development Centre (c.1995). It provides practical suggestions on some of the most difficult aspects of community tourism planning, including methods to gain representative community input into the process – a central tenet of all community planning, but the most difficult to achieve. Consequently, the material developed by this project remains relevant and valid today.

The handbook emphasises that a community has a right (in theory at least) to refuse tourism, reflecting a move from the traditional positivist economic-rationalist stance of many community tourism proponents. However, in reality, communities rarely have a say in tourism, as illustrated by the cases of film-induced tourism, where tourists will often come to see a famous site regardless of the immediate community's wishes. Such issues are addressed further in this chapter, and the theories and cases outlined above provide a good basis from which to consider the integration of film-induced tourism into the community planning process.

Applying Community Tourism Strategies to Film-Induced Tourism

As already noted, film-induced tourism can be an unexpected bonus or potentially a disaster for a community, particularly the more fragile small, rural communities whose infrastructure and ambience is often insufficient to handle an unexpected influx of visitors. By applying the theoretical tourism development models and the community planning cases illustrated above to the results of the Barwon Heads study, a series of possible future scenarios can be posited for the town, ranging from positive growth through to the collapse of the local community. Results outlined in Chapters 5 and 6 demonstrate that there is a link between the local community and regular holidaymakers who themselves have become part-time, de facto members of the broader community, and certainly stakeholders in the future of the town. This link and its associated power relations are reflected in the similar effects of each scenario on the Barwon Heads community and the holidaymaker, outlined below.

Scenario 1: Positive growth

- More visitors in off-peak times, evening out the high seasonal peaks and troughs.
- Increased accommodation range caters for all types of visitor, from the high-yield visitor through to the family budget holidaymaker.
- Economic opportunities increase for all members of the community.
- Barwon Heads receives increased support and recognition from the City of Greater Geelong.
- Services and facilities improved and maintained by the City of Greater Geelong.
- Major tourist precincts upgraded.
- Development is sympathetic to the fishing village ambience and nature.
- Heritage sites are retained and restored.
- Increase in the general population base, supporting local amenities such as schools, medical services, police, etc.

At first, the power in Scenario 1 may seem to be evenly spread amongst the local community and regular visitors, with the desires of all parties taken into account. However, in terms of political and power-relations practice, this is an unlikely scenario.

Scenario 2: Business as usual

- No further development.
- Accommodation and facilities continue to support the family budget holidaymakers.
- Everyone happy with the minor fillip to the town.
- Visitors pass though, staying in other towns able to handle the added influx, limiting the impact on the tranquillity of the area.
- Housing and rental prices remain stable.
- Traditional family holiday market continues to be welcome and catered for.

Scenario 2 sees the power residing with those in the community who like it as it is and with the long-term regular visitors. The research identified that these are the shorter-term residents, many of whom had moved to the village after visiting it as holidaymakers or tourists. This group of people is powerful owing to their political understanding and resistance to change.

Scenario 3: Back to the drawing board

- New businesses cannot be supported by numbers of residents and visitors outside the peak season.
- Shops become run-down, deserted and vacant.
- Council funds diverted to other, more lucrative tourist towns such as Queenscliff.
- Housing prices fall and rental market opens up.
- Niche accommodation for the high-yield markets not supported, forcing closures or restructuring.
- Traditional family holiday market welcome, but may move owing to the perceived downturn after the excitement of *Sea Change*.

In the third scenario, the strong anti-development groups have the power and have sabotaged any attempts at consultation and development. As with Scenario 2, this group tends to be dominated by the newer residents, with a strong representation of urban dwellers, often referred to as 'urban refugees' looking for their own private Sea Change.

Scenario 4: Losing the Pearl Bay feeling

- Regular budget holidaymakers forced out due to increased demand, prices and/or loss of amenity.

- Shops and services developed to cater for visitors – overpriced and unappealing to local residents.
- Barwon Heads changes from family holiday village to a day visitor attraction.
- Outside entrepreneurs not based in the region take over local business operations.
- Locals begin to resent the intrusion of thousands of visitors.
- Crowding severely impacts on local services.
- More Council funds required to maintain basic services used by visitors and residents.
- Housing purchase and rental prices skyrocket.
- Pressure put on natural environment – coastal and wetland areas.

In this final scenario, the regular visitors have no power and have been forced out of the region owing to the power coalition of pro-development business and economic development supporters, which may include local government. The power group is also made up of some of the long-term residents who are looking for an economic 'future' for their children.

As the Barwon Heads study looked at circumstances over a given three-year period, each of the above scenarios can be placed into a model in terms of the levels of development, tourist yield and visitor numbers, which have been the main variables considered in this book. One such model is proposed in Figure 7.2, with the current position (at the time of writing) of Barwon

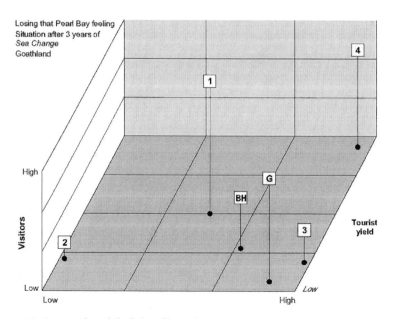

Figure 7.2 Proposed model of the effect of tourism on a community

Heads also plotted, which relates to the previous discussion on power relations. For comparison, the current position of Goathland is also placed in the model. As can be seen, the *Heartbeat* (1992–2010) series has prompted high visitor numbers, fairly high development (especially in terms of hardening the site), but very low visitor yield to the actual village, with visitors staying in other towns. Such a scenario can (and has) created ill will and resentment between residents and visitors.

Placed within the model are the four scenarios posited: Positive growth, Business as usual, Back to the drawing board, and Losing that Pearl Bay feeling, as well as the position that Barwon Heads is in after three years of the *Sea Change* phenomenon. Each of these responds differently to the three variables nominated, and they exist in very different spaces on the model. Theoretically, the optimum position would be in the centre of the cube, not far from Scenario 1's position where the yield is average, the visitor numbers are average and development is average. Such a position may not be desirable to all stakeholders or community members, but while it may represent a compromise, it allows for continued long-term positive growth. The results of the three-year study indicate that Barwon Heads is currently situated between Scenarios 1 and 4, with residents and visitors expressing the same sense of loss of atmosphere, but with general acceptance of the current state. Both groups strongly assert that they do not want any further development.

Clearly, Barwon Heads will continue to change over time, with the acceptance of developments such as the restaurant at Diver Dan's, combined with the overall desire expressed both by residents and by visitors to limit further development. Such movement may reflect earlier tourism models such as Doxey's (1975) Irridex, where residents (and in this case study, regular visitors) move from eager acceptance and adoption through to displacement, or even Butler's (1980) model of a tourist area's cycle of evolution that recognises a destination's popularity movements over time. However, unless there is a new series of *Sea Change* and/or overseas popularity, it is anticipated there will be little movement from the current state because of limited infrastructure, land availability and general community reluctance to capitalise further on the *Sea Change* effect. This prediction made in 2005 has proven to be correct, and while there are changes in the village as noted in Chapter 6, there has not been a significant shift since the early days of the so-called 'Sea Change' effect'.

There are, however, important issues that come to the fore when implementing community tourism strategies, as briefly noted in the previous chapter. The Goathland case is a good example as the managing authority, the North York Moors National Park Authority (NYMNPA), has consistently worked with the community in an attempt to gain some consensus and local empowerment when dealing with the issues. As noted in Chapter 6, community cohesion does not (nor should it) exist, even in a small community of 300, presenting a fluid (while at times somewhat stagnant) situation.

One concern often expressed by community members is the misrepresentation of their community through film. A comment heard continually during my studies in all parts of the world was 'we are not like that!' This may not be a major issue in many cases, as visitors recognise the difference between fiction and reality, but it can become a problem when the portrayals are negative. Later in the chapter we attempt to address this issue, but first we need to look further at the effect of power relations on the success of film-induced tourism. As noted in Chapter 3, Hall (2003) argues that equal access to representation is not achievable, and that the power relations in communities result in those with the power dominating any cooperative process.

The Power and the Glory: The Role of Power Relations in Film Tourism

While the relationship between film makers and tourist destinations is complex and at times can be contradictory, or even competitive, there are also instances where film and tourism organisations have worked together to their mutual benefit, sometimes initiated by the film company (Cynthia & Beeton, 2009) or the tourism industry (Beeton, 2000, 2005). Yet, all players do not have equal levels of power – in most cases, political (and at times social) power is held by those with financial influence (Beeton, 2008b). By understanding power relations, managers, marketers, organisations and communities can make decisions that contribute positively to their desired futures.

Power can exist in a hierarchical manner (which is often imposed power), or organizationally in terms of local council, state government, national government and so on, which is often seen as *political power*. (Beeton, 2006a: 81)

Based on over 30 years of direct experience relating to tourism based on film, and subsequent research, I have developed a model built on the degree of cooperation between these groups, looking at the linkages between various film makers and destinations. My goal was to understand the range of relationships between film makers and tourist destinations and operations, and secondarily to identify inhibitors/enhancers to tourism success in terms of the power conferred on each actor.

This is illustrated in Figure 7.3, which was developed from the following research studies to illustrate the relationship between certain film makers and tourist destinations, from the large studios and national tourism organisations through to independent film makers and individual tourism enterprises. As with most of my film tourism work, the majority of cases have been studied over a period of time and involve significant elements of

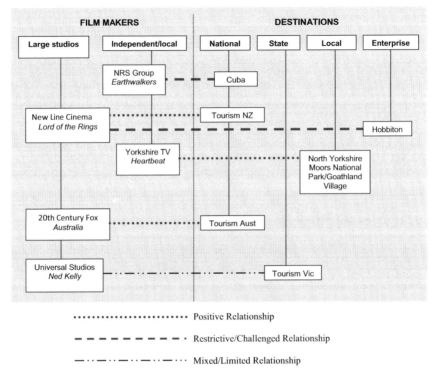

Figure 7.3 Film makers and destination partnerships

participant observation, as outlined in the discussion below, where I also comment on my level of immersion in the experiences described in each case. While many of the cases are from Australia and New Zealand, I have also included research I have undertaken in Cuba and the United Kingdom (UK). Again, these cases are illuminative and indicative.

Case One: NRS Group (*Earthwalkers*) and Cuba

The Australian independent film company, the NRS Group, produced the cable television travel programme *Earthwalkers*. The premise of the series was that it was fronted by a traveller rather than a professional, and presented from that person's perspective (Cynthia & Beeton, 2009). As a member of a tour group in Cuba, I was approached by the film crew to front one of their hour-long episodes. While travelling and filming with the crew, I was aware of the restrictions they faced from the Castro government – in many cases we were accompanied by an official government guide and were not permitted to film certain activities or areas.

Even though I had not previously seen the *Earthwalkers* series, as a presenter and tourist I became immediately immersed in this case, particularly in relation to the ways in which the film company leveraged tourism in order to access filming sites, as outlined in Cynthia and Beeton (2009). Consequently, my role here as film participant presenter required total investigator immersion.

The episode in which I was involved was potentially contentious as I was given the task to interpret the Bay of Pigs invasion, which we presented from the Cuban perspective, all the time aware of our international audience. Ultimately, whatever went to air had to be sanctioned by the government and, as such, had the potential to be somewhat overly positive towards the Cubans. However, while there were restrictions, Cuba is keen to encourage tourism, so they were not as prescriptive as some other communist countries have been in the past.

In return, the *Earthwalkers* programme was able to present a tourist's perspective of a country that is seen as exotic and remains closed to many, especially the citizens of the United States (US). The benefits to the film company are clear, as to the Cuban government. Consequently, this relationship is represented in Figure 7.3 as 'restrictive and challenged', yet it can also be seen as successful in terms of raising tourism awareness of the destination.

Case Two: New Line Cinema (*The Lord of the Rings*) and Tourism New Zealand

As we know, the movie trilogy *The Lord of the Rings* is a popular cult fantasy based on a novel set in a fictional place known as 'Middle Earth'. The New Zealand government and Tourism New Zealand recognised the potential of having a popular story that was not overtly country-specific based in their country. The opportunity to brand New Zealand as 'Middle Earth' resulted in the appointment of a government minister to oversee the relationship between the tourist commission and the film company as well as the actual filming. This resulted in numerous collaborative promotions, such as the successful 'you've seen the movie, now visit the set' programme by Tourism New Zealand. The movie and associated promotions branded the country as a place of contrasting natural beauty, fantasy and adventure, sitting well with past tourism promotions. Consequently, awareness of New Zealand as a desirable place to visit increased significantly (NFO New Zealand, 2003).

While not as obsessive as some, I have been a fan of the book since my late teens and subsequently the film, meaning that I was deeply, but not totally, immersed in the story and the tourism activity surrounding the premiere of the final episode in the trilogy, in spite of my focus on the series of movies in this book. Furthermore, after experiencing the festivities surrounding the premiere of the final episode of *The Lord of the Rings* in Wellington, New Zealand (see Chapter 8), I was impressed with the level of collaboration and cooperation between New Line Cinema and Tourism New Zealand, as discussed in subsequent chapters. However, this was not the case for all aspects of the movie, as outlined in the following.

Case Three: New Line Cinema (*The Lord of the Rings*) and Hobbiton

During and after the filming of *The Lord of the Rings*, New Line Cinema was extremely cautious about security and copyright, in spite of its collaboration with Tourism New Zealand outlined above. Extras and others involved in the filming were required to sign confidentiality agreements and not discuss any elements of the movie prior to the release of the final episode. This included the landowner on whose property the village of Hobbiton was built. Ultimately, all of the sites used by the film makers were being returned to their original state, with no evidence of the movie to remain. After two years of negotiation, the landowner was permitted to retain what remained of the partially destroyed Hobbiton and conduct tours; however New Line Cinema dictated the script that guides could use and provided the story boards for the site that it deemed appropriate.

This meant that the site of Hobbiton looks little like it did in the movie, and requires a significant level of interpretation from the guides and imagination from visitors (Beeton, 2007). Nevertheless, the power of the movie has been such that the enterprise has been extremely successful, which continues to be the case. Much of the tour tells the story of the issues the landowner faced and the relationship with New Line Cinema, which could have been a negative element, but actually adds an insiders' depth to the site, much in the same way as Grihault's Manhattan TV Tours.

While I have updated the Hobbiton experience elsewhere in this publication, I am retaining this case as it is, at the conclusion of *the Lord of the Rings* movies, rather than incorporating developments since the later filming of *The Hobbit* due to the relevance of this case to the model at this particular point in time.

As a past tour guide associated with the Australian 1980s movie, *The Man from Snowy River*, my level of immersion here was deeper than in the previous case. I remain highly engaged with visitor interpretation and storytelling, hence on the model of investigator immersion, I am totally immersed.

In this case, the relationship is expressed as being restrictive, as the film company has been not only restrictive in its permissions to use the site (which is on private land), but refused permission for some time. And, while this situation has now changed since the filming of *The Hobbit*, the relations noted above provide a valid contribution to the model.

Case Four: Yorkshire TV (*Heartbeat*) and North Yorkshire Moors National Park

As we are aware, when the quirky 1960s era television series *Heartbeat* was first filmed in the small village of Goathland in the North Yorkshire

Moors National Park in 1989, no-one expected it to be filming after 20 years (which was the case). Due to the need to regularly film there (Yorkshire TV is filming at least once a month), the film company had to gain community support in terms of accepting road closures and other disruptions during filming, but also to counteract the crowding and privacy invasion of the large number of tourists, which is still around 1 million visitors per annum. Stories from locals included a negative change in the 'type' of visitor and the need to alter their living habits, as I have noted previously, both here and elsewhere (Beeton, 2000).

To counteract a growing community dissatisfaction with the local impacts of the series, Yorkshire TV subsequently engaged with the Goathland community, supporting infrastructure development and permitted local entrepreneurs to trade off the *Heartbeat* name. This includes some sites retaining their fictional signage and a raft of souvenirs, from sweets and postcards through to clocks, model cars of the period and virtually anything else that has space to stamp the *Heartbeat* name on it, presenting what has become a positive ongoing relationship between the film makers and the destination.

In terms of my level of immersion in this case, it is complex and deep. I have an initial relationship with *Heartbeat* as a viewer with my parents, who were big fans, in particular my late father. He would have been thrilled and fascinated with my stories of visiting Goathland. Not only has the series a personal resonance, but I am also highly attracted to the era in terms of nostalgia and the place which, for me, represents quintessential rural England. When I visited, I was surprised and moved as to how 'close' the real village was to its representation in the series. I have returned a number of times and continue to study the effects of the television series on this village and its community even today. Consequently, I am deeply immersed as a film tourist in this particular case.

Case Five: 20th Century Fox (*Australia*) and Tourism Australia

The 2008/09 movie *Australia*, produced by Baz Luhrmann for 20th Century Fox, came at a time when Tourism Australia was looking for a promotional programme. Consequently, after many years of avoiding any conscious linking of film with tourism, they developed a strategy to leverage the exposure the movie would create for the country, Australia. However, they did not simply take the (historical) storyline, rather commissioned Luhrmann to develop a series of advertisements and other promotional collateral as well as commercial relationships based on the emotional elements in the film of journey and transformation (Beeton, 2009). By taking such an approach, they were not totally reliant on the 'success' of the movie, rather the 'chatter' that it would produce. While the success of this promotion in terms of tourist visitation has been mixed, the media exposure measures were impressive

(Tourism Australia, 2009), illustrating a positive relationship, with tourism success in some markets.

My level of immersion here was more of an observer researcher than a participant, experiencing the movie (which I have seen three times – once in the cinema, once on a Qantas flight and finally on television) more in terms of its marketing potential, and how Tourism Australia addressed the issue as to whether the movie would be a popular tourist drawcard or not.

Case Six: Universal Studios (*Ned Kelly*) and Tourism Victoria

Aware of the potential of film-induced tourism after the successes of *The Lord of the Rings* in New Zealand, Tourism Victoria (an Australian state-based destination marketing organisation (DMO)) produced a range of touring routes and web-based information based on the 2003 movie *Ned Kelly*, starring well-known actors Heath Ledger and Orlando Bloom. This movie was based on a historical figure, but filmed in places where he was not active. The movie was dark and did not encourage visitors to the sites of the filming – if anything, they were encouraged to seek out the authentic sites (Beeton, 2004). Consequently, while the overall relationship with the film maker was positive, the execution of the tourism programme and its relationship with the movie was unsuccessful, presenting a restricted/limited relationship outcome.

As with the previous case, I was more of an observer than participant in this case, even though I have seen the movie three times and visited the sites. All of these activities were undertaken in my role as a researcher, not as a participant.

Figure 7.3 illustrates the relationships briefly outlined in the cases above and allows us to see the effects of such relationships. A discussion of these relationships, based on a grounded theoretical approach, follows.

So, what is the common denominator in these cases that range from large film corporations and national DMOs to independent film makers and tourist enterprises? By looking at the concept of power relations, we are able to develop a theoretical response to the question.

Power relations

As already noted, the study of power relations is a complex field including inferred as well as imposed power (Hall, 2003; Marzano, 2008). In this study the type of power being considered is that which is 'imposed'.

If we consider the model in Figure 7.3 and the cases it is based on, the level and type of relationship (and in many cases, its ultimate tourism success) can be seen to relate directly to who has the power to provide or withhold permissions of use of a site (the destination) or of the creative material (the film maker) in the relationship. For example, in the *Earthwalkers* case, it is the government (of Cuba) who has the power to permit or restrict filming access to the country, whereas in the Hobbiton case, the film company (New Line Cinema) had the power to permit or prohibit the use of the site for tours and the extent of maintenance that can be done to preserve what remains of the site.

In the two cases where there is a positive relationship, this has been achieved by a collaborative process between the parties, where the power is equal – New Line Cinema and the New Zealand government developed a collaborative relationship as both parties had the power to permit or refuse access to sites (the government) and the use of film images (the film maker). As Yorkshire TV requires ongoing access to the village and land managed by the North Yorkshire Moors National Park, and the Goathland community presented a powerful social resistance to the issues created by increased film tourists, the initially unequal power relation moved to a more equal one, with each party having the power to approve or refuse access to the place and the *Heartbeat* creative material respectively.

Where there was a limited relationship, as in the case of *Ned Kelly*, the outcome was more about the connection between the movie and the places where it was filmed, and less about the power differential between the various parties. This, coupled with what is clearly a lack of understanding of film-induced tourism has resulted in the limitations (Beeton, 2004).

My aim with these cases was to uncover the range of relationships between film makers and tourism, as well as to identify various inhibitors or enhancers to tourism success. It is evident that power plays a significant role in the type of relationship between film makers and tourist destinations. By recognising where this power lies, it is possible for organisations to work proactively to achieve their desired outcomes. Where there is an uneven relationship, the use of mediators such as film and tourism commissions may ameliorate the situation.

While most film organisations see their respective film commissions as working on their behalf, and tourism operations see their tourism commissions in the same light, these organisations are often in a position to act as information sources and mediators for the other. Where the power lies with the film makers, film commissions may be seen as a mediator that can negotiate with the tourism industry to find a way that their power can be balanced. Where the power lies with the destination, the tourist commissions may perform a similar role. The rationale behind this statement lies in the ability of the commissions to represent the interests of their stakeholders from an external perspective, often more able to explain the needs from their industry's perspective to the other.

It remains rare for tourism operations to use the experience of the film commissions to assist in negotiations where there is an imbalance in the power of the actors, however it is one that can be used in a proactive manner.

There are a number of ways that film and tourism work together, areas where there is conflict and finally areas where there is no link, positive or negative. In actual fact, there is no empirical evidence to-date of people being discouraged to visit a place due to a film, in spite of media speculation of the effect of movies with negative images of a place, such as slasher movies. It has been proposed in this chapter that the power relations between the film makers is a far more important element. But, what can be done if these are too popular? This is a contentious issue, so I propose some possibilities below.

An Approach to Altering Negative Film-Induced Images

It has been well-established in this book and elsewhere that film is a most powerful imaging medium, especially when the storyline and site are closely interrelated. Such images are often retained by consumers for extended periods, as in *Last of the Summer Wine* (1973–2010), which has been influential for more than 30 years, and the Western movie, *Shane* (1953), which still resonates with visitors to Wyoming some 40 years on (Lazarus, 1999). We are now seeing many instances in Asia where tourism is increasing exponentially due to film and pop culture (Chan, 2007; Ji & Beeton, 2011; Zhang *et al.*, 2016; Kim & Long, 2012; Zhao & Timothy, 2015).

Community inclusiveness and participation are regularly overlooked in the filming decision-making process, due in part to the very nature of the film industry itself. A director of a movie or television programme is interested in producing the best product possible and is not duly concerned about the legacy with which the community may be left, such as a sudden surge in tourist numbers and changed environment (socially, economically and physically). If communities are left out of any real discussion or consultation, as is often the case, they are unable to contribute to or choose the type of community they live in – a critical aspect of community tourism planning. Such disenfranchisement and loss of community control can have dramatic long-term social effects and can also impact on the relationship between residents and visitors.

While many destinations now recognise the potential of film to induce tourism and create a powerful destination image, few have retained control over how and to whom the destination is presented through commercial films (particularly movies and television series). Producers are interested in creating the film they want, not the type of tourism image that the destination marketers or community may desire. For example, a DMO may want to encourage high-yield visitors, looking to establish images of a high-quality holiday destination, while members of the community may see their town or region as a friendly, welcoming area. These images are not incompatible, and can be incorporated into a destination marketing/imaging strategy. However, if a film studio wants to use the region to film a movie about a small-minded, allegedly racist community, which may be a simplistic stereo-type, then this image will not be congruent with either the community's or the DMO's desired (or ideal) image.

Is all publicity good publicity? Undesired imagery

There are three basic types of image that can be considered 'undesirable' by a community, the first being created by a negative storyline, such as crim-inal or bizarre activities. There are instances where community pressure has been able to deny filming access to such perceived negative storylines, but it is arguable as to whether the negative images actually repel or attract tour-ists. The example cited previously regarding the movie *Deliverance* (1972) increasing adventure tourism to the region where it was filmed in Rabun County, Georgia (notwithstanding that the storyline was set in Appalachia), is pertinent (Riley *et al.*, 1998). Linda Peterson Warren, director of the Arizona Film Commission, goes so far as to claim that 'people remember locations, beauty and don't tend to attach plot' (Radmacher, 1997: 14). This may be the case for some films, but not all, and is a complex area that requires further investigation.

Secondly, an undesired tourism image can result from one that is too successful in attracting visitors – increased visitation giving rise to negative community impacts such as loss of privacy, crowding and cultural amenity. For example, Amish country in Lancaster County Pennsylvania received a great deal of tourist attention following the popular 1985 movie *Witness*, starring Harrison Ford. Not only were the Amish portrayed in a highly-skewed manner, but also the high level of outside attention was, for such a private community, negatively received. According to Amish professor, Hostetler, the movie '...was a psychological invasion. [The Amish] took it as a kind of mockery' (*People Weekly*, 1985). The community could not undo the effect of the film, so eventually sought ways to counteract the images pre-sented. One example of how this has been achieved is most interesting: a group of Amish, who generally rejected mechanisation, movies and televi-sion, have developed a tourist site, 'The Amish Experience Theatre'. This is based around a multimedia production 'conceived in the finest tradition of Hollywood or Orlando-based special effects houses' (The Amish Experience, 2001). It has been screening *Jacob's Choice*, a 'dramatic tale of an Amish fam-ily's effort to preserve [their] lifestyle and culture' (The Amish Experience, 2001), which is used as the knowledge base and starting point for associated farm and countryside tours. This film's imagery has been adapted by the community to meet its need to counteract ill-informed movie-goers and por-tray an authentic Amish image, and in 2015 is still shown to visitors to the Amish Experience tourist attraction in Pennsylvania.

A third negative image can arise from the creation of unrealistic visitor expectations and aspects of authenticity. For example, visitors to some sites have been disappointed that the community does not behave or dress in the manner described in a film. There is also the issue of mistaken identity, when a story may be set in a particular region, but is filmed somewhere else. This is becoming more prevalent with the growth of such 'runaway productions', where sites are chosen on the basis of cost rather than authenticity (Croy & Walker, 2001). While most Americans associate *Deliverance* (1972) with the Appalachia region, and may have been disappointed if attempting to visit film sites in that region, Rabun County was able to leverage the film's popularity to promote its outdoor adventures at the same time as playing down the storyline and the 'real' region in which it was set.

So, what can a community do to alter an adverse (either negative or too successfully positive) image? While the Amish have attempted to create their own integrated image through film, communities do not generally have the funds to produce and distribute powerful film images themselves. So in order to counteract such a compelling medium as film, strategic (and even lateral) thinking must be applied by the community as part of its tourism planning. One potentially effective method is to apply demarketing theory as the basis of a remarketing/re-imaging strategy.

The second type of undesired image, one that is too successful, can be studied by looking at popular film-induced tourism sites that are experiencing large numbers of visitors and associated impacts (see Friends of the Lake District, 1996; *Economist*, 1995b; Demetriadi, 1996). While problems are evident at such sites, it appears that little is being done to proactively manage them, with the tourism managers (and DMOs) continuing to focus solely on economic aspects, with little community input. Demarketing techniques are proposed as both management strategies and re-imaging techniques. Being part of the marketing mix, demarketing is able to reach visitors prior to their visit, much as film does.

First coined by Kotler and Levy (1971), 'demarketing' has been applied widely in the public health care field in an effort to handle excessively high demand, and its effectiveness and ethics have been debated in many different forums (see Reddy, 1989; Kindra & Taylor, 1990; Malhorta, 1990; Borkowski, 1994). While it has not been extensively applied to tourism, there are cases where demarketing has been consciously or even unconsciously applied (see Clements, 1989; Beeton, 2001a, 2003; Beeton & Benfield, 2002; Dolnicar *et al.*, 2008; Armstrong & Kern, 2011; Orchiston & Higham, 2016). Demarketing in tourism is a powerful tool, as it is able to incorporate visitor management techniques at the marketing stage of an operation, before people visit – the stage when expectations are created and decisions on destinations and activities are made. Demarketing strategies range from pricing strategies and entry controls, to behavioural education and even a total reduction in marketing and promotion, some of which can be utilised on a community basis (see Beeton, 2001c; Benfield, 2001).

Film-induced tourism demarketing strategies

Beeton and Benfield (2002) propose a wide range of possible demarketing strategies, the most relevant to the film-induced tourism cases being:

- increasing entry fees;
- increasing advertising that warns of capacity limitations;
- reducing sales and promotion expenditure;
- separate management of large groups;
- educating potential visitors regarding appropriate behaviour at point of information gathering and within marketing and promotional literature;
- educating journalists and associated media regarding appropriate behaviour;
- encouraging specific ('desirable') markets through the style and information provided in the destination's promotional material;
- discouraging certain ('undesirable') markets through the style and information of destination promotional material;
- notifying visitors of banned activities and access at the point of information gathering and in promotional literature;
- permitting certain activities or access only under supervision of appropriately educated personnel (such as accredited commercial operators).

These strategies fall into three basic categories: limiting supply by making access more difficult (both physically and financially), limiting demand by restricting advertising, or educating potential visitors at the point of decision-making (through marketing material). The first two can be considered prescriptive and somewhat difficult due to the lack of influence that destination marketers and communities have over commercial film imaging, whereas the third can have some effect by dealing with visitor attitudes and expectations prior to their actual visit.

In order to ascertain the extent to which demarketing tools are being used to alter responses to film-induced images, popular US movie sites and UK television sites were examined. All the sites are promoted as filming destinations in either the Californian (California Tourism, 2001) or British Tourist Authority's (BTA, 2001b) *Movie Maps* and have received recognised visitor attention from the associated filming. The sites selected were the towns of Intercourse (Amish movie *Witness*), Mt Airy (setting for *The Andy Griffith Show*, though it was not filmed there), and Dyersville (*Field of Dreams*) in the US, and Holmfirth (*Last of the Summer Wine*), Luss (*Take the High Road*) and Goathland (*Heartbeat*) in the UK. The longevity of many of these series or interest in the movies (up to 30 years) provides the opportunity to consider the long-term effects of film-induced tourism.

The relevant tourist associations were approached, as well as the associated National Parks Authority (NPA) in the UK, as many of the villages and sites there are located in regions managed by the NPA. Table 7.1 summarises the responses to questions regarding visitor problems, community issues and the strategies taken to address them. There is a distinct variation in the degree and type of impacts as well as the strategies to handle them, but there was a common consensus that the community shared some resentment towards the influx of tourists. Barwon Heads currently uses fewer demarketing strategies from the longer established film-tourism sites in the UK and US, which supports the thesis that visitor management has been reactive, with destinations waiting until the problems are manifest before dealing with them. Restrictions and attempts to modify visitor behaviour are only introduced after community and environmental issues become apparent. The key to demarketing is that it is proactive, educating and managing potential tourists before as well as during their visit.

In spite of the recognised impacts on the community, the conscious application of strategies to handle the issues of crowding and loss of privacy at the point of promotion varies for each community, as demonstrated in Table 7.1. In order to examine this further, a basic socio-semiotic analysis of the marketing material indicated little in terms of demarketing, with the analysis outlined in Table 7.2. In order to study what a potential visitor would receive, a request for brochures was emailed to the respective tourist offices of the five sites identified in the UK and the US. Promotional brochures were requested from all the offices, but only one of them actually forwarded material. Such reluctance to forward hard copies of tourism information forces international visitors to rely heavily on the unregulated internet as an information source, where individual businesses and movie fans themselves are able to extensively publicise film sites, with no control or input from the community or government agencies (see Melissa's Heartbeat Page, Classic TV and SeaChange websites in the Bibliography). All the regions had tourism internet sites and these were used as the main source of accessible visitor information, along with the most relevant commercial sites of businesses directly benefiting from film-induced tourism. In addition, brochures obtained during site visits were utilised.

Many of the so-called 'demarketing strategies' that have been identified in Table 7.2 also come under the realm of 'visitor management'. The difference between them is not so much the actions taken, but when the actions occur on the visitor experience continuum from initial decision to travel, information gathering and choice of destination through to travel to the destination and the experience at the destination. Visitor management, as the term suggests, takes place when the visitors are actually on-location, whereas demarketing strategies are those that occur during the information gathering process. Such a distinction is more than mere semantics as there are few destinations (including national parks) that proactively target visitor behaviour before the visitor arrives. This is becoming more apparent in fragile environments such as some national parks, with some literature notifying

Table 7.2 Destination marketing material for film tourism sites

Town: Series/movie	Type of promotional material		Refs to series/movie	Position of references			Images from series	Map of sites	Demarketing strategies			
	www	Brochure		Front/www home	Back	Inside/www link			Limit access	Go elsewhere in area	Fee	Education re privacy
United Kingdom												
Holmfirth: Last of the Summer Wine	TB					✓						
	LG			✓						✓		
	C		✓✓✓✓	✓✓✓		✓	✓✓✓					
		Film location guide				✓✓✓	✓✓✓✓✓					
		Region visitor guide	✓✓			✓	✓	✓				
		Holmfirth brochure	✓✓✓			✓✓✓	✓	✓		✓		✓
Goathland: Heartbeat	C		✓			✓						
	NPA					✓				✓		
	.com						✓✓✓✓✓✓✓					
		Visitor brochure	✓	✓								
		Guide for research	✓	✓						✓		✓

(Continued)

Table 7.2 (*Continued*)

Town: Series/movie	Type of promotional material		Refs to series/movie	Position of references			Images from series	Map of sites	Demarketing strategies			
	www	*Brochure*		*Front/www home*	*Back*	*Inside/www link*			*Limit access*	*Go elsewhere in area*	*Fee*	*Education re privacy*
Luss: *Take the High Road*	C		✓	✓								
Road	NPA		✓			✓				✓		
		Luss brochure	✓			✓						
USA												
Intercourse: *Witness*	LG		✓			✓						✓
	C		✓			✓						✓
	.com		0									
Mt Airy: *Andy Griffith Show*	LG		✓			✓						
Dyersville: *Field of Dreams*	LG				✓✓						✓	
	.com		✓	✓								
Australia												
Barwon Heads: *Sea Change*	NPA		✓	✓								
	C		✓✓✓	✓✓		✓						

Note: TB = Tourism Board; LG = Local Government/Council; C = Community; NPA = National Parks Authority/Public Land Management Agency (Aust); .com = Commercial site.

potential visitors of banned activities and other restrictions, but it is rarely treated in a conscious proactive manner (Beeton, 2003). It is important for destinations affected adversely by tourism to address the negative conse- quences and notify visitors of any banned activities, restrictions, costs or preferred behaviour at the information-gathering stage when expectations are developed. In the case of film-induced tourism, this is even more vital owing to the lack of community control over the filming process in the first instance. It also must be stressed that demarketing is one aspect of the mar- keting mix, not an alternative to marketing itself.

The above cursory examination of promotional material indicates the unconscious use of some demarketing strategies. Much of the promotional material mentions their related film sites but, apart from those that focus specifically on film (such as the *TV and Film Location Guide* for the Kirklees region, which includes Holmfirth), promotion of the filming sites is extremely limited. The film sites promoted in the guide include the settings for series such as *The League of Gentlemen, Where the Heart Is* and *Wokenwell* as well as movies including *Blow Dry, Duncan Wayne: World Number One* and *Distress Signals*. Apart from *Blow Dry*, the other movies were not hits, so it is the television series that tend to attract most visitors, especially *Last of the Summer Wine*, which received prominent exposure in the brochure.

As noted in Chapter 4, while much of the *Heartbeat* information (such as numerous guidebooks) were prominently displayed in Goathland, it was not used more extensively or on the NYMNPA website. Such limited use of the promotional power of film indicates use of a general demarketing strat- egy of limiting the promotion of the towns as film sites. Much of the mate- rial promotes other activities and sites to visit away from the film areas, while only four out of the 22 promotional media comment on issues such as respecting residents' privacy. Only one site charges a fee (*Field of Dreams*), which is for entry to a maze, leaving the rest of the site with no entrance fee. The *Field of Dreams* site is interesting in that it is split between two private property owners, with one providing a less developed experience than the other, which includes the maze and 'costumed' baseball entertainers.

Proposed demarketing strategies for film tourism sites

Levels of resident dissatisfaction are suggested by media stories that report concerns over images portrayed in storylines as well as increased pres- sures on infrastructure and lifestyle at many film sites (see *Economist*, 1995b; Demetriadi, 1996; *Friends of the Lake District Report and Newsletter*, 1996). While the media have a tendency to latch on to negative stories, research undertaken at many sites around the world supports this proposition (see the previous chapters). An integrated demarketing strategy is proposed as a means to address the issues that have been identified. A model for re-imaging

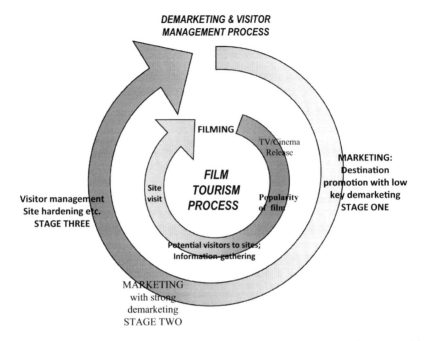

Figure 7.4 Integrated demarketing strategy assists in future tourism planning, with particular emphasis on film-induced tourism and communities

a destination through demarketing is proposed in Figure 7.4, which will which will assist in future tourism planning, with particular emphasis on film-induced tourism and communities.

The model incorporates demarketing into the marketing process at the stage of destination marketing when run concurrently with the release of a movie or television series as well as at the information-gathering stage. Initially, at the destination marketing stage, the demarketing would be minor, possibly in the realm of notifying potential visitors whether sites are publicly accessible, and if not, what limitations there may be. The second stage of demarketing may require more information, such as costs, time or number restrictions and appropriate behaviour towards residents, bringing it more into line with visitor management that comes into effect once the visitors are on-location (Stage 3).

While not all issues that a community or small town faces regarding film-induced tourism can be addressed by demarketing, there are strategies that can aid the process. These should not be seen as stand-alone strategies, rather they are most effective when incorporated into visitor and environmental management as well as part of the marketing mix. Tables 7.3, 7.4, 7.5 and 7.6 outline the issues that have been identified in the study of marketing practices at the sites listed in Table 7.2, and the proposed demarketing tools,

Table 7.3 Social demarketing options for film-induced tourism

Issue	Strategy	Stage
Loss of privacy		
Taking photos of residents	• Educate visitors in protocol for picture-taking.	2
	• Accredit 'sensitive' tour operators.	1, 2, 3
	• Train and accredit local guides.	1, 2, 3
	• Establish specific areas for photo taking.	1, 2, 3
Souveniring private property	• Educate visitors.	2
	• Offer facsimiles of popular items for purchase.	3
	• Increase security.	3
	• Accredit 'sensitive' tour operators.	1, 2, 3
	• Train and accredit local guides.	1, 2, 3
Accessing private areas	• Educate visitors.	2
	• Introduce signage.	2, 3
	• Design access paths to avoid private areas.	3
	• Increase security.	3
	• Accredit 'sensitive' tour operators.	1, 2, 3
	• Train and accredit local guides.	1, 2, 3
	• Encourage activities in other areas of the town/region.	2, 3
Crowding	• Limit numbers.	2, 3
	• Notify visitors of limitations or best times to visit.	2
	• Allocate staggered times for bus tour groups.	2
	• Accredit 'sensitive' tour operators.	1, 2, 3
	• Train and accredit local guides.	1, 2, 3
	• Introduce fees.	2, 3
	• Encourage activities in other areas of the town/region.	2, 3
Loss of atmosphere & ambience	• Accredit 'sensitive' tour operators.	1, 2, 3
	• Train and accredit local guides.	1, 2, 3
	• Encourage activities in other areas of the town/region.	2, 3
Other		
Reduced safety, esp. from car accidents	• Reduce traffic in popular areas.	2, 3
	• Increase pedestrian crossings.	2, 3
Crime – petty theft	• Educate visitors and locals to be vigilant.	2, 3
	• Increase policing.	3

along with the stage (1, 2 or 3) in the integrated demarketing strategy from Figure 7.4 at which they could be introduced. The issues have been divided into social (Table 7.3), economic (Table 7.4), environmental (Table 7.5) and tourism (Table 7.6). They also include positive aspects of film-induced

Table 7.4 Economic demarketing options for film-induced tourism

Issue	Strategy	Stage
Limited economic		
Visitors staying in other towns	• Encourage longer stays through offering local guided tours, attractions & activities that are time-consuming (yet interesting).	1, 2
	• Provide accredited tour operators with special packages/deals.	2
Benefits only to traders	• Educate locals on the economic multiplier effect, esp. via local media.	ongoing
Housing price increases	• Difficult to control – work with local government to assist.	ongoing
Infrastructure		
Limited vehicle parking	• Increase parking options.	3
	• Encourage park and ride on public transport.	2, 3
Increased pressure on public toilets	• Increase number of public toilets.	3
	• Continuous needs assessment and monitoring.	ongoing
	• Consider design of toilets.	ongoing
Waste disposal	• Increase council services (who pays?).	ongoing

Table 7.5 Environmental demarketing options for film-induced tourism

Issue	Strategy	Stage
Environmental		
Increased rubbish	• Educate visitors.	2
	• Introduce signage.	2, 3
	• Design access paths to pass by rubbish bins.	2, 3
	• Study habits for appropriate placement and style of bin.	3
	• Increase number of bins and collection services.	3
	• Accredit 'sensitive' tour operators.	1, 2, 3
	• Train and accredit local guides.	1, 2, 3
Erosion of paths and roads (heavy vehicles)	• Limit access to sensitive areas.	2, 3
	• Temporary closure of roads and paths.	2, 3
	• Offer alternatives – park and walk, free public transport/shuttles.	2, 3
	• Harden the site.	3
Pollution from vehicles	• Offer 'green' alternatives – park and walk, free public transport/shuttles.	2, 3
	• Limit time of day for vehicle access.	2, 3

Table 7.6 Tourism demarketing options for film-induced tourism

Issue	Strategy	Stage
Tourism		
Displacement of traditional holidaymakers	• Provide services, activities and facilities that they find attractive.	2
Effect of students researching the phenomenon	• Limit research activities by requiring community approval.	ongoing
	• Inform institutions of the problem & suggest other areas/towns to study.	2

tourism, which in spite of the term demarketing should also be incorporated at these planning stages.

Many of the issues outlined in Table 7.3 may be more perceived than actual; nevertheless they have a major effect on relationships between tourists, residents and regular visitors alike, and as such are very real. Social impacts are highly perceptual and open to constant change and reassessment, so they must be addressed and reinforced throughout the entire marketing/demarketing process.

Economic impacts have a significant effect on the future survival of a community, consequently the positive impacts need to be encouraged, with an awareness of the negative issues, particularly in terms of a shift in the visitation patterns of existing tourists.

One of the problems with many environmental impacts (Table 7.5) is that they are not evident until the environment is damaged, often irrevocably. Numerous researchers into environmental sustainability have noted that the major problem with establishing carrying capacity is that it is rarely recognised or understood until it has been exceeded. When outlining the problems of establishing carrying capacity, Stankey and Lime note that '...when you get down to specifics – how many, what kinds, when, for whom, etc. – the discussion bogs down' (Stankey & Lime, 1975: 174). It is essential to establish desired levels of visitation and activities of visitors from the outset.

Tourism issues in Table 7.6 relate to the changes that film-induced tourism may bring to the existing tourism market and infrastructure. While there are not as many such tourism aspects compared with the social, economic and environmental issues outlined in the previous tables, they should not be overlooked. For example, the effect of film-induced tourism on traditional holidaymakers may well compound the negative economic and social impacts. Also, interest by students in studying a new tourism phenomenon has created a new type of visitor to film sites who has different requirements, and may well be more socially intrusive than all other visitors.

Each community needs to assess the proposed strategies outlined in the above tables in light of their own goals and vision, integrating them into the community tourism planning and development process. The stronger and more inclusive the community vision, the easier it is for communities to decide on the most appropriate strategies and the more beneficial they become.

Some of the options require funding, whereas others can be relatively cost-neutral, while others even generate revenue, such as accrediting operators and guides. While individual travellers cannot always be successfully restricted or educated, the concept of accrediting and training tour operators and local guides and using such accreditation in the marketing material can be of some merit. Accreditation of tour operators has been successfully applied in many national parks, especially in Australia where operators must gain (and pay for) a permit to operate in national parks. Conditions attached to the permits include safety as well as knowledge of the environment (through approved seminars and other programmes). Operators have at times also been authorised to notify the land management agency of groups or individuals behaving irresponsibly. By providing training opportunities and other benefits, the operators view accreditation as a benefit to themselves and as a strong marketing tool. There is no evidence of such a programme being undertaken in filming towns, yet there is a good case to consider such an option. Geelong Otway Tourism did offer to train locals at Barwon Heads to become 'Sea Change specialists', but there was no interest – once again a reflection of the general ambivalence and reluctance of residents to identify with the series.

In a survey conducted by the Yorkshire Tourist Board and the NYMNPA (YTB & NYMNPA, 1997) about the impact of filming on Goathland residents, many of the residents made suggestions that are, to all intents and purposes, demarketing strategies. This includes recommendations to promote other areas of the national park, away from Goathland, to refrain from any tourism promotion of Goathland, and for the television company (Yorkshire TV) to also refrain from referring to Goathland. There were also suggestions about targeting 'appropriate' tourists and restricting access to the village.

This demonstrates that many of the demarketing concepts are not new, with elements being proposed and used by destination communities, albeit in a reactive, unconscious manner.

The potential of demarketing as a tool to re-image a destination and manage visitor movement and behaviour has been demonstrated in the above discussion. The proposed strategies can be incorporated into many development plans and utilised by commercial as well as community groups. Demarketing can also be used as a tool in empowering members who may have lost control of their community through unplanned film-induced tourism.

Community Tourism Planning Revisited

It has become evident through comparing the results of the Barwon Heads study in Australia with the data available in the US and the UK that, while film-induced tourism is a common and growing phenomenon, it is not as extensive or intrusive in Australia. Also, it appears that movies may have more impact in the US, while the UK sites most affected by tourism are those from television series or based on popular books.

Regardless of the type, film is a powerful image-maker, and while it would be advantageous to be able to incorporate filming into community planning, in reality this is rarely the case. We are finding that communities are often left to face the results of a too-successful or negative image with limited resources and unequal power relations and coalitions. The concepts of demarketing can be used to work towards re-imaging these communities, empowering them and creating a more sustainable future.

The Barwon Heads community's general ambivalence towards *Sea Change* has unconsciously self-imposed a limit on film-induced tourism visitation to the town as well as maintaining a reasonable level of positive development (apart from some increasing property values). Such an unconscious limiting of visitors may not always be successful or even desired, which is where community tourism planning comes into its own. For example, if the series had received the level of screening of other Australian series in the UK, such as *Neighbours* (1985–) and *Home and Away* (1988–), the subsequent tourist visitation would have been far greater.

Issues of community cohesion have been raised in the *Heartbeat* discussions, which have indicated that at times the media has over-emphasised some of the discordant views within the village. Such misrepresentation may serve to heighten what were initially minor tensions. However, healthy communities are vibrant, multi-faceted, changing groups that cannot be treated as a single, static entity, and some friction is a necessary component. By proactively planning for the tourism aftermath of filming a popular television series, potential issues such as overcrowding and even economic loss to other towns/regions (such as the Goathland case) may be avoided. Also, planning enables a community to truly take advantage and control of those aspects of film-induced tourism that they desire, not merely what the media represents.

The next section moves on from looking at film-induced tourism on location to tourism that is connected with the production studios themselves, that is, off-location film tourism.

Part 3

Off-Location Film Studio Tourism

The previous section looked at film-induced tourism from the aspect of people visiting the sites that are featured in television programmes and movies, introduced in Chapter 1 as on-location film tourism. The two chapters in this section go to the film production studios to look at film-induced tourism in terms of the studios themselves ('off-location').

Film is a great motivator, not only for tourism, but also for additional commercial consumption that may not necessarily be directly related to the film itself. Product placement has become an accepted aspect of television programmes and movies, and at times has verged on the extreme, as in programmes such as the television series *Baywatch* (1989–2001), where the sponsors' names feature in the script, interfering dramatically with what storyline there is.

Also, many of the on-location filming sites are promoted in conjunction with opportunities to purchase film-related souvenirs, in addition to the products used by the characters in the film or even by the actors in real life. For example, the Hong Kong Tourist Association's *Movie Map* links film sites with up-market shopping by featuring the stores that are used as backdrops in popular Hong Kong movies (Yan, 2000). Tourism New Zealand and Air New Zealand both promote the places where *The Lord of the Rings* stars had coffee (Air New Zealand, 2003b), not unlike the so-called 'quaint' Barwon Heads blackboards exhorting visitors to 'have coffee and cake like Sigrid' (see Chapter 4). The development of film studio theme parks and their concomitant merchandising and souvenir sales has taken advantage of this fascination with filming and celebrity endorsement off-location at the film production studios themselves.

8 From Themed Events to Film Studios

In the context of this publication, film production studios are considered to be 'off-location', even though many are filmed entirely in the studios, with no on-location filming in the field. This is especially true of many television programmes, which may have only their initial establishing images filmed at the location of the story. Table 8.1 summarises the elements that constitute the two terms, on-location and off-location.

In terms of 'authenticity', on-location sites are not necessarily authentic, in that many places are filmed in such a way that they appear quite different from 'real life' (larger, smaller or more extensive, for example), or may even be presented as a completely different place (known as runaway productions). The term, off-location, relates to filming undertaken in a set constructed within the confines of the production unit, away from a naturally occurring setting such as a town, coastal area or desert, and at first glance may be considered to be totally in-authentic, yet for the post-tourist is quite 'real'. For example, films that use Paramount Studios' famous painted sky wall or Main Street facades are considered to be just as 'off-location' as those using the closed sound stages and studios, regardless of how they appear on film. Tourism at those sites can also be considered as 'industrial tourism' with visitors gazing at the film industry while it is at work.

Industrial tourism is broadly recognised as being an aspect of a venture whose core activity is the production of non-tourism goods and/or services (Otgaar, 2012; Vargas-Sánchez, 2015). Tourists gaze at the actual production process, such as chocolates being made in a chocolate factory or beer brewing at the brewery – the core activity is the production, with tourism an added diversification. Film studios can be classified in this area, as their core activity is film production. However, if the visitor is taken to a separate site to experience a constructed replication (or simulacrum) of the filming process, this is not strictly industrial tourism. Such tourism attractions belong to the realm of the theme park, and include film studios such

Table 8.1 Elements of on-location and off-location film sites

On-location		Off-location	
Description	Example	Description	Example
Existing buildings	Castles, cottages, hotels	Constructed set	Closed film studio sound stages
Built landscapes	Main streets	Separate from the naturally occurring setting of the film, such as the generic street sets in film studios	External facades constructed at a studio site (often representing a main street)
Natural landscapes	Mountains, fields, lakes, ocean	Representation of natural landscapes through computer imaging, modelling, etc.	Vistas such as Paramount Studios' blue sky wall (in a staff carpark)

as Warner Brothers Movie World and Fox Studios Backlot in Australia, Disney in Florida, Anaheim, France, Hong Kong and Japan and Universal Studios in Japan and Singapore as well as in Burbank, California and Florida, among others. While this appears to be a predominantly Western-based development, there are some constructed theme parks and film studio experiences in Asia such as Studio Gibley in Japan, with more mooted for the future.

Much of the success of such tourism ventures lies in the clear segregation of the working studio and tourist facilities with its playful take on authenticity through obvious fictional representations of fantasy – the public are part of the joke. Visitors would be closer to the film-making process watching a video of *Back to the Future* at home than on the public ride of the same name at Universal Studios, yet they are prepared to pay more than a movie ticket price for simulated movie experiences. This is the ultimate postmodern construct, aptly fitting Baudrillard's (1983) 'hyper reality', a term that is taken up in the following discussion on the postmodern paradigm.

Film studio tourism such as at Universal Studios is not a component of industrial tourism, but is more related to theme park theory and postmodern developments such as Hannigan's (1998) 'Fantasy City'. Hannigan (1998) describes Fantasy City as possessing six central features:

(1) it is based around a single or multi-theme (drawn from popular entertainment, sport, history or the city's geographic locale);
(2) it is aggressively branded with sponsors and highly reliant on licensed merchandise sales;
(3) it operates day and night;

(4) it is modular (mixing and matching an array of standard components such as themed restaurants, cinema megaplexes and high tech amusements);

(5) it is solipsistic (that is, self-contained and physically, economically and socially isolated from its locale);

(6) it is postmodern in that it is constructed around simulations, virtual reality and the 'thrill of the spectacle' (Hannigan, 1998: 3–4).

Such elements are integral parts of theme parks, particularly film studio theme park enterprises and, as Hannigan notes:

> ...as motion picture and amusement park technologies merge to produce a new generation of attractions, the space between authenticity and illusion recedes, creating the illusion of 'hyper reality' described by such postmodern writers as Umberto Eco and Jean Baudrillard. (Hannigan, 1998: 4)

We return to these concepts and themes throughout the next chapters. However, as much of the academic discourse on theme parks comes from a postmodern paradigm, some comment on this perspective is required. Taking a brief look at such a complex area is fraught with the dangers of over-simplification, and there are profound differences between the major proponents of postmodernism. The following outline must therefore be taken as a selective introduction to postmodern theory and concepts in terms of how they may relate to tourism (particularly to theme parks, film and tourism).

Postmodernism: Theoretical Paradigm or Merely a Place in Time?

The term 'postmodernism' can be confusing, not only because of its over (and mis)use in today's society, but also because of its dual meanings and applications. On the one hand, the term signifies that it comes after ('post') modernism, and represents a moving-on in time and a break with the modern (Featherstone, 1988). Hence, it is easy to see postmodernism as a place in time, following the modernist era of the 19th and 20th centuries, which in turn followed the Renaissance period. The use of modernisation to represent economic progress also tends to create the impression that post-modernisation is also economically based.

On the other hand, postmodernism has come to represent far more than a social or economic era, and as such is seen by many postmodernists as a way of looking at the world – reflecting developments in post-structural philosophy (Hassard, 1999). Urry (2002) refers to postmodernism as a particular set of cultural developments that led to a new paradigm. He considers it to be a 'system of signs or symbols, which is specific in both time and space' (Urry, 2002: 75).

In the context of numerous discourses, including film-induced tourism, postmodernism is more than an era, it is a theoretical paradigm or epistemology. According to Hassard (1999: 174), '[p]ostmodern epistemology suggests that the world is constituted by our shared language...[where] meaning is constantly slipping through our grasp'. Postmodernism recognises and even celebrates the existence of multiple realities and changing 'meaning', but it does not attempt to provide a meta-discourse to explain all language forms, meanings and realities (Lyotard, 1984). Postmodernists recognise that this is not possible, nor even desirable, with blurring, ambiguity and contradiction accepted as integral elements of reality.

Supporting the view that postmodernism is an epistemological discourse, one of its key figures, Jean Baudrillard (1983) argues that models constitute the world (rather than merely representing it), blurring the distinction between the real and apparent, resulting in the notion of hyper reality. There are countless tourism examples for this notion, as noted later. Baudrillard (1983: 146) claims that '...the real is not only what can be reproduced, but that which is already reproduced, the hyper real'. Copies or representations of objects, referred to as 'simulacra' constitute this reality of Baudrillard's. Featherstone (1988) goes on to summarise the central features of the works of the leaders of postmodernism (Baudrillard, Derrida, Foucault, Habermas and Jameson) as:

> [t]he effacement of the boundary between art and everyday life; the collapse of the hierarchical distinction between high and mass/popular culture; a stylistic promiscuity favouring eclecticism and the mixing of codes; parody, pastiche, irony, playfulness and the celebration of the surface 'depthlessness' of culture... (Featherstone, 1988: 203)

Such abstract concepts are not readily embraced by all, particularly by many positivist researchers who are looking for measurable absolutes, not what they may see as 'capricious concepts'. However, as we start to think about tourism and film, it becomes clear that they are both abstract concepts in their own right, often representing something else (simulacra) while still being part of the 'real' world. Such notions of film and tourism lend themselves to postmodern consideration.

Postmodernism and post-tourism

Key postmodern terms such as 'representation' and 'other', as used by Baudrillard, Lyotard, Derrida and Cooper, have become central to the tourism discourse. The notion of replacing so-called 'facts' with 'representations' has been an early theme of postmodernism, and suggests that 'attempts to discover the genuine order of things are both naive and mistaken' (Hassard, 1999: 181). Many tourists become representations of something, or someone, else (the 'other') when travelling. A classic, all-encompassing example is that, by not having to work, they are living a representation of a wealthy aristocrat.

If we take this postmodernist paradigm and consider it in terms of tourism, 'post-tourism' becomes a logical concept. At the extreme, Ritzer and Liska (1997) describe the post-tourist as one who finds it unnecessary to leave home to travel (the classic 'armchair traveller') and who sees touring as a game where there are no 'authentic' tourism experiences. Rojek (1993) describes this in terms of the site traveller ('out of the armchair') who, as a post-tourist, accepts commodification. Tourism is seen as an end in itself, not as a means to the loftier goals of personal development, cultural interaction or education. Rojek argues that the postmodernism view of heritage tourism, for example, is that we cannot preserve the past, merely represent it, as the mobility of all things is a constant state. Urry and Larsen (2011) reaffirm much of the post-tourist developments, explaining that the post-tourist revels in playfulness, variety and is conscious of the various contradictions inherent in the tourist experience. Venkatesh (1992) described postmodern society as one of spectacle and media, which suggests that film-induced tourism plays a significant role, being a form of media that creates (representations of) spectacles.

Taking this further into the realm of tourism, Teo and Yeo (2001) support the concept of post-tourism as introduced by Ritzer and Liska (1997), seeing it as the recognition that all products (including culture) can be commodified, advertised and sold, rendering any expectations of 'authenticity' to be moot – it cannot be found, having been substituted by simulacra. Mura and Tavakoli (2014) reaffirm the continued relevance of post-tourism from an Asian perspective, particularly when considering the concept of social capital. Much of these discussions are reminiscent of the theming and solipsistic elements of Hannigan's 'Fantasy City' outlined at the beginning of this chapter. Such simulations do not have to be the same as those in our day-to-day lives – they can be inversions of the everyday simulacra, which provide the tourist with difference and escapism – two strong tourist motivators. Baudrillard (1983) uses an example of the caves of Lescaux in France, which have been closed, with an exact replica (inverted simulation) being constructed and open to the public. There are also numerous cases of places that visitors cannot enter being filmed and broadcast in real-time, such as with wild, shy or endangered animals.

Taking up these arguments, Ritzer and Liska (1997: 107) go so far as to argue that 'many tourists today are in search of inauthenticity'. Previously, MacCannell (1976), long recognised as one of the major figures in developing and discussing aspects of authenticity, argued that tourists *are* searching for authentic experiences. As appealing as MacCannell's view is of a highly developed tourist primarily concerned with reality and authenticity, in relation to theme parks and film, Ritzer and Liska's argument resonates more soundly. They argue that, if we accept Baudrillard's claim that we have been raised in a postmodern world dominated by simulations, there is an increasing tendency to both want and to insist on simulations when on holiday (Ritzer & Liska, 1997).

Urry (1990, 2002) ties this discourse in with another postmodern concept, that of the 'gaze'. His pioneering 1990s work took the concept of the gaze from medicine and brought it into tourism where the 'tourist gaze' is now a firmly entrenched postmodern sociological concept. Urry (2002) also notes the link between the postmodern notion of signification (representations and reality) and film and other elements of popular culture. 'People know that the media, for example, are a simulation, and they in turn simulate the media...[W]hat is fake can often seem more real than the real' (Urry, 2002: 77). Urry and Larsen also note that the notion of postmodernism includes de-differentiation, where 'each implodes into the other, and most involve visual spectacle and play' (Urry & Larsen, 2011: 98).

MacCannell, Boorstin and Eco have contrasting opinions regarding the post-tourist's interest in simulacra (and elements of 'authenticity'). While MacCannell (1976) contends that the tourist seeks (but usually fails to find) authenticity, Boorstin (1972) feels that the tourist does not care if the experience is authentic or not. In what is seen by some as a criticism of the post-tourist, Eco (1983) maintains that tourists are happiest when experiencing that which is completely inauthentic, that is, the hyper real tourist site. Urry (1990: 100) also supports Eco's view, stating that 'the post-tourist knows that they are a tourist and that tourism is a game...with multiple texts and no single, authentic tourist experience'. Theme parks and fantasy cities are outstanding examples of such hyper real experiences.

An example that further challenges MacCannell's impression that tourists search for authenticity and supports Eco's and Urry's views of the significance of hyper real tourism, is the Sega arcade/theme park in London. Here, visitors are offered simulated rides of an already simulated ride from Disney World, taking them even further into hyper reality (Ritzer & Liska, 1997).

In what is now considered a hoax, in 1994 *The Bulletin* reported that a Berlin concert manager had plans to build 'Ossi Park', a 500-acre replica of East German life, complete with '...badly stocked stores, snooping state secret police, and scratchy toilet paper known as "Stalin's Revenge"' (*The Bulletin*, 1994). The idea of such a bizarre simulation appealed to post-modernists such as Ritzer and Liska, who even cited it from another source as 'fact' (Ritzer & Liska, 1997). It is doubtful that they saw the proposed logo, which might have alerted them to the hoax – as it bore a striking resemblance to *Jurassic Park*. This also raises issues of the power of again and again reporting what another has reported until it becomes accepted as genuine or 'authentic'. Such is the nature of so-called 'urban myths', some of which eventually move into folklore, becoming part of the heritage of a culture. This is also an element of media reporting that, at times, results in cases of misrepresentation, or reporting simulacra as truth. It is a far too easy trap to fall into.

Many of the aspects of combining film with tourism can be studied in the postmodern paradigm, not in the least because of the co-existence of such opposing concepts as authenticity and fantasy, hyper reality and inversion, simulacra and reality. For example, a 2002 exhibition at the Smithsonian's Cooper-Hewitt, National Design Museum titled, 'New Hotels for Global Nomads' presented hotels in the themes, Urban Hotels, Hotels as Global Business, Fantasy Hotels, Natural Hotels and Hotels on the Move. One of the hotels explored in the exhibition is The Hotel in Lucerne, which expresses itself as a cinematic experience by recreating movie scenes on the ceilings of the guests' rooms (Smithsonian Cooper-Hewitt, 2002). Not only is this an interesting (and potentially strong commercial) concept from the hotel's point of view, the real fascination lies in that it also forms part of a museum exhibition in New York. Such inversions provide enormous scope for students of hyper reality as well as for the tourist gaze and have become even more prevalent in recent years.

Simulacra and representation do not always come together in a seamless integration; however the postmodern tourist is aware of this. In essence, the postmodern tourist accepts and even expects multiple representations and simulacra, relishing such dissonance. This was evident during the weekend preceding *The Lord of the Rings* world premiere in Wellington. A Medieval Fair was held that weekend, which was not directly linked to *The Lord of the Rings* movies, but provided a contextual backdrop for many of the visitors to the city. At one stage several men acting as 'ogres' were fighting a man armed with a whip as a 'taster' to encourage people to visit the fair. There were many comments and discussions in the audience as to this particular 'act' and its relationship with *The Lord of the Rings*. Numerous audience members were heard to comment, 'No, they're not real', meaning that the men were not *The Lord of the Rings'* characters. Such notions of reality are direct cases of hyper reality at work in our society. Inside the fair, there were countless other hyper real situations, from watching a group consisting of a Maori, Japanese and two Pakeha (Caucasian New Zealanders) playing Japanese drums to being able to purchase elf ears and watch *Zena, Warrior Princess*-styled women perform on horseback.

This is not the only hyper real experience I have had, but it was the first one where I was conscious of the various realities operating simultaneously. As noted in Chapter 2, film landscapes have become so pervasive that even the destinations are transformed into *mediaworlds* where fans, in their desire to find the reality of a movie or television series, take pilgrimages to the film locations and studios as well as participating in re-enactments and tangentially associated activities, confusing model and reality (Urry & Larsen, 2011).

Film-Themed Events

One-off events such as film premieres and festivals can act as tourism generators, in much the same way as other forms of festival. As noted in Chapter 1, Riley and Van Doren (1992) have likened movies to hallmark events, and this idea is also studied by Cousins and Andereck (1993). However, neither group of researchers has looked at the clear links between film festivals and premieres and festivals in general.

Falassi (1987) argues that there are two closely related elements of festivals and events, namely a social function and symbolic meaning, both relating to and reflecting the community's ideology, social identity, historical continuity and physical survival. Film festivals and movie premieres, such as that for *The Return of the King*, the final movie in *The Lord of the Rings* series and the more recent *Oddball* (2015) premieres, fulfil such roles, albeit differently from community-based festivals. These aspects are explored below.

Film festivals

Many cities host film festivals, from the internationally acclaimed Cannes Film Festival, where film-makers take their work for exposure and future profit, to smaller, more audience-focused festivals. A festival such as the Cannes Film Festival, where many of those attending are industry professionals hoping to sign distribution (or other) contracts, is very much an industry event, more in the line of a convention or trade show than a public festival. It is not easy for the general public to gain access to such an event, because limited tickets and the high cost of attendance and accommodation effectively filter them out.

However, there are hundreds of audience-based film festivals around the world, from generic style festivals that may have a 'fringe' attachment for the more avant-garde films, to themed festivals such as science fiction film festivals, or even *Star Trek* festivals. They all contain elements of symbolic meaning and social function, often reflecting a community's view of its place in the world through the films that are selected (and prove to be the most popular) for the festival. The number of film festivals grows daily, but an example of the range of such events is illustrated in Beeton (2008c), where I look at the role of international film festivals and awards ceremonies in terms of international business, re-presented in Table 8.2.

Many such festivals attract domestic visitors and international film industry personnel, and often combine professional conferences and

Table 8.2 Selected international film festivals

Festival	Month(s)	Venue
Del Plata International Film Festival	March	Buenos Aires, Argentina
Brisbane International Film Festival	July/August	Brisbane, Australia
Heart of Gold International Film Festival	October	Gympie, Australia
Melbourne International Film Festival	July/August	Melbourne, Australia
World of Women International Film Festival	October	Sydney, Australia
Viennale – Vienna International Film Festival	October	Vienna, Austria
Mumbai International Film Festival	January	Mumbai, India
Dublin International Film Festival	February	Dublin, Ireland
Galway Film Fleadh	July	Galway, Ireland
River to River Florence Indian Film Festival	December	Florence, Italy
MIFF – Milano International Film Festival	March/April	Milan, Italy
Shanghai International Film Festival	June	Shanghai, China
Osaka European Film Festival	November	Osaka, Japan
Wood Green International Short Film Festival	March	London, England
BFM International Film Festival	September	London, England
Boston Motion Picture Awards	December	Reading, US
Sundance Film Festival	January	Utah, US
San Francisco International Film Festival	April/May	San Francisco, US
AFI Fest – Los Angeles International Film Festival	November	Los Angeles, US

Source: Beeton (2008c: 265). Adapted from www.britfilms.com.

business with those for whom the works are made – the general public. However, there has been little emphasis on film festivals as tourism attractions, enhancers or generators, and this certainly needs to be considered further. The tourism field has paid even less attention to movie premieres; however, considering the changing nature of such events, this will have to change.

Movie premieres

While festivals tend to occur regularly (annually, bi-annually and so on), events tend to be one-off or transient, with every event being a unique blending of its duration, setting, management and people. The term 'special' event is often used, and this is distinguished by being an event outside the normal programme or activities of the sponsoring or organising body. For the customer, it is the opportunity for a leisure, social or cultural experience outside the normal range of choices or beyond everyday experience.

Film premieres in general have not been seriously considered in terms of tourism generation, by either the organisers or tourism professionals. The majority of the large, blockbuster movies (many of which ultimately attract tourists) are produced by Hollywood studios, and are premiered in that town. However, with the expansion of many Hollywood studios and associated creative production expertise to other parts of the world, this situation is changing. While Fox Studios Australia did not succeed with its Backlot enterprise, they have produced some significant blockbuster films, including some that had their world premieres in Sydney. These include *Mission Impossible II* (2000) and *Moulin Rouge* (2001) – the former features the sites of Sydney, while the latter was filmed virtually entirely in Fox Studios. Both premieres were what may be considered standard fare, with the stars turning up for a brief red-carpet walk and relatively little interaction with fans. Hollywood premieres may have a little more attached to them, such as the traditional setting of hands in concrete outside Mann's Chinese Theatre on Hollywood Boulevard. However, they tend to be media focused, with an emphasis on providing some glamorous images of the stars, some special celebrity guests and a few brief sound bites from the producer and lead actor.

When the decision was made to premiere the final *Lord of the Rings* movie, *The Return of the King*, in New Zealand in 2003, Hollywood had little idea of how this would change the format of future world premieres. The capital of New Zealand, Wellington, which had been the base during the 18-month filming process, hosted what was a special, three-day event, not just a film screening of a few hours followed by an elitist party. The city re-positioned itself as the home of 'real' Middle Earth, with even the airport decked out with movie characters. I must admit to feeling a little disoriented when we touched down in Wellington and the Air New Zealand pilot welcomed us to 'Middle Earth'. This sense of being part of something very surreal did not leave me until I flew out after the premiere. After all, *The Lord of the Rings* is a fantasy, yet here I was in a place where reality and fantasy had somehow been reversed.

Even as one who is fascinated in and celebrates the postmodern elements of simulacra and pastiche, I found myself becoming disorientated and confused by some of the juxtapositions between reality and fantasy that I witnessed. For example, at the aforementioned Medieval Fair, the performance of Japanese drumming was in sight of modern-day fairground rides, in the shadow of the country's national museum, Te Papa. This multi-tiered representation of reality became increasingly difficult to internalise without a strong sense of dislocation and this feeling was intensified when the stars of *The Lord of the Rings* regularly appeared at the places I also visited.

Over the three days, there was a series of special activities, including the above-mentioned Medieval Fair, CD signings by the composer of the movie soundtrack, book signings by some of the actors, free concerts and screenings of the previous *Lord of the Rings* movies as well as many themed parties and functions. It was relatively easy to have some contact with the stars, who were open and very friendly with their fans wherever they went. Such accessibility is, I believe, unprecedented, and the entire event was handled with the utmost humour from all involved, from the security guards through to the stars and their fans (Figure 8.1).

The whole three days was crowned by the parade of the stars and other actors through the city of Wellington, finishing at a red carpet some 450 metres long. They all walked down the carpet, signing autographs and talking to the fans. For those who couldn't get to the actual red carpet, the proceedings were displayed on a large public screen on the waterfront.

The New Zealand government took advantage of the international media in town, and hosted a special event at Te Papa featuring the best of the country's produce, and also provided special tours along with the standard media packages. Cross-promoting the country, its produce and tourism have become integral to many international events, such as sporting events in Australia including the Australian Open tennis, the Rugby World Cup and the 2000 Olympics.

As noted in Chapter 4, the world premiere of *The Return of the King* cost the government NZ$2 million, with expectations that it will be worth significantly more. However, the only economic figures available were the

Figure 8.1 Film-induced leveraging: Starbucks also joined the fray of *The Lord of The Rings* for tourists visiting Wellington, New Zealand, during the world premiere

estimates made some 12 months previously, which suggest the premiere of *The Return of the King* alone would add NZ$7 million to the Wellington economy (Wellington Regional Council, 2002). As demonstrated in other sections of this book (particularly in the next chapter), estimates can often be wrong. Also, media exposure of the films was estimated to be equivalent to NZ$25 million worth of advertising for Wellington, which is also a questionable figure, as much of it may not be the type of media appropriate for tourism advertising in the first instance (see Chapter 5).

The activities in Wellington (which not only renamed its region 'Middle Earth', but has become known colloquially as 'Wellywood') for the world premiere have certainly 'upped the ante' for such future events. The close ties with tourism and proactive national marketing are also a first for a movie premiere. There was speculation about a *Lord of the Rings* theme park being created adjacent to producer Peter Jackson's studios, but this has been dismissed by the tourism authorities, who claim that 'all of New Zealand is the theme'. Nevertheless, when we look at theme park theory below, and consider some of Jackson's upcoming projects, including a remake of *King Kong* and the movies of the *Narnia* fantasy series, such a venture should not be dismissed outright.

There are now special premieres that focus even more on the locations and local communities rather than simply the stars and major city events. The recently released Australian movie *Oddball* (2015) not only had its premiere in a major city (Melbourne), but also a pre-release screening in the town in which it was set and filmed, the Victorian coastal city of Warrnambool. As related in Chapter 6, this was an invitation-only event, complete with red carpet and the director, writer and star of the movie in attendance. The difference here was that this was presented as a 'thank-you' to the local community who had been so supportive of the filming. This event was significant for the town, receiving news reports from around the country, yet was a relatively low-key event, sitting nicely with the nature and story of the movie.

Exhibitions and fan events

In the publication *Travel, Tourism and the Moving Image* (Beeton, 2015), I spend some time looking at a range of special exhibitions related to film that attract tourists to the towns in which they are shown. I focus particularly on the Australian Centre for the Moving Image (ACMI) which not only houses the Australian film archives, but also presents (and creates) many popular exhibitions related to the moving image, in particular film. Some include the extremely popular 2011 *Tim Burton Exhibition*, *Game Masters* in 2012, *DreamWorks Animation* (in 2014) and a smaller exhibit of the sets from the movie *Australia*. As well as events based around major film and moving image activities, ACMI also presents more focused video-art related experiences such as Julian Rosenfeldt's *American Night* (first shown in 2009), based around images of the Western movie genre.

Table 8.3 The 10 largest North American anime conventions of 2014

Convention		Visitor numbers
1.	Anime Expo	86,000 warm bodies
2.	Otakon	33,929 paid attendees
3.	Anime Central	29,675 warm bodies
4.	Anime North	28,509 paid attendees
5.	A-Kon	26,377 warm bodies
6.	Anime Boston	25,493 warm bodies with 24,798 paid attendees
7.	Sakura-Con	approximately 22,000 paid attendees
8.	Anime Weekend Atlanta	20,311 paid attendees
9.	Anime Matsuri	19,412 warm bodies
10.	Otakuthon	17,661 warm bodies

Source: AnimeCons. See http://animecons.com/articles/article.shtml/1478/Ten_Largest_North_
American_Anime_Conventions_of_2014

We are now also seeing conventions and events being presented purely for (and often by) fans of a movie, series or particular genre. For example, Comic Con celebrates animated, comic book characters, where participants dress as their favourite character, and are able to meet some of them in person. Usually held over a few days, Comic Cons are now big business, with hundreds of events being held around the world, from the US and Australia to India, the UK and Eastern Europe. While many Comic Cons include anime, there are a number of specialised events such as the Sydney Manga and Anime Show (SMASH), while Japan hosts many anime related events, with fans dressing up at almost any opportunity. While there are also hundreds of websites dedicated to anime conventions, AnimeCons has a detailed list of many of the events around the world, including anime, sci-fi, comics, costumes, gamin, toys and television at http://animecons.com/events. As a brief indication of the tourism potential of these events, AnimeCons lists the top 10 US Anime Cons for 2014 with visitor numbers (Table 8.3).

Such events present powerful tourism attractions for the duration of their exhibition, with the destination often leveraging such exposure and benefiting into the future. Yet they remain an under-studied aspect of film-induced tourism. In many ways they have created a place for fans to experience the 'reality' of a film where often there are no 'real' locations as a form of post-tourism, which is also an element of the theme park as discussed next.

Theme Parks

Established in 1955, Disneyland is generally recognised as the world's first theme park, albeit a descendent of the turn-of-the-century open-air museums such as Skansen in Stockholm, amusement parks such as Coney Island and England's Brighton Pier, combined with elements of celebration and spectacle found in the World's Fairs (Teo & Yeo, 2001). It is the classic example of a 'Fantasy City' and, as the first, it is seen by many as the most successful of its kind, and is a model for theme park development.

While Disneyland's genesis is shrouded in myth (when, how and why did Walt Disney come up with the concept?), what is more verifiable, yet rarely noted, is the park's intimate relationship with film and television from its very beginning. During the construction phase, Disney required a substantial cash injection to complete Disneyland, so he formed a lucrative partnership with ABC Television Corporation to create the Mickey Mouse Club. The club assisted Disneyland in its construction and ongoing publicity, while Disneyland promoted ABC and increased the company's ratings exponentially. Consequently, the park was 'the first place ever conceived simultaneously with a TV series' (Sorkin, 1992b: 206) – Disneyland is television's first 'real' place. Confirming its place in the world of television, the official opening of Disneyland in 1955, *Dateline Disneyland*, was telecast live on a coast-to-coast television hook-up (Marling, 1994).

Sorkin (1992b) also recognises that television and theme parks such as Disneyland have numerous similarities, including the means of extracting, reducing and recombining elements of history and fantasy, reality and simulation, to invent a new, self-contained, anti-geographical space (even though theme parks are sited geographically in a physical sense). Film-studio tourism is an even finer example of being able to create anti-geographical space, as their theme parks celebrate populist films that are set anywhere and can be viewed anywhere in the world, hence reducing the need to consider the park's geographical appropriateness or its cultural relationships to the theme.

It is a small conceptual step from the filmic relationship between the Disney-style theme park and television to a film-studio theme park. However, the significance of this early aspect of Disneyland's development has not been sufficiently recognised, particularly in terms of film-induced tourism. The concept of on-location film-induced tourism may have been recognised from the early days of movies with visits to sites such as Monument Valley (the striking backdrop for *Stagecoach* in 1935, starring John Wayne, and used in many other Westerns). However, the link between television and theme parks has, up until now, been ignored in academic literature.

In response to public requests to visit his studios, Disney had long entertained the idea of developing a customised theme park adjacent to his film studio, as he felt that visitors would soon find the actual film-making process tedious and boring, needing more 'colour and movement' (Marling, 1994). He believed that the tourists wanted to be a part of the illusion but did not want to take hours to see just a few seconds of footage being filmed. So, when Disney built his new Burbank Studio in 1940, a park of eight acres was to be set aside for guests. By 1948 preliminary plans for a

Disney backlot park next to the Burbank Studio had been developed, including a glorified self-guided studio tour with sets depicting the Old West, the farm, a Main Village, model railway and the 'Gay 90s'. Unfortunately for Disney, he was ahead of the times, as the Burbank City Council rejected the concept as having the atmosphere of a carnival, not the family-centred entertainment complex that Disney claimed it to be (Marling, 1994).

Therefore, in order to understand and study off-location film tourism at the studio, we need to consider the various elements that constitute a theme park in general, including those coming from the postmodern paradigm outlined by Hannigan earlier in the chapter. In spite of the much-lauded success of many theme parks, numerous tourist attractions that may be considered as such tend to shy away from using the term, in part as a response to the negative connotations often attached to mass entertainment and tourism. Entertainment for the masses is regularly decried by numerous academic-based social commentators as bland, insipid, unchallenging, unsustainable and inauthentic, yet it remains a mainstay of the tourism industry (see Boorstin, 1972; MacCannell, 1976; Eco, 1983; Horne, 1992; Craik, 1991). For example, Horne (1992: x) notes that work by '…sociologists, anthropologists and semioticians…treat tourism as a disease requiring appropriate classification before being eliminated'.

In an attempt to encompass the broad range and increasing influence of theme parks, in a somewhat generic explanation, Camp (1997) outlines three main elements of a theme park in the late 20th century. These are that it is an outdoor attraction combining rides, attractions and shows, is designed around a central theme or group of themes, and charges a pay-one-price admission fee to visitors.

However, such a definition is too general, crude and incomplete. Camp did not adequately incorporate concepts such as those articulated by Hannigan (1998), or many of the other (post-tourist/postmodern) elements of theme parks, such as the prevalence of inverting reality and fantasy – a significant element of postmodern society. An example of this is the inversion of transport – where the ride is the destination (or attraction), not the means of getting there, as it is in 'real life'. Camp's simplistic description may have been an attempt to describe a shift in theme park style towards entertainment as its main focus, but theme parks remain more than merely themed amusement park entertainment.

Challenging the traditional view of theme parks as merely re-created amusement parks, Roberts and Wall (1979) describe a theme park as being distinguished by its particular goal of integrating public entertainment with conservation and historical preservation. One tourism product that fits this description is Sovereign Hill in Victoria's historic gold fields region. This is a purpose-built site representing a pivotal decade in Australia's gold rush (the 1850s), housing recreated buildings, mines, shops and dwellings with a host of costumed interpreters (W. Taylor, 1999). It is set in an historic mining town, still riddled with underground mines. However, Sovereign Hill goes to great lengths to distance itself from its theme park origins, preferring to promote itself as 'Australia's foremost outdoor museum' (Sovereign Hill, 2001). There is much debate regarding the current and future understanding of what constitutes a museum, outdoor or indoor, especially when museums adopt high technology and virtual reality to create more interactive spaces of more interest to today's youth – taking on many attributes of a theme park or Fantasy City. Horne is critical of the current state of technological reliance in our new museums, arguing that:

> [w]e do not need museums to dazzle us with modern electronic equip-ment...[W]e need museums that provide some vision of humanity differ-ent from the vision put forward by every advertising agency and political speech. (Horne, 1992: 196)

Those film studios that have consciously incorporated tourism into their product can be seen to contain aspects of the above theme park elements, including conservation in terms of cultural (media) heritage as well as ele-ments of Hannigan's Fantasy City. Sorkin adds support to the theme park as Fantasy City concept, in that:

> [t]he theme park presents its happy regulated vision of pleasure...as a substitute for the democratic public realm, and it does so appealingly by stripping troubled urbanity of its sting, or the presence of the poor, of crime, of dirt, of work. (Sorkin, 1992a: xv)

In order to achieve this 'happy regulated vision of pleasure', theme parks have become completely self-contained, solipsistic environments – versions of towns that have been constructed to be nice, clean and free of crime. Sorkin cites the head of Disney's movie division, Jeffrey Katzenberg as saying that 'we think of Disney World as a medium-sized city with a crime rate of zero' (Sorkin, 1992a: 231).

Contributing to the theme park literature, Weaver and Oppermann (2000) identify four paradoxes typical of theme parks that can be considered in relation to the Fantasy City, particularly regarding themocentricity, modu-larisation, solipsism and postmodernism:

(1) The 'dangerous' adventure rides are provided in one of the safest, con-trolled and sanitised tourist environments possible.
(2) Theme parks are portrayed as providing total freedom to wander at will, while they have high security, crowd control techniques and regulation of activities.
(3) There is a contrast between their emphasis on spontaneity, fantasy and escapism and the highly orchestrated nature of the actual experience.

(4)   Marketing theme parks as 'unique' experiences, yet most features are similar to (if not direct copies) of other theme parks, creating an impression of placelessness. (Weaver & Oppermann, 2000: 172)

A further paradox or issue that does not relate solely to theme parks, but in which they play a significant role, is the loss of public space. This has been occurring on many levels, such as the privatisation of public school grounds, and the sale of publicly-owned enterprises such as now-redundant mental institutions to developers. Page (2011) expresses concern over the equity issues of controlling entry and participation to once-public entertainment areas by tariffs and entry fees where a 'theme park' has been supplanted on to a public site. This has been an issue at Fox Studios Australia – one that has left the public with greatly reduced amenity and access. Public aspects of the Fox case are examined in the next chapter.

Understanding Film Studio Theme Parks: Concepts and Models

Issues of authenticity and reality become blurred and at times inverted in the theme park, and even more so in the film-studio theme park, which is a representation of what was a fantasy or construction in the first instance. In developing a model for such attractions, the anthropological literature and models of authenticity can be utilised, even though visitors to film-based theme parks may not be in search of 'authenticity' in terms of the earlier postmodern discourse. In the 1970s, MacCannell (1973) developed a six-stage frontstage/backstage model of authenticity that can be applied to theme parks as well as to other tourist sites. Pearce (1982b) furthered this dichotomous model of authenticity by developing a nine-fold classification incorporating people's motivations and needs in terms of encounters. In anthropological terms, the backstage areas referred to by MacCannell and Pearce are the private living areas of residents, and are out of limits to visitors. However, Pearce and other researchers realise that tourists have a great desire to experience the back areas (which MacCannell identified as 'no-go' areas for visitors), using terms such as 'getting off the beaten track' and 'meeting the real people' (Craik, 2001). Where MacCannell saw the backstage tourist spaces as areas off-limits to the public gaze, Pearce conceded that the pressure from tourists to undertake backstage encounters has altered the host–visitor landscape. Pearce included backstage areas in his model as areas that visitors can, at times and under certain conditions (usually as a mediated experience), access. Even so, there are still areas beyond Pearce's (1982b) 'backstage' that are strictly off-limits to tourists, such as engine rooms and rubbish collection areas – the former for safety and security reasons and the latter for reasons of

Table 8.4 Pearce's nine-fold classification

First	Backstage people in a backstage region;
Second	Frontstage people in a frontstage region;
Third	Frontstage people in a backstage region;
Fourth	Backstage people in a frontstage region;
Fifth	Encounters with backstage people (region not important);
Sixth	Encounters with frontstage people (region not important);
Seventh	Backstage region (people not important);
Eighth	Frontstage region (people not important);
Ninth	Front or backstage irrelevant.

Source: Pearce (1982b).

maintaining the desired 'image'. Pearce's classifications of encounters is shown in Table 8.4.

Taking the elements of theme parks as described by Camp, Roberts and Wall, and incorporating them with MacCannell and Pearce's models of authenticity as well as direct participant-observation of film studio theme parks, allows us to propose a film studio theme park model outlining the major elements (Figure 8.2).

The *frontstage* regions of the film studio theme park model are the general public areas such as walkways, restaurants, amenities, rides and theatres, while *backstage* regions incorporate the actual film sets where the 'hosts' work. The frontstage personnel at a film studio theme park are the traditional theme park service staff as well as professional actors who work in the frontstage region, while the backstage area presents staff employed in the film production process, from technical staff through to the film actors themselves. While a film set may be constructed in the same manner as a theme park site is constructed, the tourist's relationship to the set is different. Where the traditional theme park is accepted as a frontstage construct, the film set, while constructed, is viewed as a workplace, or backstage.

Many film studio theme parks claim to present a 'real' backstage experience yet provide it as a frontstage activity – for example Universal Studios' tour of the 'Backlot' takes visitors into film sets created to simulate theatrical experiences, rather than into the actual sets. Such a blurring of authenticity requires the model to be viewed with a third region between front and back, namely *midstage* (or simulated backstage).

There is still an inaccessible backstage off-limits to the public, as at Disneyland where a labyrinth of tunnels provides services for and staff access to the public activities above (Sorkin, 1992b). This is referred to in the model as 'deep backstage', and in a film setting equates with the 'real' working places of the film's creative and production staff as well as the invisible service aspects for visitors.

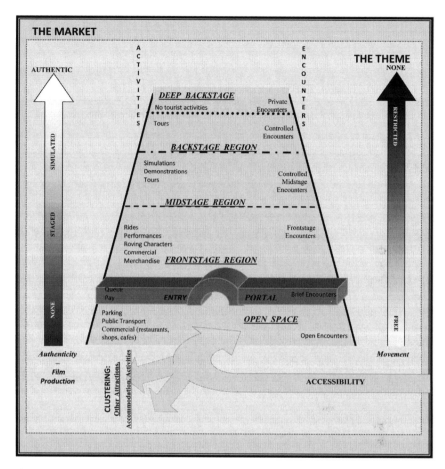

Figure 8.2 Model of film-studio theme parks

Two more regions have also been identified, both physically situated before the frontstage – that of the open (general public) space before entering the theme park and the entry portal. These are two distinct regions, one creating anticipation, the other a sense of arrival. In the cases of Universal Studios (Universal City Walk) and Fox Studios Australia (Bent Street), the open spaces incorporate a commercial, public precinct of shops and restaurants, whereas at other parks the open space may be the parking lot or street frontage. Universal has an imposing entry portal that creates not only a sense of arrival but also a sense of occasion and fantasy and differentiates the public open space from the more secretive fantasy world of film-making, as did Fox Studios for part of its existence. This model has been conceptualised in Figure 8.2 with more in-depth discussion of each region following.

Accessibility to the park site is crucial to its success – simply put, if people cannot get there, there will be no visitors. Accessibility relates not only to physical amenities such as public transport services, road quality, parking and drop-off places for tour buses and disabled facilities, but also to the more psychological aspects of access. For example, is the site on a recognised tourist route or near other facilities? Aspects of centrality relate more to perception than to physical centrality; if the site is clustered with other attractions or activities it is considered 'central' in the sense that there are other activities available (including accommodation) that increase the value of the price:time ratio – the higher the price, the more time a visitor feels should be spent in order to justify the cost. This also requires that there be sufficient activities and entertainment to fill the 'required' time. For example, Disneyland incorporated accommodation into its product range in order to give people the time to experience all on offer and to ameliorate the time–distance barrier from central Los Angeles and the airport. Apart from being a sound business proposition, this improved the price:time ratio, or at least the perceived ratio, for the customer.

The vertical arrows in Figure 8.2 represent levels of authenticity and freedom of movement through the various stages of the site. Levels of authenticity depend primarily on the structure of the park and the decisions made by management regarding the physical and personal encounters provided. Public access moves through each region with varying degrees of difficulty, from the most open access in the open space region, to the frontstage and through the midstage to the controlled backstage. Access to each of these regions becomes more difficult, requiring payment, queuing and/or reserving places (seen as providing a cost-benefit) as they go up the model, with the experience becoming increasingly mediated.

The likelihood of personal encounters with those in the film industry also increases as one moves from the open space region, through the others, to the backstage region, at the same time these encounters become more controlled. In fact, encounters are most likely in the midstage region, which presents itself as a backstage where visitors can participate in simulated film activities and demonstrations of production skills and techniques and where they may interact with production staff such as camera operators, sound technicians, Foley (sound effects) artists and make-up artists. However, as these encounters are expected, planned and controlled, they do not have the resonance of accidental encounters with stars or their associates – the less the likelihood, the greater the value. Hence, the visitor greets unplanned encounters in the open space or frontstage regions with great excitement. While deep backstage has been listed as offering no access or encounters, there is still the opportunity for those who are particularly well-connected or influential to be taken into those regions – with a high probability of personal encounters with all levels of film worker, usually on a one-to-one basis. Such access and encounters have enormously high cachet and are sought after, owing to their rarity and their relationship with the 'cult of celebrity'. Exclusive tour companies trade on their ability to secure such access, for an equally impressive price.

The activities offered differ in each of the spaces, in direct relationship to the personal encounters and access aspects. In the open spaces, publicly available commercial activities are offered, from car parking to restaurants, cafés and shops or booths that are often set up to promote the theme park within, selling merchandise, entry tickets and providing promotional material. Cinemas can also be part of the open space region, where they can be used to promote the studio theme park through association as well as merchandising. These spaces are also often used to encourage the local community to utilise the region – there is no cover charge to open space, so local people can regularly visit the stores and restaurants. Promoted as being 'community friendly', such regions have the ability to raise the awareness of locals to the theme park, increasing the probability of repeat visitation to the park itself, especially in the lucrative family and visiting friends and relatives markets.

Next is the entry portal – physically small, yet in so many ways the most important space of all, as it is here that a sense of arriving and passing through from one world into the other is generated. According to Sorkin:

> The element of arrival is especially crucial, the idea that one is not passing through some intermediate station but has come to someplace where there is a definite 'there'. (Sorkin, 1992b: 215)

It can be argued that the element of arrival is even more critical at film studio theme parks, which already centre on a culture of fame and fantasy that creates high expectations of 'otherness'. In order to maximise Sorkin's 'element of arrival', the entrance must provide a sense of magical anticipation and arrival at a special place outside the everyday world – a place where anything can happen. Usually constructed to permit tantalising glimpses of the world within and to celebrate the grandeur of the film industry and its concomitant fame, the entry portal becomes more than merely a place for divesting visitors of their cash.

The most highly promoted aspect of most theme parks is the frontstage region, which includes activities such as commercial outlets (including merchandising stores), theatrical-style variety shows, photo opportunities with roving characters and rides from virtual reality to roller coasters, in particular the popular 'white-knuckle rides'. However, film studio theme parks also heavily promote their midstage activities, which can be differentiated from frontstage (and other more general theme parks) by their industrial basis, while the frontstage is entertainment based. One of the main features of frontstage regions is the promotion of the high-speed rides, which are often used in an iconic sense and are based on major box office hits. Warner Brothers Movie

World (2001b) heavily promotes its high-speed, 'heart-thumping thrill rides like *Lethal Weapon*' and the 'high tech, high speed showdown' on the *Batman* ride; while Universal Studios features *Jurassic Park* as a ride that '...could take a turn for the worse, putting you right in the path of a rampaging T-rex and down an 80-foot waterfall!' (Universal Studios, 2001b).

The enduring popularity of the high-speed, white-knuckle roller coaster rides has received attention from numerous postmodern commentators, especially in terms of 'inversion' and 'difference'. One aspect of inversion between theme parks and reality has already been mentioned – where the transport medium becomes the attraction or destination at the theme park, instead of transport being the means to get to a destination. This concept of inversion is particularly interesting when considered in terms of the high-speed rides where people happily queue for extensive periods (in a 'traffic jam') in order to travel on a roller coaster (like a train, composed of carriages), to end up back where they were (at the end of the queue). Sorkin (1992b: 216) summarises this phenomenon by suggesting that '[g]etting there, then, is not half the fun: it's all the fun'. Rojek (1993) enters the postmodernist theme park rides discourse by referring to concepts of our preoccupation with endless motion, inversion in terms of inverting the body (defying gravity), identifying difference and speed as sources of pleasure.

In a description of the Disney-MGM theme park, Sorkin outlines further levels of authenticity and inversion at a film studio theme park with the following example, reminiscent of Baudrillard's hyper reality:

> If postmodern culture can be said to be about the weaving of ever more elaborate fabrics of simulation, about successive displacements of 'authentic' signifiers, then the Japanese family sitting in front of the Sony back in Nagasaki, watching their home videos of the Animatronic re-creation of the creative geography of a Hollywood 'original', all recorded at a simulacrum of Hollywood in central Florida, must be said to have achieved a truly weird apotheosis of raw referentiality. (Sorkin, 1992b: 229)

While the frontstage encompasses the entertainment and commercial aspects of the park, the midstage is presented as a more educative, industry-based region. The midstage region is particular to film studio theme parks in that it provides an additional level of immersion and encounters not available in general theme parks that do not have an industrial aspect to them. The activities are directly related to the process of filmmaking, but are carefully controlled and scripted to maintain a distance between the real process and the demonstrations/simulations. The closest that visitors may come to reality is some contact with production staff who have worked on films and have themselves met the stars – supporting the attractiveness of fame by association. Visitors may have the opportunity to volunteer to participate, though at times actors take on the more complex or embarrassing aspects of audience participation, this time playing the role of visitors, not stars. This is one of the rare occasions where the audience is not 'in' on the joke – it is usually unaware that the actor is not real. Tours of so-called backlot or backstage areas are often not real themselves, and take visitors through sound stages and sets that have been specifically built or adapted to provide a visitor experience. The midstage areas not only compress time and space as described by Rojek (1993) when looking at theme parks, but show us how it is done, conspiring with the visitor by providing the opportunity to participate in the creation of filmic simulacra.

Further evidence of the enormous tourism appeal of film and the public's acceptance of a midstage (or simulated backstage) experience can be seen at Universal Studios' range of theme parks in America and Japan. Universal places a strong emphasis on the midstage region at all its sites, the success of which is evident in its visitor numbers. For example, Universal Studios Japan broke all theme park attendance records when it opened in March 2001 with one million visitors in its first month and it is experiencing strong continuing visitation (Universal Studios, 2001a). While the population in Japan is intensely urbanised and technologically advanced, with committed movie fans providing a large existing market base, such high visitation is still remarkable. The use of space in the park once again touches on the postmodernist discourse of inversion – the Universal Studios theme park inverts the Japanese concepts and methods of utilising space in their 'real' world.

The next region in the model, the backstage, is presented as a special site, with access not only restricted to greatly-mediated guided tours, but often limited because of the actual work of making films. Most of the encounters are still with the production and creative staff, not with the stars. The reality of the filming and production processes is that they are tedious and time-consuming, and are not readily made for visitor gazing – another reason for the existence of the constructed midstage region that can provide information on the film industry in an entertaining manner. The industry presented by a true backstage experience can disappoint visitors who find they do not wish to go so far in stripping away the effects of the fantasy.

As already stated, a visit to the deep backstage region holds enormous kudos owing to its apparent inaccessibility and the opportunity to actually encounter and interact on a one-to-one basis with the staff and the stars. However, the general public rarely accesses this region, as it is a working environment that is sensitive to external eyes for security as well as creative reasons. The film-making process is not conducive to gazing because of the tedium and detail involved, let alone the confined nature of most sets which simply could not cope with excess bodies wandering about. Consequently, the more that visitors move towards 'authenticity', the more they move away from entertainment and enjoyment. Even educational opportunities are arguably best gained in a specifically constructed midstage environment, which is where most of them have been sited.

As part of Disney World Florida, the Disney-MGM Studios have utilised the concept of front–backstage encounters to the extent that the 26,000 workers at Disney World are considered to be 'cast members', moving them from the frontstage to the much-lauded backstage arena in terms of market perception. The Disney-MGM theme park relies heavily on the structure of the model, with simulated backstage ('midstage') spaces and controlled encounters limited to a few 'genuine' backstage experiences through tours of some of the actual film sets (Sorkin, 1992b). Most of the Disney-MGM Studios theme park is a simulated, controlled, staged and safe midstage experience.

In a bizarre twist to these structured moves between frontstage, midstage and backstage, Disney has begun to develop movies based on its theme park attractions, which takes a frontstage ride or attraction into a mid- or even backstage experience. By 2002, three such movies were in production: *The Country Bears*, a musical comedy based on the animatronic bears at Walt Disney World Florida, *Pirates of the Caribbean*, a big-budget romantic action adventure released in 2003, and *The Haunted Mansion*, which is loosely based on the Disneyland attraction of the same name (Verrier, 2002). Such postmodern inversions seem to thrive in the film, tourism and theme park world. On its release over the US Thanksgiving holiday weekend, *The Haunted Mansion* took US$25.3 million at the box office (Reuters, 2003). Whether some of this popularity flows on to the Disneyland ride is not easy to measure, but Disney's expertise at cross-promotion suggests that this could be significant.

Surrounding all this is the theme, without which the theme park would not exist. Appropriate, creative and consistent theming is crucial to the ongoing success of any theme park. Creating a mood, establishing a recognisable brand and telling a story are all aspects of theming. Read (1997) looks at theming as a historic activity, claiming that the arts commissioned by Church and State were acts of theming, where the theatre, painting and music culminated in exhibitions of pomp and ceremony, providing people with entertainment and escapism and spiritual solace. According to Read, modern times have seen business replace the role of the Church and State in providing entertainment, using themes such as the physical world, cultures, images of fantasy, science and space as well as Westerns and movie stars. Film and theming are interesting as '[i]n theme parks as well as film the object of the theme is to provide an overall visual direction and content for a production' (Read, 1997: 11). Consequently, a theme park based on film has theming, branding and attractiveness built in – it is 'simply' a case of deciding which films will provide the most appropriate themes. Such decisions have been based around box office success, with the most popular movies, cartoons and television shows featuring in successful film studio theme parks. Owing to the universal appeal of the box office 'blockbusters', cultural differences in establishing film-based theme parks are not as significant as in other theme parks – a ride based on the movie *Jurassic Park* is as relevant in Japan as in Burbank.

Theming also creates a powerful visual and spatial reorganisation of public space and shapes consumption spaces. Theme park visitors are able to 'see the world' and recall their experience by purchasing souvenirs and merchandising, with thematic motifs continued throughout the entire experience, even into nearby hotels (Teo & Yeo, 2001). In effect, 'site is sight' (Zukin, 1995: 57) in theme parks such as Disney World.

It has also been suggested that in the future theme parks may combine with shopping malls, as evidenced by the development of the Mall of America in Bloomington, which is America's largest shopping mall and incorporates Lego's Space Station, dinosaurs and a medieval castle as well as Knott's Camp, Snoopy and numerous rides. At West Edmonton Mall in Canada (the world's largest shopping mall), shoppers (or visitors) can view sharks from a submarine, visit a replica of Columbus' ship *Santa Maria*, gamble at roulette tables, or soak in a spa near a volcano (Goeldner *et al.*, 2000). As theme parks incorporate more commercial shopping opportunities and shopping malls introduce theme-park-style entertainment, the closer to each other they become. The theme park and shopping experiences are coming ever closer to the 'Fantasy City', with the main differentiating factor being the pay-one-price admission of theme parks as defined by Camp (1997).

Industrial film studio theme parks

While Universal Studios, Disney-MGM, Warner Brothers Movie World and Fox Studios Australia have all created a backstage theme park experience, there are examples where off-location film tourism has developed virtually organically, providing a more authentic (but arguably less exciting), industrial-type tourism experience. Paramount Studios in Los Angeles offers guided tours of operational television and film sets where access is dictated by what is being filmed at the time, with the tours and tourists being content to accommodate industrial rhythms. Generally, visitors accept this as they recognise (and it is also made clear to them by their guides) that they are on a working film-lot and many of them will have just come from being the audience for a series or pilot shooting.

In South Africa, a set known as Shakaland was constructed for the filming of the television series *Shaka-Zulu*, which was one of the most successful ever cable television releases in the US (Tomaselli, 2001). Following the end of the series, the South African Rural TV Network used the site for film production. After a slump in the South African film and television industry, the set became a tourism theme park. The site was promoted as an educational and conservation site, attracting day-trippers and overnight visitors to the region. While this site cannot be truly considered a theme park, neither is it an industrial tourism site – it is an example of 'industrial heritage tourism' with a film theme where the front and back stages have been artificially joined to present a historical film industry perspective.

In spite of the above examples from Paramount and Shakaland, the constructed, 'purpose-built' film tourism theme park now dominates off-location film-induced tourism, and attracts the big tourist numbers. This supports and reflects Disney's early belief from the 1950s that people are more interested in an exciting fantasy than boring reality – simulacra and commodified experiences are more important to many film tourists than authenticity.

The theme park market

The final element in the model is the market, without which the park cannot survive financially. Theme parks, with their sense of playfulness and escape, are not solely the realm of children – at Disneyland, three visitors in every four are adults. Nevertheless, family groups are a significant market, and as research has shown, if family members have to spend more than two hours together, they tend to squabble, which is an issue admirably addressed by theme parks (McClung, 2011). Being closed, gated environments, safety and cleanliness can be maintained. Consequently, the most successful theme parks are planned with a range of activities that not only cater to the different interests of family members, but allow them to separate from one another with reduced concerns about safety and security. If children go missing or become lost, the parks have developed efficient and friendly 'lost children' centres, usually located near the entrance, and with a high number of roving staff, lost children are quickly identified and cared for. Universal Studios even provides kennel boarding for that other important family member – the family pet.

While the need to vary the entertainment and attractions at theme parks is recognised as a basic tenet of theme park management, it is also important to identify the factors that influence a visitor's theme park selection in the first instance. In a North American domestic study, McClung (2011) found that children's desires rated higher than price, with climate the overriding factor in theme park choice. However he concludes that 'predicting theme park attendance and recognising potential market segments is difficult' (McClung, 2011: 242). This may have been in part due to the broad nature of McClung's study and methodology, which did not look at specific theme parks. Examinations of individual parks may provide richer data and identify more concise methodologies for future broad-scale studies. However, McClung did find that visitors to theme parks were generally younger (with children under 18) and had a higher income than non-visitors.

Theme parks are no longer the exclusive realm of North America or even Western society. Some research has been undertaken to see what differences there may be in the needs and expectations of different cultures and between the various ethnic groups, especially in the Asian market. Page (2000) believes that if ethnic divisions within a society are not sensitively integrated into the subject matter of theme parks, the potential for inter-ethnic conflict increases. Kau (2011) conducted a study in Singapore on the Tang Dynasty Theme Park, where he found that there were some differences in the theme park needs of the two groups surveyed (Caucasians and Asians), but he did not examine inter-ethnic differences per se. The theme park includes three television and movie filming studios, as well as an underground Chinese city, pagoda, temple, shopping arcade and dining areas.

Asian and Caucasian visitors to Singapore were surveyed prior to the theme park's completion, with a far greater proportion of Asians wanting high-tech rides and amusements – 60% expressed such an attitude, compared with 34% of the Caucasian sample (Kau, 2011). Such findings do not augur well for Fox Studios, as illustrated in the following chapter. The Asians also expressed a high level of interest in motion-picture making, with the Caucasians slightly lower. The areas that the Caucasians were most interested in were the more cultural Chinese aspects of the park. These findings are logical, in that Chinese culture is not 'exotic' for Asian visitors, whereas it will be for Caucasians. Likewise, high-tech rides and entertainment are more familiar to the more urban-based Caucasians than Asians, unless they live near major centres that have already built such attractions.

Film-based theme parks may not suffer such cultural problems as they are based on fantasy to start with and focus on those box office hits and television programmes with mass appeal. This is supported by Kau's (2011) work where, when given a choice of marketing slogans for Universal Studios in Japan, some 15% of the Asian sample responded with 'Universal Studio of the East'. Even though, at the time of writing, it is still relatively early days for this venture, the initial success of Universal Studios in Japan indicates the universality and cultural transferability of film, especially in a culture such as Japan, which had an aggressive introduction to American culture during the occupation after World War II, but which also has its own vibrant film-making industry. Perhaps we will see Japanese movie theme parks develop alongside the Western models.

Applying the model

The film studio theme park model has been developed in order to describe the complex frontstage–backstage relationship between film, fantasy and tourism. This has been based upon the work of numerous postmodern theorists such as MacCannell, Eco, Baudrillard and more recently Urry and Larsen, Pearce, Camp, Roberts and Wall as well as my ongoing personal research. As a theoretical model, this suggests ways that film studio theme parks can be conceptualised, as well as building on previous general theme park theory. However, it is important to ascertain how such models can be applied, so in the next chapter a range of cases of film studio theme parks are studied – with a focus on two in Australia, with one being a continuing success, the other a spectacular failure. As well as these, the model is tested against some more recent theme park activities including *The Wizarding World of Harry Potter* along with some of the increasingly geographically-spread Disney parks.

9 Film Studio Theme Park Success and Failings

The previous chapter ended with a lead-in to a discussion on the use of models in tourism research and practice. They are used extensively in econometric analysis, especially to establish economic impacts and undertake related research. In the social sciences, there are basically two types of models – prescriptive or descriptive. Prescriptive models are strongly theoretically focused, explaining what should happen in an ideal situation, as opposed to descriptive models that take as a starting point what actually occurs (Hall & Page, 1999). Some descriptive models also have the potential to predict future behaviour or events based on analysis of past events.

The model presented in the previous chapter is based on actual visits to various film studios as well as on general theme park theory. In order to test the predictable aspects of the model, long-term study of film studio theme parks is required. To test the model's descriptive and predictive ability, the spectacular failure of Fox Studios Australia (after less than two years of operation) is outlined in this chapter and compared with the successful Warner Brothers Movie World on the Australian Gold Coast (after more than 10 years of operation), with a postscript on Dockland Studios in Melbourne. The focus on Australia here is intentional, as it enables a strong comparative study. Nevertheless, the more recent developments of *The Wizarding World of Harry Potter* at Universal Studios have been included here to consider how this model can be applied elsewhere Other *Harry Potter* tourist sites and studios (such as in the UK) have not been included due to the theme park nature of this research. In order to provide further context before the cases and model are examined, a discussion on business failure follows. Learning from failure is important for students as well as entrepreneurs, yet appropriate cases are hard to find, as noted by numerous educators, including Sheldon and Fesenmaier who posit that '[p]romoting a culture of creativity that acknowledges and seeks to learn from failure encourages students to move…towards new possibilities and originality' (Sheldon & Fesenmaier, 2015: 158–159).

Understanding business failure relies on how 'success' is defined because, as pointed out by Frost (2001), 'Failure is rarely absolute…' Economically, business failure may relate to financial bankruptcy, inability to meet stated economic goals, or to respond adequately to shocks in the economy. Often ascribed to their propensity for risk-taking, entrepreneurs can experience failure, but they also often demonstrate a high level of resilience, learning from their own mistakes as well as those of others (Singh, 2011). In addition, a business may fail on environmental or social grounds, depending on the aims of the operation. Environmental and social considerations are especially pertinent to tourism, where such attributes play a central role. A so-called 'failed' enterprise may still continue to trade, propped up by government assistance, a parent company, reduced staffing, services and amenities, and so on. Table 9.1 outlines the range of reactions to a sustained failure to meet business objectives as identified by Frost (2001).

Numerous reasons are attributed to business failures, including inadequate or inappropriate business expertise, planning and market research. In a case study on the Big Banana tourism enterprise at Coffs Harbour in Australia, Leiper (2002) identifies management consultants' inadequate feasibility studies as contributing to the failure of the enterprise. Leiper

Table 9.1 Responses to failing to meet business objectives

	Responses
1	Bankruptcy, liquidation, mortgagee's sale, closure.
2	Sale as going concern.
3	Capital injection, either from owners' reserves or by attraction of new partners, public share issue, etc.
4	Seeking reduced rent, royalties, etc.
5	Reducing employee numbers.
6	Reducing opening hours or operating only at weekends or in high tourism seasons.
7	Seeking government grants, including conversion of seeding or one-off grants to a repeated subsidy.
8	Greater emphasis on increasing returns from commercial activities such as café, restaurant, gift shop, etc.
9	Sub-letting space to outside operators.
10	Postponement or dropping of projected later stages in the development.
11	Changes in admission prices.
12	Refocusing of attraction/site themes in order to make them more appealing. May include name changes.
13	Hiring of management consultants as managers or advisers.
14	Unscheduled revision of business, strategic or marketing plan.

Source: Frost (2001).

comments on the optimistic predictions used by the consultants, resulting in an enormous over-estimation of the feasibility of the business.

According to Leiper (2002), the Big Banana, constructed in 1965 as a symbol for the local banana industry, a produce outlet and short stop-over for road-based visitors to purchase local produce and take a break, proved a successful enterprise for its first 24 years. In 1988 the Big Banana was taken over by a large horticultural company who had plans to establish a horticultural theme park. Two experienced tourism and business consulting firms were engaged to conduct feasibility studies. Visitation estimates were based on the optimistic tourist predictions prevalent at the time. The late 1980s had seen enormous growth in international tourism thanks to a combination of factors such as the World Expo in Brisbane and Australia's Bicentennial in 1988, and the impact of movies such as *Crocodile Dundee, Mad Max* and *The Man from Snowy River*. Australia was 'the flavour of month' and nothing could stop us! Estimates of over one million visitors per annum to the Big Banana were considered realistic and achievable. By late 1989, initial high visitation had dropped off and the company became technically insolvent, being placed into receivership in mid 1990. The Big Banana had been a successful roadside stop for transiting tourists, not a theme park that needed to offer visitors enough to justify an entrance fee and a visit of some hours. Visitors did not have (or allow) the time they felt the cost necessitated, resulting in a high price:time ratio that could not be justified (Leiper, 2002).

Over-optimistic tourism assessment continues to be a significant contributor to business failure and is an aspect that is considered in this chapter's case study analysis of the Fox Studios Backlot in Sydney, Australia. Examination of the reaction of film studio theme parks to business failure and the application of the model is preceded by a description of the two cases examined, including my own personal experiences of the site visits. A detailed discussion on the development of the Fox Studios Backlot follows, tracing its progress and controversy.

Studying the failure of a commercial enterprise is problematic in that access to commercial-in-confidence information is rarely possible. (There are few businesses that want to make their errors well-known!) Fox Studio Owners, Lend Lease and News Corp are public companies, so access to Annual Reports and Stock Exchange notices forms the factual basis of this study. Even so, the Fox Studios data were buried in the enormous and broad interests of the News Corp companies, concealing even the public data. Their partner, Lend Lease, was not able to this, and as it is an Australian-listed company, access to its public records was much easier. Because of these issues and the reluctance of Fox Studios to communicate with me, much of the material in the following discussion was obtained through media reports, supported by Lend Lease's public records wherever possible. Participant-observation at the studio also enabled some confirmation and triangulation of the data.

Fox Studios Australia

When Fox Studios Australia, a joint venture between News Corp and Lend Lease Corporation, was launched in November 1999, the Australian Tourist Commission (ATC, 2000) claimed that it would welcome 1.5 million domestic and international visitors to the Backlot area in its first year of operation. Even though this proposed figure is significantly lower than earlier claims from California-based marketing consultants Pritchard Marketing Inc. that a 'conservative estimate' would be 5 million visitors per year (Zoltak, 1997), it was still greater than actual visitors to the well-established Warner Brothers Movie World on the Gold Coast (1.1 million visitors in 2000). It is certainly greater than the eventual visitor numbers to the theme park element of the site, known as the Backlot. According to media reports, actual visitation for the first six months of operation was around 55% of the projected figures, much reduced from the original projections (Emmons, 2000). Such estimates were so far off the mark that they raise questions, not only in relation to what went wrong at Fox, but also as to how an internationally lauded and awarded tourist commission could fall for its own rhetoric – or, at the very least, blithely accept and publicise the claims of others, even highly paid consultants.

Fox Studios Australia was ripe for media attention, not only because of the high profile of the movie industry and Rupert Murdoch's ownership of Fox through News Corp, but also because of the site selected for the studios and attraction – the Sydney Showgrounds, a 260-acre site 10 minutes east of the central business district. A high-profile group, 'Save Our Showground for Sydney' had been formed to argue for public ownership and access to this large site so close to the centre of town. The group included at least two judges and numerous independent film makers and was supported by 60 metropolitan and rural councils, with multi-millionaire Sinclair Hill giving the group a high-profile public face. The group mounted an unsuccessful challenge to the re-zoning of the area, citing Fox's lack of public consultation and environmental impact studies, as well as the company's contempt for planning procedures (Nicklin, 1997). Fox Studios threatened to take the film studios to Melbourne or elsewhere if extra land was not provided for a theme park in the agreement with the state government. The lobbying by the Save Our Showground group had some success in that it encouraged the developers to restore several historical buildings and to drop plans to build a so-called 'Hollywood-style' theme park on the site, opting instead for a potentially more authentic walking tour precinct christened the Backlot. The site was also subject to the New South Wales Heritage Act, providing the group with some legal leverage in their heritage lobbying.

As noted in the previous chapter, heritage and conservation (in conjunction with entertainment) are considered to be major elements of a theme park by some commentators, such as Roberts and Wall (1979). However, preservation of historic sites is not in itself an aim of many theme parks, with heritage more often presented in a postmodernist constructed, compressed form for today's entertainment market. In a strong indictment, Hannigan (1998) sees theme parks as destroying public space and historical architecture – an argument made by the Save Our Showground group, who did not want to see the public space of the Sydney Showgrounds subsumed by the private operations of the studios and the theme park.

Fox Studios Australia was a rare foray into entertainment management for Lend Lease Development, a company that has made its mark in providing real estate and financial services, being a joint venture between Lend Lease and News Corp's Fox Entertainment Group. The vision of the developers was to create a working studio, a Backlot Studio tourist area and what they refer to as a 'family entertainment centre facility' (FEC), in the style of Universal City Walk in Hollywood. Despite the similarities, they continually stressed that this was not a theme park in the sense of the Queensland Warner Brothers Movie World – there would be 'no white-knuckle rides…[rather]…a walking tour on various aspects of the movie-making industry' (Zoltak, 1996: 21–22). The Backlot and FEC were central to the development, with Chief Executive of Fox Studios Australia, Kim Williams, conceding that the public-access facilities will be a 'key revenue and profit generator' (Shoebridge, 1997: 40). However, at Lend Lease's 2000 Annual General Meeting one year after its opening, Managing Director David Higgins responded to a question regarding the Backlot by stating that '[w]e originally looked at entertainment and leisure as an area for growth…however we no longer have that view' (Lend Lease Corporation, 2000c: 18).

Even though Williams cited a lack of white-knuckle rides, the enterprise still had more similarities with the Universal Studios style of theme park than the Paramount Studios industrial tourism, outlined in the previous chapter. Elements of a theme park, introduced in Chapter 8, were evident at Fox, including theming, pay-one-price entrance fees, entertainment in the form of attractions and shows, as well as the site being self-contained, safe and clean.

The funding of the development and the incentives provided to Fox Australia came under public and industry criticism, as the State and Federal governments not only spent A$35 million on repairing services to the site, but also provided a stamp duty exemption (valued at A$460,000), seven-year exemptions on payroll and land taxes (capped at A$6.1 million), as well as a rent-free period of four years (Shoebridge, 1997). While information on the costs of developing the tourist site have been difficult to isolate, the original A$150 million estimate blew up to A$480 million prior to the opening of the Backlot in November 1999. In July 2000, Lend Lease made a pre-tax provision of A$96.8 million against the project's initial trading losses (Lend Lease Corporation, 2001c). The major loss-making area of the Studio was the

Backlot 'theme park/walking tour', which failed to attract the expected patronage (Lend Lease Corporation, 2001c), sinking the expectations of the developers that the Backlot would bring in 60–70% of Fox Studio Australia's income (Walkley, 1999).

The import of the Backlot's losses to the financial health of Fox Studios Australia lies in the cost of producing movies. While the production facilities are booked for up to two years in advance, and Fox has had major box office hits with *Mission Impossible II* (2000) and *The Matrix* (1999), such movies are extremely expensive to produce and cannot immediately offset the costs of establishing the studios. The Backlot, with its relatively low running costs (compared with the studios) was to provide the venture's operating profit. Fox Studios Chief Executive Kim Williams is quoted as stating that '[l]ike any factory, a film studio is a cost centre, not a profit centre' (Shoebridge, 1998: 80).

The price for admission to the Backlot precinct ranged from A$22.95 per child to A$37.95 per adult, with no family ticket offered, in spite of Chief Executive Kim William's statement that '...entertainment is an ever-increasing part of the diet of families...' (Sweaney, 1999: 13). The attractions centred on staged interactive demonstrations, two live shows, and two large attractions – 'The *Simpsons* Down Under', featuring motion capture technology and 'The *Titanic* Experience', a walk-through simulation promoted as giving visitors the experience of being an extra on the set.

The breakdown of visitors was anticipated to be 29% from overseas, 21% interstate and 50% from New South Wales (Schulze, 1999). While it is generally recognised that the Backlot has not been getting anywhere near the projected visitation levels of 1.5 million per annum, actual figures or the breakdown of attendance have not been released by Fox Studios. Media reports indicate that visitation to the Backlot is between 500 and 1300 people per day, a significant drop from the high of 6000 visitors per day in January 2000 (Cummins & Morris, 2000). Using this media data and averaging the 11 months outside of January at 1000 per day gives us a very rough estimate of around 520,000 visitors per annum; while such an estimate is not reliable or 'official', it is significantly below Fox's early estimates. The only figures that Fox Studios are prepared to provide are for Bent Street, which has been successful in attracting around 80,000 visits each week. However, as this is a commercial precinct with shops, eateries, cinemas and offices, the income to Fox Studios is limited to rental fees and a small percentage of income from the businesses (Kermode, 2000; Lend Lease Corporation, 2000b).

Actual visitor figures for other Sydney attractions are significantly lower than Fox's planned 1.5 million, which raises questions as to what data the predicted visitation was based on. For example, the Powerhouse Museum attracted 624,331 visitors in 1998 (Powerhouse Museum, 2001), while the National Maritime Museum attracted 315,498 in 1997–1998, 280,759 in 1998–1999 and 428,343 in 2000 (the Sydney Olympic year) (Australian

National Maritime Museum, 2001). While these attractions may not immediately seem comparable to the Fox Backlot, they are competing for the same disposable income in similar markets and are based in the central Sydney area. In addition, two out of three of the most popular exhibitions at the Powerhouse at that time were film-related (*Star Trek* and Audrey Hepburn), providing direct competition for the tourist dollar (Powerhouse Museum, 2000). Wonderland Sydney, a theme park 45 minutes from central Sydney, is a Disney-style park with seven themed lands, regularly featuring film themes such as *Shrek* and various comic strip characters (Tourism New South Wales, 2001). According to promotional material, its annual visitor figures are just over 1 million visitors (Wonderland Sydney, 2001).

On 1 November 2000, just one year after opening the Backlot, in an attempt to address the low visitation for the precinct (which was intended to bring in such a large proportion of Fox's income), Fox announced major changes. These included reducing the admission price for Backlot attractions to A\$24.95 for adults and A\$14.95 for children (but still no family ticket). They also took out the entry portal separating the Backlot from the popular commercial precinct (Bent Street), allowing free movement around the whole site. After the integration of the Backlot and Bent Street, trading losses ran at some A\$1 million per month, requiring a further pre-tax provision of A\$88.8 million, following the A\$96.8 million provision made in July 2000 against its share of expected losses. This reduced Lend Lease's carrying value of the Backlot to A\$15 million (Lend Lease Corporation, 2001c). Such announcements resulted in an immediate fall of 10% in the Lend Lease share price, with further falls anticipated (Harley, 2001). In 2000, the property development arm of Lend Lease contributed a meagre A\$3.3 million to the corporation, down from A\$89.6 million the previous year, which was seen largely as a result of the Fox Studios' losses and provisions (Lend Lease Corporation, 2001b).

Staff cutbacks in the Backlot followed and an application was made to extend trading hours in Bent Street, the third change from the original master plan in this area alone. In the first 12 months of operation, Fox Studios made 15 applications to vary the master plan approved by the New South Wales State Government in May 1996, indicating some 'teething problems' in spite of their 'extensive' research (Morris, 2001).

An indication of the political power of Fox Studios and the clash between two major tourist concerns in a major city is that they exerted influence over the planning for the Sydney Olympic Games by strongly requesting (and succeeding in that request) that the road cycling races be relocated to avoid a five-day shut-down of the studio (*The Bulletin*, 1999). However, in spite of the political 'power' of the organisation, the Backlot tourist enterprise was shut down without warning on 16 October 2001. It was proposed that part of the space would be used to extend Bent Street, with the rest being incorporated into the film studio. Lend Lease sold its half share in the A\$430 million plus development for between A$8 million and A$10 million to the Fox Entertainment Group.

So, what happened? Fox Studios undertook what they considered to be extensive market research by Californian consulting firm Pritchard Marketing and feasibility consultants, ERA, who surveyed more than 1200 people during the development phase and reportedly continued to survey visitors to the site. Exit surveys and brand tracking were undertaken by Sydney-based market research firm Newspoll (Emmons, 2000), a company experienced in political polling and market research, so how could they have got it so wrong? It is not possible to examine the research methodology used by private consulting firms as such details are commercial-in-confidence, and requests for data or information have been denied. Consequently, desk research and participant–observation were employed in an attempt to uncover some possible reasons. The outcomes were then applied to the film studio theme park model in an attempt to identify areas of weakness in the enterprise.

Site visits to Fox Studios

The overall experience of my first visit to the site in June 2000 was enjoyable enough. I found it a cross between the Hollywood tours of Paramount Studios and the theme parks of Universal Studios and Warner Brothers Movie World. The controlled, safe environment of the theme park was evident, as was the use of front, mid and backstage regions. But, there was a major element missing at all visits – people.

Due at least in part to the wet weather, the numbers at the site were low, well below the large crowds that the site could cope with, making the area seem a little desolate. Visitors included families and young couples, some middle-aged American tourists, but no elderly people. A large proportion of Asian and Japanese tour groups dutifully queued up for the scheduled shows then left via the souvenir store.

Fox Studios is set in the old Sydney Showgrounds, and on arrival visitors proceed through the Bent Street retail and restaurant precinct up a sloping hill towards the Backlot entrance. The entrance was constructed in a likeness of the old amusement park portal, complete with turnstiles, beneath a 'coat of arms' featuring an emu, kangaroo, kookaburra and other native animals replete with movie cameras and megaphones. The style was interwar populist with an art deco influence, in line with many of the historical buildings in the area, providing an amusing, humorous and entertaining sense of arrival and anticipation (Figure 9.1).

The Backlot area consisted of a series of sound stages and American themed cafes that were no more than poor imitations of Middle America streetscapes. Unfortunately, inclement weather on the day made visiting the site unappealing as, once through the gates to the Backlot, there was little

Figure 9.1 Fox Backlot entry portal (June 2000), replete with a movie version of the kangaroo and emu coat of arms crowning Australiana

relief from the wind and rain, which made the much-touted self-guided walking tour deeply unattractive. This was not really an all-weather site, despite publicity to the contrary.

The working backstage region proved disappointing and boring, as the working sets were all closed off with blinds and shutters owing to the imminent production work on *Star Wars*. So the only 'behind the scenes' encounters were those taken out of the working studio areas into the midstage of the Backlot construct. Those demonstrating make-up and Foley (sound effects) had worked on some productions, giving a perception of authenticity to the encounters. The live shows were typical of a theme park performance, even if they had an extremely corny Australian theme.

Fearing disappointment, I braved the main attraction, The *Titanic* Experience, where approximately one-quarter of the participants were returning for their second 'experience' that day. This was because there are actually two separate *Titanic* experiences – half of the group head down into the ship and 'die', while the other half get to the lifeboats and 'survive'. The experience itself was controlled, enjoyable and well put together. However, it was nothing like the promised backstage experience of being an extra on the film (as promoted); rather it was a surprisingly similar experience to the virtual reality *Back to the Future* ride at Universal Studios in Hollywood, even though different technology was applied. The visitors clearly enjoyed the experience, but few took advantage of the high-priced commemorative photographic merchandise available on the way out, provided by major sponsor Kodak.

The staff were generally courteous and the costumed 'customer relations' staff worked hard to entertain those waiting in (the mercifully short) queues, and chatted to those travelling alone. While they were costumed, these staff did not represent specific film characters (as is the case at Warner Brothers Movie World), rather they were a pastiche of Australiana (young men in Drizabone coats and Akubra hats) and slapstick entertainers in the nature of the Keystone Cops. This lack of utilising known characters is most likely due to some confusing licensing problems that Fox Australia appears to be experiencing, but it does little to create any sense of backstage or celebrity encounters. Information on the licensing issues is anecdotal and incomplete, with staff informing me of this problem in whispered, conspiratorial tones and may not be totally reliable, yet it is hard to find another explanation that fits.

There certainly seemed to be enormous problems at the site regarding licensing issues, and few actual Fox movie themes featured. Even the set for *Babe, Pig in the City* is a static, dead site without any interpretation, even in the form of storyboards. In order to side-step its limited access to interactive film material (a rights issue), the Backlot relies heavily on *Simpsons* characters (for which there are no licensing problems), from life-size free standing cut-outs to decorated burger stands and hot dog vans (all of which were closed on the day of my visit).

As further evidence of licensing difficulties, over half of the Fox Souvenir Shop was dedicated to *Simpsons* merchandise, with the rest made up of a small range of Fox Studio souvenirs, and some *Star Wars* and *Titanic* merchandise. There were few souvenirs specific to Fox Australia (apart from clothing with the Fox name), and no postcards or other photographic memorabilia, even though (or maybe because) Kodak is a major sponsor. Frontstage encounters with the staff in the shop were pleasant, but unenthused.

After the removal of the entry gates and lowering of entry fees to the Backlot in November 2000, I made return visits to see what effect this had had on numbers to the site and on the activities of visitors. I wondered whether, by taking away the pay-one-price admission and allowing free movement around the Backlot, the enclosed, safe theme park feeling might be lost. The site now gave the impression of an entirely retail venture, lacking any identifiable theatrical or cinematic theme. The 'experience' started at the retail area of Bent Street with its cafes, Italian and Swiss restaurants, a Sanity music store, Dymocks Bookstore and cinema complex, and moved on to the (now open) Backlot area, with no physical entrance or sense of arrival, reducing even the simulated backstage to a purely 'open space' experience. The entry portal that had provided a theatrical sense of arrival had been dismantled and moved to the side of one of the streets in the Backlot. The photos in Figure 9.2 illustrate the effect on the entrance of the removal of the Backlot entry portal.

People were wandering aimlessly through the site then leaving, not interested in eating or drinking in the pitiful imitation American-style diners, unless

Figure 9.2 Changes to Fox Backlot entrance. The top picture (June 2000) shows the original entry portal. The lower one (May 2001) shows the entrance after the portal had been removed

they had purchased an all-inclusive ticket to the 'shows' and Backlot studios. This ticket enabled attendees to visit each attraction only once and could not be used to make repeat visits to an 'experience', as is the case at other theme parks. The themed hosts I noted in the previous visit (June 2000) were not evident, and the only midstage/frontstage character interaction was with a mute Homer Simpson who was transported around Bent Street and the Market area on a small cart. The children were thrilled, but not enough to persuade their parents to take them to any of the separately priced attractions.

Those actually attending the paid attractions on both the Friday and Saturday were almost entirely Japanese tour groups. Observation indicated there were about 80% Japanese and Asian visitors, 10% other international visitors (American with some French and Germans) and a maximum of 10% domestic visitors. In spite of media reports of Fox's plan to make regular changes to the entertainment, the shows and other paid attractions had not been changed in the past 12 months, indicating no desire to encourage repeat visitation, instead relying on the one-off international visitor. As the Backlot had not been the anticipated gold mine, there may have been no additional funds allocated to facilitate changes to the entertainment programme. However, without this Fox was unable to attract repeat visitors, especially in the local market – a key to successful tourism enterprises.

The staff were all friendly and happy to talk, especially as they appeared quite bored owing to the lack of visitors, and were a valuable source of information. There were no costumed hosts visible, leaving the casual visitor with little desire to move from the free frontstage region (which is more akin to an open space region now that the entry portal has been removed), to the simulated, commercial midstage and backstage experiences.

At the Fox Souvenir Shop, a staff member explained that they were totally reliant on Japanese tour groups for souvenir sales. No postcards featuring the site were available, apparently because of the aforementioned licensing issues. The shop was still dominated by *Simpsons* merchandise, with some *Star Wars* and *Titanic* items. The same staff member also confirmed that Fox is no longer marketing the Backlot to Sydney, but is focusing almost exclusively on the Asian market. He commented that he felt the situation was better since the gates had been removed, as at least there were more people wandering around, though they were not actually buying any merchandise.

The licensing problems observed on the previous visit have not been resolved. The site now boasts a plethora of *Simpsons* characters, but virtually nothing else. The hot dog vans and hamburger stands were again closed (it was a Saturday).

A farmers' market was now held every Wednesday and on Saturdays in conjunction with the weekend market. According to a long-time stallholder, the takings from shops on Bent Street on Wednesdays increased by up to 50%. The farmers' market has now been introduced on Saturdays (this site visit coincided with the second Saturday since introduction) in an attempt to increase visitation and broaden the appeal of the weekend market. The market had been originally planned to consist of local produce and movie memorabilia, but this had been replaced by Chinese massage, Tarot readings, Asian imports, very average pottery and jewellery along with one stall selling Elvis merchandise. The ultimate success of the market to visitors outside the local population is questionable, as it is in direct competition for tourist dollars with the highly popular and diverse Paddington and Rocks markets. Paddington has the depth of a long-established market, while the Rocks offers a carefully formulated mix of goods aimed at both domestic and international visitors.

Originally the market and the site were promoted Sydney-wide, but Sydneysiders did not appear interested in travelling to the eastern suburbs to shop for high-priced boutique produce. So, Fox began to promote the market to residents of local eastern suburbs and this, according to the stallholders, has worked better. This local, almost entirely middle-class, clientele showed little interest in the Backlot.

A Fox on the run?

When we consider the current trend towards blurring differences between shopping and theme parks (as outlined in the previous chapter), Lend Lease's move into the entertainment field, especially theme parks, would appear to be a logical step, yet it proved disastrous. The reliance on feasibility consultant ERA and a marketing consultant from California (Pritchard Marketing) appears foolish. It has already been noted that Pritchard's estimated visitor numbers of five million per annum was a ludicrous guess, eventually amended by Fox to 1.5 million – still a gross overestimate. Fox had anticipated 29% of visitors would be from overseas, 21% from interstate, and the remainder from New South Wales (Schulze, 1999). While actual figures have not been released, 29% international visitors was a high estimate, as the well-established Sydney Wonderland (2001) obtained such an international visitation only after 16 years of operation, and only 6% of its visitors are from interstate, making the local market critical. As already discussed, Fox alienated its local market and failed to successfully counteract local resentment and concern over the theme park development, so it may have experienced a high proportion of overseas visitors, but within a very small total number of visitors.

Fox and Lend Lease also contracted a high-profile market research company, Newspoll, to conduct ongoing research, yet seem to have continually operated on a trial-and-error basis, with very patchy success. The continual propping up of the Backlot site through the additional provision of more than A$145 million is a most damning indictment of the project. Lend Lease earnings per share were down by 58% for the half year ending December 2001, due in no small part to the Fox Backlot failure (Lend Lease Corporation, 2001b).

The final indictment for the Backlot came at 5.32pm on 16 October 2001 when a joint media release announced that the Backlot would close immediately, with News Corp paying Lend Lease a sum between A$8 million and A$10 million for its share of the Backlot (Lend Lease Corporation, 2001a). The space was to be used to extend the studio area and the commercial Bent

Street precinct. Chief Executive of Fox Studios Australia Kim Williams commented that 'the closure of the Backlot...is a source of disappointment' (Lend Lease Corporation, 2001a).

According to media reports from the News Corp-owned *Australian* newspaper, the terrorist attacks in the United States (US) on September 11 2001 and the anticipated reduction in tourism 'pushed shareholders to resolve the Fox Studios structure' (Elliot, 2001: 35). However, the Backlot was never a success and, rather than the US terrorist attacks precipitating its downfall, they gave Fox Studios an excuse to close the already failing area and Lend Lease a reason to divest itself of an unprofitable liability. The simple observation and informal conversations undertaken on my site visits to the studios yielded a depth of information that would have provided Fox and Lend Lease with a richer form of data than exit surveys and tracking, and may have revealed positive ways in which to improve the Backlot's fortunes.

The elements claimed by Fox Studios as contributing to the Backlot's demise have been expressed in terms that infer they were externally based, and out of Fox's control. Chief Executive Kim Williams claims that '...the worsening economic situation and lack of public interest...[combined] with an expected downturn in tourism...[mean there is] no light on the horizon' (Rochfort & Cummins, 2001: 1). The term 'lack of public interest', as quoted in the *Sydney Morning Herald* newspaper, suggests that the failure was through no fault of Fox – the public were just not interested. This belies the demonstrated interest in and power of film-induced tourism – any 'fault' lies firmly with Fox Studios, its consultants and management, not with external uncontrollable factors.

Williams refused to publicly consider reasons for the Backlot's demise, stating that '...I don't intend to go into a retrospective forensic process about the Backlot. As of tonight, it's shut' (Rochfort & Cummins, 2001: 1). Some five months later, a more open Kim Williams told the media that '...we made some mistakes...[and]...one day I'll write about what happened there...' (*The Australian*, 2002: 5). However, the impact of such failures goes beyond the business itself and the jobs lost (90 full time and 50 part time) – the flow-on economic effects and levels of investor confidence can be significant. As Leiper states in his concluding remarks on the failure of the Big Banana theme park:

> Losses such as these are paid for, indirectly, by everyone with any sort of interest in the Australian economy: wage earners, consumers, businesses, investors, tax payers and borrowers. That is why large business losses should be matters of public interest and why decisions behind failed investments should be studied. (Leiper, 2002: 265)

Finally, in 2003 Lend Lease made moves to get out of Fox Studios completely, announcing its intention to sell its share of the commercial Bent Street precinct (Cummins, 2003). This announcement has raised further concerns from the local community, as evidenced by a letter from the local parliamentary member Clover Moore to the Minister for Infrastructure and Planning:

> These proposals are a breach of the public trust over this significant public site…[and] the Bent Street precinct is of ever-reducing relevance to the film studio complex…[resulting] in the original master plan being effectively abandoned. (Moore, 2003)

Warner Brothers Movie World

In order to consider the effect of external pressures on Australian film studio theme parks, another (more successful) enterprise, Warner Brothers Movie World (Movie World) on the Queensland Gold Coast, was examined. Were the start-up and operating difficulties of the Fox Studios Backlot analogous to Movie World, and could this information be used to develop a predictive theme park model?

Movie World's significance as a tourism operation is reflected by its success in winning tourism awards, the judging of which is primarily based on business success and growth. Movie World won the national award for the Best Major Tourist Attraction for three consecutive years (1994, 1995 and 1996), and consequently has become a member of the Australian Tourism Awards' Hall of Fame (Warner Brothers Movie World, 2001a). The awards are not only prestigious but are an affirmation of business success, as the judging process considers aspects such as business operations and links with the broader tourism industry.

Movie World, a three-way partnership between Warner Brothers, Village Roadshow Limited and Sea World Property Trust, opened in June 1991. It is one of a group of three theme parks owned by the partnership, the other two being Sea World (opened in 1971) and Wet 'n' Wild Water Resort (1991). The parks are situated in close proximity to each other (Movie World is next door to Wet 'n' Wild) and are promoted cooperatively, with special passes to all three as well as other package offers including airfares and accommodation.

Site visit to Movie World

Unlike Fox Studios and the Universal Studios standard format, Movie World does not have a commercial restaurant and shopping precinct in its open space. Moreover, it is situated outside the major urban precinct of the Gold Coast on the Brisbane–Gold Coast Highway, only 45 minutes' drive from metropolitan Brisbane, and within an hour's drive of two-thirds of Brisbane's population of 1.6 million. On entry to the park, visitors can choose from a range of activities and entertainment options for an all-inclusive entry fee of A\$52 per adult.

As with Universal Studios, visitors can take a studio tour past (but not into) operating sound stages, then on to a special effects stage that is set up for visitors only. While viewing the set of a 'typical Aussie bar', participants are selected from the audience to experience the antics of a Foley (sound) artist at the special effects stage. As at Universal Studios, visitors only get as far as a midstage or simulated backstage experience, and do not interact with actors or production staff.

Visitors are also able to have their photos taken (either professionally or using their own cameras) with so-called 'stars' such as Marilyn Monroe, Elvis, Batman and various cartoon characters. This is in effect a frontstage celebrity encounter – visitors get to meet actors pretending to be other actors or characters. Scheduled performances, from cabaret-style acts with the 'stars' through to film-based shows, such as the *Police Academy Stunt Show*, provide a frontstage experience with the audience quite separate from the performers who are once again pretending to be other actors. While 'voluntary' guests may be included in their programmes, they are often planted staff – a ruse also employed at Fox Studios.

Unlike at Fox, where there were no theme-park-style roller coaster rides, at Movie World rides are available, ranging from white-knuckle movie-based adventures (*Batman, Lethal Weapon*) to more sedate children's rides (*Looney Tunes*). All rides at the park are popular, with the white-knuckle rides having by far the longest queues. Planning regulations and resident lobbying did not permit Fox to offer such attractions, which undoubtedly affected the domestic and family popularity of its theme park. Luna Park, in the inner suburban area of Sydney, had also been dogged by planning and noise issues. Being unable to get permission to open its 'Big Dipper' for evening rides because of noise complaints and legal action from local residents, Luna Park's cash flow was undermined to the point where it had to close (Robinson, 1999).

During the last few years of the 1990s, the Gold Coast region experienced a series of tourism problems, particularly in terms of the Asian economic downturn, which began to take effect in late 1997/98, and severely reduced the numbers of Japanese visitors to the region. Businesses solely reliant on the Japanese market suffered, but those that could move (or already had moved) to other markets were able to survive. Following the Asian economic crisis, two years of bad weather in 1998 and 1999 also impacted on Gold Coast tourism.

The three theme parks experienced a combined downturn in their turnover from the 1997/98 financial year, but were able to come back strongly in a relatively short time. In 1999/2000 they contributed A\$8 million to Village Roadshow's (2001b) operating profit, growing to A\$13.7 million for 2000/01 with overall visitors growing by 5.4% (Village Roadshow, 2001a). Unlike Fox Studios, the Village Roadshow theme parks (including Movie World), have established a strong domestic market by regularly changing and updating their attractions, and providing entertainment for all family members. By tying their product to domestic promotions, the theme parks have developed a high domestic profile. As proudly stated by their Chief Executive, John Menzies, 'A family can have a different experience every day of their holiday and still return the following year for something completely new again' (Village Roadshow, 2000). Menzies also commented on the strength of the domestic market and its importance to the theme parks.

The 5.4% increase in visitation to all three theme parks during 2000/01 was driven by the growth in the domestic market. This has been attributed to a range of factors, including improved access due to the upgrading of the Gold Coast Highway, increases in discount flights to the Gold Coast, the weaker Australian dollar discouraging outbound travel, and a run of fine and warm weather (Village Roadshow, 2001a). International visitor numbers in 2000/01 were still affected by the soft Japanese market, but did see some growth from China, South Korea and other emerging markets.

However, Movie World did not fare as well as the other parks in the group for 2000/01, with lower attendances after a strong previous year when a new ride (the *Wild West Adventure Ride*) had been installed. In response, overheads were reduced which partially offset the lower returns and work commenced for a new ride (*Scooby Doo's Spooky Castle*) 'to correct the downturn' (Village Roadshow, 2001a: 9). In addition, the release of the movie, *Harry Potter and the Philosopher's Stone* and an associated theme park ride at the end of 2001 has revived Movie World (Lawson, 2001). Prior to the release of the movie and launch of the ride, the park's website heavily featured Harry Potter.

Clustering three different theme parks means that a downturn at one can often be carried by the growth of the others, allowing the operators some room to move. In addition, the theme parks have been able to work together in a region that was not in a major city (yet was still close enough to Brisbane to attract day visitors). This means they do not have to compete directly with traditional urban leisure activities such as cinema, theatre, shopping and sport and so on.

Recognising the range of both positive and negative external factors outlined above, and responding to them in a timely manner, Village Roadshow demonstrates a good understanding of the tourism industry and market. However, in order to maintain the domestic market, it seems new and updated rides and attractions must be continually introduced.

Movie World has coped with a series of negative, externally generated global and local issues (the Asian economy and poor weather) through strong theming, strategic planning, product development and a recognition of the importance of the domestic market – something that Fox Studios ignored. Even though Movie World suffered a recent downturn in business, it has not followed the downward slide of the Fox Studios Backlot, which had no periods of growth.

Table 9.2 Responses by Fox Studios and Movie World to failures to meet objectives

Movie World	Fox Studios	Action
	x	Closure.
	x	Writedown of equity.
		Sale as going concern.
x		Capital injection, either from owners' reserves or by attraction of new partners, public share issue, etc.
		Seeking reduced rent, royalties, etc.
x	x	Reducing employee numbers.
		Reducing opening hours or operating only at weekends or in high tourism seasons.
		Seeking government grants, including conversion of seeding or one-off grants to a repeated subsidy.
	x	Greater emphasis on increasing returns from commercial activities such as café, restaurant, gift shop, etc.
	x	Subletting space to outside operators.
	x	Postponing or dropping projected later stages in the development.
	x	Changing (reducing) admission prices.
	x	Introduction of special events and festivals to encourage domestic visitors.
x		Introduction of new activities/attractions in the park in order to attract greater domestic market.
x		Refocusing of attraction/site themes in order to attract new international markets.
		Hiring of management consultants as managers/advisers.
x	x	Unscheduled revision of business or marketing plan.

Earlier in this chapter, Table 9.1 listed the possible responses of businesses that fail to meet their objectives (compiled by Frost, 2001). Table 9.2 is an adapted version of that table, summarising and comparing the actions taken by Fox Studios and Movie World when their operations were failing to meet their business objectives, particularly in relation to profitability, visitor numbers and target markets.

Table 9.2 lists the numerous responses from Fox Studios regarding the problems experienced at the Backlot, whereas Movie World's responses appear to be fewer and more targeted. The number of different strategies Fox employed to counter its failures may be part of its problem – the responses appear to be knee-jerk, uncoordinated and non-strategic.

The responses from Movie World that differed from those of Fox were in areas relating to the introduction of new activities and attracting a greater domestic market and/or new overseas markets. Movie World turned to the emerging international markets of China and South Korea as well as strengthening its domestic visitation by providing new activities for repeat (usually domestic) visitors. Movie World was successful in its attempts to counter the external economic and climatic matters it encountered, whereas Fox was not.

However, Table 9.2 does not go far enough in discovering the critical factors that Fox may have neglected. It merely looks at Fox's reaction to certain events (some beyond Fox's control), whereas the model developed in Chapter 8 looks at the structure of a film studio theme park and so provides us with an opportunity to analyse the structural differences between the Fox and Warner Brothers theme parks. Such differences are related to the responses shown in the table in that they necessitated some of the responses.

Critical Success Factors for Film Studio Theme Parks

The film studio theme park model introduced in Chapter 8 has been modified in Table 9.2 to indicate the structure of each operation (Fox Backlot and Movie World), particularly in terms of the levels of encounters and activities and the access to and existence of each region. For the Fox Backlot there are two versions – an initial model (Figure 9.3) and a revised model after the entry portal was removed (Figure 9.4).

When the Fox Backlot first opened, it resembled the standard film-park model, with a few marked exceptions – there were no roving characters or rides in the midstage region apart from a group of actors dressed in costumes that were not intended to represent any specific character. Even though the movie set of *Babe, Pig in the City* was in the frontstage region, visitors had no interaction with characters or creative staff (and certainly not with stars) until they entered the midstage region, apart from the costumed hosts who had no recognisable association with celebrity or fame. Apart from the antics of the costumed hosts, there were no performances in the frontstage region. Instead, the midstage region hosted the various performances ('Lights, Camera, Chaos!', '*The Simpsons* Down Under') tours (TV Tour), demonstrations (Sound Stage and Star Dressing Room) and activity (The *Titanic* Experience). The demonstrations were led by staff who had worked on some of the Fox Studio films. While not actively promoted, a tour of the working areas was possible, giving a form of access to the backstage region. This tour was strictly controlled and could not provide any real insight into the film-making process as all the studios were blacked out because of security surrounding the up-coming filming of *Star Wars*. The guide compensated by describing what it is usually like and that some actors even wave at the tourists – hardly an 'encounter'. As to be expected, there appeared to be no possible access to 'deep backstage'.

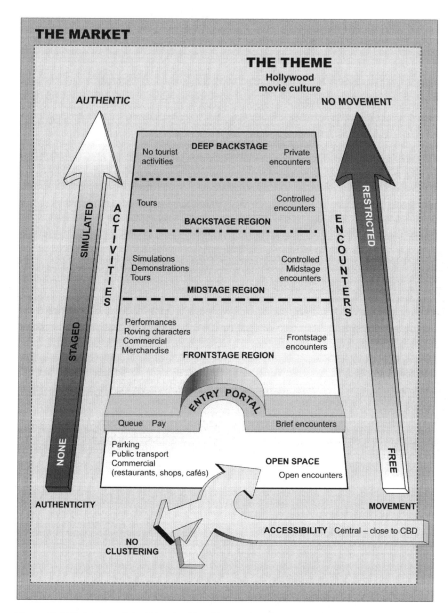

Figure 9.3 Initial model of Fox Backlot film studio theme park

After the gates had been removed and entry prices reduced, the Fox Backlot, minus its entry portal, looked like Figure 9.2.

Once the entry portal was removed, there was no differentiation between the open space and frontstage regions, which merged into one open space. Consequently there was no sense of arrival, no entrance and no welcome to

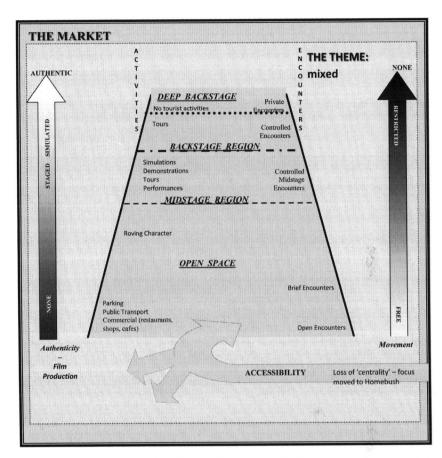

THE MARKET

THE THEME: mixed

AUTHENTIC

ACTIVITIES

ENCOUNTERS

NONE

STAGED SIMULATED

DEEP BACKSTAGE
No tourist activities

Private Encounters

Tours

Controlled Encounters

BACKSTAGE REGION

RESTRICTED

Simulations
Demonstrations
Tours
Performances

Controlled Midstage Encounters

MIDSTAGE REGION

Roving Character

OPEN SPACE

Brief Encounters

NONE

Parking
Public Transport
Commercial (restaurants, shops, cafes)

Open Encounters

FREE

*Authenticity
–
Film
Production*

ACCESSIBILITY

Movement

Loss of 'centrality' – focus moved to Homebush

Figure 9.4 Model of Fox Backlot film studio theme park after removal of entry portal

visitors to the Backlot. Visitors paid to enter the various performances, tours, etc., as listed previously, but did not have repeat access to them – they could visit each site only once, whereas previously they could visit as many times as they liked in the same day. There were no costumed hosts, but one roving character was wheeled out and briefly taken around the open space region, namely Homer Simpson. The midstage and backstage regions remained the same (no new or updated performances), except for increased restriction to the midstage region as already discussed.

Figure 9.5 outlines the Movie World structure in terms of regions, access, encounters and activities. The only significant deviation from the standard model at Movie World is the lack of commercial outlets in the open space, which is limited to car parking and transport collection.

At Movie World, there is a far greater sense of being at a working studio, with the backstage tour providing a controlled, yet seemingly open

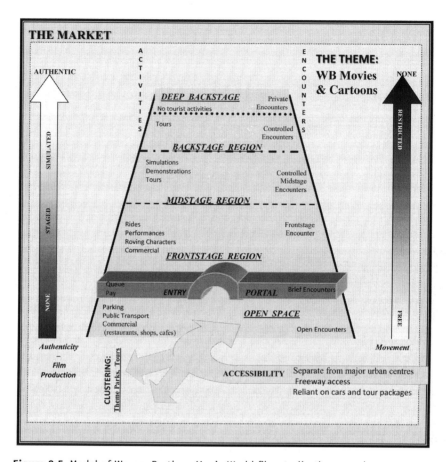

Figure 9.5 Model of Warner Brothers Movie World film studio theme park

experience – people movers take visitors around the lot to view the outside of the sound stages, then visitors are taken to a sound stage set up for tourists, simulating the backstage experience. In this way, the visitor moves between backstage and midstage within a single tour/experience.

So, what can we learn from a comparison of these models? While aspects, such as strategic planning and research, have played a role in the success (or failure) of the two theme parks, we have demonstrated the critical areas for a film studio theme park. Listed below are the areas where Movie World differs from the Fox Backlot:

- an entry portal, creating a sense of arrival, welcome and anticipation;
- opportunities for encounters in all regions, even those with actors playing characters;
- strong frontstage atmosphere with shows and characters;
- strong backstage activities combined with midstage;

- clustering of products and services;
- strong, consistent theming;
- diverse market – not reliant on one, volatile market.

The differences are significant and relate directly to the responses outlined previously in Table 9.2, so they can be considered as the main critical success factors.

The final curtain?

Kim Williams' 'key revenue and profit generator' (Shoebridge, 1997: 40) did not live up to its hype, and serves as a timely warning for those wishing to capitalise on the apparent add-on power of film. The abject failure of the Backlot demonstrates the risk of relying on boosterist consultants who tell clients what they want to hear, especially given the volatility of predicting tourism success. Without the Asian tour groups and special events, the Backlot's troubles would have been apparent within months of opening. Such reliance on a single market has proven disastrous historically and goes against all recognised business strategies (including Movie World's). So it is extraordinary that Fox focused so much on a particular segment of the Asian market – one that responds swiftly to global economic trends beyond the control of the operator. The anticipated negative tourism fallout from the September 11 2001 terrorist attacks in the US is further evidence of the inadvisability of relying on international markets and of disregarding, if not failing to understand, the domestic market.

In addition, the opening of Universal Studios Japan in March 2001 may have redirected Asian visitors from the Australian film studio tourism market towards Japan (Universal Studios, 2001a). Early visitor figures for the Japanese site are staggering (1 million in the first month), though they may settle as the novelty wears off, unless Universal regularly introduces new attractions for the domestic Japanese market. It is reasonable to assume they will, as they have done so at their other operations in Los Angeles and Florida.

Contemplating the community benefits of theme parks, Page (2011: 228) points out that 'theme parks...have been criticised as the high technology playgrounds of the middle classes, of little benefit to local communities'. In spite of Fox Studios' rhetoric, this has been the case regarding the Backlot development, which not only provided little benefit for the local community but provided negative returns for the hapless shareholders of Lend Lease (in particular) and News Corporation.

Still, the question arises as to why Fox Studios failed to live up to its tourism expectations. A possible reason is that, in its attempts to get tourism recognised as a valuable industry and to gain public funds to develop and maintain the public infrastructure that is so necessary for tourism, the industry over-estimated the economic contribution of tourists as opposed to resident visitors to theme parks. This certainly appears to be the case when Fox Studios estimates 60–70% of its income from tourism, and the original Studio City proposal for Docklands (Melbourne) cites a A$200 million benefit from tourism. This is of great concern and urgently requires more research and investigation. Such concern is also expressed by Leiper (2002) when considering the over-estimated tourism advice that the Big Banana theme park received from its management consultants in the late 1980s.

In spite of the publicity spin put on the success of Fox Studios, the working studios had not yet moved into profit in December 2001, and Lend Lease declared a loss on its investment (Lend Lease Corporation, 2001b). Recent filming at the studios includes *The Wolverine* (2013), *The Great Gatsby* (2013), *Mad Max: Fury Road* (2015), and television programmes including *The Great Australian Spelling Bee* (2015) and *The Voice Australia* (2012–). Since Lend Lease divested its interest in the development, it has not been possible to obtain such detailed financial information, making it difficult to trace the fortunes of the site. By 2015, the entertainment quarter that Lend Lease and Fox sold off in 2004 had been purchased by a consortium of private interests for further development, which may include a hotel, but interestingly, one of the investors, retail mogul Gerry Harvey, told the media that it was a 'matter of creating a place with ambience and also involving the community' (Cummins, 2014; smh.com. au/business/property/john-singleton-gerry-harvey-mark-carnegie-buy-enter tainment-quarter-for-80m-20140604-39j0k.html#ixzz3mEdohKSa).

Many of the critical success factors that eluded Fox could have been met, while others merely required simple counter-measures to overcome them, as they were primarily based on misunderstandings of visitor motivations and community perceptions. The false predictions of the popularity of the Backlot by Fox Studios and its consultants were compounded by insufficient and incorrect reactions to problems at Fox, resulting in its failure.

Such over-estimates and tourism failures undermine the credibility of tourism planning and funding as well as the broader economic and social effects. As we start to see tourism academics join private consultancy businesses, new standards in disinterested analysis need to be promulgated if tourism research is to remain credible.

A Missed Tourism Opportunity: Docklands 'Studio City' in Victoria, Australia

The Victorian State Government took great interest in the Sydney Fox Studios development, recognising the economic importance of the film industry and the tourism flow-on. In August 1999, a few months before the opening of the Fox Backlot, the Docklands Entertainment Precinct in Melbourne was unveiled. To be called Studio City, it was to consist of a Paramount

Studios adventure theme park, an entertainment and retail precinct and the Docklands Studios. The similarities between Fox Studios did not end there – the state government claimed that increased tourism to Melbourne due to Studio City would inject more than A\$200 million into the economy, while the film industry would be boosted by A\$50 million. Once again, the estimated tourism-generated income far exceeded the film revenue. According to the precinct consortium head, Paul Hameister, the theme park (which was to feature three roller coaster rides and a 50-metre high Ferris wheel) '...will be the first of its kind built in the centre of a city' (Taylor, 1999: 7).

However, by June 2001, the Docklands plan had been drastically revised, due in part to the failure of the original plan because of the financial collapse of one of the partners, Studio City – the developer of the proposed theme park (Schulze, 2000). For the revised development, state government support of A\$40 million has been promised for the development of film and television studios in the Docklands precinct. According to the Office of the Premier (2001), there was no theme park or other tourism attraction planned for the site. The state government indicated that the reasons for this decision were partly related to the problems facing Fox Studios and to the film industry's focus on production and film development as opposed to any direct tourism participation. This general attitude was reflected in the report of the Victorian Film and Television Industry Task Force (2000), which recognised the tourism flow-ons of film, but did not recommend direct involvement, particularly in terms of a theme park at the Docklands site. Unlike in other parts of the world where tourism and film offices have been placed under the one roof, Tourism Victoria and Film Victoria remain both operationally and spatially separate, which I feel has resulted in a missed opportunity; where the Docklands Studio in 2015 was an active filming site with five sound stages, filing movies including *Charlotte's Web* (2006), *Patrick* (2013), *The Dressmaker* (2015) and *Oddball* (2015), as well as numerous television programmes, its potential as a tourist attraction remained unrealised. As one of only three major sound stages in Australia, and the site of some highly popular films and television shows, the potential for industrial-based tourism exists; however, as seen, it needs careful planning. The site promotes its facilities for events, product launches such as fashion and cars, and corporate events, but has no tourism agenda.

While a theme park may not be the appropriate film-tourism product, an option might be guided tours combined with audiences at television shoots in a format similar to that at Paramount Studios in Los Angeles. At Paramount, anyone participating in an audience-based programme (especially pilots) is given a complimentary tour of the studios, with access to operating sound stages and sets. This type of tour may provide the most authentic backstage experience of all studio-based theme parks, yet the question remains: are visitors searching for authenticity, or just an array of entertainment and escapism as proposed by postmodernist theorists?

While on the surface this may appear to be a wise move in view of the Fox Backlot failure, the power of film as a tourism generator and the public demand for film tourism experiences should not be so lightly passed off. In a North American study of general managers from over 100 theme parks, Milman (2001) found that they saw movies and television shows as the third-highest ranking theme for future theme parks and attractions, out of a list of 16 significant themes. Such optimism is reflected in the general interest in film and television around the world, as noted throughout this work and has only increased over the past 10 years.

Studio Theme Park Tourism Ten Years On: *The Wizarding World of Harry Potter*

While studio-based theme parks have been around since the early days of Disneyland in the 1950s, and arguably earlier in the form of movie ranches (see Rothel, 1990, as well as Beeton, 2015 for a detailed discussion of this phenomenon), we are now seeing some outstanding creative collaborations which actually develop a destination for stories that are not based in a physical space, such as animation (Yamamura, 2011). While not an animated film, the movies based on J.K. Rowling's Harry Potter books have had an entire village set created by Universal Studios for their theme parks, known as *The Wizarding World of Harry Potter*. I have experienced this attraction in Orlando, Florida, in 2010 and Osaka, Japan, in 2014, within the first few weeks of both sites opening.

While still part of the overall Universal Studios theme park, the Wizarding World has been set up with its own major entry portal along with creative frontstage, midstage and backstage experiences, perfectly reflecting the model introduced and discussed in this publication. This was clear in both the US and Japan, with the sites virtually the same (Figure 9.6). The attention to detail in the development delights visitors of all ages, and as I took the time to sit and observe, I became even more aware of the small touches, such as a cello that plays itself, and enjoyed watching as others also discovered them. The major ride, *Harry Potter and the Forbidden Journey*, was one of my all-time favourite experiences, so I found myself deeply immersed in the magic of the entire experience in both countries, and even on reflection find little to be critical about. It seems that the fantasy of Harry Potter and opportunity to dress in costume sits very well with Japanese fans, who I found were also deeply immersed in their experience and shown in the photos in Figure 9.6.

This is a great example of a highly popular experience that positively supports the model in terms of a successful venture, and I believe it will remain popular for many years to come; however, it will need periodic updating as visitors return. Already, a 2014 expansion in Florida has created a second site, Diagon Alley, separate from the original site which is now known as Hogsmeade.

Entry Portal, Orlando Florida, US

Entry Portal, Osaka, Japan

Diagon Alley, Osaka, Japan

Diagon Alley, Orlando, Florida, US

Hogwarts, Orlando, Florida, US

Hogwarts, Osaka, Japan

Figure 9.6 The Wizarding Worlds of Harry Potter

Conclusion

Film studio theme parks are growing in their numbers, size and complexity, and are a major element that has not previously been studied in the context of film-induced tourism, and remains dramatically under-studied. These chapters are an introduction to thinking about film studio theme parks as a separate type of tourist attraction, not merely as another theme park. Their tie-in with the particular fantasy that film creates is significant, and differentiates them from other theme parks.

The two chapters in this section have primarily taken a business approach, developing and testing a model that describes the structure and operation of theme parks associated with film studios. By combining the application of the model with business theory on failure, a number of critical success factors have been established within the Australian context, indicating the model's ability to predict as well as describe.

Since studying the Fox Backlot and Movie World cases in the early 2000s, I have undertaken a series of site visits to the main Hollywood studios in most parts of the world, including Disney Hong Kong, Tokyo, Anaheim and Orlando, Universal Studios Burbank, Orlando, Singapore and Osaka as well as Studio Ghilbli in Japan, arguably not a full theme park, but still a constructed film-based tourist attraction. A number of these experiences are covered in *Travel, Tourism and the Moving Image* (Beeton, 2015). In spite of their movie triumphs, as shown in the Fox Studios case, the success of many of these theme parks is not guaranteed and they have had varying degrees of success over a period of time; but, unlike the Fox Backlot, they have tended to respond proactively to issues they have faced and demonstrate an understanding of their markets and tourism.

The failure of the Fox Backlot may well have affected studio-based film-related tourism overall, particularly in terms of business development and investment in tourism. It has traditionally been difficult for many tourism businesses to obtain financial support, and this has often been attributed to the highly publicised tourism enterprise failures (Leiper, 2002). The film industry itself is extremely fickle and volatile, which only exacerbates the situation. Public failures such as the Backlot may discourage financiers from supporting film tourism investment, yet it is precisely this diversification that may assist the overall film industry and reduce some of its own volatility. This was one of the aims of Fox Studios when it established the Backlot; however, as has been demonstrated, a poor understanding of tourism, and knee-jerk responses to problems, relegated the project to the realms of farce and ultimate failure.

Part 4

Conclusion

I hadn't yet realized that, imagining other worlds, you end up changing this one
(Eco, 1983: 99, *Baudolino*)

Since I began formally studying film-induced tourism in 1999, fascination in participating – however vicariously – in the fantasies and magic of film production has increased dramatically. All cultures and people have put meaning and depth into spaces to make them *places*. They are given stories – our own stories of experiences in that space, the stories of others we care about (or are influenced by), or perhaps imaginary stories created by us or by others. Fantasy and dreams are significant elements of the human psyche, and they are both recognised in many societies as integral to one's well-being. Popular culture as reflected in poetry, music, literature and film can all contribute to our fantasies and dreams, and in turn to our sense of place. According to Brown (1997: 185), 'With space defeated by cars, the SST, fibre optics, and the internet, people react by linking to place, and the idea of places.'

For some time now, it has been convincingly argued that 'reality' is socially constructed through our stories (see Schutz, 1962; Berger & Luckman, 1966; Hall, 1997), and making sense or meaning out of everything integral to the human psyche. Consequently, we view movies through ourselves in such a way as to gain some personal meaning within a constructed reality. We put ourselves into the story, sights, sounds and emotions of the movie through our personal experience, knowledge and analogy. As tourists, we also attempt to find personal meaning in (or create it from) what we are gazing at or experiencing, even if that meaning is purely 'fun'.

So, what happens when we go to the place we experienced in a film? Why do some of us have such a strong desire to do so in some circumstances, but not others? While these questions are part of the underlying motivational question of 'what makes people want to visit film sites', they also illustrate some of the complexities underlying such a supposedly simple question. In this book, various motivators have been proposed and illustrated; however this complex area needs ongoing (and continual) deep investigation, particularly in terms of our evolving social and cultural constructs.

For example, the mountains of Australia are stunning, but cannot compare on a picturesque level with those of Europe, Asia and America. It was the Banjo Paterson poem *The Man from Snowy River* that gave them meaning, emotion and depth for many Australians. The legend of the common man and his horse against the odds was rich with meaning, metaphor, fantasy and dreaming. This was reinforced by the two extremely popular movies based on the poem, *The Man from Snowy River* and *The Man from Snowy River II*. The story is very much about 'place' and is demonstrated in the movie when the mountain cattlemen talk about having to 'earn your right to live here' and Jessica's statement 'I can see why you love it' after being frighteningly lost in the mountains – it is the *place* that rules. Such a place has been imbued with meaning and metaphor, becoming much more than a site upon which to gaze.

The genesis of this study came from personal experience based on the elements noted above – *The Man from Snowy River* movies spawned an adventure horseback industry at a time when, as a keen horse rider, I was looking for adventure and challenge and as an Anglo-Saxon Australian, longed for the romance associated with our bush legends and pioneering horses. The sudden popularity of adventure horseback riding tours introduced me to tourism, both as a concept and as a profession. The influence of the movies on tourism and on my own research in the tourism field (imaginatively, professionally and academically) has been central to my life over the past 35 years. Combined with an increasing interest in, and recognition of the importance of, community tourism development, this interest in film and its varying effects on small, often fragile, communities has grown. Hence the initial focus on communities and film in the early chapters of this work, with the interest in movie theme parks coming later, sparked by the initial fanfare and subsequent failure of Fox Studios Backlot and professional visits to film studios in Japan, Hong Kong and Singapore as well as Australia and the United States.

10 Emerging Issues and Future Directions

Writing a second edition of a book that relates to early research in this field has been quite sobering – while we have seen many people undertake research in this area, much of it remains relatively light in terms of theoretical and practical development. However, there are those who have contributed significantly and continue to do so, including many to whom I have referred to in this publication. In particular, the work of Roesch (2011, 2016), Reijnders (2007, 2009, 2015, 2016), Tzanelli (2007, 2015), Frost (2006, 2008, 2010, 2014, 2016), Hudson and Ritchie (2006a, 2006b), Connell (2005, 2012), Kim (2010b, 2012, 2015), Sugawa-Shimada (2015) and Yamamura (2011) has contributed significantly to our understanding of film as a form of place promotion, product placement, meaning-making and an experience for tourists and fans alike, while also sounding a warning of the potential business, social and environmental perils.

From the fans' and tourists' perspective, newspapers and websites feature articles on filming sites in their own country as well as overseas. For many film communities, it is the media publicity that has 'put them on the map', and all the communities in this study confirm the power of the media in this respect. Many are also promoted via social media and the internet on specific movie and fan sites as well as the detailed Internet Movie Database (IMDb). There are now also smartphone apps (applications) such as Location Scout that searches for filming sites at your current location and links them to IMDb, as well as specific film guides such as ParisHugo, TS Filming (Times Square), GoT (Game of Thrones Filming Locations), with Global Movie Trails presenting a series of film location trails based around certain films. The growth in visitor-generated ranking and advisory sites such as TripAdvisor also presents visitors' experiences of film sites. For example, I related my most recent experience of Hobbiton as outlined in Chapter 5 on TripAdvisor, curious to read others' comments, which ranged from uncritical, unbridled joy through to my own more circumspect entry.

Ten years ago few actual filming locations in Australia actively promoted themselves as such, yet some were finding themselves dealing with the consequences of film-induced popularity. More recently, the community where the movie *Oddball* (2015) was set and filmed took a more proactive approach, reflecting a maturing of understanding the pros and cons of film-induced tourism. Their ongoing research of visitors will also assist us to increase our understanding on a practical as well as theoretical level.

Overall, New Zealand has been far more proactive in terms of supporting film-induced tourism, particularly in relation to *The Lord of the Rings* (2001–2003) and *The Hobbit* (2012–2014) series of movies. It is usually extremely difficult for tourist agencies and groups to convince governments to commit public moneys to long-term imaging exercises, as these are difficult to measure, particularly in terms of return on investment. However, the New Zealand government committed significant funds towards the promotion of New Zealand as the 'home of Middle Earth'. The extent of public moneys being put into the tourism promotion associated with one type of imaging tool in a country of less than 4 million people and an annual international visitation of 2 million (compared with Australia's 5 million visitors and the UK's 24 million) appears to be a little out of sync. The resulting economic 'benefit' from the high level of tax breaks made available to film makers in New Zealand combined with this promotional expenditure has been questioned by the Organisation for Economic Co-operation and Development (OECD, 2003). However, the ensuing years and sustained passionate championing of New Zealand by Sir Peter Jackson demonstrate that it can be worthwhile. Nevertheless, in light of the studies in this book, caution needs to be taken when committing large sums of money to a phenomenon that is still so little understood. This is not to say that such investment is not viable, but we need to monitor and research public investment in tourism promotion and private enterprises such as the Fox Backlot.

The approach in the UK lies somewhere between the Australian and New Zealand examples, with VisitScotland, the North York Moors Tourism Association and other regional tourist boards in Scotland and England taking an active stance in developing and promoting precincts based on film. However, the issue remains that the already large numbers of visitors to many tourist areas and potential for dramatically sharp increases in tourist numbers can be problematic, as evidenced in Goathland. There seems to be little concern for the social and environmental impacts that have become evident, particularly in the case of the Yorkshire Moors, examined in some detail in this publication. The tourist boards are primarily interested in increasing visitor numbers, which is anathema to the developing interest in sustainable tourism enterprises. Instead of finding themselves with a tourism boon from film, these regions may soon find that they are being avoided by the higher-yield market that is developing a sense of responsibility towards travel and its associated impacts.

Film tourism in Asia has grown exponentially, particularly when seen as part of the pop culture phenomenon such as the Korean Hallyu, Japanese

Contents Tourism and anime as studied by Kim (2012), Kim and Nam (2015), Sugawa-Shimada (2015) and Yamamura (2011), along with a growing number of studies on historical dramas in China (Zhang, 2014; Zhang *et al.*, 2016) and Japan (Seaton, 2015).

While the material outlined in this book indicates that less-populated countries such as Australia and New Zealand do not suffer from the obvious impacts of a massive, unsupportable increase in tourism and research due to film as can occur in the US and the UK, this may not always be the case. Australia and New Zealand are in a position to plan for on-location film tourism and to learn from the issues facing other sites around the world that have not had the luxury of taking a proactive stance, requiring them to cope with an unanticipated flood of tourists. It is crucial that they both monitor their film locations and plan for the possibility of increased interest in tourism to, and research in, these areas.

The main reason that there has not been the flood of tourists to Australian and New Zealand on-location film sites compared with locations in Europe and America has been their distance from the major tourism-generating regions of Europe and the US. There are indications that this psychological barrier may weaken as Australian film bodies work to increase overseas exposure and screenings, and as the appeal of Australia and New Zealand as relatively safe and accessible tourist destinations increases.

Australian film studios are already successful in the international movie market, and the increasing number of runaway productions (filmed in one place, but pretending to be another) moving from Canada to Australia has seen towns such as Daylesford in rural Victoria being used in the stead of American locations (as in *Ponderosa* (2001–2002), the prequel to the popular US television series, *Bonanza* (1959–1973). New Zealand is also courting the runaway film market, with movies such as *The Last Samurai* (2003) starring Tom Cruise being filmed there in place of Japan.

While visitors may not be interested in visiting such 'fake' sites, there has still been limited research into the phenomenon, apart from some work by Frost (2009) and passing comments from others such as Croy (2010), Durmaz *et al.* (2010), Seaton and Yamamura (2015) as well as myself, both here and elsewhere (see Beeton, 2011). If we look at work from other disciplines, researchers such as Mayer tend to consider tourism only briefly in terms of 'residual economic gain' (Mayer, 2015: 392) when discussing the cultural impacts of runaway filming. Consequently, we cannot be unequivocally certain of visitor motives, particularly if we accept the postmodern arguments regarding simulacra, authenticity and hyper reality. An indication of the tourism potential of runaway productions can be seen with the aforementioned movie, *The Last Samurai*, in New Zealand. Visits to the sites for the movie are still incorporated into some tour companies' itineraries and remains popular with Japanese visitors. Regardless of the success of such on-location tours, visitors may still be interested in visiting the production studios.

Of the in-depth cases studied, the Australian cases of Fox Studios Backlot and Barwon Heads differ in terms of scale, setting, longevity and capital investment, yet both raise issues about community attitudes and the loss of public amenities. While Barwon Heads has benefitted overall from filming in the town, the Fox Studios Backlot failed, even though the studios themselves continue to flourish in terms of movie projects and awards. These two cases demonstrate the implications of film-induced tourism in quite different circumstances, illustrating the complexity of the phenomenon.

The Fox Studios Backlot had an inadequate sense of location, both spatially and imaginatively – the local community did not embrace the Backlot enterprise and Fox failed to appeal to the imagination of the rest of Sydney, instead focusing on one main international market, the Japanese. There was no incentive for repeat visitation, as the Japanese groups came through once and headed home. Fox ignored the local market until it was too late. The studio's attempts to 'improve' the Backlot by taking away the entry portal and focusing on *The Simpsons* cartoon characters were reactive, inadvisable and unsuccessful.

Sea Change (1998–2000) coincided with a number of factors that not only made the television series so successful, but also aided the township of Barwon Heads. There has been a major public re-evaluation of small towns close to urban centres as places to live, and an increasing focus on the environmental quality of life, with people longing for clean air, the freedom of the ocean and a perceived sense of belonging in a small community. Lifestyle priorities are also undergoing re-evaluation, with people starting to consider other aspects of their life and well-being apart from work. Another, related serendipitous social phenomenon that affects not only the appeal of the series, but also Barwon Heads, is that those in the baby boomer generation are now moving into their early retirement years, and seaside towns close to major urban centres (Barwon Heads is 15 minutes from Geelong, Victoria's largest regional centre) are becoming popular early retirement centres. As stated by Kotler *et al.*:

> [f]rom quality of life considerations to charm, culture and ambience, the quest for livable, investible and visitable places is a perpetual search for the new and vibrant, an effort to stay clear of the sullen and depressed. (Kotler *et al.*, 1993: 2)

There is a synergy between the *Sea Change* story and the town, which enhanced Barwon Heads' appeal and 'put it on the map' as a place in an attractive setting and with small-community appeal. Barwon Heads had previously been perceived as boring – surrounded by swamp, prone to flooding and a place only for family holidaymakers and surfers, with most other visitors bypassing the town on their way to the grand 19th-century town of

Queenscliff or heading down the Great Ocean Road to fashionable Lorne. The television series showed the appealing and attractive aspects of the region and added a hitherto missing romantic appeal through its storyline, changing such perceptions and expectations, and constructing a new 'reality'.

Yet Barwon Heads did not capitalise on *Sea Change* as much as it could. The residents were deeply suspicious of their local government agency, the City of Greater Geelong and its bureaucratic constructs and want to retain their own sense of locality. They saw themselves as part of the rural/coastal Bellarine Peninsula, not the urban centre of Geelong, under whose local government jurisdiction Barwon Heads exists. Also there was an abiding local suspicion of the tourist board, Geelong Otway Tourism, which they regarded as more interested in promoting the Great Ocean Road than their region. Such attitudes are evidenced by the point that no locals took up Geelong Otway Tourism's offer to train locals as 'Sea Change specialists' at the time. In 2014, the tourist board was at last changed to Geelong and Bellarine Tourism, which sits better with the community. It will be interesting to see how they will respond if a similar opportunity presents itself in the future.

Certainly *Sea Change* was not a conscious developmental or promotional tool for Barwon Heads – all the beneficial changes are truly serendipitous. By contrast, the Fox Backlot was a specific tourist venture, yet all the planning, research and massive capital investment could not produce a viable tourist theme park. This raises an important question regarding film-induced tourism – film is a powerful medium, but on its own is it a strong enough tourist motivator? The answer seems to depend on a series of factors as uncovered in this study.

While in many ways the situation described in the village of Goathland in the UK is similar to that in Barwon Heads, there are two major differences that have affected the village significantly, namely the actual number and type of visitors attracted by their respective television series. The implications of the overall planning and community impact issues that have been raised by the studies on Goathland, Barwon Heads and other film-induced communities are summarised in the following section.

On-Location Tourism: Community Impacts and Planning

In the past, film-induced tourism has been incidental to the film itself, with little consideration given to the long-term effects that filming may have on a community. While such tourism can provide a significant economic fillip to a community, especially in a marginalised rural area, the community may not be prepared or willing to deal with the changes associated with film-induced tourism. With decreasing government intervention in local community issues and needs, the increased pressure on individuals to take on community responsibilities places community well-being at the forefront of their concerns.

When we consider the extent of tourism associated with movies and television series along with the lack of preparedness of many of the smaller communities to consider and plan for the latent tourism growth, there is need for us to be concerned. This creates an imperative to work towards understanding the phenomenon more comprehensively.

While communities are never totally homogenous, a divided community with powerful, disenfranchised clusters will not operate in the best interests of that community. Issues such as future development, crowding and congestion, changing real estate values, community pride and economic benefits must be considered in conjunction with one another and with the 'head in the sand' attitudes of those who hope everything will go away and leave them as before. By recognising and considering the potential costs and benefits of on-location film-induced tourism, a community has the opportunity to use the benefits to strengthen it and ameliorate the costs.

Such a solution may appear simplistic, which it is certainly not – the complexities of the communities in which we live, play and work are increasing, not decreasing. Alternative ways of uncovering and understanding complex communities, such as through social representation theory, provide an opportunity to develop our understanding of community processes in relation to film-induced tourism. Community planning models must consider film-induced tourism as a component of the tourism aspects of a community and not merely hope for serendipitous outcomes.

Spin-off tourism businesses such as guided tours appear to have a strong future, especially in cities such as New York and regions such as Hawaii that support numerous film projects where a certain longevity and variety of product (stories and sites) is assured. Also of interest here are the published guides such as maps and books, heralding a new field for the written word – that of writing about film and tourism. Souvenirs are rarely treated in any depth in tourism research and publications, yet they are a significant commercial element of the business of tourism, providing insight into how visitors and hosts view themselves and the 'places' they visit and inhabit (Paraskevaidis & Andriotis, 2015). The notion of film as a souvenir was introduced in Chapter 1, but it goes beyond merely returning home with a marker or representation of the holiday. Viewing a television series or movie takes on additional elements once the sites, sets and studios have been visited. For some, the dissonance between reality and fiction may detract from the viewing experience, but for many it appears that having knowledge of the process imbues that person with some cultural cachet. Through knowing the inconsistencies between reality and fiction, the person becomes an 'insider' to certain knowledge that was, in the past, the reserve of those in the industry. This in turn adds a dimension not only of knowledge but also of celebrity to the person involved – by merely being there, one's personal worth increases.

Off-Location Tourism: The Film Studio Theme Park Model

Studying failures can prove just as illuminating as considering successes – at times even more so. One of the most significant outcomes from the study of the failure of the Fox Studios Backlot and the comparison with successful film studio theme parks has been the development of a model that outlines the elements of such an enterprise, as discussed in the preceding chapters. Combined with the critical success factors noted in those chapters, the model provides a template with which to consider the planning and development of such enterprises as well as to assess and improve current ventures. The importance of reducing such high-profile tourism failures goes beyond the individual enterprise and affects business attitudes and investment.

While those purporting to be looking for 'authenticity' denigrate theme parks, the demand for structured, safe tourism experiences is expected to increase, along with the public's insatiable desire for contacts with celebrities (people, places and characters), no matter how vicarious. Film studios are, by their very nature, inauthentic in that their goal is to present images and representations as 'real', and it is the desire of many to have some entrée into this world of images and fantasy that has resulted in the development of studio tours and theme parks. Furthermore, through the use of new technologies such as augmented reality (Jung et al., 2015), they are now creating 'authentic' imaginary places for us to experience.

For as long as families holiday together, while the nature of attractions and experiences within theme parks may alter, their appeal will not dissipate. Places that provide security, while simultaneously offering a certain freedom and range of experiences from taking a ride based on a film to participating in some of the production processes, appeal to groups with diverse demographic and psychographic profiles, such as within many families.

At the same time as this study has provided applied models for theme parks and community tourism development, it has also demonstrated the extent of film-induced tourism in today's film-obsessed society, along with our limited understanding of many elements of film-induced tourism. Such aspects are outlined in the following section.

Destination Marketing and Film

In today's market the competition for tourists is fierce, particularly in places that traditionally have a mono-economic base such as many agricultural areas, particularly those engaged in cereal production. However, many of the landscapes associated with large-scale agriculture (or in arid regions) can appear monotonous to an outsider. Festivals and events have long been considered tools that can differentiate a place and give 'life' to nondescript sites (see Getz, 1991; Hall, 1992; Janiskee & Drews, 1998). Such re-imaging has been the aspiration of numerous locations, particularly in rural areas where, to a visitor, one pastoral landscape can easily replace another in terms of enjoyment, need and desire.

While Butler (1990) suggests that film is little more than a historical development of visual place promotion, following on from the Grand Tour paintings and seaside postcards to posters and photographs, film also contains a significant literary element. It is this combination of story, mood and visual stimuli that makes movies and television programmes more powerful than any other incidental tourism promotional tool. The influence of film, and television series in particular, in re-imaging rural areas has proven to be extremely important, as illustrated by *Heartbeat* (1992–2009) in Goathland, *Hamish Macbeth* (1995–1996) in Plockton, *Sea Change* (1998–2000) in Barwon Heads, *The Andy Griffith Show* (1960–1968) in Mayberry, and more recently with programmes such as *Doc Martin* (2004–) in Cornwall and even *Game of Thrones* (2011–) in relation to Northern Ireland and Iceland. Hudson and Ritchie (2006a, 2006b) have looked at this concept via the framework of product placement, arguing that destinations can be proactively used as the product being placed in a movie.

However, such imaging potential is not restricted to rural areas. Urban centres that may not have immediate aesthetic appeal, such as industrial towns, or neglected areas within cities such as disused (or used) shipping ports and other transport and freight locations, recognise the benefits of being filmed. Some, such as the London Film Commission, have even gone so far as to suggest that '[e]ven a scuzzy housing estate is of interest' to film makers (English Tourism Council, 2000). Glasgow, a city that has in many ways moved from an industrial ship-building town with coal-blackened buildings to a major European arts centre, still produces movies and television series based on its industrial past and its remaining precincts. These include the acclaimed 2003 movie *Young Adam* and the television series *Taggart*.

While large urban centres such as New York already attract significant visitors, they also attract a large number of films, from movies to television series. These cities may not need to use film to differentiate themselves, but the presence of film sites provides an added attraction and activity that may keep visitors longer, take them to different precincts, and/or encourage their return. The sheer number and breadth of television and movie sites in New York, from those related to *Seinfeld* (1989–1998) and *Sex and the City* (1998–2004) to *Breakfast at Tiffany's* (1961) and *King Kong* (1976) is somewhat overwhelming.

The application of film images and storylines (where appropriate) to destination marketing is one of the most recognised uses of film in relation to tourism. Emotionally-based images from movies and television series can provide some differentiation of places, and help them to compete in what can be a crowded marketplace. Some destinations appear to place an inordinate amount of faith in the power of film as a primary tourism motivator, not merely as an image-maker. This is not yet proven sufficiently, and many of those currently studying this phenomenon are expressing concern at the seemingly unquestioning reliance on film as a primary motivational tool. On the other hand, there are those who consider film-induced tourism to be a 'flash in the pan' that does not have any longevity. There is certainly a case to argue that, in light of our rapidly changing and unpredictable global environment, film-induced tourism may have an effect as long as, if not longer than, most other destination promotion/imaging exercises.

Also, as has been demonstrated in the studies outlined in this publication, increased tourist visitation is not an automatic response to filming, and where this occurs the consequences may not always be desirable.

Film-Tourism Guidebooks

While the internet and social media have provided many new ways for us to explore film sites, physical guidebooks continue to be published at an amazing rate. Where they were once quite simple listings of places and brief explanations of what happened there in the film, many are far more creative in their approach. Instead of being published primarily to promote the destination, film buffs, fans and other artists are writing and presenting these publications. Some examples of this include the Museyon Guides: Film + Travel series which are curated (as opposed to written) by film educators, reviewers, producers, directors, historians and location specialists who 'elucidate the ways in which the silver screen has framed a region...or transformed it... Museyon is the guidebook written by pedants for dilettantes' (Museyon, 2009: 7). They have guides for North-South America, Asia-Oceania-Africa and Europe. The World Film Locations series presents movie maps along with related essays on film making in the particular region, described in the New Orleans publication as 'a brief trip through the city as seen through the eyes of the film-makers who flock to it' (Harris, 2012: 5). As well as New Orleans, the series includes books on Glasgow, Beijing, Shanghai, Boston, Las Vegas, Marseilles, Paris, Prague, Malta, Singapore, Dublin, Liverpool, Reykjavík, Vienna, Chicago, New York, Sydney, Melbourne, Rome, Mumbai and more. The Film Lover's Guide to Paris (Boespflug & Billon, 2013) is another publication that presents the city from a fresh and primarily personal perspective, compiled by a director of entertainment at a media agency, a publicity director of an advertising agency and photographer. They present their book via the places (or famous addresses) and then discuss the films made there, rather than looking at all of the places where a particular film was made, sub-titling their book, 101 legendary addresses that inspired great movies.

However, not all of the interesting publications are as recent as those discussed above. Another example of a guidebook that presents more than the tourist's perspective is *The Complete Guide to the Quiet Man* (MacHale, 2000), a 300-page book that relates the development of the story, reprinting the original tale, which appeared in the newspaper *The Saturday Evening Post*, through to the making of the movie, the film itself and various influences. Consequently, the book not only provides some tourism detail, but adds to the experience when visiting sites in Ireland. Filmed in 1952, *The Quiet Man* is another example of the longevity of film-induced tourism.

The Future of Film-Induced Tourism

The first edition of this work left many questions unasked and unanswered, yet only a few have been adequately addressed in subsequent years, in spite of the increase in studies around film and tourism. In order to look at this further, it is worth reconsidering the model on the development of film tourism knowledge discussed in the introduction to this edition. If we look at it again in light of the preceding discussions (Figure 0.3), we can see that, while there is a maturing in the approaches and ways that we think about film-induced tourism, particularly as we engage with other disciplines, we still need to study each element. As I have stressed, this is a snapshot of the way I experienced the development of my knowledge of film-induced tourism, but as we move up the pyramid, we still need to keep reinforcing and building the foundations, especially from the more practical, business-based perspective, which has been the primary orientation of this book.

The need to ascertain how, when and why a film (movie or television series) inspires people to visit a particular locality is an important aspect that still requires more study. My own work indicates that the most important aspect for sustainable longevity is the correct 'fit' between the film's story-line and the tourism potential of (and market for) that region. The recent Australian family movie *Oddball* (2015) fits well here as the town where it is set and filmed (Warrnambool in Victoria Australia) has a primary tourism market of families, so we can expect to see an overall positive outcome, as long as the sheer numbers can be managed, as discussed earlier. This can potentially reduce social conflict with the local community as well as the existing tourist market.

Is film merely a variant of destination marketing (but without the formal strategy or advertising budget) at the time of release? It does not appear to be so in all situations. We need to consider what aspects people relate to and if it is their empathetic attachment to a story or place that facilitates tourism. Once again, while this may have some merit, it is already clear that it is not the only reason. The general public's desire for contact with 'celebrities' has also been suggested as a powerful tourism motivator. Is it the opportunity to live the fantasy of the celebrity status of film? Over a six-year period of guiding adventure horseback tours, I have witnessed and helped hundreds of would-be 'Men from Snowy River' play at being legendary Australian bushmen, yet celebrity or character fantasy alone is not an adequate answer to the question of film-induced tourism's varying influence.

While not registering on the all-time film lists as far as box office returns, *Lawrence of Arabia* (1962) was nevertheless critical to the way two generations have thought about desert landscapes, mainly owing to its continued presence on television and its status as a classic, even a cult, movie. Such an influence on image and perception may well be reflected in tourists' desire to visit desert regions in general as well as in their attitude and approach. Likewise, the original *Blues Brothers* (1980) movie gave Chicago a centrality for people in many countries that it had previously enjoyed only in America. Such generic influences of film-induced tourism on landscapes have not been studied in great depth by many scholars; however I have been fascinated with this aspect, writing about it in Beeton (2008a, 2010b) and Beeton and Cavicchi (2015) as well as in *Travel, Tourism and the Moving Image* (Beeton, 2015).

Following are some additional aspects within the film tourism field that also deserve further consideration as introduced in earlier chapters. The example in Chapter 1 of Washington DC's response to the decimation of its tourism industry after the September 11 2001 terrorist attacks cries out for some thought about where we are going in relation to what and who influences us. When fictional characters are deemed to be more persuasive than real people, are we becoming disassociated from reality? Or, is this a contemporary mediatised postmodern manifestation of humankind's traditional acceptance and development of myth and legend?

Chapter 3 notes the emergence of the genre of animation as a tourist destination marketing tool and is also looked at in terms of the theme park. However, the relationship between film studios and destination marketing organisations (DMOs) has been shown to be problematic, particularly in commercial licensing terms. Further study into the business relationships between studios and DMOs regarding leveraging the destination as a form of product placement in animation is being done particularly in terms of Japanese anime, but more is needed. The fortunes of these tie-ins will also benefit from longitudinal studies. Nevertheless, far too much tourism research is short term, which does not allow us to truly ascertain the nature of this industry.

One area of particular interest not covered here is that of 'toddler tourism' and film. Preschool-age children have remarkable power and influence over family travel decisions. Connell (2005) and Connell and Meyer (2009) have been studying the effect on the Isle of Mull in Scotland of the toddler television series *Balamory* (2002–2005). This television show has become a primary motivator for families with preschool children to visit the Isle of Mull. This in itself is significant, as it is one of the few cases where primary motivation through film has clearly been demonstrated. Visitor expectations and activities (of parents and toddlers) may be quite different from those of other film-induced tourists, yet Connell has found that there has been a significant increase in such tourism to the Isle of Mull, requiring consideration of yet another element of film-induced tourism, on which I am currently working.

Fictional film provides a window into contemporary mores regarding self-image and tourism over the past 100 years or so, since the development of film in the late 19th century. The Australian movie, *The Story of the Kelly Gang*, filmed in 1906, is purportedly the world's first feature film, and the first in a series of so-called 'bushranger' films. Analogous to the Western movie from the US, the Australian bushranger films fell from sight around 1915 because of censorship rulings – these films were considered to influence young men into committing crimes (Routt, 2001). However, the legend and story of the bushranger Ned Kelly has been filmed as a movie on numerous occasions, and the 2003 production starring Australian actor Heath Ledger was consciously tied in to tourism promotion in Australia (Tourism Victoria, 2003). By studying these films we are able to trace the imaging process through them and to compare them with contemporary tourism images and visitation, providing another historical view of tourism and film (see Beeton, 2004). In much the same way, other films that were strong on imaging and message such as those produced during (and shortly after) World War I and II may also have influenced tourism at the time (and may continue to do so) and this would benefit from further consideration. The emerging concept of 'dark tourism' is also linked with modern-day as well as historic war movies.

Motion picture cameras of the early silent period were drawn to exotic juxtapositions, such as that found when Western and other cultures meet, which also constitutes a tourism experience. Many of the turn-of-the-(20th)-century films focused on the contrast between privileged travellers on luxury ships or newly built railroads and their non-Western ('exotic') hosts who met them with donkeys and rowing boats (Strain, 1996). Among these earliest films was another type of travelogue known as 'phantom rides', where the movie travelled through picturesque landscapes that were devoid of people. For example, the *Panorama of Gorge Railway*, filmed in 1903, had the camera strapped to the top of a train as it travelled through the landscape surrounding Niagara Falls (Verhoeff & Warth, 2002). It can be assumed that such films, while being attractions in their own right during this early stage of cinema, did much to introduce the images of the Niagara region to a new audience, many of whom would desire to visit and travel that same railway (Beeton, 2015). The brief examples cited above illustrate the significance of travel and tourism in film, particularly in terms of the travelogue, all of which are considered in more depth in *Travel, Tourism and the Moving Image* (Beeton, 2015). This form of filming has evolved not only into travelogues where the host narrates his or her personal travel experiences, but also the raft of television travel programmes.

These programmes are similar to the written travel stories and guide-books, providing on the one hand tales of personal adventure, and on the other purporting to be a source of information for travellers. In addition, many of the 'lifestyle' programmes that focus on cooking and/or wine contain elements of travel and the exotic. Celebrity chefs take us to different parts of the world chasing authentic regional cuisine in exotic surroundings. Programmes that take us to wineries invariably involve travel, and incorporate touristic elements of the surrounding regions.

In addition to the travelogue and travel programmes, documentaries have been recognised as motivators for travel since the days of the *National Geographic* magazines and films from the early 20th century through to the 'Discovery' Channel of the present day. While films that cover wildlife and indigenous communities have received a great deal of attention in the literature, an area of documentary-making that has recently gained media and tourism attention in Australia is one that focuses on complex human communities. Such a case is demonstrated by the 2001 film, *Cunnamulla*, an award-winning documentary about life in a small town in central Australia that has been criticised by some sectors of its community as being unbalanced, showing only '...the life of social misfits, we would call it, who have chosen to drop out' (ABC TV, 2001). However, the film and ensuing controversy has created interest in the remote town of 1500 people, with anecdotal evidence indicating an increase in visitors since the release of the documentary. Ethical questions of film maker responsibility need to go beyond the portrayal of its characters to the considerations relating to film-induced tourism. For example, if the documentary is about the 'underbelly' of a community (as in the case of *Cunnamulla*), is this what visitors will seek out? Will they be happy with a superficial tour of the 'better' aspects of the town and region, or will they want to experience the darker, private side? And how could that possibly be done, short of seeing a staged fight in a country pub or visiting a community shelter house? Once again, the local community does not control what is being filmed, and stands to find itself the focus of an extremely intrusive tourist gaze.

The genres of travelogues, documentaries and television programmes noted above have not been considered in this publication, which has focused on fictional media. Nevertheless, as can be seen from this brief discussion, they are worthy of further examination, along with the impact of the growth in reality television on our images of place, and subsequent tourism, and are being addressed (Tessitore *et al.*, 2014).

Science fiction has inspired generations of thinkers and readers alike, with the influential 1968 movie *2001: A Space Odyssey* describing a world where the now-defunct Pan American Airlines runs shuttle services to the moon as easily as it then flew around the world. While the images created by our science fiction authors are removed from the reality of space travel as it currently exists, they have created a romantic longing for a space experience. Images from and references to *2001: A Space Odyssey* were used in media reports when billionaire Denis Tito accompanied a Russian space flight to the International Space Station in 2001, becoming the first 'space tourist' (Crouch, 2001). We are now seeing more elements of space tourism coming into reality, with much of the publicity relating it back to a science fiction film (Cole, 2015; Chang, 2015). Space tourism remains expensive (Tito is rumoured to have paid US$20 million for his trip), yet early research indicates that many people (up to 80% in some surveys) are interested in space tourism, and a significant number would be prepared to pay large sums of money for the experience (Crouch, 2001). While there may be no 'host communities' in space (at least as far as we know), the effect of science fiction imaging on tourist expectations should be examined, especially at this early stage of space tourism. Exhaustive examination of current research into space tourism indicates that such a link has not been explored or considered at any level.

Runaway productions have been mentioned in passing throughout this work. However, apart from the aforementioned New Zealand tours for *The Last Samurai* and the Irish sites used for Scotland in *Braveheart*, they have generally been dismissed by those wanting to use film as a destination marketing tool as not encouraging tourism because the sites used 'pretend' to be something else, often set in another country. Yet, such is the fascination of film that we may find post-tourists coming to such locations, not looking to re-live their film-induced fantasies, but to see how such deception was achieved (not unlike the postmodernist interest in film studios). The example referred to earlier of *Ponderosa*, the prequel series to *Bonanza*, a popular US Western of the 1960s, being filmed near the southern Australian town of Daylesford, could be one such case. Visitors may have been drawn to see how the Australian bush was made to resemble the American West. However, nothing is known about whether such a motivator exists and if it would be strong enough to lure tourists, and if so, what kinds of tourists. Also, due to cutting short the filming of the prequel due to the September 11 2001 terrorist attacks in the US, it has not been possible to actually study this case sufficiently (Beeton, 2015).

In a sense, *The Lord of the Rings* fits into this category – the story is set in a fictional 'Middle Earth', not in New Zealand. Fantasy and science fiction stories that create new worlds will always be filmed somewhere in which they are not set, creating further dissonance between the reality of the places in which they were filmed and their on-screen personas. New Zealand has gone so far as to promote itself as the 'home of Middle Earth', which provides countless opportunities to further the discussion/debate on authenticity, fantasy and simulacra.

The dramatic growth of the 'Bollywood' (Indian) film industry deserves separate investigation. The Indian sagas sell over 800 million cinema tickets annually (CNN, 2001). Many Indian movies and television soap operas include lavish settings with extended displays of place as central to their stories. Australian locations have started to feature in Indian movies and soap operas, conveniently coinciding with an emerging growth of tourism interest in Australia from India (ATC, 2003b). Most of the locations used by Bollywood producers are iconic tourism sites. In addition, in 2003 the Australian Tourist Commission began working with the Australian Trade Commission to further promote Australia to the Indian Film Industry (*Travel Daily News*, 2003), which continues today.

Australia is not the only country embracing the tourism potential of Bollywood. The British Tourist Authority has produced a *Bollywood Movie Map* of sites in the UK for Indian tourists. Locations such as castles and stately homes feature in many of the 150 Bollywood productions filmed in the UK (Josiam *et al.*, 2014). Switzerland Tourism also launched a Bollywood guide, *Switzerland for the Movie Stars*, in order to encourage further filming in their country and popularise Switzerland as a tourist destination (Munshaw, 2003). Recognising the tourism flow-on, New Zealand, Singapore and Mauritius have also heavily promoted their destinations to Bollywood (Fernz, 2001).

The media reports on the Bollywood film and tourism phenomenon indicate an ad hoc approach to attracting film-induced tourism at any cost, and with some 5 million middle-class Indians, the market potential is enormous. Such a frenzy of activity deserves and requires further investigation, particularly in light of the studies outlined in this publication (Beeton, 2008c).

Celebrity cults

Film-induced tourism links with the cult of celebrity around places endowed with the 'magic' of movie-making, such as Hollywood Boulevard. However, during the last decades of the 20th century, the millions of visitors to the Boulevard found little to do apart from gaze at the stars in the footpath and their foot and hand prints outside Mann's Chinese Theatre. Souvenir and T-shirt shops, seedy tattoo parlours and homeless youths, rather than the glamorous home of Hollywood cinema that tourists had expected, occupied the Boulevard. After taking a few photos and wandering aimlessly around the area, tourists left, dissatisfied, along with their unspent dollars (Gardetta, 1999). While the power of film and the 'Hollywood dream' was recognised by councils and some residents, attempts to create the Hollywood visitors expected were poorly envisaged. Efforts made in the 1980s to revive Hollywood failed to address issues of public safety, which left the strip in an even more perilous state.

In the late 1990s the Hollywood Chamber of Commerce and associated tourism and community groups recommenced the rebirth of Hollywood Boulevard, taking a more holistic community-centred stance (Raphael, 2000). A self-guided walking tour was developed, explaining the history of the Boulevard and related buildings as well as identifying the positions of all the pavement stars, providing visitors with reasons to linger (Hollywood Historic Trust, 1999). Heritage buildings have been restored and a US$567 million retail-restaurant-entertainment complex, 'Hollywood and Highland', opened in 2001, becoming the first permanent home of the Academy Awards (*TravelTrade,* 2001). This fact is surprising to many tourists (among others) for whom the Academy Awards have a regular place in their imagination, and who had assumed that they also have a physical place in Hollywood. The degeneration and regeneration of Hollywood Boulevard may well reflect the varying fortunes of film and tourism alongside American capitalism, with the recent resurgence indicating the growth and/or recognition of the significance of film-induced tourism.

The whole realm of Hollywood, celebrities and tourism would also benefit from further study in the film-induced tourism paradigm. The entire notion of celebrity and its transference from the actors to the places in the films is one that appears to be closely related to film-induced tourism motivation.

Re-visiting the Main Success Factors

As discussed throughout this publication, it is not easy to identify a clear set of success factors for film-induced tourism; however, there are some that have shown to be consistent in their effectiveness. I summarise them here:

Repetition:
- A television series that allows people the time (usually years) to gain a personal engagement with the stories, people and places (such as *Heartbeat* and *Neighbours*);
- A movie series that also allows such engagement.

Existing fan base:
- A movie or television series based on a popular (or cult) book (such as *The Lord of the Rings*).

Sheer number of films:
- A site where many movies or television series have been filmed over a period of time (such as New York and Hawaii).

Commercial openness:
- Willingness of the film company to engage with the destination in terms of tourism (such as *Oddball*).

Power relations:
- The location needs to be in a position of power where certain elements, such as the commercial openness noted above, can be negotiated.

Market synergies:
- Match between the audience for the film and the touristic appeal of (and market for) the destination. If this match does not exist, it is unlikely that film-induced tourism will succeed in terms of sitting well within the destination.

I have not noted the actual storyline or the beauty of the destination here, as so often these elements do not translate into film tourism, and while they are certainly part of the mix, infact they are not reliable factors. However, none of these will work without the support of the local host community as dramatically illustrated by the Fox Studios Backlot failure.

The Study of Film-Induced Tourism

The increase in the number of undergraduate and postgraduate students taking an interest in this field has grown in line with the media interest, which introduces unforeseen community and research problems, such as a plethora of intrusive research techniques administered by often inexperienced and at times poorly guided researchers. This raises serious methodological concerns, necessitating the long-overdue development of new approaches to tourism research. We can no longer unquestioningly rely on self-completion questionnaires and unsolicited intercept interviews, as responses to them have become potentially flawed, due to what can be termed 'interviewee burnout'. Moreover, many tourists simply resent being asked questions when they are on holiday. Ethnographic, participant observation techniques must not only be developed and refined, but need to be treated with greater respect and credence by the tourism research field itself. Quantitative data alone is rarely sufficient to illuminate the expectations and subsequent experiences of postmodern film-induced tourists.

Academic research tends to take one of two basic approaches, applied or theoretical. Applied research is problem-driven, looking for answers to specific issues, while theoretical research tends to open up further questions and areas for study. This examination of film-induced tourism has combined those approaches, dealing with applied problems as well as theoretical questions. At the applied level, this study demonstrates the importance of incorporating film-induced tourism (both on-location and off-location) into tourism and destination marketing planning, especially in small communities that are most sensitive to development. While many scholars, including myself, have continued to study film-induced tourism, many of the questions that came to light at the end of the first edition still need to be further addressed, from both theoretical and practical perspectives. These include:

- What really drives film-induced tourism – what are the elements that make a film 'create' film-induced tourism and how are they combined?
- What are the psychological and emotional drivers in a film that encourage tourist visitation?
- How does the growing fan culture and focus on pop culture affect film-induced tourism?
- What role does the 'cult of celebrity' play in relation to tourism?
- How can local communities achieve their goals through film-induced tourism?
- Are runaway production sites of interest to tourists? How can they best be presented?
- Are there cultural differences in film-induced tourism markets?
- What is the effect of other types of film on tourism, such as real-life documentaries and science fiction?

Whether they be real-life documentaries or the fantasies of fictional tales, films have always been a way for audiences to encounter other places. The future of film as a major form of entertainment, our rapacious appetite for celebrities, and increasing levels of tourism have come together to form a new tourism segment, that of film-induced tourism. All indications are that it stands to grow exponentially; consequently our need to understand the nature of this segment is crucial to the future of community and commercial well-being. Long-term, ongoing study and research is necessary in all the areas outlined in this work, particularly in relation to the questions posed above.

A further aspect that has not been adequately addressed in this book is that of non-Western cultures and film-induced tourism, particularly the significant Asian market. While some mention has been made of India through the Bollywood movies, the Korean Hallyu and Japanese contents tourism, the response of those outside a Western hegemony has not been examined here in any true depth. With the pervasiveness of Hollywood, it may be reasonable to assume some similarities in touristic responses to film, but this needs to be investigated.

As well as academics, researchers and students, local and regional tourism associations, film producers and community representatives have all expressed interest in the results of elements of this work. They will no doubt use them to support everything from new investment decisions to demands that film tourism towns be reclaimed by permanent residents once filming is over, rather than being overrun by day-trippers. However, where the results come into their own is as a community, tourism and business planning tool for future filming locations and studios. It is imperative that considerations beyond immediate economic benefits are taken into account by communities (and their councils) considering filming in their region. In spite of the serendipitous effects noted earlier, the *Sea Change*, *Heartbeat* and Fox Studios research has illuminated aspects that have the potential to divide and destroy the community as it is today, such as differing attitudes towards tourism, economic development, costs of living, crowding and increased pride and amenities.

This book builds on the pioneering work of Riley, Tooke, Baker and Van Doren from the mid- to late-1990s, and explores ideas of place marketing and community tourism development. Theme park development theory as espoused by MacCannell and others has also been developed to consider the specialised area of film studio theme parks, recognising the particular nature of film as a tourist attraction. For too long, the industry and academia have been over-estimating the economic and community gain from tourism without considering the consequences. For the tourism industry to remain financially and socially viable, film-induced tourism must be considered soberly, rationally and realistically.

To reiterate a point made previously, the long-term influence of film on destinations and tourism is more significant in our current global environment than in the more globally stable past. It can be argued that changes precipitated by political events are occurring far more rapidly than changes in fashion and taste. Consequently, filmic images (and emotions) may well remain relevant for a far longer time than any other form. Furthermore, the effects that social media has had are continually expanding while at the same time reinforcing the pervasiveness of film-induced tourism. This can be seen in the ever-increasing obsession with taking photos and sharing them immediately, to fans and tourists creating their own filmic versions of their experiences as well as parodies and homages, becoming what has been termed 'pro-consumers' – consumers who also produce.

The costs and benefits of film-induced tourism, including furthering our understanding of who pays, who gains and who might lose out, still need to be closely studied. While the case study is a strong research tool and one that I use extensively, other methodological approaches are required, both qualitative as well as quantitative. Consequently, while scholars such as Reijnders have taken a strong theoretical approach by looking at film tourism through a more personal lens of the tourist or fan's imagination, theoretical paradigms and models that explain and maximise the benefits and ameliorate the problems must be further developed. Only then can tourism come close to being an industry that serves its communities and environments as well as living off them.

Bibliography

ABC (1999) Viewers of *Sea Change*. Unpublished report. Australian Broadcasting Corporation.

ABC (2000) *Sea Change*: Summary of audiences. Audience research. Unpublished report. Australian Broadcasting Corporation.

ABC TV (1999) Tourists and developers seek out their own Pearl Bay. *7.30 Report*, 21 July.

ABC TV (2001) Facing the music in Cunnamulla. *7.30 Report*, 22 January.

ABS (1997a) Basic community profile, 3227. *1996 Census of Population and Housing*. Catalogue Number 2020.0. Canberra: Australian Bureau of Statistics.

ABS (1997b) Basic community profile, Australia. *1996 Census of Population and Housing*. Canberra: Australian Bureau of Statistics.

Adelman, C., Jenkins, D. and Kemmis, S. (1983) Rethinking case study: Notes from the second Cambridge conference. *Case Study Methods* (2nd edn; pp. 1–10). Waurn Ponds: Deakin University.

Air New Zealand (2003a) *Air New Zealand*. Auckland: POL (NZ).

Air New Zealand (2003b) Insider's guide to star spotting in Middle-Earth. Media release, 15 November.

Air New Zealand (2003c) Picture story: Middle-Earth fleet is complete. Media release, 26 November.

Air New Zealand (2003d) The Lord of the Rings beauty completes 'Airline to Middle-Earth' themed Fleet. Media release, 26 November.

Alderman, D.H., Benjamin, S.K. and Schneider, P.P. (2012) Transforming mount airy into mayberry: Film-induced tourism as place-making. *Southeastern Geographer* 52 (2), 212–239.

American Academy of Paediatrics (2002) *Some Things You Should Know About Media Violence and Media Literacy*. See www.aap.org/advocacy/childhealthmonth/media. htm (accessed August 2002).

Amish Experience (2001) F/X Theatre. *The Amish Experience Theatre*. See www.amishexperience.com/theater.html (accessed 20 November 2001).

Anholt, S. (2010) *Places: Identity, Image and Reputation*. Basingstoke: MacMillan.

Anime Pilgrimage (2015) *Anime Tourism*. See http://en.anime-tourism.com/index.htm (accessed August 2015).

ANPA (2003) Association of National Park Authorities. See http://anpa.gov.uk (accessed November 2003).

Ap, J. (1992) Residents' perception of tourism impacts. *Annals of Tourism Research* 19 (3), 665–690.

Argyll and the Isles, Loch Lomond, Stirling and Trossachs Tourist Board (2001) *Hollywood Legends*. See www.scottish.heartlands.org/brave/brave.htm (accessed July 2001).

Armstrong, E.K. and Kern, C.L. (2011) Demarketing manages visitor demand in the Blue Mountains National Park. *Journal of Ecotourism* 10 (1), 21–37.

Ashenden, D. and Milligan, S. (2001) *The Good Universities Guide*. See www.thegood guides.com.au (accessed March 2002).

Ashworth, G. and Kavaratzis, M. (2010) *Towards Effective Place Brand Management: Branding European Cities and Regions*. Cheltenham: Edward Elgar Publishing.

ATC (2000) Fox Studios Australia. *Australian Tourist Commission News and Views*, January, p. 5.

ATC (2003a) Finding Nemo promotion. ATC media release, 14 November.

ATC (2003b) Sydney to star in Indian TV soaps. *ATC Online: News Centre*. See http://atc. Australia.com/newscentre.asp?art=3836 (accessed May 2003).

The Australian (2002) Reality bites at Fox Studios. *The Australian: Media*, 14–20 March.

Australian Film Commission (2000) *Top 50 Films of All Time*. See www.afc.gov.au/ resources/online/gtp_online/Top_films (accessed February 2002).

Australian National Maritime Museum (2001) *Annual Report 1999–2000*. Commonwealth of Australia. See www.anmm.gov.au (accessed February 2001).

Australian Travel Reporter (1996) Movies mean tourism dollars. August, p. 19.

Baptista, J.A. (2012) Tourism of poverty. *Slum Tourism: Poverty, Power and Ethics* 32, 125.

Barwon Coast Committee of Management (1999) *Proposed Management and Business Plans*. Barwon Heads: Barwon Coast Committee of Management.

Baudrillard, J. (1983) *Simulations*. New York: Semiotexte.

Bawden, L. (ed.) (1976) *The Oxford Companion to Film*. London: Oxford University Press.

Beeton, S. (1998a) *Ecotourism: A Guide for Rural Communities*. Melbourne: Landlinks Press.

Beeton, S. (1998b) Horseback tourism in Victoria. Masters' thesis, Monash University.

Beeton, S. (2000) It's a wrap! What happens after the film crew leaves? An examination of community responses to film-induced tourism. In *Lights! Camera! Action!* (pp. 127–136). TTRA National Conference proceedings. Burbank, CA: TTRA.

Beeton, S. (2001a) Cyclops and sirens: Demarketing as a proactive response to negative consequences of one-eyed competitive marketing. In R.N. Moisey, N.P. Nickerson and K.L. Andereck (eds) *2001: A Tourism Odyssey* (pp. 125–136). TTRA 32nd Conference Proceedings. Myers, FL: TTRA.

Beeton, S. (2001b) Lights, camera, re-action. How does film-induced tourism affect a country town? In M.F. Rogers and Y.M.J. Collins (eds) *The Future of Australia's Country Towns* (pp. 172–183). Bendigo: Centre for Sustainable Regional Communities, La Trobe University.

Beeton, S. (2001c) Smiling for the camera: The influence of film audiences on a budget tourism destination. *Tourism, Culture and Communication* 3 (1), 15–26.

Beeton, S. (2003) Swimming against the tide: Integrating marketing with environmental management via demarketing. *Journal of Hospitality and Tourism Management* 10 (2), 95–107.

Beeton, S. (2004) Rural tourism in Australia: Has the gaze altered? Tracking rural images through film and tourism promotion. *International Journal of Travel Research: Special Issue on Rural Tourism* 6, 125–135.

Beeton, S. (2005) The case study in tourism research: A multi-method case study approach. In B. Ritchie, P. Burns and C. Palmer (eds) *Tourism Research Methods. Integrating Theory and Practice* (pp. 37–48). Oxfordshire: CAB International.

Beeton, S. (2006a) *Community Development through Tourism*. Collingwood: Landlinks Press.

Beeton, S. (2006b) Understanding film-induced tourism. *Tourism Analysis* 11 (3), 181–188.

Beeton, S. (2007) The good, the bad and the ugly: CSR, film and tourism. Two cases of filming in a small community. *Tourism Review International* 11 (2), 145–154.

Beeton, S. (2008a) From the screen to the field: The influence of film on tourism and recreation. *Tourism Recreation Research* 33 (1), 39–47.

Beeton, S. (2008b) Location, location, location: Film corporations' social responsibilities. *Journal of Travel and Tourism Marketing* 24 (2–3), 107–114.

Beeton, S. (2008c) Partnerships and social responsibility: Leveraging tourism and inter-national film business. In T. Coles and C. Michael Hall (eds) *International Business and Tourism: Global Issues, Contemporary Interactions* (pp. 256–272). Oxon: Routledge.

Beeton, S. (2010a) The advance of film tourism. *Tourism Planning and Development* 7 (1), 1–6.

Beeton, S. (2010b) Landscapes as characters: Film, tourism and a sense of place. *Metro Magazine: Media & Education Magazine,* (166), 114–119.

Beeton, S. (2011) Tourism and the moving image – Incidental tourism promotion. *Tourism Recreation Research* 36 (1), 49–56.

Beeton, S. (2015) *Travel, Tourism and the Moving Image.* Bristol: Channel View Publications.

Beeton, S. and Benfield, R. (2003) Demand control: The case for demarketing as a visitor and environmental management tool. *Journal of Sustainable Tourism* 10 (6), 497–513.

Beeton, S. and Cavicchi, A. (2015) Not quite under the Tuscan sun...The potential of film tourism in Marche Region. *Almatourism: Journal of Tourism, Culture and Territorial Development* 6 (4), 146–160.

Beeton, S., Yamamura, T. and Seaton, P. (2013) The mediatisation of culture: Japan's contents tourism and pop culture. In J.-A. Lester and C. Scarles (eds) *Mediating the Tourist Experience* (pp. 139–154). Farnham: Ashgate.

Benfield, R. (2000) Good things come to those who wait: Market research and timed entry at Sissinghurst Castle Garden, Kent. In *Lights! Camera! Action!* (pp. 226– 234). TTRA National Conference proceedings. Burbank, CA: TTRA.

Benfield, R. (2001) Turning back the hordes: Demarketing research as a means of manag-ing mass tourism. In R.N. Moisey, N.P. Nickerson and K.L. Andereck (eds) *2001: A Tourism Odyssey* (pp. 137–150). TTRA 32nd Conference proceedings. Myers, FL: TTRA.

Benjamin, S., Schneider, P.P. and Alderman, D.H. (2012) Film tourism event longevity: Lost in Mayberry. *Tourism Review International* 16 (2), 139–150.

Berger, P. and Luckmann, T. (1966) *The Social Construction of Reality.* Garden City: Anchor Books.

Beritelli, P. and Laesser, C. (2011) Power dimensions and influence reputation in tourist destinations: Empirical evidence from a network of actors and stakeholders. *Tourism Management* 32 (6), 1299–1309.

BFI (2001) *All Time Top Films at the UK Box Office.* British Film Institute. See www.bfi.org.uk/facts/stats (accessed February 2002).

Bodey, M. (2003) Falling hook, line and Sydney, 28 August 2003. See http://entertain ment.news.com.au/ (accessed October 2003).

Bodey, R. (1999) *Bodey's Summer Report 1998/9.* Barwon Heads: Bodey Real Estate.

Boespflug, B. and Billon, B. (2013) *The Film Lover's Paris: 101 Legendary Addresses that Inspired Great Movies,* translated from French by Anne McDowall, Editions du Chene, Hachette Livre.

Boley, B.B., McGehee, N.G., Perdue, R.R. and Long, P. (2014) Empowerment and resident attitudes toward tourism: Strengthening the theoretical foundation through a Weberian lens. *Annals of Tourism Research* 49, 33–50.

Boorstin, D.J. (1972) *The Image: A Guide to Pseudo Events in America.* New York: Atheneum.

Borkowski, N.M. (1994) Demarketing of health services. *Journal of Health Care Marketing* 14 (4), 12.

Bramwell, B. (2003) Maltese responses to tourism. *Annals of Tourism Research* 30 (3), 581–605.

Bramwell, B. and Lane, B. (2000a) Collaboration and partnerships in tourism planning. In B. Bramwell and B. Lane (eds) *Tourism Collaboration and Partnerships: Politics, Practice and Sustainability* (pp. 1–19). Clevedon: Channel View Publications.

Bramwell, B. and Lane, B. (2000b) Collaborative tourism planning: Issues and future directions. In B. Bramwell and B. Lane (eds) *Tourism Collaboration and Partnerships: Politics, Practice and Sustainability* (pp. 333–341). Clevedon: Channel View Publications.

Breakell, B. (1994) Goathland car parking. Unpublished survey report, 12 July. North Yorkshire Moors National Park Authority.

Breakell, B. (1996) *Heartbeat:* The crisis out of the drama. Media headlines and National Park action regarding the TV-generated tourism in Goathland. Unpublished working notes, North Yorkshire Moors National Park Authority.

Breakell, B. (2002) Missing persons: Who doesn't visit the people's parks? *CRN* 10 (1), 13–17.

Brisbane City Council (2002) *ourbrisbane.com: Your City Online.* See www.ourbrisbane.com (accessed August 2002).

Brodie, I. (2002) *The Lord of the Rings: A Location Guidebook.* Auckland: Harper Collins Publishers.

Brodie, I. (2004) *The Lord of the Rings Location Guidebook* (2nd edn). Auckland: Harper Collins Publishers.

Brodie, I. (2011) *The Lord of the Rings Location Guidebook: Extended Edition.* Auckland: Harper Collins Publishers.

Brodie, I. (2014) *The Hobbit Motion Picture Trilogy Location Guidebook.* Auckland: Harper Collins Publishers.

Brown, L. (2015) Tourism and pilgrimage: Paying homage to literary heroes. *International Journal of Tourism Research* 18 (2), 167–175.

Brown, R.L. (1997) *Ghost Dancing on the Cracker Circuit.* Jackson: University Press of Mississippi.

BTA (2001a) *Bollywood Movie Map.* British Tourist Authority. See www.visitbritain.com/moviemap/bollywood (accessed November 2001).

BTA (2001b) *Movie Map.* British Tourist Authority. See www.visit britain.com/moviemap (accessed October 2001).

Buchmann, A., Moore, K. and Fisher, D. (2010) Experiencing film tourism: Authenticity & fellowship. *Annals of Tourism Research* 37 (1), 229–248.

Buckley, R. (2015) Autoethnography helps analyse emotions. *Frontiers in Psychology* 6, 209. See http://doi.org/10.3389/fpsyg.2015.00209

Buckley, R. and Pannell, J. (1990) Environmental impacts of tourism in recreation in national parks and conservation reserves. *The Journal of Tourism Studies* 1 (1), 24–32.

Buhalis, D. (2000) Marketing the competitive destination of the future. *Tourism Management* 1 (21), 97–116.

The Bulletin (1994) Communism as theme park. *The Bulletin* 50 (1).

The Bulletin (1999) Australia this week. *The Bulletin* 117 (6176), 16.

The Bulletin (2000) Business briefs. *The Bulletin* 118 (6234), 62.

Burrowes, G. (1982) Introduction. In A.G. Simmons (ed.) *The Man from Snowy River Film Poems* (pp. ix–xiii). Cheltenham: Judy Simmons Publications.

Busby, G. and Klug, J. (2001) Movie-induced tourism: The challenge of measurement and other issues. *Journal of Vacation Marketing* 7 (4), 316–332.

Bushell, R. (1999) Hollywood movie damages Thailand National Park. Unpublished email correspondence.

Butler, R.W. (1980) The concept of a tourism area cycle of evolution: Implications for management of resources. *Canadian Geographer* 24, 5–12.

Butler, R.W. (1990) The influence of the media in shaping international tourist patterns. *Tourism Recreation Research* 15 (2), 46–53.

Butler, R.W. and Hall, C.M. (1998) Imaging and reimaging of rural areas. In R. Butler, C.M. Hall and J. Jenkins (eds) *Tourism and Recreation in Rural Areas* (pp. 156–165). Chichester: John Wiley & Sons.

Byrnes, P. (1988) Good weekend. *The Age*, 29 April.

California Tourism (2001) *California Movie Maps*. See www.gocalif.ca.gov.movies (accessed December 2001).

Camp, D. (1997) Theme parks in Europe. *Travel and Tourism Analyst* 5, 4–21.

Cater, E. (2001) The space of the dream: A vase of mistaken identity? *Area* 33 (1), 47–54.

Chan, B. (2007) Film-induced tourism in Asia: A case study of Korean television drama and female viewers' motivation to visit Korea. *Tourism Culture & Communication* 7 (3), 207–224.

Chang, Y.W. (2015) The first decade of commercial space tourism. *Acta Astronautica* 108, 79–91.

Chon, K. (1991) Tourism destination image modification process: Marketing implications. *Tourism Management* 12 (1), 68–72.

Christianson, R. (1995) The spectator. Cited in P. Spearritt and J. Baker (eds) *AUS1040 Introduction to Tourism* (pp. 63–64). Melbourne: National Centre for Australian Studies, Monash University.

City of Greater Geelong (1998) *Geelong Economic Indicators Bulletin 1997/8*. Geelong: City of Greater Geelong.

City of Greater Geelong (1999) *Geelong Economic Indicators Bulletin 1998/9*. Geelong: City of Greater Geelong.

Classic TV. Unofficial website. See http://classictv.about.com/msub20.htm?once=true& (accessed November 2002).

Clements, M.A. (1989) Selecting tourist traffic by demarketing. *Tourism Management* 10 (2), 89–94.

Climent, M. (2014) *TOMM Kangaroo Island Committee, Visitor Exit Survey, 2013/2104*. Parkside: Colmar Brunton.

Clogg, R. (1992) *A Concise History of Greece*. Cambridge: Cambridge University Press.

CNN.com (2001) British tourism welcomes Bollywood. *CNN.com/WORLD*, 10 April. See http://edn.cnn.com (accessed 25 May 2003).

Cobb, K. (1996) Lights! Camera! Profits! *Fedgazette* 8 (2), 6–8.

Cohen, E. (1988) Traditions on the qualitative sociology of tourism. *Annals of Tourism Research* 15, 29–46.

Cohen, E. (2000) Pilgrim. In J. Jafari (ed.) *Encyclopedia of Tourism* (p. 438). London: Routledge.

Cohen, E. (2005) The beach of 'The Beach': The politics of environmental damage in Thailand. *Tourism Recreation Research* 30 (1), 1–17.

Cohen, J. (1986) Promotion of overseas tourism through media fiction. In *Tourism Services and Marketing: Advances in Theory and Practice* (pp. 229–237). Proceedings of the Special Conference on Tourism Services. Cleveland, OH: TTRA.

Cohen, J. (2002) The contemporary tourist: Is everything old new again? *Advances in Consumer Research* 29, 31–35.

Cole, S. (2015) Space tourism: Prospects, positioning, and planning. *Journal of Tourism Futures* 1 (2), 131–140.

Collins, D. (1987) *Hollywood Downunder: Australians at the Movies: 1896 to the Present Day*. North Ryde: Angus and Robertson.

Connell, J. (2005) 'What's the story in Balamory?': The impacts of a children's TV programme on small tourism enterprises on the Isle of Mull, Scotland. *Journal of Sustainable Tourism* 13 (3), 228–255.

Connell, J. (2006) Toddlers, tourism and Tobermory: Destination marketing issues and television-induced tourism. *Tourism Management* 26 (5), 763–776.

Connell, J. (2012) Film tourism – Evolution, progress and prospects. *Tourism Management* 3 (5), 1007–1029.

Connell, J. and Meyer, D. (2009) Balamory revisited: An evaluation of the screen tourism destination-tourist nexus. *Tourism Management* 30 (2), 194–207.

Cooper, R. (1983) The other: A model of human structuring. In G. Morgan (ed.) *Beyond Method* (pp. 202–218). London: Sage.

Corlis, R., Harbison, G. and Ressner, J. (1999) Amazing anime. *Time* 54 (21), 94–96.

Couldry, N. (1998) The view from inside the 'simulacrum': Visitors' tales from the set of *Coronation Street*. *Leisure Studies* 17, 94–107.

Cousins, A. and Andereck, K. (1993) Movie generated tourism in North Carolina: Two case studies. In *Expanding Responsibilities, A Blueprint for the Travel Industry* (pp. 81–88). TTRA National Conference Proceedings, October.

Craig, J. (1998) Driveway drive-bys. *Sun Media*, 2 May.

Craik, J. (1991) *Resorting to Tourism: Cultural Policies for Tourist Development in Australia* North Sydney: Allen and Unwin.

Craik, J. (2001) Cultural tourism. In N. Douglas, N. Douglas and R. Derrett (eds) *Special Interest Tourism* (pp. 113–139). Milton: John Wiley and Sons Australia.

Crawford, R.M. (1960) The birthplace of a culture. In C. Wallace-Crabbe (ed.) *The Australian Nationalists: Modern Critical Essays*. Melbourne: Oxford University Press.

Creswell, J.W. (1994) *Research Design: Qualitative and Quantitative Approaches*. Thousand Oaks, CA: Sage Publications.

Crofts, S. (1989) Re-imaging Australia: Crocodile Dundee overseas. *Continuum: The Australian Journal of Media and Culture* 2 (2), 129–142.

Crompton, J.L. (1979) An assessment of the image of Mexico as a vacation destination and the influence of geographical location upon that image. *Journal of Travel Research* 17 (4), 18–23.

Crouch, G.I. (2001) Researching the space tourism market. In R.N. Moisey, N.P. Nickerson and K.L. Andereck (eds) *2001: A Tourism Odyssey* (pp. 411–419). TTRA 32nd Conference Proceedings. Myers, FL: TTRA.

Croy, W.G. (2010) Planning for film tourism: Active destination image management. *Tourism and Hospitality Planning & Development* 7 (1), 21–30.

Croy, W.G. and Walker, R.D. (2001) Tourism and film: Issues for strategic regional development. In M. Mitchell and I. Kirkpatrick (eds) *New Dimensions in Managing Rural Tourism and Leisure*. Conference Proceedings, CD-ROM. Auchincruive: Scottish Agricultural College.

Croy, W.G. and Walker, R.D. (2003) Rural tourism and film-issues for strategic regional development. In D. Hall, L. Roberts and M. Mitchell (eds) *New Directions in Rural Tourism* (pp. 115–133). Farnham: Ashgate Publishing.

Cummins, C. (2003) Gandel keen to buy Fox Studios. *Sydney Morning Herald*, 15 October.

Cummins, S. (2014) John Singleton, Gerry Harvey, Mark Carnegie buy entertainment quarter for $80m, *Sydney Morning Herald*, 4 June. See www.smh.com.au/business/property/john-singleton-gerry-harvey-mark-carnegie-buy-entertainment-quarter-for-80m-20140604-39j0k.html#ixzz3mEdohKSa (accessed June 2015).

Cummins, C. and Morris, L. (2000) Rough ride at Fox Backlot as backers drop $80m. *Sydney Morning Herald*, 14 July.

Curtis, J.R. (1981) The boutiquing of Cannery Row. *Landscape* 25, 44–48.

Curtis, J.R. (1985) The most famous fence in the world: Fact and fiction in Mark Twain's *Hannibal*. *Landscape* 28, 8–14.

Cynthia, D. and Beeton, S. (2009) Supporting independent film production through tourism collaboration. *Tourism Review International* 13 (2), 113–119.

Dancis, B. (2001) Python grail laid bare. *Scripps Howard News Service*, 16 November.

Davidson, J. and Spearritt, P. (2000) *Holiday Business: Tourism in Australia since 1870*. Melbourne: Melbourne University Press.

Davin, S. (2005) Tourists and television viewers: Some similarities. In D. Crouch, R. Jackson and F. Thompson (eds) *The Media and the Tourist Imagination; Converging Cultures* (p. 1). Oxon: Routledge.

De Botton, A. (2002) *The Art of Travel*. London: Hamish Hamilton.
DEFRA (2002) *Review of English National Park Authorities*. London: DEFRA Publications.
DEFRA (2003) *Wildlife and Countryside*. Department of Environment, Food and Rural Affairs. See www.defra.gov.uk/wildlife-countryside (accessed October 2003).
Demetriadi, J. (1996) The tele tourists. *Hospitality*, October/November, pp. 14–15.
Denzin, N.K. (1997) *Interpretive Ethnography: Ethnographic Practices for the 21st Century*. Thousand Oaks, CA: Sage.
Denzin, N.K. and Lincoln, Y.S. (1994) Introduction: Entering the field of qualitative research. In N.K. Denzin and Y.S. Lincoln (eds) *Handbook of Qualitative Research* (pp. 1–7). Thousand Oaks: Sage.
Department of Conservation (2003) About DOC. See www.doc.gov.nz (accessed December 2003).
Diary, W.H. (2000) Python's Doune deal. *Scotland on Sunday*, 30 July, p. 15.
Dirks, T. (2002) *All-Time USA Box Office Leaders*. See www.filmsite.org/boxoffice.html (accessed February 2002).
Dixon, B. and Bouma, G. (1984) *The Research Process*. Melbourne: Oxford University Press.
DNRE (1996) Permit issuance for season of 1996. Unpublished, Department of Natural Resources and Environment.
Dolnicar, S., Crouch, G.I. and Long, P. (2008) Environment-friendly tourists: What do we really know about them? *Journal of Sustainable Tourism* 16 (2), 197–210.
Doxey, G.V. (1975) A causation theory of visitor–resident irritants: Methodology and research inferences. *TTRA Sixth Annual Conference Proceedings* (pp. 195–198). San Diego: TTRA.
Dredge, D. (2006) Policy networks and the local organisation of tourism. *Tourism Management* 27 (2), 269–280.
Durmaz, B., Platt, S. and Yigitcanlar, T. (2010) Creativity, culture tourism and place-making: Istanbul and London film industries. *International Journal of Culture, Tourism and Hospitality Research* 4 (3), 198–213.
Echtner, C.M. and Ritchie, J.R.B. (1993) The measurement of destination image: An empirical assessment. *Journal of Travel Research* 31 (4), 3–13.
Eco, U. (1983) *Travels in Hyperreality*. San Diego, CA: Harcourt Brace Jovanovitch.
Economist (1995a) Rob Roy to the rescue. *The Economist* 335 (7914), 57.
Economist (1995b) The sewers of Madison County. *The Economist* 336 (7933), 32.
Economist (1998a) Lures and enticements. *The Economist* 346 (8059), 28–29.
Economist (1998b) Wallaby-Wood. *The Economist* 347 (8070), 80.
Edgell, D.L. and Haenisch, T.R. (1995) *Coopetition: Global Tourism beyond the Millennium: Charting the Course for Education, Government, and Commerce*. International Policy Publishing.
Edgell Sr, D. L. (2013) *Managing Sustainable Tourism: A Legacy for the Future*. London: Routledge.
Edgington, D. (1996) The Iowa Passage. *Des Moines Business Record* 92 (22), 16.
Ellingwood, K. (2001) Fox opens movie park in Baja. *Los Angeles Times*, 21 May.
Elliot, G. (2001) Lend Lease takes cut and quits no-show operation. *The Australian*, 17 October, p. 35.
Emmons, N. (1999) $261 million Fox Studios Australia to open Nov. 7. *Amusement Business* 111 (44), 3.
Emmons, N. (2000) Fox Studios Australia aims to fix problems causing slack attendance. *Amusement Business* 112 (34), 34.
English Tourism Council (2000) Rolling benefits: Providing a location for film, television and commercial work allows three takes on a very lucrative script. *NewsETCetera*, 5 July.
Errigo, A. (2003) *The Rough Guide to The Lord of the Rings*. London: Penguin Books.

Espinosa, G. and Herbst, D. (2002) Sex on wheels: Georgette Blau and the City bus trips let tourists follow in the stilettos of Carrie. *People*, 13 May, p. 228.

Evans, M. (1997) Plugging into TV tourism. *Insights March D35–38*. London: English Tourist Board.

Falassi, A. (1987) Festival: Definition and morphology. In A. Falassi (ed.) *Time Out of Time: Essays on the Festival*. Albuquerque: University of New Mexico Press.

Fawcett, C. and Cormack, P. (2001) Guarding authenticity at literary tourism sites. *Annals of Tourism Research* 28 (3), 686–704.

Featherstone, M. (1988) In pursuit of the postmodern: An introduction. *Theory, Culture and Society* 5 (2–3), 195–215.

Fernz, C. (2001) Tourism boards target Bollywood to boost outbound market. *Express Travel and Tourism, India's Travel Business Magazine*, 1–15 August.

Finucane, R.C. (1977) *Miracles and Pilgrims*. Totowa, NJ: Rowman and Littlefield.

Firmat, G.P. (2014) *A Cuban in Mayberry: Looking Back at America's Hometown*. Austin: University of Texas Press.

Frew, E.A. and Shaw, R.N. (1999) Industrial tourism attractions: A conceptual and empirical identification. In J. Molloy and J. Davies (eds) *Tourism and Hospitality: Delighting the Senses, 1999 Part 1* (pp. 211–218). Proceedings of the Ninth Australian Tourism and Hospitality Research Conference. Canberra: Bureau of Tourism Research.

Friends of the Lake District Report and Newsletter (1996) The Darcy effect. Autumn, pp. 41–42.

Frost, J. (1997) That's eat-ertainment. *Australian Leisure Management*. August/September, p. 18.

Frost, W. (2001) The financial viability of heritage tourism attractions: Three cases from rural Australia. In M. Mitchell and I. Kirkpatrick (eds) *New Dimensions in Managing Rural Tourism and Leisure*. Conference Proceedings, CD-ROM. Auchincruive: Scottish Agricultural College.

Frost, W. (2006) Braveheart-ed Ned Kelly: Historic films, heritage tourism and destination image. *Tourism Management* 27 (2), 247–254.

Frost, W. (2009) From backlot to runaway production: Exploring location and authenticity in film-induced tourism. *Tourism Review International* 13 (2), 85–92.

Frost, W. (2010) Life changing experiences: Film and tourists in the Australian outback. *Annals of Tourism Research* 37 (3), 707–726.

Frost, W. (2016) Heritage in the digital era: Cinematic tourism and the activist cause. *Journal of Policy Research in Tourism, Leisure and Events* 8 (1): 93–94.

Frost, W. and Laing, J. (2014) Fictional media and imagining escape to rural villages. *Tourism Geographies* 16 (2): 207–220.

Frost, W. and Laing, J. (2015) On the trail of Errol Flynn: Explorations in autoethnography. *Tourism Analysis* 20 (3), 283–296.

Fullagar, S., Markwell, K. and Wilson, E. (eds) (2012) *Slow Tourism: Experiences and Mobilities*. Bristol: Channel View Publications.

Furano Tourism Association (2102) *Furano Area Guide, 2012*. See https://furanozone.files.wordpress.com/2013/01/furano-guide-2011-2012.pdf (accessed April 2016).

Fyfe, M. (2000) What's in a name? Just look at the papers. *The Age*, 22 March.

Gardetta, C. (1999) Will success spoil Hollywood Boulevard? *Los Angeles Magazine*, March.

Gartner, W.C. (2014) Brand equity in a tourism destination. *Place Branding and Public Diplomacy* 10 (2), 108–116.

Geelong Otway Tourism (2001) *Geelong Otway Tourism Strategic Business Plan*. Geelong: Geelong Otway Tourism.

Gerrard, D. (c.2000) *Classic Heartbeat Country*. England: David Gerrard.

Getz, D. (1991) *Festivals, Special Events and Tourism*. New York: Van Nostrand Reinhold.

Goeldner, C.R., Ritchie, J.R. Brent and McIntosh, R.W. (2000) *Tourism. Principles, Practices, Philosophies* (8th edn). New York: John Wiley & Sons.
Goh, H.K. and Litvin, S. (2000) Destination preference and self-congruity. In *Lights! Camera! Action!* (pp. 197–203). TTRA National Conference Proceedings. Burbank, CA: TTRA.
Gordon, B. (1986) The souvenir: Message of the extraordinary. *Journal of Popular Culture* 20 (3), 135–146.
Graburn, N.H. (1989) Tourism: The sacred journey. In V.L. Smith (ed.) *Hosts and Guests: The Anthropology of Tourism* (2nd edn; pp. 21–36). Pennsylvania: University of Pennsylvania Press.
Graml, G. (2004) (Re) mapping the nation: Sound of music tourism and national identity in Austria, ca 2000 CE. *Tourist Studies* 4 (2), 137–159.
Gray, H. (1998) *TV Country Favourites from the BBC and Yorkshire TV.* Skipton: Atlantic Publishers.
Grihault, N. (2003). Film tourism – The global picture. *Travel & Tourism Analyst* (5), 1–22.
Grihault, N. (2007) Set-jetting tourism-international. *Travel & Tourism Analyst* (4), 1–50.
Gritten, D. (1999) Battle of the beach. *Electronic Telegraph*, 13 March. See www.portal.telegraph.co.uk
Gunn, C.A. (1988) *Tourism Planning* (2nd edn). New York: Taylor and Francis.
Gupta, V. (1999) Sustainable tourism: Learning from Indian religious traditions. *International Journal of Contemporary Hospitality Management* 11 (2–3), 91–95.
Gustafsson, E., Larson, M. and Svensson, B. (2014) Governance in multi-project networks: Lessons from a failed destination branding effort. *European Planning Studies* 22 (8), 1569–1586.
Hadgraft, C. (1963) Literature. In A.L. McLeod (ed.) *The Pattern of Australian Culture.* New York: Cornell University Press.
Hahn, D. and Robins, N. (2008) *Oxford Guide to Literary Britain and Ireland.* London: Oxford University Press.
Hall, C.M. (1992) *Hallmark Tourist Events: Impacts, Management and Planning.* New York: Halstead Press.
Hall, C.M. (1998) *Introduction to Tourism in Australia, Development, Dimensions and Issues* (3rd edn). Melbourne: Longman.
Hall, C.M. (2003) Politics and place: An analysis of power in tourism communities. In S. Singh, D.J. Timothy and R.K. Dowling (eds) *Tourism in Destination Communities* (pp. 99–114). Wallingford: CABI Publishing.
Hall, C.M. and Jenkins, J. (1995) *Tourism and Public Policy.* Routledge: London.
Hall, C.M. and Page, S.J. (1999) *The Geography of Tourism and Recreation: Environment, Place and Space.* London: Routledge.
Hall, C.M., Croy, W.G. and Walker, R.D. (2003) Imaging and branding the destination. In C.M. Hall (ed.) *Introduction to Tourism: Dimensions and Issues* (4th edn). Frenchs Forest: Pearson Education.
Hall, S. (1997) The work of representation. In S. Hall (ed.) *Representation: Cultural Representations and Signifying Practices* (pp. 13–74). London: Sage Publications.
Hannigan, J. (1998) *Fantasy City: Pleasure and Profit in the Postmodern Metropolis.* London: Routledge.
Harley, R. (2001) More bad news from Lend Lease. *Australian Financial Review*, 29 May, p. 64.
Harris, R. and Leiper, N. (eds) (1995) *Sustainable Tourism: An Australian Perspective.* Australia: Butterworth-Heinemann.
Harris, S.J. (ed.) (2012) *World Film Locations – New Orleans.* Bristol: Intellect Books.
Hassard, J. (1999) Postmodernism, philosophy and management: Concepts and controversies. *International Journal of Management Reviews* 1 (2), 171–195.

Hawaii Tourism Authority (1999) Ke Kumu: Strategic directions for Hawaii's visitor industry. Draft, June 29. See www.hawaii.gov/tourism

Heath, E. and Wall, G. (1992) *Marketing Tourist Destinations*. New York: John Wiley and Sons.

Heeley, J. (2015) *Urban Destination Marketing in Contemporary Europe: Uniting Theory and Practice*. Bristol: Channel View Publications.

Heitmann, S. (2010) Film tourism planning and development – Questioning the role of stakeholders and sustainability. *Tourism and Hospitality Planning & Development* 7 (1), 31–46.

Herbert, D.T. (1996) Artistic and literary places in France as tourist attractions. *Tourism Management* 17 (2), 77–85.

Herbert, D.T. (2001) Literary places, tourism and the heritage experience. *Annals of Tourism Research* 28, 312–333.

Heseltine, H.P. (1964) 'Banjo' Paterson: A poet nearly anonymous. *Meanjin Quarterly* 23 (4), 386.

Higgins-Desbiolles, F. (2001) Battlelines on 'The Beach': Tourism and globalisation. *Policy, Organisation and Society Special Edition: Different Globalisations* 20 (2), 116–138.

Hills, M. (2002) *Fan Cultures*. London: Routledge.

Hills, M. (2014) Doctor Who's textual commentators: Fandome, collective memory and the self-commodification of fanfac. *Journal of Fandom Studies* 2 (1), 31–52.

Hilty, A. (1996) Tourism and literary connections: How to manage the image created. In M. Robinson *et al.* (eds) *Culture as the Tourism Product*. Newcastle-upon-Tyne: Northumbria University Centre for Travel and Tourism.

Hoaglin, D.C., Light, R.L., McPeek, B., Mosteller, F. and Stoto, M.A. (1982) *Data for Decisions: Information Strategies for Policymakers*. Cambridge, MA: Abt Books.

Hodgson, P. (2003) Govt ready for 'The Return of the King', Lord of the Rings funding. Media release, 24 October. See www.behive.ovt.nz (accessed December 2003).

Holcomb, B. (1993) Revisioning place: De- and re-constructing the image of the industrial city. In G. Kearns and C. Philo (eds) *Selling Places: The City as Cultural Capital, Past and Present* (pp. 133–143). Oxford: Pergamon Press.

Hollinshead, K. (1996) The tourism researcher as bricoloeur: The new wealth and diversity in qualitative inquiry. *Tourism Analysis* 1, 67–74.

Hollywood Historic Trust (1999) *Walk the Walk: The Hollywood Walk of Fame and Walking Tour*. Brochure and signage produced by the Hollywood Historic Trust.

Holt, N.L. (2003) Representation, legitimation and autoethnography: An autoethnographic writing story. *International Journal of Qualitative Methods* 2 (1), 18–28. See www.ualberta.ca/~iiqm/backissues/2_1final/htm/html/holt/html (accessed November 2007).

Hong Kong Tourism Board (1999) *Hong Kong Movie Map*. Singapore: MPH Magazines.

Hoppen, A., Brown, L. and Fyall, A. (2014) Literary tourism: Opportunities and challenges for the marketing and branding of destinations? *Journal of Destination Marketing & Management* 3 (1), 37–47.

Horne, D. (1992) *The Intelligent Tourist*. McMahons Point: Margaret Gee Publishing.

Hudson, S. and Ritchie, J.B. (2006a) Film tourism and destination marketing: The case of Captain Corelli's Mandolin. *Journal of Vacation Marketing* 12 (3), 256–268.

Hudson, S. and Ritchie, J.B. (2006b) Promoting destinations via film tourism: An empirical identification of supporting marketing initiatives. *Journal of Travel Research* 44 (4), 387–396.

Huesmann, L.R. and Moise, J. (1996) Media violence: A demonstrated public health threat to children. *Harvard Mental Health Letter* 12 (12), 5–7.

Idle, D. (2003) *Filming On and Around the North Yorkshire Moors Railway*. Pickering: North Yorkshire Moors Railway.

Ife, J. (1995) *Community Development: Creating Community Alternatives: Vision, Analysis and Practice*. South Melbourne: Longman.

Im, H., Chon, K.S., Peters, M. and Weiermair, K. (1999) *Movie-Induced Tourism: The Case of the Movie 'Sound of Music'*. Proceedings of the First Pan-American Conference: Education, Investment and Sustainability, Panama City, May.

The Independent (2002) Celluloid castles: Where were those baronial scenes filmed? *The Independent (London)*, 4 May, p. 7.

Inside Tucson Business (1998) Tucson's future oughta be in (motion) pictures. *Inside Tucson Business* 8 (8), 4.

Jack, L. (2000) *Development and Application of the Kangaroo Island TOMM (Tourism Optimisation Management Model)*. Proceedings of the First National Conference on the Future of Australia's Country Towns, July. Bendigo: La Trobe University, Centre for Sustainable Regional Communities. See www.regional.org.au/au/countrytowns/options/jack.htm

Jafari, J. (1989) An English language literature review. In J. Bystrzanowski (ed.) *Tourism as a Factor of Change: A Sociocultural Study* (pp. 17–60). Vienna: Centre for Research and Documentation in Social Sciences.

Jafari, J. (2002) Retracing and mapping tourism's landscape of knowledge. *ReVista: Tourism in the Americas, Harvard Review of Latin America*. Winter 2002. See www.fas.Harvard.edu/~drclas/publications/revista/Tourism (accessed 1 June 2002).

Jamal, T.B. and Getz, D. (1995) Collaboration theory and community tourism planning. *Annals of Tourism Research* 22 (1), 186–204.

Jamal, T. and Getz, D. (2000) Community roundtables for tourism-related conflicts: The dialectics of consensus and process structures. In B. Bramwell and B. Lane (eds) *Tourism Collaboration and Partnerships: Politics, Practice and Sustainability* (pp. 159–182). Clevedon: Channel View Publications.

Janiskee, R.L. and Drews, P.L. (1998) Rural festivals and community reimaging. In R. Butler, C.M. Hall and J. Jenkins (eds) *Tourism and Recreation in Rural Areas*. West Sussex: John Wiley and Sons.

Japan National Tourism Organisation (JNTO) (2015) *Japan Anime Map: Sacred Places Pilgrimage*. See www.jnto.go.jp/eng/animemap/index.html (accessed August 2015).

Jennings, G. (2001) *Tourism Research*. Milton: Wiley and Sons Australia.

Jennings, G. and Stehlik, D. (2001) Mediated authenticity: The perspectives of farm tourism providers. In R.N. Moisey, N.P. Nickerson and K.L. Andereck (eds) *2001: A Tourism Odyssey* (pp. 85–92). TTRA 32nd Conference Proceedings. Myers, FL: TTRA.

Jet (1995) African village says it did not profit from Alex Haley's 'Roots'. *Jet* 87 (22), 26–27.

Ji, Y. and Beeton, S. (2011) Is film tourism all the same? Exploring Zhang Yimou's Films' potential influence on tourism in China. *Tourism Review International* 15 (3), 293–296.

Jopp, M. (1996) Sustainable community tourism development revisited. *Tourism Management* 17 (7), 475–479.

Josiam, B.M., Spears, D., Dutta, K., Pookulangara, S.A. and Kinley, T.L. (2014) 'Namastey London': Bollywood movies and their impact on how Indians perceive European destinations. *FIU Hospitality Review* 31 (4), 2–22.

Jung, T., Chung, N. and Leue, M.C. (2015) The determinants of recommendations to use augmented reality technologies: The case of a Korean theme park. *Tourism Management* 49, 75–86.

Junker, B.H. (1960) *Fieldwork: An Introduction to the Social Sciences*. Chicago: University of Chicago Press.

Kau, A.K. (2011) Evaluating the attractiveness of a new theme park. In C. Ryan and S. Page (eds) *Tourism Management: Towards the New Millennium* (3rd edn; pp. 259–271). Oxford: Pergamon.

Keeble, J. (1999) Picture perfect. *Electronic Telegraph*, 20 March. See www. travel.telegraph. co.uk

Keenan, A. (1999) Driving for pearls: Melbourne heads to Barwon for a change. *The Sunday Age Property*, 3 October, pp. 1–2.

Kelly, I. and Nankervis, T. (2001) *Visitor Destinations*. Milton: John Wiley and Sons Australia.

Kelly, M. (2011) Is 'K-Lit' the Next Korean wave? *Speakers Corner, Visit Korea*. See http:// english.visitkorea.or.kr/myeyes.kto?cmd=view&md=enu&lang_se=ENG&bbs_sn= 1633928 (accessed August 2015).

Kermode, P. (2000) Studio value has venture partners Foxed. *Australian Financial Review*, 2 November.

Kim, S. (2010a) Extraordinary experience: Re-enacting and photographing at screen tourism locations. *Tourism and Hospitality Planning & Development* 7 (1), 59–75.

Kim, S. (2010b) The production and consumption of experience: Inter-Asian responses to small screen tourism in Korea. Unpublished PhD thesis, Leeds Metropolitan University.

Kim, S. (2012) Audience involvement and film tourism experiences: Emotional places, emotional experiences. *Tourism Management* 33 (2), 387–396.

Kim, S. and Long, P. (2012) Touring TV soap operas: Genre in film tourism research. *Tourist Studies* 12 (2), 173–185.

Kim, S. and Nam, C. (2015) Hallyu revisited: Challenges and opportunities for the South Korean tourism. *Asia Pacific Journal of Tourism Research* 21 (5), 524–540.

Kindem, G. (1979) Pierce's semiotic and film. *Quarterly Review of Film Studies* 4 (1), 61–70.

Kindra, G.S. and Taylor W. (1990) A marketing prescription for Canada's health care. *Journal of Healthcare Marketing* 15 (2), 10–14.

King, E. (1997) *Introducing William Wallace: The Life and Legacy of Scotland's Liberator*. Fort William: Firtree Publishing.

Kirklees Economic Development Service (c.2001) *It's a Wrap in Kirklees: TV Film and Location Guide*. Huddersfield: Kirklees Economic Development Service.

Kotler, P., Haider, D.H. and Rein, I. (1993) *Marketing Places*. New York: The Free Press.

Kotler, P. and Levy, S.J. (1971) Demarketing, yes demarketing. *Harvard Business Review* 49 (6), 74–80.

Krippendorff, K. (1987) Paradigms for communication and development with emphasis on autopoiesis. In D.L. Kincaid (ed.) *Communication Theory: Eastern and Western Perspectives* (pp. 189–208). New York: Academic Press.

Kylänen, M. and Mariani, M.M. (2014) Cooperative and coopetitive practices: Cases from the tourism industry. In M.M. Mariani, R. Baggio, D. Buhalis and C. Longh (eds) *Tourism Management, Marketing, and Development: Volume I: The Importance of Networks and ICTs, 1* (pp. 149–178). New York: Palgrave Macmillan.

Laing, J. and Frost, W. (2012) *Books and Travel: Inspirations, Quests and Transformations*. Bristol: Channel View Publications.

Lankford, S.V. and Howard, D.R. (1994) Developing a tourism impact attitude scale. *Annals of Tourism Research* 21, 121–139.

LaPage, W.F. and Cormer, P.L. (1977) Images of camping: Barriers to participation. *Journal of Travel Research* 15, 21.

La Trobe University Bendigo (2001) *Community Profiler*. See http://ironbark.bendigo. latrobe.edu.au/cp/ (accessed January 2002).

Lawson, A. (2001) It's downs and ups at village. *The Age*, 21 November, Business p. 1.

Lazarus, P.N. (1999) Location filming: A study of its impact on tourism. *Florida Hotel and Motel Journal*, May, 20–22.

Lee, S. and Bai, B. (2016) Influence of popular culture on special interest tourists' destination image. *Tourism Management* 52, 161–169.

Lee, Y. and Weaver, D. (2014) The tourism area life cycle in Kim Yujeong Literary Village, Korea. *Asia Pacific Journal of Tourism Research* 19 (2), 181–198.

Leiper, N. (1979) The framework of tourism: Towards a definition of tourism, tourist, and the tourist industry. *Annals of Tourism Research* 6 (4), 390–407.

Leiper, N. (1999) What is tourism worth? Some alternative approaches and techniques for finding answers. In K. Corcoran, A. Allcock, T. Frost and L. Johnson (eds) *Valuing Tourism, Methods and Techniques* (pp. 122–133) Canberra: BTR.

Leiper, N. (2002) *Tourism Management* (2nd edn). Melbourne: Pearson Education Lend.

Leiper, N. (2004) *Tourism Management* (3rd edn). Malaysia: Pearson Education Australia.

Leiper, N., Stear, L., Hing, N. and Firth, T. (2008) Partial industrialisation in tourism: A new model. *Current Issues in Tourism* 11 (3), 207–235.

Lend Lease Corporation (2000a) Fox Studios joint venture. ASX announcement, 1 November. Sydney: Lend Lease Corporation.

Lend Lease Corporation (2000b) Fox Studios joint venture. Stock Exchange announcement, 13 July. Sydney: Lend Lease Corporation.

Lend Lease Corporation (2000c) Report of the Annual General Meeting, 2 November. Sydney: Lend Lease Corporation.

Lend Lease Corporation (2001a) Annual consolidated financial report, June. Sydney: Lend Lease Corporation.

Lend Lease Corporation (2001b) Joint media release with Fox Studios Australia. ASX announcement, 16 October. Sydney: Lend Lease Corporation.

Lend Lease Corporation (2001c) Lend Lease Corporation half year results for period ending 31 December 2000, 15 February. Sydney: Lend Lease Corporation.

Lennon, J. and Foley, M. (2000) *Dark Tourism*. London: Continuum.

Levine, F. (1997) Producer aims to bring TV spotlight back to SoBe. *South Florida Business Journal* 17 (21), 3–4.

Lewins, F. (1992) *Social Science Methodology: A Brief but Critical Introduction*. South Melbourne: MacMillan Education Australia Pty.

Lickorish, L.J. and Jenkins, C.L. (1997) *An Introduction to Tourism*. Oxford: Butterworth Heinemann.

Love, L.L. and Sheldon, P.S. (1998) Souvenirs: Messengers of meaning. *Advances in Consumer Research* 25, 170–175.

Lyotard, J-F. (1984) *The Postmodern Condition: A Report on Knowledge*. Minneapolis: University of Minnesota Press.

McCabe, V., Poole, B., Weeks, P. and Leiper, N. (2000) *The Business and Management of Conventions*. Brisbane: Wiley & Sons Australia.

MacCannell, D. (1973) Staged authenticity: Arrangements of social space in tourism settings. *American Journal of Sociology* 79 (3), 357–361.

MacCannell, D. (1976) *The Tourist: A New Theory of the Leisure Class*. New York: Shocken Books.

McClung, G.W. (2011) Theme park selection: Factors influencing attendance. In C. Ryan and S. Page (eds) *Tourism Management: Towards the New Millennium* (3rd edn; pp. 232–245). Oxford: Pergamon.

MacHale, D. (2000) *The Complete Guide to the Quiet Man*. Belfast: Appletree Press.

MacKay, K. and Fesenmaier, D.R. (2000) An exploration of cross-cultural destination image assessment. *Journal of Travel Research* 38 (May), 417–423.

McKenzie, A.F. and McKenzie, S. (1988) *Doune Postcards form the Past*. Stirling: Forth Naturalist and Historian Editorial Board, University of Stirling.

Maddox, G. (2003) Hollywood dishes up ocker shark Down Under. *Sydney Morning Herald*, 3 June.

Madrigal, R. (1993) A tale of two cities. *Annals of Tourism Research* 20, 336–353.

Malhorta, N.K. (1990) Reducing health care cost by demarketing benefits. *Journal of Health Care Marketing* 10 (2), 78–79.

Maltby J. and Day, L. (2011) Celebrity worship and incidence of elective cosmetic surgery: Evidence of a link among young adults. *Journal of Adolescent Health* 49, 483–489.

Maltby, J., Houran, J., Ashe, D. and McCutcheon, L.E. (2001) The self-reported psychological well-being of celebrity worshippers. *North American Journal of Psychology* 3, 441–452.

Maltby, J., Houran, J. and McCutcheon, L.E. (2003) Locating the stages of celebrity worship within Eysenck's theory of personality. Unpublished working paper, University of Leicester.

Manidis Roberts Consultants (1997) *Developing a Tourism Optimisation Management Model (TOMM): A Model to Monitor and Manage Tourism on Kangaroo Island, South Australia.* Adelaide: South Australian Tourism Commission.

Marling, K.A. (1994) *As Seen in TV: The Visual Culture of Everyday Life in the 1950s.* Cambridge, MA: Harvard University Press.

Marzano, G. (2008) Power, destination branding and the implications of a social network perspective. In N. Scott, R. Baggio and C. Cooper (eds) *Network Analysis and Tourism: From Theory to Practice* (pp. 131–144). Clevedon: Channel View Publications.

Marzano, G. and Scott, N. (2009) Power in destination branding. *Annals of Tourism Research* 36 (2), 247–267.

Mason, P., Johnston, M. and Twynam, D. (2000) The World Wide Fund for Nature Arctic Tourism Project. In B. Bramwell and B. Lane (eds) *Tourism Collaboration and Partnerships: Politics, Practice and Sustainability* (pp. 98–116). Clevedon: Channel View Publications.

Masubuchi, T. 2010 *What is Contents Tourism? Monogatari wo tabi suru hitobito.* Tokyo: Sairyusha.

Mayer, V. (2015) The cultural impacts of runaway film production. In Toby Miller (ed.) *The Routledge Companion to Global Popular Culture* (pp. 388–396). London: Routledge.

Melissa's Heartbeat Page. Unofficial website. See www.netspace.net.au/~capefrog/heartbeat/heartbeat.html (accessed November 2002).

Merriam, S.B. (1998) *Qualitative Research and Case Study Applications in Education.* San Francisco: Jossey-Bass Publishers.

Michael, I., Brown, R. and Michael, N. (2004) Luring Indian tourists to destination Australia: The role of Bollywood. In *Tourism: State of the Art II.* Conference Proceedings, CD-ROM. Glasgow: University of Strathclyde.

Miles, M.B. and Huberman, A.M. (1994) *Qualitative Data Analysis: An Expanded Sourcebook* (2nd edn). Thousand Oaks: Sage Publications.

Miller, D.M.S. (2008) Disaster tourism and disaster landscape attractions after Hurricane Katrina: An auto-ethnographic journey. *International Journal of Culture of Tourism and Hospitality Research* 2 (2), 115–131.

Milman, A. (2001) The future of the theme park and attraction industry: A management perspective. *Journal of Travel Research* 40, 139–147.

Ministry of Economic Development (2004a) *VOTE Tourism B.7.* New Zealand: Ministry of Economic Development.

Ministry of Economic Development (2004b) *VOTE Tourism B.5* (Vol. II). New Zealand: Ministry of Economic Development.

Ministry of Land, Infrastructure, Transport and Tourism (MLITT) (2005) *Eizō tō kontentsu no seisaku katsuyō ni yoru chiiki shinkō no arikata ni kansuru chōsa hōkokusho.* See www.mlit.go.jp/kokudokeikaku/souhatu/h16seika/12eizou/12eizou.htm (accessed 26 September 2011).

Mitchell, P. (2003) Nemo-led recovery hope. *The Age,* 4 June.

Moore, C. (2003) Future of Fox Studios 'Family Entertainment Complex'. Letter to Minister for Infrastructure and Planning on Member for Bligh website. See www.clovermoore.com/issues/development/major/fox/031022_knowles.htm (accessed 26 November 2003).

Moore, T. Inglis, (1962) The red page Rhadamanthus: A.G. Stephens. In J. Jones (ed.) *Image of Australia (Texas Quarterly,* summer edition). Austin: University of Texas.

Mordue, T. (1999) Heartbeat Country: Conflicting values, coinciding visions. *Environment and Planning* 31, 629–646.

Mordue, T. (2001) Performing and directing resident/tourist cultures in Heartbeat Country. *Tourist Studies* 1 (3), 233–252.

Morris, L. (2001) Residents to fight Fox Studios over late hours. *Sydney Morning Herald,* 11 January.

Moscovici, S. (1972) Society and theory in social psychology. In J. Israel and H. Tajfel (eds) *The Context of Social Psychology* (pp. 17–68). London: Academic Press.

Moscovici, S. (1984) The phenomenon of social representations. In R.M. Farr and S. Moscovici (eds) *Social Representations* (pp. 3–69). Cambridge: Cambridge University Press.

Moser, C. (1989) Community participation in urban projects in the Third World. *Progress in Planning* 32 (2), 81.

Motion Picture Association of America (MPAA) (2015) *Theatrical Market Statistics, 2014.* Los Angeles: MPAA.

Müller, D.K. (2001) Literally unplanned literary tourism in two municipalities in rural Sweden. In M. Mitchell and I. Kirkpatrick (eds) *New Dimensions in Managing Rural Tourism and Leisure.* Conference Proceedings, CD-ROM. Auchincruive: Scottish Agricultural College.

Munshaw, S.W. (2003) Switzerland Tourism launches Bollywood guide. *Express Travel and Tourism, India's Travel Business Magazine,* 1–5 April.

Mura, P. and Tavakoli, R. (2014) Tourism and social capital in Malaysia. *Current Issues in Tourism* 17 (1), 28–45.

Muresan, A. and Smith, K.A. (1998) Dracula's castle in Transylvania: Conflicting heritage marketing strategies. *International Journal of Heritage Studies* 4 (2), 73–85.

Murphy, P.E. (1981) Community attitudes to tourism: A comparative analysis. *International Journal of Tourism Management* 2 (September), 189–195.

Murphy, P.E. (1985) *Tourism: A Community Approach.* New York: Methuen.

Murphy, P.E. (1991) Data gathering for community-oriented tourism planning: A case study of Vancouver Island, British Columbia. *Leisure Studies* 10 (1), 68–80.

Murphy, P. (1994) Tourism and sustainable development. In W. Theobold (ed.) *Global Tourism: The Next Decade* (pp. 274–290). Oxford: Butterworth-Heinemann.

Murphy, P. and Murphy, A. (2001) Regional tourism and its economic development links for small communities. In M.F. Rogers and Y.M.J. Collins (eds) *The Future of Australia's Country Towns* (pp. 162–171). Bendigo: Centre for Sustainable Regional Communities.

Museyon (2009) *Film + Traveel, North America > South America.* New York: Museyon.

Neale, S. (1994) Tom Kershaw: Everybody knows his name. *Boston Business Journal* 14 (22), 18.

Newsome, D., Moore, S.A. and Dowling, R.K. (2002) *Natural Area Tourism. Ecology, Impacts and Management* (1st edn). Clevedon: Channel View Publications.

New Zealand Herald (2001a) Extra $4.5m to help NZ cash in on 'Lord of the Rings'. *New Zealand Herald,* 7 November.

New Zealand Herald (2001b) Minister of the Rings. *New Zealand Herald,* 7 September.

NFO New Zealand (2003) *Lord of the Rings* market research summary report. Prepared for Tourism New Zealand, 4 April. NFO World Group.

Nichols, K. (2002) Disney talks raise concern with top tourism officials. *Honolulu Advertiser,* 7 June.

Nicklin, L. (1997) The show must not go on. *The Bulletin,* 22 April, p. 13.

Nielsen, C. (2001) *Tourism and the Media: Tourist Decision-Making, Information and Communication.* Melbourne: Hospitality Press.

Noy, C. (2003) The write of passage: Reflections on writing a dissertation in narrative/ qualitative methodology. *Forum of Qualitative Social Research* 4 (2). See http://www. qualitative-research.net/index.php/fqs/article/view/712. (accessed June 1, 2008).

Noy, C. (2004) 'The trip really changed me'. Backpackers' narratives of self-change. *Annals of Tourism Research* 31 (1), 78–102.

Noy, C. (2007) The language(s) of the tourist experience: An autoethnography of the poetic tourist. In I. Ateljivic, A. Pritchard and N. Morgan (eds) *The Critical Turn in Tourism Studies* (pp. 349–370). Amsterdam: Elsevier.

Nunkoo, R. and Ramkissoon, H. (2012) Power, trust, social exchange and community support. *Annals of Tourism Research* 39 (2), 997–1023.

NYMNPA (c.2001) *Research and Studies into Visitor Impact in Goathland*. Information brochure. Helmsley: North York Moors National Park Authority.

NYMNPA (2003) North York Moors National Park. See http://moors.uk.net. (accessed November 2003).

Oberin/Trayling, G. and Flick, B. (1999) Bigger picture. *The Echo:* Letters section, 4 August, p. 13.

O'Connor, N., Flanagan, S. and Gilbert, D. (2008) The integration of film-induced tourism and destination branding in Yorkshire, UK. *International Journal of Tourism Research* 10 (5), 423–437.

OECD (2003) *OECD Economic Surveys: New Zealand*. Vol. 2003, Supplement 2.

Office of the Premier (2001) Bracks announces film studio for Victoria. Victorian State Government media release, 28 June.

Office of the Valuer-General (2001) *A Guide to Property Values, Victoria*. Melbourne: Department of Natural Resources and Environment.

Okamoto, T. (2015) Otaku tourism and the anime pilgrimage phenomenon in Japan. *Japan Forum* 27 (1), 12–36.

Ooi, N., Laing, J. and Mair, J. (2015) Social capital as a heuristic device to explore sociocultural sustainability: A case study of mountain resort tourism in the community of Steamboat Springs, Colorado, USA. *Journal of Sustainable Tourism* 23 (3), 417–436.

Orchiston, C. and Higham, J.E.S. (2016) Knowledge management and tourism recovery (de) marketing: The Christchurch earthquakes 2010–2011. *Current Issues in Tourism* 19 (1), 64–84.

O'Regan, T. (1988) 'Fair Dinkum Fillums': The Crocodile Dundee phenomenon. In E. Jacka and S. Dermody (eds) *The Imaginary Industry: Australian Film in the late 80s* (pp. 155–175). Sydney: Australian Film Television and Radio School and Media Information.

Oregon Progress Board (1999) Achieving the Oregon Shines vision: The 1999 Benchmark Performance Report. Report to the Legislative Assembly, March.

Otgaar, A. (2012) Towards a common agenda for the development of industrial tourism. *Tourism Management Perspectives* 4, 86–91.

Page One Books (c.2000) *TV & Film Locations Guide*. London: Page One Books.

Page, S. (1995) *Urban Tourism*. London: Routledge.

Page, S. (2011) Theme parks. In C. Ryan and S. Page (eds) *Tourism Management: Towards the New Millennium* (3rd edn; pp. 228–232). Oxford: Pergamon.

Palmer, V. (1971) The legend. In C. Wallace-Crabbe (ed.) *The Australian Nationalists: Modern Critical Essays*. Melbourne: Oxford University Press.

Papadimitriou, L. (2000) Travelling on screen: Tourism and the Greek film musical. *Journal of Modern Greek Studies* 18, 95–104.

Papandrea, F. (1996) *Measuring Community Benefits of Australian TV Programs*. Canberra: AGPS.

Paraskevaidis, P. and Andriotis, K. (2015) Values of souvenirs as commodities. *Tourism Management* 48, 1–10.

Patton, M.Q. (1990) *Qualitative Evaluation and Research Methods* (2nd edn). Newbury Park: Sage Publications.

Pearce, P.L. (1982a) Perceived changes in holiday destinations. *Annals of Tourism Research* 9 (2), 145–164.

Pearce, P.L. (1982b) *The Social Psychology of Tourist Behaviour*. Oxford: Pergamon Press.

Pearce, P.L., Moscardo, G. and Ross, G.F. (1996) *Tourism Community Relationships*. Oxford: Elsevier Science.

People Weekly (1985) John Hostetler bears witness to Amish culture and calls the movie *Witness* 'a mockery'. *People Weekly* 23 (11 March), 63–64.

Perdue, R.R. and Pitegoff, B.E. (1994) Methods of accountability research for destination marketing. In R.J.R. Brent Ritchie and C.R. Goeldner (eds) *Travel, Tourism and Hospitality Research: A Handbook for Managers and Researchers* (2nd edn; pp. 555–571). New York: John Wiley and Sons.

Petty, T. (2003) Bring out your dead! Monty Python fans flock to castle. *Associated Press*, 8 September.

Peyser, M. and Gordon, D. (2001) Why the Sopranos sing. *Newsweek*, 2 April, p. 48.

Pike, S. and Page, S.J. (2014) Destination marketing organizations and destination marketing: A narrative analysis of the literature. *Tourism Management* 41, 202–227.

Pine, B.J. and Gilmore, J.H. (1998) Welcome to the experience economy. *Harvard Business Review* 76, 97–105.

Pine, B.J. and Gilmore, J.H. (1999) *The Experience Economy: Work is Theatre & Every Business a Stage*. Boston, MA: Harvard Business Press.

Pizam, A. (1978) Tourism's impacts: The social costs to the destination community as perceived by its residents. *Journal of Travel Research* (Spring), 8–12.

Pizam, A. (1994) Planning a tourism research investigation. In R.J.R. Brent Ritchie and C.R. Goeldner (eds) *Travel, Tourism and Hospitality Research: A Handbook for Managers and Researchers* (2nd edn; pp. 91–104). New York: John Wiley and Sons.

Platt, J. (1992) Case study in American methodological thought. *Current Sociology* 40, 21–35.

Plog, S.C. (1974) Why destination areas rise and fall in popularity. *The Cornell Hotel and Restaurant Administration Quarterly* 15, 13–16.

Portegies, A. (2010) Places on my mind: Exploring contextuality in film in between the global and the local. *Tourism and Hospitality Planning & Development* 7 (1), 47–58.

Powerhouse Museum (2000) Powerhouse Museum wins at tourism awards with Audrey Hepburn Exhibition. Media release, 27 July. See www.phm.gov.au (accessed December 2001).

Powerhouse Museum (2001) Facts and figures. See www.phm.gov.au (accessed December 2001).

Powers, W. (2001) Thanking our stars. *The Atlantic Online*, 2 May. See www.theatlantic.com/politics/nj/powers2001-05-02.htm (accessed June 2001).

Prentice, R. (1993) Community-driven tourism planning and residents' perceptions. *Tourism Management* 14 (3), 218–227.

Quiglen, J. (2002) No one famous slept here: A bus tour of TV buildings. *Columbia News Service*, 3 April.

Radmacher, K. (1997) Publicity seldom bad, film-industry officials say. *Inside Tucson Business* 7 (10), 14.

Raphael, J. (2000) Future's past: Welcoming the new millennium. *Discover Hollywood*, Winter 1999/2000, 4–10.

Rapoport, R. and Rapoport, R.N. (1975) *Leisure and the Family Life Cycle*. London: Routledge.

Read, A. (1997) In the mood. *Australian Leisure Management*, August/September, 11–12.

Reddy, A. (1989) Reducing healthcare costs by demarketing benefits. *Health Marketing Quarterly* 6 (4), 137–145.

Reed, M.G. (1997) Power relations and community-based tourism planning. *Annals of Tourism Research* 24 (3), 566–591.

Regional TAM, OzTAM and Nielsen (2015) *Australian Multi-Screen Report, Q1 2015*. Sydney: Regional TAM, OzTAM, Nielsen.

Reijnders, S. (2011) *Places of the Imagination: Media, Tourism, Culture*. Farnham: Ashgate Publishing.

Reijnders, S., Bolderman, L., van Es, N. and Waysdorf, A. (2015) Research note: Locating imagination. *Tourism Analysis* (Forthcoming).

Reilly, M.D. (1990) Free elicitation of descriptive adjectives for tourism image assessment. *Journal of Travel Research* 28 (4), 21–26.

Reuters (2003) Murphy scares off the competition. *Reuters News Service*, 1 December.

Richardson, J. (1993) *Ecotourism and Nature-based Holidays*. Marrickville: Choice Books.

Riley, R.W. (1994) Movie-induced tourism. In A.V. Seaton (ed.) *Tourism: The State of the Art*. Chichester: John Wiley & Sons.

Riley, R., Baker, D. and Van Doren, C.S. (1998) Movie induced tourism. *Annals of Tourism Research* 25 (4), 919–935.

Riley, R. and Van Doren, C.S. (1992) Movies as tourism promotion: A 'pull' factor in a 'push' location. *Tourism Management*, September, 267–274.

Rinaldi, C. and Beeton, S. (2015) Success in place branding: The case of the Tourism Victoria Jigsaw Campaign. *Journal of Travel & Tourism Marketing* 32 (5), 622–638.

Rings Scenic Tours (2002) *Hobbiton Movie Set Official Tour Guide*. Matamata: Rings Scenic Tours.

Ritchie, J.B. (1984) Assessing the impact of hallmark events: Conceptual and research issues. *Journal of Travel Research* 23 (1), 2–11.

Ritchie, J.R. Brent and Crouch, G.I. (2000) The competitive destination: A sustainability perspective. *Tourism Management* 21, 1–7.

Ritchie, J.R. Brent and Crouch, G.I. (2003) *The Competitive Destination: A Sustainable Tourism Perspective*. Wallingford: CABI Publishing.

Ritchie J.R. Brent and Goeldner, C.R. (1994) *Travel, Tourism, and Hospitality Research: A Handbook for Managers and Researchers* (2nd edn). New York: John Wiley and Sons.

Ritzer, G. and Liska, A. (1997) McDisneyization and post-tourism: Complementary perspectives on contemporary tourism. In C. Rojek and J. Urry (eds) *Touring Cultures: Transformations of Travel and Theory* (pp. 96–109). London: Routledge.

Roberts, C. and Wall, G. (1979) Possible impacts of Vaughan theme park. *Recreation Research Review* 7 (2), 11–14.

Robertson, J.P. and Radford, L.A. (2009) The private uses of quiet grandeur: A meditation on literary pilgrimage. *Changing English* 16 (2), 203–309.

Robinson, M. (1999) The ride was all downhill. *Sydney Morning Herald*, 10 July, p. 38.

Robinson, P. and Boniface, M. (1997) *Tourism and Cultural Conflicts*. Oxford: Oxford University Press.

Rochfort, S. and Cummins, C. (2001) Fox's white elephant fades to black. *Sydney Morning Herald*, 17 October, p. 1.

Roesch, S. (2007) There and back again: Comparative case studies of film location tourists' on-site behaviour and experiences. Doctoral dissertation, University of Otago.

Roesch, S. (2009) *The Experiences of Film Location Tourists*. Bristol: Channel View Publications.

Rogers, M. (2001) Triple bottom line audit: A framework for community-based action. In M.F. Rogers and Y.M.J. Collins (eds) *The Future of Australia's Country Towns* (pp. 135–145). Bendigo: Centre for Sustainable Regional Communities.

Rojek, C. (1993) *Ways of Escape*. Basingstoke: MacMillan.

Rosten, L. (1941) *Hollywood: The Movie Colony: The Movie Makers*. New York: Harcourt and Brace.

Rothel, D. (1990) *An Ambush of Ghosts: A Personal Guide to Favorite Western Film Locations.* Madison, NC: Empire Publishing.

Routt, W.D. (1996) The Australian land in Australian films. *Australian Movie Map.* New South Wales: Denise Corrigan.

Routt, W.D. (2001) More Australian than Aristotelian: The Australian bushranger film, 1904–1914. *Senses of Cinema* 18. See www.senseofcinema.com (accessed June 2003).

Ryan, C. (2002) Equity, management, power sharing and sustainability: Issues of the 'new tourism'. *Tourism Management* 23, 17–26.

Ryan, T. (2002) Lilo & Stitch want to take over your wallet. *Honolulu Star-Bulletin*, 13. See http://Starbulletin.com (accessed July 2002).

Ryan, T. (2003) HCVB to drop 'Lilo & Stitch' marketing pact with Disney. *Honolulu Star-Bulletin*, 14 January. See http://Starbulletin.com (accessed February 2003).

Ryllis Clark, M. (1999) Lou Stinson's Barwon Heads. *The Sunday Age: Escape* section, 13 June, p. 4.

SACF (2004) South Australian Film Corporation publications and resources. See www.safilm.com.au (accessed December 2004).

Schofield, P. (1996) Cinematographic images of a city: Alternative heritage tourism in Manchester. *Tourism Management* 17 (5), 333–340.

Schulze, J. (1999) Fox chief queries Viacom's park claims. *The Age*, 17 September.

Schulze, J. (2000) Fun park collapse to kill off studios. *The Age*, 10 February.

Schutz, A. (1962) *Collected Papers: The Problem of Social Reality*, M. Natanson (ed.). Boston, MA: Hague.

Scottish Daily Record (2003) Featured attraction: Doune Castle. *Scottish Daily Record*, 14 June.

Scottish Executive (2002a) Housing benefits for film-makers. Scottish Executive news release SE5133/2002, 9 January.

Scottish Executive (2002b) Launch of pocket guide to Scottish film. Scottish Executive news release Setc038/2002, 10 October.

SeaChange. Unofficial website. See http://users.bigpond.net.au/champion/SeaChange/right.htm (accessed November 2002).

Seaton, A.V. (1998) The history of tourism in Scotland: Approaches, sources and issues. In R. MacLellan and R. Smith (eds) *Tourism in Scotland* (pp. 1–41). London: International Thomson Business Press.

Seaton, A.V. and Hay, B. (1998) The marketing of Scotland as a tourist destination. In R. MacLellan and R. Smith (eds) *Tourism in Scotland* (pp. 209–239). London: International Thomson Business Press.

Seaton, P. (2015) Taiga dramas and tourism: Historical contents as sustainable tourist resources. *Japan Forum* 27 (1), 82–103.

Seaton, P. and Yamamura, T. (2015) Japanese popular culture and contents tourism – Introduction. *Japan Forum* 27 (1), 1–11.

Semley, N. and Busby, G. (2014) Film tourism: The pre-production perspective. A case study of Visit Somerset and the Hollywood story of Glastonbury, *Journal of Tourism Consumption and Practice* 6 (2), 23–53.

Shakespeare, W. (1611) 'The Tempest'. In J.M. Farrow (ed.) *The Collected Works of Shakespeare*. See www.it.usyd.edu.au (accessed August 2002).

Sheldon, P. and Fesenmaier, D.R. (2015) The tourism education futures initiative: Current and future education influences. In D. Dredge, D. Airey and M.J. Gross (eds) *The Routledge Handbook of Tourism and Hospitality Education* (pp. 155–170). London: Routledge.

Shoebridge, N. (1997) Fox creates a stir at venue for a show. *Business Review Weekly*, 13 October, pp. 40–41.

Shoebridge, N. (1998) Fox looks for original attractions. *Business Review Weekly*, 5 November (17), pp. 78–80.

Simmons, J. (1995) The censoring of *Rebel Without a Cause*. *Journal of Popular Film and Television* 23 (2), 56–63.

Simpson, P. (ed.) (2002) *The Rough Guide to Cult TV: The Good, the Bad and the Strangely Compelling*. London: Penguin Books.

Singh, S. (2011) Experiencing and learning from entrepreneurial failure. Doctoral dissertation, University of Waikato. See http://researchcommons.waikato.ac.nz/handle/10289/5965 (accessed August 2015).

Singh, S., Timothy, D.J. and Dowling, R.K. (2003a) *Tourism in Destination Communities*. Wallingford: CABI Publishing.

Singh, S., Timothy, D.J. and Dowling, R.K. (2003b) Tourism and destination communities. In S. Singh, D.J. Timothy and R.K. Dowling (eds) *Tourism in Destination Communities* (pp. 3–18). Wallingford: CABI Publishing.

Singh, T.V. and Singh, S. (1999) Coastal tourism, conservation and the community: Case of Goa. In T.V. Singh and S. Singh (eds) *Tourism Development in Critical Environments* (pp. 65–76). New York: Cognizant Communication Corporation.

Sirgy, M.J. and Su, C. (2000) Destination image, self-congruity, and travel behavior: Toward an integrative model. *Journal of Travel Research* 38 (4), 340–352.

Slee, B. (1998) Tourism and rural development in Scotland. In R. MacLellan and R. Smith (eds) *Tourism in Scotland* (pp. 93–111). London: International Thomson Business Press.

Sloan, G. (2002) Ah to walk a mile in their Jimmy Choos. *USA Today*, 1 August.

Slocum, J.D. (2000) Film violence and the institutionalization of the cinema. *Social Research* 67 (3), 649–660.

Smithsonian Cooper-Hewitt (2002) National Design Museum, 'New Hotels for Global Nomads', 29 October 2002–2 March 2003. Media release, August.

Sofield, T.H.B. (2003) *Empowerment for Sustainable Tourism Development*. Oxford: Pergamon.

Sony Pictures (2003) *Monty Python and the Holy Grail*. Official website. See www.sonypictures.com/cthe/montypython (accessed 18 September 2003).

Sorkin, M. (1992a) Introduction: Variations on a theme park. In M. Sorkin (ed.) *Variations on a Theme Park* (pp. xi–xv). New York: Noonday Press.

Sorkin, M. (1992b) See you in Disneyland. In M. Sorkin (ed.) *Variations on a Theme Park* (pp. 205–232). New York: Noonday Press.

Sovereign Hill (2001) About Sovereign Hill. See www.sovereignhill.com.au (accessed December).

Spenceley, A. and Meyer, D. (2012) Tourism and poverty reduction: Theory and practice in less economically developed countries. *Journal of Sustainable Tourism* 20 (3), 297–317.

Sperati, J.P. (2010) *Harry Potter on Location: An Unofficial Review and Guide to the Locations Used for the Entire Film Series*. Cambridge: Irregular Special Press.

Squire, S.J. (1994) The cultural values of literary tourism. *Annals of Tourism Research* 21, 103–120.

Stake, R.E. (1983) The case study method in social inquiry. In *Case Study Methods I* (2nd edn: pp. 73–76). Waurn Ponds: Deakin University.

Stake. R.E. (1995) *The Art of Case Study Research*. Thousand Oaks, CA: Sage Publications.

Stankey, G. and Lime, D. (1975) Carrying capacity: Maintaining outdoor recreation quality. In *Proceedings of the Forest Recreation Symposium* (pp. 174–184). Upper Darby, PA: Northeast Experiment Station.

Stephens, U. (2001) *Strengthening Rural Communities*. Sydney: NSW Premier's Department.

Sterry, P. (1998) Serial soap addiction: From screen viewing to pilgrimage. In J.M. Fladmark (ed.) *In Search of Heritage: As Pilgrim or Tourist?* Papers presented at the Robert Gordon University Heritage Convention 1998. Shaftsbury: Donhead.

Stone, W. (1977) *The Best of Banjo Paterson*. Melbourne: Summit Books.

Strain, E. (1996) Exotic bodies, distant landscapes: Touristic viewing and popularized anthropology in the nineteenth century. *Wide Angle* 18 (2), 70–100.

Sugawa-Shimada, A. (2015) Rekijo, pilgrimage and 'pop-spiritualism': Pop-culture-induced heritage tourism of/for young women. *Japan Forum* 27 (1), 37–58.

Surry Arts Council (2003) *Mayberry Days*, 25–27 September. See www.surryart.org/MayberryDays (accessed December 2003).

Suzuki, D. (1993) *Time to Change*. Toronto: Allen & Unwin.

Sweaney, K. (1999) Inside the movies. *Australian Leisure Management*, Dec 1999/Jan 2000, pp. 12–14.

System Three (1997) *Impact of Films Study: Final Report*. Stirling: Stirling Council/Forth Valley Enterprise.

Tapachi, N. and Waryszak, R. (2000) An examination of the role of beneficial image in tourist destination selection. *Journal of Travel Research* 39 (1), 37–44.

Taylor, K. (1999) Film and TV studios focus of $500m plan. *The Age*, 21 August, p. 7.

Taylor, W. (1999) After the Goldrush. *Australian Leisure Management*, August/September, pp. 52–54.

Teo, P. and Yeo, B.S.A. (2001) Negotiating global tourism: Localism as difference in Southeast Asian theme parks. In P. Teo, T.C. Chang and K.C. Ho (eds) *Interconnected Worlds: Tourism in Southeast Asia* (pp. 137–154). Amsterdam: Pergamon.

The Age Green Guide (1999) The ABC counts. 23 September, p. 7.

Tessitore, T., Pandelaere, M. and Van Kerckhove, A. (2014) The amazing race to India: Prominence in reality television affects destination image and travel intentions. *Tourism Management* 42, 3–12.

Timothy, D.J. and Tosun, C. (2003) Appropriate planning for tourism in destination communities: Participation, incremental growth and collaboration. In S. Singh, D.J. Timothy and R.K. Dowling (eds) *Tourism in Destination Communities* (pp. 181–204). Wallingford: CABI Publishing.

Tokyo National Film Festival (2003) A look at the promotion tactics of the closing film, *Finding Nemo* which will be released in cinemas in December in Japan after being screened at TIFF 2003, 4 September. See www.tiff-ipnet (accessed November 2003).

Tomaselli, K. (1985) Cybernetics, semiotics and meaning in the cinema. *Communicare* 4 (1), 48–62.

Tomaselli, K.G. (2001) Semiotics of the encounter: The staging of authenticity via cultural tourism, theme parks and film and TV series in the Kalahari Desert and KwaZulu-Natal, South Africa. *Annual Bulletin of International Union of Anthropological and Ethnological Sciences Commission on Urgent Anthropological Research*. Vienna. See www.und.ac.za/und/ccms/anthropology/urgent

Tooke, N. and Baker, M. (1996) Seeing is believing: The effect of film on visitor numbers to screened locations. *Tourism Management* 17 (2), 87–94.

Torchin, L. (2003) Location, location, location. The destination of the Manhattan TV tour. *Tourist Studies* 2 (3), 247–266.

Tourism Australia (2004) ATC online marketing. See www.tourism.australia.com (accessed December 2004).

Tourism Australia (2009) New campaign attracts record number of commercial partners. *Tourism Australia News Release*, 12 March.

Tourism New South Wales (2001) Wonderland Sydney. See www.sydneyaustralia.com (accessed December 2001).

Tourism New Zealand (2001a) New Zealand tourism gets into the ring. *Tourism New Zealand*. See www.tourisminfo.govt.nz/cir_news (accessed 11 December 2001).

Tourism New Zealand (2001b) The Lord of the Rings Tourism feature popular offshore. See www.tourisminfo.govt.nz/cir_news (accessed 18 December 2001).

Tourism New Zealand (2003a) *Corporate History*. Auckland: Tourism New Zealand.

Tourism New Zealand (2003b) Locations best seller for Brodie. *Tourism News*, March.

Tourism Northern Ireland (c.2015) *Tour Operator Guidelines: Game of Thrones*. See www.tourismni.com/Portals/2/Tour%20Operator%20Guidelines%20for%20Game%20of%20Thrones.pdf (accessed January 2016).

Tourism Northern Ireland (2016) The *Game of Thrones*: The starring role of screen tourism and how it can put your business into the spotlight. See www.tourismni.com/BusinessSupport/Culture%2cHeritageandActivityTourism/GamesofThrones.aspx (accessed April 2016).

Tourism Research Council, New Zealand (2004) *International Visitor Survey*. See www.trcnz.govt.nz/Surveys/International+Visitor+Survey (accessed December 2004).

Tourism Victoria (1993) *Strategic Business Plan, 1993*. Melbourne: Tourism Victoria.

Tourism Victoria (c.1996) *Domestic Market Research*. Melbourne: Tourism Victoria.

Tourism Victoria (1997) *Strategic Business Plan, 1997–2001, Building Partnerships*. Melbourne: Tourism Victoria.

Tourism Victoria (2000) Tourism Victoria industry site. See www.tourismvictoria.com.au (accessed December 2000).

Tourism Victoria (2001) *Visitors to Bays and Peninsulas: Summary Results Year Ending December 1999*. See www.tourismvictoria.com.a (accessed December 2001).

Tourism Victoria (2003) *Welcome to Victoria, The Official Site for Melbourne, Victoria, Australia*. See www.visitvictoria.com (accessed November 2003).

Travel Daily News (2003) Australian Tourist Commission and Austrade sign Memorandum of Understanding. *Travel Daily News.com*. See http://www.traveldailynews.com (accessed 25 May 2003).

TravelTrade (2001) Hollywood's big opening. *TravelTrade*, 13 June, p. 34.

Tzanelli, R. (2004) Constructing the 'cinematic tourist'. The 'sign industry' of The Lord of the Rings. *Tourist Studies* 4 (1), 21–42.

Tzanelli, R. (2007) *The Cinematic Tourist: Explorations in Globalization, Culture and Resistance*. London: Routledge.

Tzanelli, R. (2015) On Avatar's (2009) semiotechnologies: From cinematic utopias to Chinese heritage tourism. *Tourism Analysis* 20 (3), 269–282.

Universal Studios (2001a) Press kit: Universal Studios Recreation Group. See www.universalstudios.com (accessed October 2001).

Universal Studios (2001b) Universal Studios theme parks. See www.universalstudios.com (accessed December 2001).

Urry, J. (1990) *The Tourist Gaze: Leisure and Travel in Contemporary Societies*. London: Sage Publications.

Urry, J. (1995) *Consuming Places*. London: Routledge.

Urry, J. (2002) *The Tourist Gaze* (2nd edn). London: Sage Publications.

Urry, J. and Larsen, J. (2011) *The Tourist Gaze 3.0* (3rd edn). London: Sage Publications.

Usakli, A. and Baloglu, S. (2011) Brand personality of tourist destinations: An application of self-congruity theory. *Tourism Management* 32 (1), 114–127.

Uysal, M., Chen, J.S. and Williams, D.R. (2000) Increasing state market share through a regional positioning. *Tourism Management* 21, 89–96.

Vagionis, N. and Loumioti, M. (2011) Movies as a tool of modern tourist marketing. *Tourismos: An International Multidisciplinary Journal of Tourism* 6 (2), 353–362.

Vargas-Sánchez, A. (2015) Industrial heritage and tourism: A review of the literature. *The Palgrave Handbook of Contemporary Heritage Research*, 219–233.

Veal, A.J. (1997) *Research Methods for Leisure and Tourism: A Practical Guide* (2nd edn). London: Financial Times Pitman Publishing.

Venkatesh, A. (1992) Postmodernism, consumer culture and the society of the spectacle. *Advances in Consumer Research* 19, 199–202.

Verhoeff, N. and Warth, E. (2002) Rhetoric of space: Cityscape/landscape. *Historic Journal of Film, Radio and Television* 22 (3), 245–251.

Victorian Film and Television Industry Task Force (2000) The film and television production industry in Victoria. Report, September.

Vieh, J. (1997) Movies bring excitement, dollars to Arizona. *Business Journal Serving Phoenix and the Valley of the Sun* 17 (26), 47.

Vukonic, B. (1996) *Tourism and Religion*. Oxford: Pergamon.

Village Roadshow (2000) Mammoth theme park expansion. Media release, 28 July. See www.villageroadshow.com.au (accessed August 2000).

Village Roadshow (2001a) *Attachment to Preliminary Final Report: 30 June 2001*. Oxenford: Village Roadshow Limited.

Village Roadshow (2001b) Village group profile. See www.villageroadshow.com.au/profile (accessed December 2001).

VisitBritain (2015) Britain on Film. See www.visitbritain.com/en/Things-to-do/Culture/ Britain-on-film.htm (accessed August 2015).

Volo, S. and Irimiás, A. (2015) Film tourism and post-release marketing initiatives: A longitudinal case study. *Journal of Travel & Tourism Marketing*, 1–17.

Walkley, P. (1999) Peering into a Fox hole. *The Bulletin* 117 (6199), 67.

Wallace-Crabbe, C. (1971) Introduction. In C. Wallace-Crabbe (ed.) *The Australian Nationalists: Modern Critical Essays*. Melbourne: Oxford.

Walle, A.H. (1997) Quantitative versus qualitative tourism research. *Annals of Tourism Research* 24 (3), 524–536.

Walmsley, D.J. and Jenkins, J.M. (1992) Tourism cognitive mapping of unfamiliar environments. *Annals of Tourism Research* 19 (2), 268–286.

Walmsley, D.J. and Young, M. (1998) Evaluative images and tourism: The use of personal constructs to describe the structure of destination images. *Journal of Travel Research* 36 (3), 65–69.

Ward, R. (1963) The social fabric. In A.L. McLeod (ed.) *The Pattern of Australian Culture* (pp. 12–41). New York: Cornell University Press.

Ward, R. (1966) *The Australian Legend* (2nd edn). Melbourne: Oxford University Press.

Warhol, A. (1968) *Exhibit Catalog*. Stockholm: Moderna Museet.

Warner Bros Movie World (2001a) Corporate info. See www. movieworld.com.au/corpo rate_info (accessed October 2001).

Warner Bros Movie World (2001b) Rides and attractions. See www. movieworld.com.au/ rides_attractions/ride.cfm (accessed December 2001).

Watson, N.J. (2006) *The Literary Tourist: Readers and Places in Romantic and Victorian Britain*. Basingstoke: Palgrave Macmillan.

Watson, N.J. (2009) Introduction. In N.J. Watson (ed.) *Literary Tourism and Nineteenth-Century Culture* (pp. 1–12). Basingstoke: Palgrave Macmillan.

Weaver, D. and Oppermann, M. (2000) *Tourism Management*. Milton: John Wiley and Sons Australia.

Weir, D.T.H. (2002) Neville Shute and the landscape of England: An opportunity for literary tourism. In M. Robinson and H.C. Anderson (eds) *Literary and Tourism: Explorations of Tourism Writers and Writing* (pp. 119–142). London: Continuum.

Wellington Regional Council (2002) *Regional Outlook: Region Faces Growth Challenge*. Wellington: Wellington Regional Council.

Western Rural Development Centre (c.1995) *Community Tourism Assessment Handbook*. Logan, UT: Western Rural Development Centre. See http://extension.usu.edu/wrdc/ ctah (accessed January 2002).

Westwood, S. (2005) Out of the comfort zone: Situation, participation and narrative interpretation in tourism research. *The First International Congress of Qualitative Inquiry*, University of Illinois at Urbana-Champaign, CD ROM.

Whipp, G. (2001) The full Monty: The story of the writing of the film that says 'Ni'! *Daily News of Los Angeles, LA Life*, 14 June, p. L3. See ww.newslibrary.com (accessed December 2004).

Wilkinson, K.P. (1991) *The Community in Rural America*. New York: Greenwood Press.
Wonderland Sydney (2001) General educational information, November. Sydney: Wonderland Sydney.
Wright, D.M. (1918/1973) *Poetical Works of Henry Lawson*. Sydney: Angus and Robertson.
WTO (1999) *New Global Ethics for World Tourism*. Madrid: World Tourism Organisation.
Wu, N. (2003) Cross-promotions give the islands some prime exposure. *Pacific Business News (Honolulu)*, 13 October.
Yamamura, T. (2011) *Anime, manga de chiiki shinkō*. Tokyo: Tokyo Hōrei Shuppan.
Yan, Chow Tsz (2000) Star-spangled journey: Hong Kong movie-induced tourism. *The Hong Kong Anthropologist* 13, 27–33.
Yeabsley, J. and Duncan, I. (2002) Scoping the lasting effects of *The Lord of the Rings*. Report to the New Zealand Film Commission. Wellington: NZ Institute of Economic Research.
Yin, R.K. (1994) *Case Study Research. Design and Methods* (2nd edn). Thousand Oaks, CA: Sage Publications.
Yin, R.K. (2013) *Case Study Research: Design and Methods* (5th edn). Thousand Oaks, CA: Sage Publications.
Yoon, Y., Kim, S.S. and Kim, S.S. (2015) Successful and unsuccessful film tourism destinations: From the perspective of Korean local residents' perceptions of film tourism impacts. *Tourism Analysis* 20 (3), 297–311.
Young, A.F. and Young, R. (2008) Measuring the effects of film and television on tourism to screen locations: A theoretical and empirical perspective. *Journal of Travel & Tourism Marketing* 24 (2–3), 195–212.
Young, C. and Kaczmarek, S. (1999) Changing the perception of the post-socialist city: Place promotion and imagery in Lodz, Poland. *The Geographic Journal* (2), 183–191.
Young, G. (1973) *Tourism: Blessing or Blight?* London: Penguin Books.
YTB (2001) *Tourism Education Pack 2001*. York: Yorkshire Tourist Board.
YTB (2003) Yorkshire Tourist Board supports world and northern premieres of *Calendar Girls*. Yorkshire Tourist Board press release, 3 September. Pickering: Yorkshire Tourist Board.
YTB and NYMNPA (1997) The impact of filming on the residents of Goathland. Unpublished research report. York: Yorkshire Tourist Board and North York Moors National Park Authority.
Zhang, H., Fu, X., Cai, L. A. and Lu, L. (2014) Destination image and tourist loyalty: A meta-analysis. *Tourism Management* 40, 213–223.
Zhang, X. (2014) Grand view garden: An investigation of tourists' motivation and satisfaction. Doctoral dissertation, University of Waikato.
Zhang, X., Ryan, C. and Cave, J. (2016) Residents, their use of a tourist facility and contribution to tourist ambience: Narratives from a film tourism site in Beijing. *Tourism Management* 52, 416–429.
Zhao, S.N. and Timothy, D.J. (2015) Governance of red tourism in China: Perspectives on power and guanxi. *Tourism Management* 46, 489–500.
Zoltak, J. (1996) $89m Fox Studios Australia FEC to replace Sydney Showgrounds. *Amusement Business* 108 (5), 21–22.
Zoltak, J. (1997) Fox Studios Australia seeks corporate partners. *Amusement Business* 109 (46), 32.
Zukin, S. (1995) *The Culture of Cities*. Cambridge: Blackwell Publishers.

Index